Rocío G. Davis and Sämi Ludwi

Asian American Literature in the Inter

Contributions to
Asian American Literary Studies

edited by

Rocío G. Davis
(University of Navarre)

and

Sämi Ludwig
(University of Bern)

Volume 1

LIT

Rocío G. Davis and Sämi Ludwig, eds.

Asian American Literature in the International Context

Readings on Fiction, Poetry, and Performance

LIT

Dedicated to
the memory of
our colleague and friend
Amy Ling

Cover art: Rudolf Ammann

We thank the Faculty of Arts and Letters of University of Navarre for their financial support of this book.

Die Deutsche Bibliothek – CIP-Einheitsaufnahme

Asian American Literature in the International Context : Readings on Fiction, Poetry, and Performance / Rocío G. Davis and Sämi Ludwig, eds. – Hamburg : LIT, 2002
   (Contributions to Asian American Literary Studies ; 1)
   ISBN 3-8258-5710-7

© LIT VERLAG Münster – Hamburg – London
   Grindelberg 15a 20144 Hamburg Tel. 040 - 44 64 46 Fax 040 - 44 14 22
   e-Mail: hamburg@lit-verlag.de   http://www.lit-verlag.de

Distributed in North America by:

Transaction Publishers
New Brunswick (U.S.A.) and London (U.K.)

Transaction Publishers
Rutgers University
35 Berrue Circle
Piscataway, NJ 08854

Tel.: (732) 445 - 2280
Fax: (732) 445 - 3138
for orders (U. S. only):
toll free (888) 999 - 6778

Acknowledgements

We'd like to thank, in the first place, the participants of our panel on Asian American Literature at the EAAS Lisbon Conference, from where this volume has grown, as well as the contributors who were not at the sessions, for their enthusiasm and support for this project, and for their patience to wait until this collection of articles went into print. We are also grateful to the different anonymous readers of this manuscript and their invaluable suggestions, which have challenged our preconceptions and helped us move the volume to its editorial completion. We further want to thank Veit Hopf and LIT Verlag in Berlin for accepting our manuscript and suggesting that we turn this effort into the first volume of a series on Asian American Studies, the first series in Europe of its kind. And then we'd also like to thank Ruedi Ammann in Japan for his enthusiasm and his fine ideas for the cover design.

Since each scholar has an academic home out of which he or she works, we also want to thank the Faculty of Arts and Letters of University of Navarre for their financial support and the members of our respective departments in Pamplona and Berne for all of their direct and indirect help and encouragement. But most of all, we want to thank our families, who have borne with us, even at times when they didn't understand why we had to spend so many hours in front of the computer rather than play with them.

Rocío Davis and Sämi Ludwig   Pamplona and Berne, 20 October 2001

Table of Contents

Introduction: Asian American Literature in the International Context   9
Rocío G. Davis and Sämi Ludwig

I. Biraciality/Biculturality

Beyond Biraciality: "Race" as Process in the Work of
Edith Eaton/Sui Sin Far and Winnifred Eaton/Onoto Watanna
Carol Roh-Spaulding   21

Celebrating Ourselves in the Other, Or:
Who Controls the Conceptual Allusions in Kingston?
Sämi Ludwig   37

"Adding On," Not "Giving Up":
Ceremonies of Self in Frank Chin's *Donald Duk*
Gordon O. Taylor   57

II. Interethnic Negotiations

Funeral Rites, Ethnicity, and the Politics of Representation
in Asian American Literature
Seiwoong Oh   69

Mending the Sk(e)in of Memory: Trauma, Narrative and the
Recovery of Identity in Chao, Liu, and Kogawa
Helena Grice   81

Ceremonies of Dialogism in Asian American Poetry
Eulalia Piñero-Gil   97

III. Poetic Creation

Marilyn Chin's Poetry of "Self as Nation":
Transforming the "Lyric I," Reinventing Cultural Inheritance
Zhou Xiaojing   111

Undercover Asian: John Yau and the Politics of Ethnic Self-Identification
Dorothy J. Wang   135

The Way a Calendar Dissolves:
A Refugee's Sense of Time in the Work of Li-Young Lee
Johnny Lorenz   157

IV. Narrative Experiments

Everyone's Story:
Narrative *You* in Chitra Bannerjee Divakaruni's "The Word Love"
Rocío G. Davis   173

Otherness as Reading Process: Theresa Hak Kyung Cha's *DICTEE*
Kirsten Twelbeck   185

The "American" Voice in Asian American Male Autoperformance
Robert H. Vorlicky   203

V. (Re)Constructing Self

Rituals of Mothering: Food and Intercultural Identity in Gus Lee's *China Boy*
Alicia Otano   215

Cultural Cross-Dressing in *Mona in the Promised Land*
Amy Ling   227

Rupture as Continuity:
Migrant Identity and "Unsettled" Perspective in Bapsi Sidhwa's
An American Brat
Geoffrey Kain   237

South Asian American Women Writers in the Mythical West
Carmen Faymonville   247

Notes on Contributors   262

Introduction:
Asian American Literature in the International Context

Rocío G. Davis and Sämi Ludwig

Since the publication of Maxine Hong Kingston's *The Woman Warrior* a quarter of a century ago, we have witnessed an unprecedented growth in the literatures of Asian America, both in their creative expression and in the substantial body of criticism that seeks to discuss them in the light of contemporary identity and cultural politics. Kingston's emblematic text not only opened the way for writers to engage the complexities of their ethnicity, but also signaled a narrative boldness and maturity regarding the appropriation and subversion of traditional genres. The range of writing that comprises today's expanding Asian American canon includes the works of authors who continue Kingston's experimentation with and exploration of genre and theme, the borders between fiction and reality, issues of intercultural expression and identity, and the question of authenticity. Asian American writing has tremendously expanded its range of expression—be it in its experimental edge, as literary technique, or in the further integration of elements from its ever more diverse and complex ethnic constituencies. More and more different experiences, stories, and thematic issues are finding literary expression in innovative forms that range from words to performance. Today the cultural production of Asian America has a scope and variety that is as aesthetically complex and sophisticated as any other literature, yet maintaining a very particular flavor of its own.

Asian American literature offers a very rich field of investigation because in it we comprehend transcultural literary phenomena beyond geographic, national, ethnic, and even linguistic boundaries. Recent scholarship consistently points to the need to expand and deepen the approaches to this complex set of concerns and strategies. Shirley Lim believes that Asian American literature

> as a heuristic term is the mountain of gold to be mined by archival and scholarly labor. But as a distinct minority literature, it has become a space for cultural contestation between forces for containment and enlargement. Places under interrogation are the nature and boundaries of this body of materials, its categorization and composition, and the interpretations and evaluations brought to bear on it. (149)

Asian American writers have been aware for a long time that self-definitions and authentic cultural representation must emerge not from an easy, assimilationalist surrender to labels supplied or inspired by others, but from their own individualistic ways of coming to terms with their specific backgrounds as they learn to accept their share of the burden of personal and social histories they have embraced within the multifarious world that is the United States. Lisa Lowe's loaded statement on the positionality of this literature demands an ever-widening space for the location of the creative product: "We might conceive of the making and practice of Asian American culture as nomadic, unsettled, taking place in the travel between cultural sites and in the multivocality of heterogeneous and conflicting positions" (39). The diverse forms within the distinct ethnicities embraced by the term "Asian American culture" proffer a convergence of old traditions and new cultures, of immigrant translation and historical appropriation, that often finds creative expression in a synthesis of myth and the modern consciousness through the use of innovative forms of perception and renegotiations of cultural heritage in the plural. Its contextualization in literature inspires continued study and thus also demands a widening theoretical framework from within which to analyze particular texts. Corollary to this, the interactive processes of the creation of Asian American literature impose new strategies of reading characterized by a continual call to reorientation and a new conditioning of the determinants of meaning.

The remarkable imaginative and narrative contributions of Asian American literature have made their mark outside the boundaries of the United States as well, and in many ways the present collection of essays by international scholars is a result of this fact. Here is its history: at a first workshop on Asian American literature at the biannual conference of the European Association of American Studies (EAAS) in 1996, contacts among European scholars dedicated to this field were established. Their lively interaction inspired the publication of a special issue of Berkeley's *Hitting Critical Mass* entitled "European Perspectives on Asian American Literature" and an essay collection, *Talk-Story in Chinatown and Away*, edited by Lina Unali. Two years later we organized another workshop at the EAAS conference in Lisbon, which had as a central theme "Ceremonies and Spectacles: America and the Staging of Collective Identities." The core of the essays in this collection come from our sessions on Asian American literature entitled "Asian American Ceremonies: Continuity, Rupture, Invention?" Our aim was to discuss the manner in which contemporary writers—novelists, dramatists, and poets—deal with the ceremonies that characterize Asian America in its widest sense. Possible links with formulations of the past, emancipation from tradition, blending of the old and the new, or even invention when there was nothing that could serve, were our concern. The sessions were lively, but produced, as always in these cases, more questions than answers. We were thus inspired to continue the debate in print, which gave us an opportunity to expand the scope of our contributors into an even more international group. Contributions on other aspects of the theme were sought, to widen the discussion and clarify our concerns in more detail. Still, the frequent references in our essays to words or phrases such as "celebration," "ceremony," or "continuity, rupture, invention" reflect the origin of our project.

In their different and yet complementary perspectives, all of the essays in this collection reiterate the universal lesson of pluralism. As editors, we did not aim at establishing or requiring an overarching perspective that should define some essence of Asian Americanness. Hence, rather than a new theoretical take that tries to frame the highly complex field of Asian American literature, we offer a careful selection of specific readings that show the richness, complexity, and diversity of Asian American writing through a variety of critical and theoretical methods and approaches to different writers and genres. This concrete engagement aims at avoiding abstraction in a negative sense. The decision not to impose a defining theoretical paradigm therefore becomes, in itself, a powerful statement that studies of Asian American literature should not be limited to any one particular perspective or ideology. Instead of struggling to elaborate a general aesthetic which should reflect the experience of a particular ethnic group, we take our lesson from African American studies, where the notion of a Black Aesthetic, although influential, lost its validity as an overriding approach in the late 1970s, and yet the worthiness of African American literature as a field remains unquestioned.

Consequently, the diversity of perspectives offered by the international scholars of this book is also specifically aimed against dangerous provincialist tendencies in certain areas of scholarship and publication, which often tend to follow narrow fashions of intellectual interest and, particularly in the field of ethnic literatures, even the hedging tendencies of cultural nationalism. Through our gestures of associating critics from three different continents—Europe, Asia, and America—within the same volume and of including readings of a number of recent Asian American works that have not received adequate critical attention, we intend to acknowledge the international appeal of Asian American literature and at the same time to celebrate the exploding plurality of approaches possible in Asian American studies today. Demonstrating the continued value of interrogating Asian American writing from diverse perspectives, the essays collected here tackle oftentimes conflicting ethnic/racial perspectives and critique exclusive theoretical approaches. To limit readings of Asian American literature to a single, currently prevalent, outlook is very problematic indeed. According to our vision, Asian American studies cannot be a progressive science that moves toward a teleological future—we rather endorse a pluralistic hermeneutic that opposes all hegemonic theoretical tendencies. As such, some of the approaches included here may actually be readings against the established norm; a structure that, we hope, opens up debate and discussion. The conclusions arrived at in our essays—interethnic in their focus and concerned with innovative expression within diverse genres—emphasize a clear mood of expansion in Asian American creativity where more writing and renewed readings continuously add to a growing body of literary and cultural signification.

In the spirit of these considerations, this volume is at the same time the first book in a series which the present editors are starting for LIT-Verlag in Münster, Germany. We envision this new series, called "Contributions to Asian American Literary Studies," as a medium to create an international forum of interdisciplinary discussion. Rather than merely theorizing transcultural issues and the internationalization of research—an approach which often endorses the already hegemonic position of powerful United States academic institutions—in this series we intend to *be* international rather than talk about it and to *do the work* of presenting the research of scholars who are both inside *and* outside of the established discourse of Asian American studies as an emerging discipline. We want to foster communication among researchers of different backgrounds in order to avoid the transitionalities of theoretical fashion. Hence, we understand "difference" in the sense of discrete authors from a variety of backgrounds, whose approaches are complementary and mutually enriching, providing innovative and incisive scholarship as they understand it.

Asian American Literature in the International Context: Readings on Fiction, Poetry, and Performance is structured according to genres and diverse themes that highlight the ways in which creative expression and critical discussion have evolved and heightened our understanding and appreciation of the literature as cultural production. The first three articles center on early representations of *biraciality and biculturality* as initiatory issues within the creative and critical endeavors of Asian American writers. Carol Roh-Spaulding explores the writing of the Eaton sisters and offers a fascinating new assessment of Sui Sin Far (Edith Eaton) and Onoto Watanna (Winnifred Eaton) in which she counteracts the widely accepted notion that the younger sister, Onoto Watanna, merely imitates conventional stereotypes. Roh-Spaulding shows how both sisters explore "race" by articulating in their work "a racial self-concept that embraces not a biracial or bicultural identity but a racial indeterminacy, as they move continually between or outside of established racial, social, and national frames." "Eurasianness" becomes the Eaton sisters' "terrain"—a strategy rather than a fixed condition, analyzed through continuous or "serial" articulation of their racial selves as embodied in their fictional heroines and autobiographical representations. This highly sophisticated manner of viewing race, Roh-Spaulding argues, creates categorical ambiguity on many levels, exhausting the supposed fixity and impermeability of racial boundaries.

Sämi Ludwig presents a reading of Kingston that challenges facile categorizations by showing how easy it is to misappropriate Kingston's affinities with

Western *topoi* in *The Woman Warrior* and read many of her subtexts that come out of traditional American literature as manifestations of Chinese culture: "The modernist density of the text has been appropriated in ways that often misrecognize 'American' references as 'Chinese' in a way that does justice to neither." If we ignore how Kingston actively processes these materials, he argues, we submit to the danger of celebrating our own projections instead of understanding her creativity. Ludwig suggests that in her more recent writings, Kingston has changed her allusive aesthetic toward a more controlled textuality of *klartext* in which many of her opinions are explicit and can no longer be misconstrued so easily.

Gordon Taylor looks at the presentation of hybrid culture in Frank Chin's *Donald Duk*, arguing that each of the "ceremonial" contexts evoked—cast in the categories of dance, dream, flight, and food, all connected in turn to celebration of the Chinese New Year—centers on the problematic relations between present and past, America and China, and their contending claims on the young Chinese American protagonist's consciousness. Taylor shows how Chin's narrative gathers momentum, not of cyclical repetition but of cumulative intensification: "On the one hand, this is the density of legend or myth, a bicultural poetry-in-prose of triumph and tragedy, these outcomes at once commingled and mutually distinct. On the other hand, it is that of a counterhistory, systematically as much as subversively researched, to standard U.S. interpretations of the completion of the railroad as a watershed event in the progress of the dominant culture, a defining step in the conquest of the frontier." Taylor concludes that the experience of biculturality is more a matter of "adding on," as we have it in the cultural hyphen as a railroad cross-tie, than a subtractive "giving up." Donald Duk masters multiple "languages" or media of self-invention; layers of experience that can be made to translate. Thus Chin's aesthetic shows a creative way out of poststructuralist limitations that posit identical fragmentation through oppositional definition and paradoxical cancellation. As an old friend of the African American writer Ishmael Reed (and having been part of Reed's multicultural project of the Before Columbus Foundation), Chin thus offers an approach to hyphenated culture that is cognitive rather than deconstructive.

Another group of contributions deals with *interethnic negotiations*, i.e., with particular thematic concerns as they are treated in different groups of texts within the diverse Asian American groups. Thus Seiwoong Oh analyzes funeral ceremonies and demonstrates through a number of examples how these rites are symptomatic of the different ways in which rituals thematize the relation of Asian Americans to their respective mother countries: "In some works," Oh argues, "the rites are portrayed to be eclectic and largely perfunctory," signifying the loss of connection between the ritual and the mourners. Yet in others, he continues, "writers try to reclaim their ties to their ancestral culture by attempting to rebuild a meaningful ritual from their dim memory." Oh concludes that while some writers compromise their work to meet the "demand and expectations by staging funeral scenes as spectacles to be consumed by readers who are cultural outsiders," other writers have found various ways to deal with the ethnic signs associated with funeral customs, by suppressing the scenes, by using the scenes to develop plots or characters, or by "finding the missing link between the rituals and their meaningfulness."

Helena Grice expands our understanding of the Asian American novelistic tradition that deals with remembering. She focuses on a particular subgroup that follows the established pattern of "trauma narratives" within a context of sexual abuse and cross-cultural racism. Noting that "[r]elease from trauma can only come by confronting it, but this is always a traumatic process in itself," Grice traces translations of physical experience into narrative framing in exemplary shamanic efforts of healing trauma. She reads the novels of Aimee Liu, Joy Kogawa, and Patricia Chao as efforts to recover identity from very corporeal traumatic experiences in complex and painful processes of reframing that involve different imagery in which "memory is a wound, but it is also a thread, often broken by a traumatic event, which needs to be reconnected in order for the subject to heal."

Finally, Eulalia Piñero-Gil reads the works of Janice Mirikitani, Arthur Sze, John Yau, Amy Ling, and Nelly Wong as "ceremonies of dialogism." Observing that the corpus of Asian American poetry represents a rich tradition of dissenting voices, Piñero-Gil demonstrates that Bakhtin's theory can be applied to the hybridity and heterogeneity that characterize Asian American poetry as well as to the novel form, especially in the way that the confluence of dissenting voices in poetic texts generates gaps and silences that can subvert dominant ideologies and at the same time try to reconstruct the past of the community: "I consider that their conspicuous use of voices develops an ethnic consciousness that characterizes most Asian American poetry and confers to it a unique idiosyncrasy."

Piñero-Gil's essay leads on to the section on *poetic creation*, which centers on emblematic Asian American poets writing today, whose work is slowly gaining the recognition it deserves for its richness and originality. Xiaojing Zhou offers close readings of Marilyn Chin's poetry that show how Chin "reclaims and reinvents her Chinese cultural inheritance, and develops a voice that is uniquely her own—passionate and compelling, at times humorous, at times heartbreaking." Zhou demonstrates how Chin negotiates her own family memories with the history of Chinese immigrants and revisions of textual sources such as the historical Japanese poet Bashō or the modern Greek poet Cavafy's poem on "barbarians" in ways that objectify and at the same time creatively negotiate otherness and invent identity beyond a simple confessional mode.

Taking the infamous Yau-Weinberger debate in the *American Poetry Review* as a starting point, Dorothy Wang integrates John Yau's earlier avant-garde, and supposedly non-ethnic, experimental side with his more recent explicit embracing of Asian American identity. Wang does a masterful job of unraveling the buried assumptions about race, ethnic identity, and their role in cultural produc-

tion that have apparently caused the pervasive blind spots in the critical reception of Yau. Observing that "critics' interpretations of Yau's work often focus
narrowly on those angles that reflect their particular interests," she emphasizes
that his postmodern and more objective approach to writing the self has from the
very beginning been consistent with his rejection of solipsistic confessional poetic role models. Wang provides detailed readings, particularly of Yau's early
works, that explain the complex way in which the poet integrates his interests as
an art critic with a rigorous exploration of his own ethnic double consciousness,
for example in his benchmark poem "Carp and Goldfish."

Finally, Johnny Lorenz approaches Li-Young Lee's poetry from the angle of
Walter Benjamin's Angel of History and W.E.B. Du Bois's "double consciousness" when he analyzes the representation of the refugee's sense of time: "Lee's
work—full of echoes, heavy with ritual, stitched with the broken threads of
memory—creates intimacies across chronological distances." He illustrates how
Lee locates history as a resonance and thus creates multi-layered figures of remembering that turn faces into palimpsests of ancestry: "The ghosts that we discover in Lee's books give evidence of the past's refusal to keep still, to remain
wreckage." In his carefully crafted imagery, Lee reconstructs his identity from a
personal heritage of dislocation where, like his father, he has to metaphorically
rebuild Solomon's temple from a paper model. This exile's voice can overcome
losses and save through time fragments of identity inherited from his parents and
the places where he grew up; it can overcome alienation by braiding hairs of the
past and the present into imagery of love and even eroticism.

The section on *narrative experimentation* arises from the heightened interest
in narrative innovations that makes essays on discursive strategies imperative.
Rocío Davis analyzes Chitra Bannerjee Divakaruni's appropriation of the second-person point of view in her short story "The Word Love," illustrating how
narrative technique is used to widen the range of discourse and challenge monolithic assumptions of readership. Aware of the potential that narrative offers in
the process of constructing or re-constructing identity, the author's choice of this
perspective widens the range of referentiality of the text itself. Divakaruni's
technique "opens up possibilities on both a thematic level—as it offers a new
way of dealing with the process of subjectivity and immigrant positionality, interrogating notions of identity and choice—and on a textual level, as it challenges the traditionally accepted border between narrator and narratee, between
text and reader." Davis argues that the second person narrative articulates the
contingencies of individual and communal story, problematizing self-
representation, creating and maintaining subjectivity through literary discourse
as the writer appropriates the narrative *you* as a metaphor for the fragmentation
and multiplicity of ethnic lives.

Kirsten Twelbeck offers a subtle re-reading of Theresa Cha's *DICTEE* in
which she compares this celebrated example of postmodern autobiography to
Peter Hyun's more conventional life story *In the New World*. The two narratives

share the same basic questions, which are pronouncedly Korean American, namely the struggle for a place to call "home," language as a site for identity production, and gender as a culturally constructed limitation. One of the crucial observations that Twelbeck makes as a European outsider is her astute criticism of "ethnic ownership" in this particular case. She argues that the formal complexity of *DICTEE* and its poststructuralist author-position continuously remind the reader of his or her own modes of perception. The "pleasure" of the text "lies not so much on the cognitive level—although it is indispensable for the overall understanding of the text—but in the capacity of the reader to give her- or himself up to it." The experience of reading *DICTEE* is described as a matter of "training toward accepting 'Otherness,'" its openness and playfulness seen as textual qualities that facilitate intercultural contact by inducing a readiness to doubt and "forget" internalized cultural norms and truths. This way *DICTEE* creates an un-fixed subject beyond a self.

This section closes with an investigation by Robert H. Vorlicky of the American voice in Asian American autoperformance. Vorlicky traces the performative nature of the American "I" from its white male origins to the late twentieth-century explorations in the genre of the author-director-performer, and the experimentations of male Asian American autoperformers who have created a counter-tradition to traditional theatrical and filmic representations of Asian American men. He exemplifies this in Dan Kwong's multimedia work, which steps outside of victim identity in highly creative ways that make use of parody and celebrate this breaking of silence. Kwong stands for a new generation of Asian American theater practitioners thriving in the United States who can be seen and have their voices heard in increasingly more non-for-profit as well as commercial theaters.

The fifth and concluding section deals with issues of identity construction, i.e., with the *(re)construction of self.* Alicia Otano reads Gus Lee's autobiographical *China Boy* in terms of food as the central metaphor that explores and structures the re-telling of his boyhood. As the protagonist's life develops, food is found to define at the same time an essence of home, security, and identity as it makes possible the adoption of other cultures and thus other ways of "feeding" that suggest a radically non-essentialist identity. Hence the protagonist Kai can evolve "from the adoration of his mother to the emulation of role models at the Y.M.C.A., a multicultural America in miniature." The centrality of scenes related to food and eating within this narrative of childhood demonstrate that the narrator privileges these rituals as a vital part of the development of identity and self-affirmation. Alimentary detail, Otano affirms, "becomes part of the process of signification: it is a supplement to cultural meaning." Because moral values are attached to meals—to the giving, receiving, eating and serving of meals—food is used in *China Boy* to define various aspects of love, pride, familial and social standing, and gratitude, and the meals are carefully planned and structured to highlight and explain motivation as well as personal and cultural development.

In one of the last essays she wrote before her untimely death, Amy Ling uses the term "cultural cross-dressing" to describe what she calls a sixth freedom of all U.S. citizens, namely the "freedom of cultural choice." She finds in Gish Jen's *Mona in the Promised Land* a perfect example of the exploration of what Werner Sollors would call an identity of "consent," when Mona, daughter of the assimilationist Chinese Americans Helen and Ralph of Jen's earlier novel, decides to become Jewish. This "lateral" cultural transgression triggers the experience of many new boundaries and the perspective of old boundaries in new ways that involve the interaction with many other kinds of cultural cross-dressers: "Power and privilege are still largely a matter of descent. However, with its rollicking humor and good-natured irreverence, *Mona in the Promised Land* offers cultural cross-dressing as the means for the various peoples of the U.S. to grow in solidarity and mutual understanding."

Geoffrey Kain extends the discussion of this issue by analyzing what he calls the "unsettled perspective" in Bapsi Sidhwa's novel *An American Brat*. Kain begins his essay with a commentary on Skinner's behavioral theory as it anticipates and partially informs more recent ideas of identity relating to immigrant or diasporic identity. Sidhwa's novel, he argues, "helps us to see not only the power of culture to 'select' behaviors and values, but also invites us to ponder the struggle of immigrants to retain their hold on what they value of their native (and—over time—increasingly distant) culture and, simultaneously, to relinquish those values and behaviors that are not reinforced by their present environment." From one perspective—something of a traditional, mythically American one—*An American Brat* is a tale of continuity as it tells of the protagonist's immersion within the archetypal America of independence and individualism, with energetic improvisation becoming stronger as the novel progresses. From another point of view, the same protagonist is almost lost to her extended family, to her religion, to modes of traditional behavior, and to native place and culture as she is "swallowed" by the seductive giant of America, making the novel a tale of rupture. In many ways therefore, Kain asserts, this is a very American tale.

Finally, Carmen Faymonville traces the acquisition of identity in Sidwa and Mukherjee's novels about South Asian characters in the American West, and how it is shaped in this traditional frontier environment. She shows how these "Indians" signify on the European experience in the West and redefine the role of immigrant pioneers under radically new conditions. She problematizes the question of where the West actually begins, expanding the implication of the possible answers into the lives and struggles of the immigrant women portrayed in the novels. The conquest of the West acquires heightened and renewed meaning as it becomes part of these Asian women's cultural dialogue with America, on cultural and gender levels. Because these new pioneer women come from non-Western societies, she argues, "American frontier individualism seems somehow forced upon them. [...]. Thus, South Asian frontierswomen [...] must learn to cope with their new-found mobility, but must also negotiate the negative effects of their independence such as loss of culture and forced assimilation."

The wide variety of approaches by our authors, whose remarkable spectrum of critical, analytical, and thematic orientation reflects their training in different cultures and across cultures, showcase refreshing new perspectives in reading that combine the views of literary scholars from three different continents in the same book. Ultimately the aim of this collection of essays is to achieve an internationalization of Asian American studies, i.e., we want to create a space for discussion and commentary, of heightened appreciation and increased creativity, a forum that turns our discipline into a truly intercultural debate beyond the confines of the U.S. academy. We see this kind of internationalization as nothing less than the critical application of Shirley Lim and Amy Ling's conclusion to their groundbreaking collection of essays, *Reading the Literatures of Asian America*, that "the diversity and range of subjects, critical stances, styles, concerns, and theoretical grids compellingly demonstrate the heterogeneous, multiple, divergent, polyphonic, multivocal character of Asian American cultural discourse" (9). Our readings of fiction, poetry, and performance support that awareness of creative and intellectual pluralism, as a means of establishing uniqueness within the diverse Asian American communities, a movement that continually and effectively expands beyond borders of many different kinds.

Works Cited

Davis, Rocío, ed. *Hitting Critical Mass*. Special Issue "European Perspectives on Asian American Literature." 4.1 (1996).

Lim, Shirley Geok-lin. "Assaying the Gold; or, Contesting the Ground of Asian American." *New Literary History* 24 (1993): 147-69.

Lim, Shirley Geok-lin and Amy Ling, eds. *Reading the Literatures of Asian America*. Philadelphia: Temple UP, 1992.

Lowe, Lisa. "Heterogeneity, Hybridity, Multiplicity: Marking Asian American Differences." *Diaspora* 1.1 (1991): 24-44.

Unali, Lina, ed. *Talk-Story in Chinatown and Away*. Rome: Sun Moon Lake, 1998.

I. Biraciality/Biculturality

Beyond Biraciality: "Race" as Process in the Work of Edith Eaton/Sui Sin Far and Winnifred Eaton/Onoto Watanna

Carol Roh-Spaulding

At the close of the 20th century, demographic shifts indicated for the 21st century have influenced significantly the discussion of racial and ethnic formation in North America, and in particular the subject of biracial and bicultural identity. In Asian American literary studies, two half-Chinese sisters—one born in England and the other in Canada—from the early part of the century have made an important contribution to our thinking on the subject of mixed race. Edith Maude Eaton or Sui Sin Far, and Winnifred Babcock Eaton or Onoto Watanna, articulate in their work a racial self-concept that embraces not a biracial or bicultural identity but a racial indeterminacy, as they move continually between or outside of established racial, social, and national frames. This movement creates categorical ambiguity on many levels, exhausting the supposed fixity and impermeability of racial boundaries.

Race is scripted in absolute (white/non-white) terms in North America. While the phenotypical and genealogical prerequisites for whiteness are always changing (most often due to rising economic status of immigrant groups) the categories "white" and "people of color" endure as opposites. "Betweenness" is understood not as a viable identity alternative, but as a categorical aberration, even though few Americans are absolutely white or non-white. In American literature, stories dealing with the subject of mixed race have often centered on the disjuncture a mixed-race character experiences between a racial self-conception and a racial designation that do not fit together. Faulkner's Joe Christmas, for example, is taken for white but believes he is black, and there is no place for him. The story of mixed race in American narrative is the story of the outcast, the vilified, the abject.

Because the concept of race mixture threatens racial absolutism, it has the potential to force a re-examination of "race" and its categories. Homi Bhabha has articulated the "in-between" as a "terrain for elaborating strategies of self-hood—singular or communal—that initiate new signs of identity" (1). Rather than serving as simply a new alternative designation, however, Bhabha's "terrain" is the space, "unrepresentable in itself," in which racial self-articulation is disconnected from "primordial unity or fixity" (37). "Eurasianness" is the Eaton sisters' "terrain"—a means rather than an end, a strategy as opposed to a fixed condition. It is racial identity as process: through continuous or "serial" articulation of their racial selves as embodied in their fictional heroines and autobiographical representations, they affirm their very racial indeterminacy as the foundation of their racial being without either succumbing to the "terministic violence" of racial categorization (Spillers 167) or simply retreating into whiteness.

"The Saddest Flower of All"

The eldest daughter of a Chinese mother and British father, Edith Eaton called herself Sui Sin Far (or Seen Far), meaning "fragrant water lily," in her first published article in 1897, and published dozens of short stories and non-fiction articles using this name until her death in 1913 (Ling 28). As the first American of Chinese ancestry to write in defense of the Chinese, and as an unmarried woman who supported herself solely through her writing, Eaton has been the focus of several literary recovery projects in both Asian American literature and women's studies, most notably in the work of Amy Ling, Annette White-Parks, and Elizabeth Ammons. The only book-length work she produced is a collection of her stories, titled *Mrs. Spring Fragrance* (1912), gathered from the various popular magazines that published her work, including *Century, Good Housekeeping, Independent, Land of Sunshine* (later, *Out West*), and *Westerner.*

According to Annette White-Parks, Eaton was read in her own day primarily by a white, educated, middle-class audience likely inspired by what Howard Mumford Jones calls the "cosmopolitan spirit" of the age. Since, as Jones argues, this spirit was inspired by a taste for the exotic, as long as Eaton was careful to distinguish herself from the negative image of the Chinese in the minds of most Americans—and she was—her writing could be the focus of such attention.

The contemporary view of Edith Eaton is driven not by cosmopolitanism but by multiculturalism. Eaton is "claimed" by Asian American scholars as the first Chinese American writer. Indeed, had she not been so claimed by Asian American studies, few if any, contemporary readers would know about her. However, the label "Chinese American" has thus far produced critical readings that limit a more complete understanding of Eaton's work. Far from regarding herself as a writer with this specific ethnic label, Eaton assumed a variety of stances related to but not centered within the category "Chinese American." In her non-fiction, she acted as a sympathetic, non-Chinese "interpreter" of the Chinese in America; in her magazine fiction, she assumes the role of a Chinatown insider of indeterminate ethnicity writing stories to increase understanding about the American Chinese; in her children's stories, she becomes a Chinese Mother Goose telling tales of her homeland for American children; and in her autobiographical writing she claims a mixed Chinese/Anglo ancestry, aiming to create awareness about mixed-race Asians.

Sui Sin Far's fictional Eurasians—the particular focus, here—assume similarly fluid subject positions. While none of her heroines suffer the sublime abjection of a character like Joe Christmas, they do struggle to negotiate solutions to racial and cultural conflict in situations where there are seldom real villains or victims. These young women seem to live with the same urgent questions at heart that Sui Sin Far asked as a child. In her autobiographical essay titled "Leaves From the Mental Portfolio of an Eurasian," she recalls the questions of her childhood, which indicate that, for young Edith, being Eurasian meant being neither English nor Chinese nor some harmonious blend of these, but rather someone racially unclassifiable, a misfit: "Why are we what we are? I and my brothers and sisters. Why did God make us to be hooted and stared at? Papa is English, mamma is Chinese. Why couldn't we have been one thing or the other?" (888).

The first of Eaton's stories to feature a Eurasian character was "The Sing-Song Woman," originally published in *Land of Sunshine* in 1898. Mag-gee, the protagonist, has a name that mimics her "half-white" (Eaton does not call her half-Chinese) status, for it is pronounced like the American name Maggie, but the spelling looks like translated Chinese. Miserable at the thought of her impending marriage to a "Chinaman," the girl wants, like other American girls, to marry whom she chooses. She insists, in a rather breathless litany of characteristics, that her physical appearance and personality testify to a less racially ambiguous and decidedly white self: "I was born in America, and I'm not Chinese in looks nor in any other way. See! My eyes are blue, and there is gold in my hair; and I love potatoes and beef, and every time I eat rice it makes me sick, and so does chopped up food" (237). Mag-gee is not only in love with the idea of white America, she has internalized the race prejudice directed at the Chinese, railing, "To think of having to marry a Chinaman! How I hate the Chinese!" (237).

Her resistance pays off when her Chinese friend, an actress called the Sing-Song Woman, suggests to Mag-gee that they play a trick on her father, Hwuy Yen. The Sing-Song woman will play the part of Mag-gee the bride during the wedding ceremony, while Mag-gee runs off with her meat-and-potatoes man. The implicit irony of this scheme lies within the notion of the roles of bride-impostor and true bride. Hwuy Yen expects to betroth his daughter to a Chinese man, at which point Mag-gee will go "away forever to live in China" (237). Her father has forced her to "put the paint and powder on [her] face, and dress in Chinese clothes." She laments, "I shall be a Chinese woman next year—I commenced to be one today" (237). In other words, now that she is of marrying age, the biracial Mag-gee must assume the ethnic status of her father and her future husband. (Mothers are curiously absent in the work of both Eatons). But if being a Chinese woman is a role that she can don like a wedding gown; and if, like a wedding gown, her ethnicity is nothing but a nuptial appurtenance, then Mag-gee is decidedly not already (that is, biologically) Chinese. Mag-gee is the "real" bride in that she is the legitimate, presumably virgin daughter of Hwuy Yen. Yet her Chinese-ness is real neither to her father nor to herself. Since her father intends to pass her off as Chinese for what is, essentially, the rest of her life, the "real" bride is, ethnically, a fake.

On the other hand, the Sing-Song Woman is an "actress" by profession, a term which implies pretense, and which is probably a euphemism for prostitute (White-Parks 171). Thus, she is neither the actual daughter of Hwuy Yen nor a virgin; but because she is authentically Chinese—and because she desires to marry the bridegroom, Ke Leang—she is "real" in the way that counts. After the bride-impostor has been unveiled, Hwuy Yen demands to know where Mag-gee has gone. The Sing-Song Woman replies with "bright, defiant eyes" which "met her questioner's boldly" that Mag-gee has run off with a white man (239). Her daring seems inspired by the fact that she is only acting out of "mischief" in a "play," says she, "like the play I shall act tomorrow" (240). But, in the end, the Sing-Song Woman wins Ke Leang as a real husband by being authentic in the two respects in which Mag-gee would have had to fake it—in her desire for and her ethnic suitability for a Chinese husband.

Meanwhile, Mag-gee's father is unconcerned about his daughter once he learns she has run away. His last words concern not Mag-gee but the Sing-Song Woman, about whom he declares to his would-be son-in-law, "See how worthless a thing she is" (239). She has beat him at his own game. Presumably, both women have achieved their heart's desire because each has, in her own way, come clean. But at the end of the story, only the Sing-Song Woman's future happiness as a wife is predicted. Of Mag-gee's fate, none are the wiser. The girl's near-hysterical reaction against the Chinese might be seen as entirely unsympathetic, but her choice of a racial identity can only be empowering when it isn't compelled. If she has chosen to live her life as white, it is also the only other option available to her when she refuses to live her life as Chinese. Ultimately, her refusal to live out the ethnic fate her father intends for her results in Mag-gee's disappearance from the narrative, as though a woman who chooses self-definition as both a sexual and racial being places her literally beyond the bounds of domestic fiction. Her choosing whiteness signifies not only her familial but her textual exile: the whiteness of the blank page.

Another story by Sui Sin Far, "Its Wavering Image," illustrates a similar identity effacement by the forces of culture and community. Young Pan (whose name, in English, means "a combining" as a noun and "to join or fit together" as a verb) wavers between loyalty to her white suitor, Mark Carson, and to her community, Chinatown—between the lure of sexual maturity and the safety of her childhood as a Chinese girl. As in "The Sing-Song Woman," Pan's white mother has passed away long ago, and so Pan has grown up regarding herself as fully Chinese. But the young woman's Chinese identity is founded in a dread of the unknown rather than in a conscious decision to identify with her Chinese side. She "always turned from whites," and shrank "from their curious scrutiny as she would from the sharp edge of a sword" (85-86). Consequently, Pan is forced to deal with the conflict inherent in her racial makeup before she can freely choose any single identity.

That conflict arrives in the form of the opportunistic journalist, Mark Carson. Known as the man who would "sell his soul for a story" (86), Carson has been trying to get an inside look at Chinatown since it became part of his beat. Since Pan was "born a Bohemian, exempt from the conventional restrictions imposed upon either the white or Chinese woman" (86), she feels free to associate with this white man without threat of censure. She "led him about Chinatown, initiating him into the simple mystery and history of many things" (87).

So well does Mark win her over that this once-Chinese girl begins to regard herself as white, precipitating her internal struggle. She feels "at times as if her white self must entirely dominate and trample under foot her Chinese" (87). Were this merely a story about growing pains or a girl's coming-of-age, then Pan would eventually marry Mark, which would mean she would "choose" to become white, leaving Chinatown and her father behind. But as in "The Sing-Song Woman," such a choice does not guarantee happiness, for racial indeterminacy is not so easily resolved.[1] Her internal conflict over white and Chinese identity is not simply a symbol for the conflict between childhood and adulthood or girlhood and womanhood. Racial indeterminacy is its own conflict, disrupting the traditional coming-of-age narrative line.

Soon, Mark pushes Pan too hard. He tries to persuade her to leave Chinatown, insisting, "you do not belong here," and "you are white—white [...]. You have no right to be here, your real life is alien to them" (89). Because Pan demurs, Mark gives her an ultimatum: she must decide between living in Chinatown or in white society, and he frames this decision as the choice to be with him or without him. "Pan," Mark urges, "don't you see that you have got to decide what you will be—Chinese or white? You cannot be both!" (90). Mark's insistence that his lover leave behind her racial murkiness and "choose" to be white, and his belief that, in fact, it is possible for her to do so, is similar to the expectations of Mag-gee's father. Both cases indicate that the fulfillment of a woman's sexual role as wife and mother comes with the prerequisite of her racial clarity. As Gina Marchetti points out in *Romance and the Yellow Peril*, Eurasian women implicitly pose a threat to certain foundations of white civilization as representatives of "taboo sexuality." So Mark's insistence that Pan decide who she will be is also an insistence on "racial boundaries and traditional morality" (Marchetti 71).

---

1   The term *mulatto*, says Hortense Spillers, "tells us little or nothing about the subject buried beneath them, but quite a great deal more concerning the psychic and cultural reflexes that invent and invoke them" (166).

Nearly broken by her lover's coercion, Pan is later calmed when he sings her a song about the "wavering image" of the moon casting its broken reflection upon the water. The song declares that the image is symbolic of heaven's perfect love cast imperfectly upon the earth, but it is Pan's image of herself that is broken. Even as she weeps, Mark declares that her tears "prove that you are white" (91).

Soon, Mark has his story and publishes the secrets and mysteries of Chinatown Pan has revealed to him in the daily newspaper. When she learns of this betrayal, she retreats to her room, this time alone, and gazes up again at the moon's wavering image. "A white woman!" she whispers. "I would not be a white woman for all the world. *You* are a white man. And *what* is a promise to a white man!" (95). The true "wavering image" is Pan's own image of herself as first Chinese, then white, then Chinese. Formerly, she had not recognized that the racial identity she chose was her decision all along, not Mark's, and for that mistake she became his victim. And yet Mark is not entirely to blame; he has simply acted as the catalyst for the real growing up Pan must do, the kind that involves not simply becoming someone's wife but becoming one's true self.

Now, seeing that she might have been the agent of her own change, Pan feels only bitterness. For a while, the "element of Fire" rages "so fiercely within her that it had almost shriveled up the childish frame." But in the end she decides that both whiteness and the "wavering" she endured while in love are too much for her. She returns to identifying with "the race that remembers" (92). In the last image of the story, Pan is comforted by a friend's young Chinese daughter, who climbs onto her lap and presses her head against Pan's "sick bosom." The image is both that of Pan's former uncomplicated Chinese self and a harbinger of her future as a Chinese mother. But these identities offer no real comfort or solution; for if Pan salvages her broken identity, she does so by regressing to an innocent, "pre-wavering" self to which she can never really return. She has only the hope that her bitterness will one day pass. For contemporary readers accustomed to stories that celebrate the return to ethnic origins, this ending may seem quizzical at first. Yet for Sui Sin Far's Eurasian heroines, a deepening of ethnic identity is not the answer.

What "Its Wavering Image" suggests most strongly is that Pan's sense of herself will never be perfect or complete now that she has felt the Fire—the pain of living beyond or between racial and cultural categories. And yet, as is also true for Mag-gee, life's experiences are keenest at this border, where there is deep love, and great risk. What persists, however, in Eaton's work as a whole, is the strong presence of the wavering image—of movement itself representing the possibility of a strategic identity. Mag-gee, Pan, and others of Eaton's Eurasian heroines achieve this only in glimpses, which takes courage enough. As she declares in her autobiographical essay, "Leaves From the Mental Portfolio of an Eurasian": "I give my right hand to the Occidentals and my left to the Orientals, hoping that between them they will not utterly destroy the insignificant 'connecting link.'" For Sui Sin Far, living in-between is both dangerous and inevitable. "The hybrid flower," she writes, "is the saddest flower of all" (895). As a Eurasian, she calls herself a "pioneer." It is the wavering itself, and not any single identity, that gives meaning to her own and her characters' racial sense of self.

Turning Japanese

Edith Eaton's younger sister, Winnifred, wrote only novels and changed ethnicities like costumes. At various points in her career, she wrote under the pen names Winnifred Mooney, Winnifred Babcock Reeve, Winnifred Eaton Reeve, and Onoto Watanna, as well as under her given name, which has appeared as Winnifred and Winifred, and as Winnifred Eaton and Winnifred Babcock Eaton. The pen names helped to fashion Eaton's various literary personas as a working-class Irish American, an Englishwoman in the Canadian west, and most successfully, as the daughter of a Japanese noblewoman. (She was, in fact, the daughter of a Chinese circus-performer).

In many respects, Winnifred Eaton is the opposite of Edith. The older sister struggled throughout her career to earn enough money to support herself as a writer, and by the end of her career had produced but a single book—a collection of her previously published works. Winnifred, on the other hand, supported herself and her four children as a single mother on the proceeds of her book sales and screenplays. She produced almost a novel a year between 1901 and 1916—fourteen novels in all—and an autobiography, as well as headed the screenplay division of Universal Studios between 1924 and 1931. Edith, sickly since childhood, died in 1914 at the relatively young age of forty-nine, while her sister outlived her by thirty years.

Probably the most significant distinction that has been noted between the sisters lies in the diverging ethnic emphases in their work. As Amy Ling has described it, "since her sister had gone the Chinese route" Winnifred would "be the admired kind of 'Oriental'" (25). In other words, since Edith chose to champion the cause of the then much-vilified Chinese in America, Winnifred would don a kimono and, in an ironic twist on the "paper son" practice in which the Chinese sought to enter the country illegally after the Chinese Exclusion Act of 1882, pretended to be from across the waters. With seven novels to her credit as Onoto Watanna, an imaginary family history that contained royal blood, and even a "reasonable imitation of cursive Japanese writing" (Ling 25) in her facsimile signature on the title page of her novels, Winnifred Eaton had succeeded quite remarkably at "turning Japanese."

While Winnifred Eaton did, in fact, pretend to be Japanese in the literary world, she also engaged other ethnicities at other times—as the Irish author of *The Diary of Delilah* (1907), the British author of *His Royal Nibs* (1925), and the Canadian author of *Cattle* (1923). She also assumed her sister Sara's persona as narrator of *Marion: A Story of an Artist's Model* (1916) and a fictional persona as the narrator, Nora Ascough, in her autobiography, *Me: A Book of Remembrance* (1915). Ling was the first to note that Winnifred acted as an "ethnic chameleon," but she doesn't fully account for the significance of this "trickster" act. For Ling, Eaton's turning Japanese (and Irish and British Canadian) was a rejection of her ethnic heritage. Eaton was not, she tells us, "a challenger or protester, not a word-warrior"—the qualities most valued in contemporary critical studies of ethnic American fiction. The best that can be said about her is that she "made for herself a dazzling career by catering to and expressing [...] myths," social, sexual, and racial, "which she understood so well" (Ling 55). But in order to discover the ways in which Eaton articulated her ethnic identity, you have to look in the right place: Winnifred Eaton was not a Chinese American writer, she was a Eurasian one. She was, indeed, not a "cause" writer. But she was not so much "hiding" her Chinese affiliation as using the strategy of "ethnic chameleon" to resist any single affiliation altogether (in this crucial respect, the sisters' projects, as Eurasians, can actually be seen as allied).

As the author of seven "Japanese" novels, Winnifred Eaton could claim literary predecessors like Pierre Loti and Lafcadio Hearn, who had established an audience of mostly female readers of exoticized sentimental fiction and Orientalist portraits of the East. Eaton would have relied heavily on the work of japanophiles like Loti and Hearn, having never traveled to Japan herself, nor studied formally the culture or language. And she must have done her homework well. Ling cites Japanese critics and a Japanese student who reviewed her novels favorably, reporting that her work played an "important role in introducing things Japanese to the American public" (54). Furthermore, the "Japanese" novels underwent painstaking handiwork in order to appear authentic. The pages are faintly embossed with "Japanese" images of cherry blossoms and pagodas. Shiny gold "Japanese"-style lettering with brightly colored images decorate every jacket cover. Several full color illustrations, mostly of the Japanese or Eurasian heroines and their lovers, are included in each volume. Such elaborate orientalization lends a souvenir-quality authentication to the reading experience, a marketing strategy which Elizabeth Ammons notes was relatively unique at this time (119).

Three of Onoto Watanna's seven "Japanese" novels contain part-Japanese, part-Anglo heroines, however, and the conflicts they experience as racial outcasts are remarkably similar to those portrayed in the work of Sui Sin Far. Where Mag-gee and Pan are "wavering" figures, Watanna's Eurasians are positively elusive, literally fleeing from the constraints of social ascription at every turn. Eaton's first "Eurasian" novel, *Tama* (1910), opens with the arrival of the unlikely romantic hero, the Tojin-san (Honorable Mr. Foreigner) in a small village in Japan. He is no longer young, but he has been seized by a longing for adventure after spending his younger days as the university's "Old Grind." A social outcast because of a battle with smallpox that has left him physically ravaged, the Tojin-san hopes to begin his life anew as a teacher of the Japanese. However, the remote province of Fukui has been so little touched by Westernization that the villagers are but "fearfully and curiously holding out a grudging hand to the Western nations pressing her on all sides" (66).

The people retain superstitious beliefs in gods and spirits, and are particularly fearful of the enchanted "fox-woman," whom they blame for all of the bloodshed and poverty the city has endured since the Restoration. The fox-woman was an actual figure of legend in Japanese culture. Eaton had probably read Hearn's account of this figure in his own Fox Woman tale in his collection *Glimpses of Unfamiliar Japan* and created her own Tama, who wanders the forests, stealing food to survive. The villagers warn the Tojin-san about the woman with unnaturally gold hair and blue eyes, traits they have never seen in humans. His curiosity piqued, the Tojin-san finally catches a glimpse of this enchantress. Not only is she just a harmless girl, she is stunning as well. The book's illustrations do reveal an almost disturbing incongruousness (and biological improbability) in her features. In the frontispiece, Tama is a slight, but shapely figure in a drapey white kimono tied loosely with a high blue sash and revealing a hint of red undergarments (associated with wedding garments in Chinese culture) underneath. Her gold hair rivals Rapunzel's, sweeping the ground behind her like a veil. Yet her rounded face and slanted (though blue) eyes are unmistakably Oriental. Her ancient look of impassive resignation underlies her air of long-suffering. And the Tojin-san has decided he must have her.

The citizens are horrified. Even the supposedly more enlightened university students are sure that the visitor from America has been bewitched. Although it is far from the truth that Tama has chosen to assert her own desires in winning over her suitor, the Fukui believe this is precisely what she has done. Tama's social and racial unclassifiablity seems to indicate above all a moral threat. To the Fukui, she embodies what Gina Marchetti argues later becomes a cinematic motif spanning the century: the Eurasian "siren" acts as the "agent of social havoc and moral ruin" (71). Since the Tojin-san refuses to give her up, hostility arises against both the professor and the fox-woman he has captured and brought home. Such a union, the villagers fear, will bring disaster to the province. In one of her most direct statements about the historical encounter between East and West, Eaton writes:

> A sullen rebellious hatred for the white nations who had brought this new state of affairs about—a murderous, resentful impulse of revenge. It was the same feeling that had animated the misguided patriots of Satsume, when they fought the allied fleet at Kagoshima, but it was uglier, meaner, for its force was directed upon two individuals, who, for the Fukui mind, represented the detested nations of the West. One of these [...] was directly responsible for the disaster. She the accursed outcast... (133)

Tama is a cultural symbol for all that these Japanese fear about the invasion of the Western "barbarians." The daughter of a Japanese Buddhist nun-gone-wrong and an irresponsible foreign sailor, Tama wanders the forests, dispossessed. She remains nameless throughout most of the novel, as it is told from the point of view of the Tojin-san, who spends most of the story seeking this elusive girl. She also remains voiceless until he captures her, and when she does speak, it is arguable whether she can be said to have a language or not. Abandoned as a child and having spoken to no one since that time, Tama knows no Japanese and her English isn't much better. She remains completely marginalized by her racial ambiguity and can have no nationality in the eyes of the Fukui, who, having little experience with foreigners, have no reason to distinguish between racial and national identity. Thus, Tama is a heroine with no family, no name, no race, no voice, no language, and no country. And as if that weren't enough to be without, Tama is blind. She literally cannot see for herself those characteristics about her—namely, hair, eyes, and skin, that inspire such dread in the Fukui. She is the product of an illegal and abhorred union without place, name, or nation. To the villagers, she is inhuman, a dangerous and incomprehensible mixture of East and West. But she is also the scapegoat for all the troubles descending on them from across the sea. Symbolically and actually, Tama inhabits the territory of exile.

In his essay, "The Symbolic Element in History," Robert Darnton tells us that the ambiguous position of the taboo figure is related to its position as mediator between a culture's binary opposites. Those things which "slip in between categories, that straddle boundaries, or spill beyond borders threaten our basic sense of order" (223). Tama is such a figure for the Fukui, both revered and feared, marginal, unclassifiable, and she likely functioned as fraught cultural symbol for her American readers as well. Although the heroine is safely tucked away in a "formula romance" (as Eaton, herself, called her novels) and in a distant setting, the hostility of the Fukui is but thin disguise for the hostility of many Americans of Eaton's time toward a racial, social, ethnic misfit like Tama.

Turn-of-the-century Americans were fascinated with the Japanese as a new global power and had developed a taste for things Japanese, but as soon as the Japanese began emigrating to the United States in significant numbers, they began to be perceived as every bit the threat the Chinese were in the minds of many Americans. It is, therefore, not entirely accurate to assume that Winnifred Eaton chose to assume a Japanese literary persona simply because she wanted to be the "admired kind of Oriental." And Eaton's own dismissal of her work as mere "formula romances" belies what can be found there. Nowadays, the elder Edith enjoys far more admiring critical attention than her vastly more successful sister—an ironic reversal of fortune for the literary reputations of this pair, but one based on the erroneous assumption that Sui Sin Far's project was to embrace an ethnicity that her sister denied.

In the years immediately preceding the publication of *Tama,* anti-Japanese sentiment began to reach near-hysterical proportions on the West Coast. As early as 1907, the California legislature began hearings on a series of bills designed to prohibit landownership by Japanese immigrants. In that same year, the Asiatic Exclusion League was formed, its constitution founded on the belief that the Caucasian and the Asiatic races (which, by the end of its tenure, grew to include Koreans and Filipinos as well as Chinese and Japanese) were "unassimilable." Newspapers like the *San Francisco Chronicle* and several nationalist organizations stepped up what Ronald Takaki called their "exclusionist clamor" (201). Cecil B. DeMille's 1915 film *The Cheat* portrays the rape of an innocent blond girl by an evil and lecherous Japanese. In 1907, President Roosevelt was forced to deploy federal troops in California in order to protect the Japanese against mob violence. His concerns about a possible retaliation by the Japanese were underscored by the 1909 publication of Homer Lea's *The Valor of Ignorance*, which "worked out in startling detail a prediction of Japanese military occupation of the West coast" (202). Such was the climate in which Winnifred Eaton penned her allegedly frivolous romances.

From 1910 onward, one of the hottest issues taken up by anti-Japanese agitators was interracial marriage. Although miscegenation between Caucasians and "Asiatics" was both statistically insignificant and technically illegal in California and other states with an Asian presence, the threat posed by what Darnton calls the "collapsing of categories" was strong. Several films depicting the threat of miscegenation abounded at the height of Watanna's writing career and during her years at Universal Studios, including the well-known *Birth of a Nation* (1915), *The Cheat* (1915), a film containing a white woman threatened by a Japanese villain, and another film, *Broken Blossoms* (1918), which poses hints of sexual relations between a white woman and a kind-hearted Chinese. Imagined scenarios in which a lecherous Chinese or Japanese takes advantage of a citizen's white daughter are common throughout the published proceedings of the *Asiatic Exclusion League* from 1907 to 1913. In *The Politics of Prejudice*, Roger Daniels shares the statement of a typical anti-Japanese demonstrator concerning the union of a Japanese farmer and his white American wife. This former Congregational minister declared: "In that woman's arms is a baby. What is that baby? It isn't Japanese. It isn't white. It is a germ of the mightiest problem that ever faced this state; a problem that will make the black problem of the South look white" (quoted in Daniels 59). Perhaps even more disturbingly, a leading spokesman of the California Progressives in 1910 makes clear that even though racial discrimination was rightly seen as prejudice by many, racial mixing was yet widely considered by the state's supposedly more level-headed citizens to be a dangerous practice. The spokesman declared,

> Race [...] counts more than anything else in the world [...]. So the line is biological, and we draw it at the biological point, at the propagation of the species. Intermarriage between a Japanese and a White would be a sort of international

adultery [...]. The instinct of self-preservation of our race demands that its future members shall be members of our race. (Daniels 119)

In light of such prejudice, Eaton's *Tama* takes on more than mere sentimental significance. Since Eaton's novel is set in Japan, the threat Tama poses to racial purity is to the Japanese. But the imaginative distance between the villagers of Fukui and the Americans clamoring about miscegenation and the yellow peril is, in comparison to the geographical distance between them, slender indeed. Eaton's heroine is an outcast in both cultures—the fictional world of *Tama* and the real world of the West in 1910.

Toward the novel's end, Tama and Tojin-san are forced out of Fukui due to the growing hostility against them. They escape to the forests, where Tama teaches her lover to live in the wild. There, the outcasts spend several idyllic months together and, at one point, set up housekeeping in the temple where her mother had worshipped her Japanese gods and was visited by her father, the sailor. Here, Tama kneels in the corner before a "tattered, shabby scroll" bearing a picture of Jesus Christ—a subtle indication of her fitness for civilized life and also, given the rhetoric of Eaton's day, an assertion of her superior white blood (192). Eventually, students still loyal to the Tojin-san find him there and persuade him to return to civilization, where he and Tama can be accepted in Tokyo, if not in a remote province like Fukui.

Called back to a sense of duty and the desire for legitimation, the Tojin-san endeavors to get on with their life together among others. Tama is naturally reluctant to go with him. She has already found more acceptance with the Tojin-san than she had ever hoped for and fears losing it to the hostile Japanese. Eventually she does agree to return to the city with him, whereupon an old friend of the professor's offers to perform an operation which will restore Tama's sight. Of course, the Tojin-san fears that Tama's love for him will not be so blind once she gets a look at him. He agrees to let her have the operation, but refuses to see her after it is performed. "What you believe now to be beautiful," he explains, "may prove to be otherwise" (230).

Ostensibly, the professor's words demonstrate his love for Tama: he will not have her suffer his "horrible" face. Yet this emphasis on visual facts reveals an underlying power distinction which is exactly the opposite of what it appears. On one hand, the Tojin-san originally contradicted the Fukui belief in Tama as fox-woman because, as a heterosexual male, he could clearly see that she was beautiful, regardless of her racial makeup. But in another sense, his superior vision, which allows him to "read" Tama as a helpless, harmless beauty, is based not only in desire but in his secure racial sense of self: he reads the signs of his own race in her features and claims her as his "own," racially as well as romantically. Yet by the same token, he cannot trust that once her sight is restored Tama will claim him in the same way, for she has no racial standard of her own by which to read the features of another, and thus no power to claim another.

Forlorn, Tama returns to the forests and to her status as outcast, while her lover goes back to his work, now in Fukui, where the spirit of modernization has finally begun to take hold. Only this time, Tama can see. She will not, again, accept her banishment, not when legitimation for herself as a woman—even if the same is impossible for her as a person of indeterminate race—is that close at hand. She will not gain a better understanding of herself as a racial being, but she will gain a social definition as "wife" that will end her social exile, an exile that originated in the notion of her mixed blood. "Romantic love wins out," writes Gina Marchetti, "over the ability to define the self in a racist society" (70). She steals back to the Tojin-san, is undaunted by his physical appearance, and they are happily reunited.

Tama is an extremely appealing heroine with Caucasian features and an exotic hint of the Oriental. Her Japanese blood hardly seems the threat posed by exclusionist American visions of the degenerate Asian. Provocative as she may be, however, this romantic heroine is nothing less than an unclassified alien created in the "one-drop" era, when Americans known to have Asian ancestry were considered as "tainted" as those having African American or Cherokee "blood." *Tama* may have seemed to the *New York Times* to be "charmingly Japanese," and "fragrant, dainty, elusive" but among Eaton's contemporaries were those attempting to prove that the mixing of races would result in a "physically and psychologically mutated people" (Motoyoshi 77). For every loving (although today we would call them orientalist) depiction of Japan by Lafcadio Hearn there were dozens of stories, novels, films, and plays depicting the "yellow peril" which abounded years before Asian Americans would come to write their own stories and their own history. Tama is Eaton's response.

It is a politically significant act to claim or reclaim writers as African American, Asian American, American Indian or Latino/a (add to this list a seemingly endless proliferation of difference, including Arab American and writers of the diaspora), but reading within ethnic paradigms is something of a necessary evil. It is difficult to keep from sliding toward the notion of essence. Race is so salient, Howard Winant explains, that Americans tend to naturalize it—it becomes "real" (37). Contemporary critical readings of American ethnic literature do not consider fully non-paradigmatic articulations of racial experience. The important work of ethnic literary recovery need not limit authors to their ethnic classifications, because too often the only ticket out becomes the author's ability to address the themes that are regarded as timeless and universal in her critics' particular place and time.

By defining Eurasian experience as processual and dislocatory, the Eaton sisters declared themselves beyond racial classification and racial mixture. Sui Sin Far's own definition of the term "Chinese American" writer was probably more analogous to the term "nature writer" in her own time, the modifier describing her subject matter rather than her subjectivity. Onoto Watanna makes no direct statements about the situation of a racial and cultural hybrid, yet she succeeds in creating heroines whose fate we care about, which is surely an important form of understanding necessary for creating awareness. If their blue-eyed Asian maidens-in-distress were not recognized as the locus of ambivalent feeling and cross-cultural tension in their own age, then in our age of the global village—when national borders change almost daily and racial strife runs high, when American minority and immigrant populations are growing, and when racial and cultural blendings indicate changes for the coming century—their contributions to American literature are, if not timeless, then at least timely.

Works Cited

Ammons, Elizabeth. *Conflicting Stories: American Women Writers at the Turn into the Twentieth Century.* New York and London: Oxford UP, 1992.

—, and Annette White-Parks, eds. *Tricksterism in Turn-of-the-Century American Literature: A Multicultural Perspective.* Hanover and London: UP of New England, 1994.

Asiatic Exclusion League. *Proceedings of the Asiatic Exclusion League, 1907-1913.* New York: Arno P, 1977.

Bhabha, Homi K. *The Location of Culture.* London and New York: Routledge, 1994.

Daniels, Roger C. *The Politics of Prejudice: The Anti-Japanese Movement in California and the Struggle for Japanese Exclusion.* Berkeley and Los Angeles: U of California P, 1978.

Darnton, Robert. "The Symbolic Element in History." *Journal of Modern History* 58 (1986): 218-34.

Eaton, Edith. (Sui Sin Far). "Leaves From the Mental Portfolio of an Eurasian." *Heath Anthology of American Literature* Vol. 2. Ed. Paul Lauter. Lexington, MA and Toronto: D. C. Heath and Company, 1990. 885-95.

—. *Mrs. Spring Fragrance.* Chicago: A. C. McClurg, 1912.

Eaton, Winnifred. (Onoto Watanna). *Me: A Book of Remembrance.* New York: Century, 1915.

—. *Tama.* New York and London: Harper and Brothers, 1910.

Faulkner, William. *Light in August.* (1926). New York: Modern Library, 1968.

Hearn, Lafcadio. *Glimpses of Unfamiliar Japan.* Boston and New York: Houghton, Mifflin and Company, 1894.

Higham, John. *Strangers in the Land: Patterns of American Nativism 1860-1925.* New York: Atheneum, 1981.

Jones, Howard Mumford. *The Age of Energy: Varieties of American Experience 1865-1915.* New York: Viking P, 1971.

Lea, Homer. *The Valor of Ignorance.* New York and London: Harper and Bros, 1909.

Ling, Amy. *Between Worlds: Women Writers of Chinese Ancestry.* New York: Pergamon P, 1990.

Loti, Pierre. *Japoneries d'autumne.* Paris: Calmann-Levy, 1903.

Marchetti, Gina. *Romance and the Yellow Peril: Race, Sex, and Discursive Strategies in Hollywood Fiction.* Berkeley, Los Angeles, and London: U of California P, 1993.

Motoyoshi, Michelle M. "The Experience of Mixed-Race People: Some Thoughts and Theories." *Journal of Ethnic Studies* 18.2 (1990-91): 77-94.

Spillers, Hortense J. "Notes on an Alternative Model—neither/nor." *The Difference Within: Feminism and Critical Theory.* Eds. Elizabeth Meese and Alice Parker. Amsterdam and Philadelphia: John Benjamins Publishing Company, 1989. 171-90.

White-Parks, Annette. "The Wisdom of the New." *Legacy* 5.3: 34-49.

—. "Sui Sin Far/Edith Maude Eaton: Writer on the Chinese-Anglo Borders of America." Diss. Washington State University, 1992.

—. *Sui Sin Far/Edith Maude Eaton: A Literary Biography.* Urbana: U of Illinois P, 1995.

Winant, Howard. *Racial Conditions: Politics, Theory, Comparisons.* Minneapolis: U of Minnesota P, 1994.

Celebrating Ourselves in the Other, Or:
Who Controls the Conceptual Allusions in Kingston?

Sämi Ludwig

"Rabbits taste like chickens." (26)[1]

Maxine Hong Kingston's *The Woman Warrior* has met with phenomenal success. It has been claimed as a masterpiece by academics, been written about in major journals and taught at almost all colleges and universities. It has been read by an enormous number of readers. Ferraro maintains that "*The Woman Warrior* sells steadily, 450,000 copies to date" (219). In 1997 Kingston received the National Humanities Medal from President Clinton at the White House. This raises the question of what it is that readers find so attractive in this book. What, precisely, do all of these people understand when they read it? What insights, moreover, are being celebrated by the majority of her readers, who are outsiders to Chinese American culture? This is a particularly crucial issue because *The Woman Warrior* is a book about bicultural experience that has succeeded with an intercultural readership—one that is to a great extent not Chinese American.

Significantly, some aspects of Kingston's success have been bitter-sweet. In many circles she has been read as a culture-broker and turned into a representative of the Chinese American experience as such. Conversely, some of her Chinese American colleagues have accused her of misrepresenting the authentic Chinese tradition and selling out to Western expectations. Sensing the non-Chinese elements in *The Woman Warrior*, they have called her a "traitor" because she would tamper with the "original" form of Chinese legends, an act which Frank Chin labels a "violation of history and fact" ("The Most Popular Book" 11). Thus, at some point even Kingston herself felt the need to interfere, and commented in "Cultural Mis-readings" on how uncomfortable she was about being both criticized and praised for the wrong reasons.

My focus in this paper is mainly on the problem of allusive reference in an intercultural context. I believe that many highly complex affinities with generally Western culture and specifically American literature in *The Woman Warrior* (which is after all written in English) have been unconsciously picked up or projected and aesthetically processed in a subliminal way, but then been inter-

---

1   All page numbers in brackets refer, if not otherwise indicated, to *The Woman Warrior*.

preted as essentially Chinese. The modernist kind of density of the text has been appropriated in ways that often misrecognize the "American" references as the "Chinese" ones in a way that does justice to neither. In order to explain my case, let me first present some opinions about Kingston's book and then point out some possible Western readings in her text in order to show how certain projective celebrations are constructed. I will finally suggest that because of such appropriative readings, Kingston has changed her later writing style in significant ways, not necessarily giving up the modernist kind of allusive density, but using a more transparent referentiality in order to control meanings in ways that can no longer be misunderstood or misrepresented.

Many readers have imposed a coherent Chinese identity onto Maxine Hong Kingston, which manifests itself most forcefully when *The Woman Warrior* is read as a source of information on Chinese American life and on the "exotic" Chinese sensibility. Although Laureen Mar warns that this book "should not be read as a sociological report on Chinese-Americans, however willingly it lends itself to that cause" (quoted in Woo 177), Miller and Chang treat Kingston's memoirs as "sociological documents" (75), and Komenaka concludes her assessment by emphasizing the "rich opportunity to those sociolinguists and ethnolinguists, whether practicing scholars or students, who wish to observe their subjects in action and in context" (116). Most amazingly, such unreflected practices of appropriating a literary text as sociological data can also be found in the Modern Language Association's handbook to *The Woman Warrior*, edited by Shirley Geok-lin Lim. Some of the contributors to this volume even recommend that Kingston's artfully composed and highly figurative text should be read as a mimetic document of straightforward information. Thus McBride rejoices: "Luckily, in the field of ethnic studies, historians have valuable allies in writers emerging from the immigrant experience" (94). And Aubrey even asks students "to assume the role of armchair ethnologists" (84). What happens in a student's mind, if he or she does precisely this, is reported by Melton, who quotes a student: "[I]t really makes you just *sit* and think!" (79, original emphasis). And another student evaluates: "I was really shocked at how women within the society of the Orient were treated" (78). In my opinion such emotional reactions and simplistic attitudes of immediate *Betroffenheit* will only reify stereotypes and make the reader attribute even more Otherness to Chinese Americans. These readings provide a wry commentary on R.G. Lee's assessment that Kingston "stands Orientalism on its head" (62). Though theoretically she may "other" white Americans by describing them as "ghosts," the students' reactions indicate that ambiguous defamiliarization "really" can backfire.

As a cultural outsider I do not feel entitled to judge the Chineseness of Kingston's writing. Yet, what I find striking in this respect is how critics from China react to *The Woman Warrior*. Hongjun Su, for example, associates the villagers' white masks with the Ku Klux Klan and claims that calling the No Name Woman's hair "sexy" is an American attitude. The Chinese, according to her, think that skin is more alluring (23). She likewise relates the no name aunt's romantic inclinations to a "Western tradition" (15) and furthermore observes that "it is not a Chinese practice to throw eggs to show their resentment." Eggs are considered "good food" and are often "expensive" (22). Generally one gets the impression that Chinese readers also see in *The Woman Warrior* a "hyphenated" text, but one which gives them access to the other side of their perspective, namely the U.S. culture.[2] To them, Kingston is not Chinese but American, and this is what makes her text valuable.[3]

It may be more noticeable to foreign readers that Kingston has a strong background in American culture, not just as a self-conscious U.S. citizen, but as a trained teacher of English and American literature. She considers herself as coming from "Steinbeck's land" (Islas 16) and mentions Whitman, Hawthorne, and Woolf as her ancestors (Fishkin 790). Moreover, she tells Rabinowitz: "I think that my books are much more American than they are Chinese" (182). As I will argue, we can also find affinities with William Carlos Williams, Lewis Carroll, Emily Dickinson, T.S. Eliot, Sylvia Plath, Sherwood Anderson, and classical Western *topoi* in *The Woman Warrior*,[4] a fact which may suggest that Kingston is trying to wedge her way into and change the canon of American literature and its heritage. Still, it is not the aim of this paper to argue that any of these references, which are often simple coincidences, provide an explanation for Kingston's inspiration and creativity or furnish the "meaning" of her text. What matters is rather that vocabulary, imagery, and general structural analogies may invite certain kinds of readings. From the intercultural viewpoint, then, such understanding *can* take place, and because of that possibility it *does*—especially if we keep in mind that the majority of Kingston's readers are not Chinese Americans.

On a very general level, we can find classical Western *topoi* as we know them from Ernst Robert Curtius's investigation into the heart of Western culture. Thus there is a pastoral scene in Kingston's last description of the Chinese village before it is bombed by the Japanese: "peace and summer [....] blankets covering the wildflowers with embroidered flowers. [....] they were all together, idle above their fields, nobody hoeing, godlike; nobody weeding, New Year's in summer" (94). This world reminds one of the mythical standstill of a Golden Age. A further classical reference can be found in the mother's profession as a

---

2   Also see Ya-jie Zhang's approach as an example of a Chinese reading references in *The Woman Warrior*.

3   This does not seem to be the case with Chinese translations of *The Woman Warrior*. Kingston reports that the Chinese have adopted her as one of their own, mainly because so much of traditional Chinese culture (which they also find in *The Woman Warrior*!) has been lost during the cultural revolution (Fishkin 790).

4   Ferraro suggests the influence of Kate Chopin's *The Awakening* as well.

"midwife." She is in many ways a maieutic helper in the sense that we know from the Socratic dialogues, a "champion talker" (202) who tries to make little Maxine[5] give birth to the right kinds of words and ideas. Thus Rubenstein sees the mother "symbolically, as a midwife" (180), and Eakin calls her a "warrior woman midwife of speech" (268). For Li, "the mother Brave Orchid is both a literal and a literary midwife" ("The Production" 329).[6] This is one of the major concepts in the novel, and it clearly signifies on the Socratic usage. We may also want to associate Kingston's story of the blind "knot-maker" and the fact that her mother cut Maxine's frenum, "so you would not be tongue-tied" (164), with the legend of Alexander the Great, who cut the Gordian Knot and successfully conquered a big foreign country.[7]

We find traditional Christian motifs as well, such as the *mundus inversus*, e.g., when the Chinese aunt Moon Orchid is told about a particular brother who "doesn't obey" and hangs "upside down from the furniture like a bat" (132). Also Maxine hangs "upside down" (173) on the metal stairs in the school lavatory, this "different world" (175) where she encounters the quiet girl, her uncanny doppelgänger (another Western notion).[8] In both cases we have encounters with a reality of a totally different order, one that is well expressed in the logic of the antipodal image. On a very basic level, there is also an analogy in Moon Orchid's relationship with her American husband to the concept of a *sponsa Dei*. Her efforts in "At the Western Palace" follow the pattern of symbolic attachment to a ruling male logos that gives meaning and thus spiritual or mental life, i.e., to the *topos* of the divine bridegroom.[9] Generally the reflective kind of mirror identity as we have it in "Moon" Orchid is compatible with the notion of a Christian soul belonging to God.[10] And once we acknowledge the allusions to all of these Christian concepts, we may also notice that the traditional practice in the Chinese village of not talking at the dinner table (11) is isomorphic with the Western tradition of monastic silence.[11] All of these references come naturally to a Western reader. Whether they have been consciously

---

5   I will follow Mayer's terminology in my study and use the name "Kingston" for the adult author and the name "Maxine" for the child character in the book. Obviously at times they are difficult to keep apart, especially since Kingston tends to vary narrative distance greatly.

6   Li even sees Kingston's "subject constitution [....] intricately couched in terms of a birth metaphor" (329). On this issue, also see below, my references to Anderson's "youth."

7   Margaret Miller also associates the cut frenum with Alexander (13).

8   For a detailed tracing of the doppelgänger motif in Asian American literature, see Sau-ling Wong's chapter on "Encounters with the Racial Shadow" (*Reading* 77 ff.).

9   For examples of this image, see Matth. 9:15, II Corinth. 5:22, Revelation 21:1, and Underhill's comments (137-140).

10 Actually, Maxine's empathy with the monkey whose brain is eaten up points to the issue of monkey-like identity as a mere "aping" imitation of reality—another classical Christian image.

11 Also consider Maxine's brother's comment about their family: "Ah, you know they don't talk when they eat" (163).

or unconsciously borrowed by the author, they call up certain concepts and thus invoke functional analogies.

Other Western meanings have to do with English language puns and popular imagery. For example, Moon Orchid's exotic Chinese name makes great sense, if we see it as a premonition of her lunacy. Kingston also uses English puns, e.g., the word "dumb" meaning "silent" and "stupid" at the same time in Maxine's encounter with the quiet girl (189). More ambivalent is the Chinese character Moon Orchid's claim that the name "Maxine" sounds like "ink": Miller and Chang suggest "Maxink?" (90). However, coincidentally the Chinese word is "moshui" (literally "black water"), thus "Maxine" sounds like "ink" both in English and in Chinese. A more convincing example is the cigar store owner who "looked like a camel" (139). He provides an ethnic association which Western smokers of Camel cigarettes will consider very fitting.

There are many allusions to European history and legend in *The Woman Warrior*, interestingly even in the supposedly most Chinese episodes. For example, affinities with St. Joan in "White Tigers" are so obvious that Kingston has to explicitly deny them: "Marriage and childbirth strengthen the swordswoman, who is not a maid like Joan of Arc" (48). Still, the "beheading machine" (44) imitates a *guillotine* of the French Revolution. Fa Mu Lan's setting up a new calendar points to the same source of inspiration: "This is a new year, [...] the year one" (45). Sau-ling Wong, translating her name as "Sylvan Orchid," even finds Fa Mu Lan turning "into a Robin Hood type" ("Kingston's Handling" 31-32).[12] To point to all the implicit American cultural references is almost impossible in this context, but we should note little details, such as Fa Mu Lan asking the old Chinese couple for cookies: "'I'm starved. Do you have any cookies?' I like chocolate chip cookies" (21). And we may want to associate that foreign-sounding name "Brave Orchid" with Francis Scott Key's "home of the brave!" as an allusion to an original American kind of strength, implying an identity that is American rather than colorfully exotic.

Since Kingston's is a literary book, many of her references and allusions are to English and American literature. Pee Ah Nah's "slough" of madness is reminiscent of Bunyan[13]; the white desert in "White Tigers" in which Fa Mu Lan gets lost reminds one of T.S. Eliot's *Waste Land* as well as of Melville's famous chapter, "The Whiteness of the Whale," in *Moby Dick*. Furthermore, Lewis Carroll's Alice seems to have had a certain influence on the Fa Mu Lan story. Maxine's disappearance into a fantasy world of picture books and imagination, and her looking through a magic water gourd back onto reality "from the sky which was where I was" (22) suggests that she jumped *Through the Looking-*

---

12 R.G. Lee offers the literal translation "Wood Orchid" (58). Kingston herself claims that "White Tigers" "is not a Chinese myth but one transformed by America, a sort of kung fu movie parody" ("Cultural Mis-readings" 57).

13 This Chinese witch is, moreover, clearly modeled on imagery associated with Halloween; also see Kingston's comments in *Hawai'i* (39).

Glass into cosmology and is now exploring the realm of representation and the way it refers to reality. The No Name Woman's suicide in the family well would then be a negative and deadly version of such a leap through the mirror of a reality made out of socially constructed concepts. We may further see an oblique reference to Poe in the mentally retarded boy, this "hunching sitter" of no intelligence who becomes a prophet expressing Maxine's fear of going mad (220). And we find an echo of Twain in Moon Orchid's being "eager to work, roughing it in the wilderness" (135).

Of course, feminist icons are important in this novel. When Kingston describes her mother's life as a medical student at the To Keung School of Midwifery, her description of this community has obviously been influenced by Virginia Woolf:

> Not many women got to live out the daydream of women—to have a room, even a section of a room, that only gets messed up when she messes it up herself. The book would stay open at the very page she had pressed flat with her hand, and no one would complain about the field not being plowed or the leak in the roof. She would clean her own bowl and a small, limited area; she would have one drawer to sort, one bed to make. [...]. The Revolution put an end to prostitution by giving women what they wanted: a job and a room of their own. (61-62)

Another strong but rather oblique presence in the book is Sylvia Plath, whose imagery seems pervasive.[14] Thus the "dragon ways" in "White Tigers" can be seen as contrasting with Plath in the way they offer a positive attitude toward the fragmentary representation in Plath's "Colossus":

> I crawl like an ant in mourning
> Over the weedy acres of your brow
> To mend the immense skull plates and clear
> The bald, white tumuli of your eyes.

Compare this to how Kingston describes the dragon:

> Unlike tigers, dragons are so immense, I would never see one in its entirety. But I could explore the mountains, which are the top of its head. "These mountains are also *like* the tops of *other* dragons' heads," the old people would tell me. When climbing the slopes, I could understand that I was a bug riding on a dragon's forehead as it roams through space, its speed so different from my speed that I feel the dragon solid and immobile. (28-29)

---

14 Still, Kingston explicitly denies having been influenced by her (personal communication via email, June 1998).

Imagery of alienation is put into a context of assertion. Furthermore, Plath's idea of verbally cutting into reality with "axes" in "Words" agrees with Kingston's wanting to become a "lumberjack and a newspaper reporter" (203). Plath also anticipates Moon Orchid's notions of marrying a black-suited male Other and her empty, non-consequential "talk, talk, talk" ("The Applicant"), notions of identity approached through midwifery ("Morning Song," also "Mirror") and pregnancy ("Heavy Woman"), dying babies and destructive visions of "ash" ("Lady Lazarus"), the inability to have a voice of one's own in the face of a powerful superego ("Daddy"), panic emotions of "shrieks," "flaps" and "cries" ("Elm") and "bleeding" ("Cut"), and, most of all, a pervasive concern with the "mirror." Maxine's nightmares about a baby whose "skin tautens and its face becomes nothing but a red hole of a scream. The hole returns into a pinprick as the baby recedes from me" (87) is reminiscent of the "two wet eyes and a screech" in Plath's "Thalidomide." Kingston's imagery of wounds as an indicator of a painful but authentic self generally correlates with Plath, who is a specialist in this field.[15] We can even see Plath in the naming of the two alienated "Orchid" sisters: "The ghastly orchid / Hanging its hanging garden in the air" ("Fever 103°").

The status of these intertextual references, important in an analysis of the narrative as cultural production, nonetheless takes a back seat to their function, which may provide more important aspects of the subliminal logic of the text, as, for example, in the affinities of *The Woman Warrior* with *Winesburg, Ohio*. Though Kingston does not remember ever having read Sherwood Anderson,[16] the description of Maxine's "mysterious illness" uses some very similar images:

> The world is sometimes just, and I spent the next eighteen months sick in bed with a mysterious illness. There was no pain and no symptoms, though the middle line in my left palm broke in two. Instead of starting junior high school I lived like the Victorian recluses I read about. I had a rented hospital bed in the living room, where I watched soap operas on t.v., and my family cranked me up and down. I saw no one but my family, who took good care of me. I could have no visitors, no other relatives, no villagers. My bed was against the west window, and I watched the seasons change the peach tree. (181-82)

This can be compared to Anderson's description:

> The writer, an old man with a white mustache, had some difficulty in getting into bed. The windows of the house in which he lived were high and he wanted to look at the trees when he awoke in the morning. A carpenter came to fix the bed so that it would be on a level with the window. (21)

---

15 Also see "Tulips" ("Their redness talks to my wound") and the picture in Moon Orchid's former husband's office: "a tall black frame around white paint with dashes of red" (148).

16 Personal communication via email, June 1998.

He was like a pregnant woman, only that the thing inside him was not a baby but a youth. (22)

Though one describes a child and the other an old man,[17] both authors write about gaining understanding through some kind of sickness, about a bed artificially propped up, a person looking out of a window and watching nature before he (she) starts writing. If pregnancy of a very special kind appears in the old man as a "youth," i.e., not in a literal but in a rejuvenating conceptual sense, this ties in with the notion of Brave Orchid's cognitive midwifery that I have suggested above. It may also help us interpret the "eighteen months" that Maxine spent in bed as a figurative double pregnancy; the breaking of the "middle line" of her left palm in two points to a life split into Chinese American biculturalism.[18] Inside her grows a new identity that is based on the books she reads. If Anderson writes that it "was the young thing inside him that saved the old man" (24), a similar pupation time most probably trains Maxine to cope with her own former "quiet" side and to express herself as a writer in the future.

Moreover, in her predicament of growing up between cultures, Maxine is in danger of losing her own identity, of going crazy like her aunt Moon Orchid, and becoming "grotesque" like many of the characters in Anderson. As Anderson writes: "It was the truths that made the people grotesques. The old man had quite an elaborate theory concerning the matter. It was this notion that the moment one of the people took one of the truths for himself, called it his truth, and tried to live his life by it, he became a grotesque and the truth he embraced became a falsehood" (24). If we follow this lead, Brave Orchid's behavior in "At the Western Palace," her own "truths" turning into "falsehoods," seems "grotesque" in hindsight.[19] Grotesqueness also manifests itself in Maxine's fear of going mad when she is alienated from her Chinese parents. She worries about the "free movies" and the "adventurous people inside [her] head" to whom she talks (190), a situation very much like the one of Enoch Robinson in Anderson's "Loneliness." Andersonian grotesqueness also looms big in the scene where Maxine tries to confess her sins and desires to her ironing mother:

"Mm," she said, squeezing the starch out of the collar and cuffs. But I had talked, and she acted as if she hadn't heard.
Perhaps she hadn't understood. I had to be more explicit. I hated this. [...].
"Mm," she said, nodded, and kept dipping and squeezing. (199-200)

---

17 Actually, the writer's white mustache can be compared to the adult narrator Kingston's white hair.
18 Chua observes: "[A]s palmists will recognize, that is the Line of the Head" ("Golden Mountain" 51).
19 Also see Kingston on the Chinese village: "Or perhaps our little village had become odd in its isolation" (186). The alienating effect of crystallized Chinese conceptions is also emphasized in the exoticizing name "Brave Orchid."

Maxine's American confession is bracketed by her mother's ironing; it is threatened by the static force of Chinese starch. Like Elmer Cowley in Sherwood Anderson's "Queer," Maxine is in danger of being "washed and ironed and starched" in the laundry: "Elmer tried to explain. [...]. 'Well, you see,' he began, and then lost control of his tongue. 'I'll be washed and ironed and starched,' he muttered incoherently" (200). Unfortunately the "mother's most peaceful time" of starching "the white shirts" is not a good "time and place for the telling" (198). At this moment, she has the white ghosts under control and gets annoyed by Maxine's confessions: "Senseless gabbings every night. I wish you would stop. Go away and work. Whispering, whispering, making no sense. Madness. I don't feel like hearing your craziness" (200). My point is not that Kingston has borrowed Anderson's imagery and vocabulary in *The Woman Warrior*, but that his concepts of the "youth" and of "grotesqueness" construct a metaphorical argument that is in many ways isomorphic with Kingston's expression. This does not mean that Kingston copies Anderson, but that they both tap very similar concepts.

If in Anderson we find intertextual affinities that clearly go beyond mere decoration and involve the very meaning of Maxine's quest for an identity of her own, I think that Kingston's presentation of a Chinese village in "No Name Woman" has caused drastic mis-readings that have their source in intercultural appropriations. From early on, critics have commented on the astonishingly negative presentation of traditional Chinese village culture in this account. Melton speaks of a "misogynist culture, feudal China" (74), and R.G. Lee suggests "a Neo-confucian ideology [...] recapitulating patriarchal family relations at all levels of the Chinese polity" (56). Mayer even assesses Kingston's attitude as a stance of distancing herself from her Chinese origin.[20] Sledge, moreover, generally senses the cliché which Raymond Dawson has called the erroneous "fiction of 'eternal standstill'" that led westerners for many centuries to extol the Chinese mind for its stability, "uniformity and unvariability" and the homogeneous, family-oriented Confucian state as "an example and model even for Christians" (14-15). My point is that in Kingston's case, intercultural analogies can go full circle. Thus the world of "No Name Woman" is a sophisticated intercultural/intertextual construction, and I would even go as far as to claim that to a certain extent it is an American Puritan village dressed in Chinese clothes.

Many of the village attitudes, and even some of the imagery used in order to express them, can be intertextually traced back to American sources. First of all, Kingston's projection of a repressive "Chinese tradition" has strong affinities with patterns of familiar U.S. culture, especially with William Carlos Williams's assessment of the Puritans in *In the American Grain*, a book which Kingston is very fond of, which she regularly teaches in her creative writing classes, and which she intended to continue with her own two autobiographies: "Williams

---

20   In German: "Distanzierung zu ihrem chinesischen Ursprung" (178).

has told American History poetically and, it seems to me, truly. In a way, I feel that I have continued that book. The dates are even right. The earliest episode in my book is about 1850, which is roughly where Williams left off" (Pfaff 25).[21] Williams's Puritans also live in a closed world. They are incapable of reaching beyond their culturally determined views: "The jargon of God, which they used, was their dialect by which they kept themselves surrounded as with a palisade" (64). This is how he describes the Puritans' lack of perception—like Kingston's villagers, they assimilate their environment and are unwilling to see beyond what they know:

> The Puritan, finding one thing like another in a world destined for blossom only in "Eternity," all soul, all "emptiness" then here, was precluded from SEEING the Indian. They never realized the Indian in the least save as an unformed PURITAN. The *immorality* of such a concept, the inhumanity, the brutalizing effect upon their own minds, on their SPIRITS—they never suspected. (113, original capitals and italics)

Much of the narrow-mindedness and coercion described in Kingston's tale is anticipated in Williams's description. Williams also seems to have influenced Kingston's style in her fictionalizing approach to history and her speculations about the past.[22]

   Once we recognize Williams's influence in Kingston's construction of her Chinese village, we start noticing other possible Puritan references, both literary and theological. For example, the whole issue of an archaic, closed-system cosmic order of absolute beliefs that expresses itself in the symbolism of village "roundness" is also called "circumference": "This roundness had to be made coinsized so that she would see its circumference punish her at the birth of her baby" (13). It is precisely the aunt's "youth" which is a transgression of this rigid public order. The notion of circumference can also be found in Emily Dickinson, for example in poem 378:

---

21   For an assessment of links to *In the American Grain* in Kingston's second book *China Men* and its "debunking of the Puritan heritage," see Li ("*China Men*" 483).

22   For example, this is how Williams describes George Washington: "Here was a man of tremendous vitality buried in a massive frame and under a rather stolid and untractable exterior which the ladies somewhat feared, *I fancy.* He *must have* looked well to them, from a distance, or say on horseback—but later it proved a little too powerful for comfort" (140, my italics). When Kingston writes about her aunt's lover or rapist (we never learn which it really is), she presents many similar textual signals which indicate narrative distance:

> Some man had commanded her to lie with him and be his secret evil. *I wonder* whether he masked himself when he joined the raid on her family.
>
>   *Perhaps* she had encountered him in the fields or on the mountain where the daughters-in-law collected fuel. Or *perhaps* he first noticed her in the marketplace. [...]. *Perhaps* he worked an adjoining field, or he sold her the cloth for the dress she sewed and wore. His demand *must have* surprised, even terrified her. (6, my italics)

I saw no Way—The Heavens were stitched—
I felt the Columns close—
The Earth reversed her Hemispheres—
I touched the Universe—

And back I slid—and I alone—
A Speck upon a Ball—
Went out upon Circumference—
Beyond the Dip of Bell—

Much of this imagery might remind one of the dynamic cosmology in Kingston's birth scene. "Circumference" appears in many of Dickinson's poems, e.g., in 883, 1084, 1343, and in 1663. Her use of this concept was probably influenced by Ralph Waldo Emerson, especially his essays "The Over-Soul" and "Circles." If Emerson and Dickinson see "Circumference" as a positive structure of support, Kingston interprets it negatively, as an instance of Williams's "palisade."

Kingston herself offers Hawthorne as another Puritan link: "When I was writing 'No Name Woman,' I was thinking about Nathaniel Hawthorne and *The Scarlet Letter* as a discussion of the Puritan part of America, and of China, and a woman's place" (Rabinowitz 182). Ferraro finds "Hester Prynne reconceived as a Chinese peasant" (163), a view which would associate the aunt's projections about her daughter's future life with Pearl: "A child with no descent line would not soften her life, but only trail after her, ghost-like, begging her to give it purpose. At dawn the villagers on their way to the fields would stand around the fence and look" (15). Compare this to Hester Prynne meeting the "public gaze" when walking about town with her child "tripping along at the rate of three or four footsteps to one of Hester's" (94). Also sensing a Puritan reference, the Chinese scholar Su comments: "The image of the No Name Woman seems more an American witch in Salem than a victim of Chinese female virtues" (16). We find Hester used as the figure of an archetypal kind of feminist witch. The subtext in that sense even points beyond Hawthorne.

The villagers who punish the aunt's family for her breach of the traditional system of values are typical religious hypocrites. Once we acknowledge the strong influence of Puritanism, at least via classical literary sources in "No Name Woman," we can also find a Puritan streak in the typology of female role models as they are experienced by the protagonist. Chua divides these women up in "two dialectically opposed types," i.e., "her mother, Brave Orchid, type Fa Mu Lan, and her natural aunt, Moon Orchid—type No Name Woman" ("Two Chinese" 64), the kind of categorization which Ling defines as "victor and vanquished" (157). In Puritan terms, these types signify either salvation or damnation. Thus Maxine can be seen as struggling to figure out in which category she will ultimately end up. Though Chinese on the surface, this system of choices imposing itself on her is very much an affair of values and principles that a Western reader will easily understand.

Generally one can say that in this "exotic" tale Kingston uses many references that are recognizable to a Western reader. However, this does not mean that she simply sells out to Western readers' expectations and their background; to say this would be a way of reasoning which commits the mistake of defining her world as Chinese only and ours as Western, and of reducing the complex and dynamic conceptual heterogeneity of her text to a translation from one closed cultural entity to another. Kingston's strategies of familiarization are not merely a crutch for the reader, but they openly trace the definition of self in a multicultural environment. Thus they reflect an act of identity-finding and point to the elements used in this process.

My point is that Maxine in *The Woman Warrior* is portrayed as a protagonist growing up in response to a great variety of influences. If I have concentrated on showing Western affinities, I have mainly done so in order to warn against readings that celebrate access to the Other when they actually merely reflect a subtext of Western understanding. Such projections celebrate themselves rather than give access to the conceptualizations of other people. In a complex and multicultural text, the danger of such cultural appropriation is particularly challenging. Allusions, i.e., vague and rather uncontrollable references, and even simple coincidences will be used in ways that gratify the reader, in our case especially European American readers who form most of Kingston's audience.

If an intercultural text wants to communicate, it has to offer familiar material, but there is a certain risk if we believe like Arturo Islas that "it is instructive to see how she [Kingston] taps her sources, which are Chinese, in such a way as to make that world accessible to those that are not at all familiar with it" (12). Particularly in the case of the Puritan Chinese village, the familiar context can dominate and be mis-recognized as the Other. This can even, in the extreme case, end up in a situation in which readers understand the logic that makes a traditional Chinese village tick in a way that is more American and Puritan than Chinese. These seekers of "China" are not aware that they are actually finders of "America" (although, considering the case of Columbus, such a gesture may actually be typically American). In short, Kingston has often been praised for the wrong reasons, a fact about which she bitterly complains in "Cultural Misreadings." In this comment on her readers' comments on her work, she attempts to clarify many of her references and points to the shortcomings of the many Orientalist interpretations imposed on her book: "*The Woman Warrior* is an American book. [...]. Don't you hear the American slang? Don't you see the American settings?" (56, 58).

Let me suggest, in addition to all of the attitudinal prejudices she mentions, that Kingston's intercultural text has also become the victim of an allusive modernist style. The sophisticated density of her writing coincides with standards set by the modernist practice at American universities in her youth. Says she: "I even write for my old English professors of the new criticism school in Berkeley" ("Cultural Mis-readings" 65). But her problem is that as a minority author she implies a cultural context with which few are familiar: she cannot just aesthetically "hint" at meanings and talk indirectly in terms of "pointing" and polysemic insinuations. If she merely alludes to things, or implies them, she cannot, like the great Western writers, count on an audience that knows The Great Tradition. Writing for "loro che sanno" will only reach few, most of whom will pick up the wrong references. Moreover, she is at the mercy of given interpretive traditions that appropriate her creativity even if isomorphic metaphors happen to be merely coincidental. Ethnic U.S. authors who tell the truth "but tell it slant" will be misunderstood by traditional critics who radically trust the tale and not the tellers. Woo writes that "there is little tolerance for creative styles which leave certain facts ambiguous" (183), and she adds: "In no small way, what Kingston may have hoped to achieve by her deliberately artful reconceptualization of myth eludes her control" (185).[23] If one leaves too many things ambiguous, Euro-American majority critics will have their way and impose their own readings. Hence Sau-ling Wong writes that a "weightier task awaits [Kingston], namely, educating the reader about the reality of Chinese American life. To this end, only one translation, with all the 'right' connotations, is acceptable" ("Necessity" 35). The problem of Kingston is that she publishes in a discursive environment which forces her to delimit her use of connotations and secondary meanings, to *turn away from the modernist ideal of "ambiguity" and provide textual structures which more narrowly define what they really mean.* As a result, in her recent work she has chosen what I think are different and more explicit ways of writing.

We can observe that after the publication of *The Woman Warrior*, Kingston has tried to counteract its patronizing kind of appropriation in her second book *China Men*. For example, her rendering of "The Adventures of Lo Bun Sun" even quotes the least expected statements verbatim from Defoe. It is so obviously based on *Robinson Crusoe* that simple familiarization becomes uncanny. Yet in view of the above observations it seems symptomatic to me that critics are less infatuated with Kingston's second autobiography and even more at a loss with *Tripmaster Monkey*, a book in which Kingston tries more actively to control the Western discourse rather than merely allude to it. Thus Furth writes about the "consternation and confusion that greeted the publication of *Tripmaster Monkey* and the deafening silence from scholarly literary journals" (36). I believe that this is the case because in this "novel"[24] Kingston no longer contents

---

23 On the appropriation of Kingston's "indeterminacies" by the wrong people, also see Sau-ling Wong ("Ethnic Dimensions" 282).

24 As opposed to her previous two "autobiographies" Kingston clearly has *Tripmaster* labeled as

herself with a formalist semiotics of "ambiguity" or "indeterminacy." Neither a new critical nor a deconstructive aesthetics can appreciate certain qualities of this text that have to do with referentiality and intention.

Let me therefore conclude my paper by showing how Kingston puts many of her earlier complaints from "Cultural Mis-readings" into this book in order to argue with a new fictional language that I can only call expository *klartext*. Such a way of writing may point in the direction of a new, non-formalist multicultural aesthetics. In "One Man Show," the concluding chapter of *Tripmaster Monkey*, the protagonist Wittman Ah Sing (a clear allusion to the singer about himself, Walt Whitman) includes the reviews of his play in the performance and makes his own comment on them part of what is presented on stage:

> "Come on, you can't like these reviews. Don't be too hastily made happy. Look. Look. 'East meets West.' 'Exotic.' 'Sino-American theater.' 'Snaps, crackles and pops like singing rice.' 'Sweet and Sour.' Quit clapping. Stop it. What's to cheer about? You like being compared to Rice Krispies? Cut it out. Let me show you, you've been insulted. They sent their food critics. They wrote us up like they were tasting Chinese food. Rice, get it? 'Savor beautious Nanci Lee,' it says here. That's like saying that LeRoy Jones is as good as a water melon." (307)

And he goes on for a few more pages, complaining about "East is east and West is west": "Nobody says 'twain shall,' except in reference to us. We've failed with our magnificence of explosions to bust through their Kipling. I'm having to give instruction. There is no East here. West is meeting West" (308). Wittman is offended: "I've read my Aristotle and Agee, I've been to college; they have ways to criticize theater besides sweetness and sourness. They do laundry reviews, clean or dirty. Come on. What's so 'exotic'?" (308). Or: "This other piece says that we are *not* exotic. 'Easily understood and not too exotic for the American audience.' Do I have to explain why 'exotic' pisses me off? They've got us in a bag, which we aren't punching our way out of" (308). There is a dose of Frank Chin (who has been one of Kingston's severest critics) in this character, in his way of staging himself and in his trying to wedge his way into a pluralist kind of American identity that exists beyond the exotic:

> "We should have done a soap opera that takes place in a kitchen about your average domestic love agonies and money agonies. The leading lady is in hair curlers and an apron, and her husband, who has a home haircut like mine, stomps in, home from work. [...]. No ching-chong music, no epic costumes, you understand? [...]. You know what the *Tribune* will say? 'Exotic.' Or they'll say, 'Waddya know? Not exotic. The inscrutables are explaining themselves at last. We are allowed into their mysterious oriental world.'" (309)

"her first novel" in the appended "note about the author."

Wittman's improvization escalates, ending with the scream "Aieeee!," quoting the stereotypical funnies about the Chinese and at the same time the title of the ground-breaking anthology on Asian American literature co-edited by Frank Chin.

Kingston ends *Tripmaster Monkey* in a virtuoso performance that is in many ways more comment on the representation of Chinese American culture, a self-reflective meta-commentary in a breathless monologue, than what we traditionally associate with a fictional narrative. She names names when she has Wittman review movies and TV series, *Shane, Krapp's Last Tape, Year of the Dragon, Breakfast at Tiffany's*, D.W. Griffith's *Broken Blossoms*, invented Chinese sayings in *Vertigo*, Charlie Chan, "he doesn't grab his client-in-distress and kiss her hard, pressing her boobs against his gun. [...]. Confucius say this. Confucius say that. Too clean and too good for sex" (320). Kingston puts the finger directly on the scenes that are debasing: "[T]his guy with tape on his eyes [...] played by Nils Aster" is "alone in his palace with Barbara Stanwick and one last slave girl, Anna May Wong, whom he has locked up and plans to kill slowly" (321). She notes all the sexual innuendo of the camera work, which makes us assume that he will force the innocent white maiden to have sex with him: "The general could have looked down, as the camera does, and seen pretty far down her décolletage. She's wet with tears again" (321). Wittman comments: "The audience is catching thrills. Are they going to make out? Are the tails of that silk handkerchief tickling her neck and the top of her tits? Are his lips going to land on her lips in an inter-racial kiss?" (322). But then: "He picks up his teacup and drinks, and quietly leans back in his throne. And dies. He has poisoned himself before he can defile her. The name of that movie was *The Bitter Tea of General Yin*. They named him that to castrate us" (322). Kingston here comments very directly on real pictures in a non-fictional reality beyond her own "novel" in a way that cannot be misunderstood. If she picks up Frank Chin's criticism of the demasculinization of Chinese American men in American culture, she does, however, not fall into the trap of advocating one-sided phallic manliness. Instead, she has her protagonist suggest more of an interactive kind of sexuality, the oral communion of kissing: "Charlie Chan doesn't kiss. And Keye Luke doesn't kiss. And Richard Look doesn't kiss. We've got to kiss and fuck and breed in the streets" (322). Even kissing contests are suggested and Wittman has his audience practice to become "champion kissers" (330).

Kingston also puts her old argument about the hyphen in "Chinese-American" (and the reason why she wants to leave it out) into Wittman's speech:

> "You do mean 'Chinese' as short of 'Chinese-American,' don't you? We mustn't call ourselves 'Chinese' among those who are ready to send us back to where they think we came from. But 'Chinese-American' takes too long. Nobody says or hears past the first part. And 'Chinese-American' is inaccu-

rate—as if we could have two countries. We need to take the hyphen out—'Chinese American.' 'American' the noun and 'Chinese' the adjective. From now on: 'Chinese Americans.'" (327)

Compare this to her earlier reflections in "Cultural Mis-readings":

> And lately, I have been thinking that we ought to leave out the hyphen in 'Chinese-American', because the hyphen gives the word on either side equal weight, as if linking two nouns. It looks as if a Chinese-American has double citizenship, which is impossible in today's world. Without hyphen, 'Chinese' is an adjective and 'American' a noun; a Chinese American is a type of American. (60)

What we have in *Tripmaster Monkey* is a way of writing that is still very dense, very allusive, and very modernist in its sensibility, but at the same time also very referential in its comments on the extrafictional world, and at times very clear and even polemical in the way it comments on reality. Thus it is (in a postmodernist way) "realistic" out of a need to be understood correctly in an intercultural communicative situation. Such a pluralistic realism is not merely the mimetic confirmation of a hegemonic majority ideology as a whole, but one of referentiality and intention that asserts a specific local opinion.

We can actually find in the work of Kingston's Berkeley writer colleague Ishmael Reed a similar tendency toward more explicitness. Reed, who at one point created a "Neo-HooDoo Aesthetic" for himself and whom we may consider the dean of American multiculturalism, has also suffered from being praised as an expert on exotic Voodoo mysteries when all he wanted to do was to argue a point. This has made him write in more directly referential ways, turning to a more familiar vocabulary (e.g., "zombis" turn into "body snatchers," and "possession" turns into "ventriloquism"). In his recent novel, *Japanese by Spring,* many important figures of contemporary history are mentioned by name and important things are not just hinted at but named directly. Even "Ishmael Reed" himself appears in the book and is focalized through himself so that his views are not to be mistaken: "Ringleader Ishmael Reed has never called anybody a traitor to anybody's race and not only hasn't opposed black women writing about black male misogyny but published some of it" (24). In a private conversation, Reed even suggested for his most recent kind of writing the name "essel," a combination of essay and novel. He thus conceives of a kind of fiction that is opinionizing, clearer in its reference, more controlled, and arguing points.

Let me summarize my argument: As an American, Kingston makes abundant use of Western traditions, ideas, and images in her books in order to weave from this material and from her own heritage and experience a new "text" that does justice to her multicultural experience. But the fact that in the tradition of a formalist aesthetics mere allusions and even metaphorical coincidences tend to be misappropriated by a majority readership—who will only pick up a very selective part of the subtext—forces ethnic writers who actively engage in intercultural negotiations and multicultural issues to be very specific in their references and intentions. Kingston's more recent fictional discourse is a typical example of such a tendency of writerly control and *klartext*, a new stylistic strategy which may indicate a shift in aesthetic sensibility toward a new kind of postpoststructuralist realism that reaches beyond formalist predicaments.

Works Cited

Anderson, Sherwood. *Winesburg, Ohio*. 1919. London: Penguin, 1982.

Aubrey, James R. "Woman Warriors and Military Students." Lim 80-86 .

Chin, Frank. "The Most Popular Book in China." *Quilt* 4 (1984): 6-12.

—. "On Amy Tan, David Hwang, Maxine Hong Kingston. An Essay." *Konch* 1.2 (1990): 25-28.

—. "This Is Not an Autobiography." *Genre* 18 (1985): 109-30.

Chua, Chen Lok. "Golden Mountain: Chinese Versions of the American Dream in Lin Yutang, Louis Chu, and Maxine Hong Kingston." *Ethnic Groups* 4.1-2 (1982): 33-59.

—. "Two Chinese Versions of the American Dream: The Golden Mountain in Lin Yutang and Maxine Hong Kingston." *MELUS* 8.4 (1981): 61-70.

Curtius, Ernst Robert. *European Literature and the Latin Middle Ages*. New York: Harper, 1963.

Dickinson, Emily. *The Complete Poems of Emily Dickinson*. Ed. Thomas H. Johnson. Boston, Toronto: Little, Brown, 1960.

Eakin, Paul John. *Fictions in Autobiography: Studies in the Art of Self-Invention*. Princeton: Princeton UP, 1985. 181-278.

Ferraro, Thomas J. "Changing the Rituals: Courageous Daughtering and the Mystique of *The Woman Warrior*." *Ethnic Passages. Literary Immigrants in Twentieth-Century America*. Chicago and London: U of Chicago P, 1993. 154-90.

Fishkin, Shelley Fisher. "Interview with Maxine Hong Kingston." *American Literary History* 3 (1991): 782-91.

Furth, Isabella. "Beee-e-een! Nation, Transformation and the Hyphen of Ethnicity in Kingston's *Tripmaster Monkey*." *Modern Fiction Studies* 40.1 (1994): 33-49.

Hawthorne, Nathaniel. *The Scarlet Letter*. 1850. New York: Washington Square P, 1967.

Islas, Arturo. "Interview with Maxine Hong Kingston." *Women Writers of the West Coast Speaking of their Lives and Careers*. Ed. Marilyn Yalom. Santa Barbara, CA: Capra P, 1983. 11-19.

Kingston, Maxine Hong. *China Men*. New York: Knopf, 1980.

—. "Cultural Mis-readings by American Reviewers." *Asian and Western Writers in Dialogue: New Cultural Identities.* Ed. Guy Amirthanayagam. London: Macmillan, 1982. 55-65.

—. *Hawai'i One Summer.* Illus. Deng Ming-Dao. San Francisco: Meadow P, 1987.

—. "Personal Statement." Lim 23-25.

—. *Tripmaster Monkey: His Fake Book.* New York: Knopf, 1989.

—. *The Woman Warrior: Memoirs of a Girlhood Among Ghosts.* New York: Knopf, 1975.

Komenaka, April R. "Autobiography as a Sociolinguistic Resource: Maxine Hong Kingston's *The Woman Warrior.*" *International Journal of the Sociology of Language* 69 (1988): 105-18.

Lee, R.G., "*The Woman Warrior* as an Invention in Asian American Historiography." Lim 52-63.

Li, David Leiwei. "*China Men*: Maxine Hong Kingston and the American Canon." *American Literary History* 2.3 (1990): 482-502.

—. "The Production of Chinese American Tradition: Displacing American Orientalist Discourse." *Reading the Literatures of Asian America.* Eds. Shirley Geok-lin Lim and Amy Ling. Philadelphia: Temple UP, 1992. 319-31.

Lim, Shirley Geok-lin, ed. *Approaches to Teaching Kingston's* The Woman Warrior. New York: MLA, 1991.

Ling, Amy. "Thematic Threads in Maxine Hong Kingston's *The Woman Warrior.*" *Tamkang Review* 14.1-4 (1983-84): 155-64.

McBride, Paul W. "*The Woman Warrior* in the History Classroom." Lim 93-100.

Mayer, Susanne. "Maxine Hong Kingston: Die Autobiographie als poetische Anthropologie." *Die Sehnsucht nach den Anderen. Eine Studie zum Verhältnis von Subjekt und Gesellschaft in den Autobiographien von Lillian Hellman, Maya Angelou und Maxine Hong Kingston.* Frankfurt am Main, Bern, New York: Lang, 1986. 175-225.

Melton, Judith M. "*The Woman Warrior* in the Women's Studies Classroom." Lim 74-79.

Miller, Lucien, and Hui-chuan Chang. "Fiction and Autobiography: Spatial Form in *The Golden Cangue* and *The Woman Warrior.*" *Tamkang Review* 15.1-4 (1984-85): 75-96.

Miller, Margaret. "Threads of Identity in Maxine Hong Kingston's *The Woman Warrior.*" *Biography* 6.1 (1983): 13-32.

Pfaff, Timothy. "Talk With Mrs. Kingston." *The New York Times Book Review* 15 June 1980: 1+.

Plath, Sylvia. *The Collected Poems.* Ed. Ted Hughes. New York: Harper & Row, 1981.

Rabinowitz, Paula. "Eccentric Memories: A Conversation with Maxine Hong Kingston." *Michigan Quarterly Review* 26.1 (1987): 177-87.

Reed, Ishmael. *Japanese by Spring.* New York: Macmillan, 1993.

Rubenstein, Roberta. "Bridging Two Cultures: Maxine Hong Kingston." *Boundaries of the Self: Gender, Culture, Fiction.* Urbana: U of Illinois P, 1987. 164-89.

Sledge, Linda Ching. "Maxine Hong Kingston's *China Men*: The Family Historian as Epic Poet." *MELUS* 7.4 (1980): 3-22.

Su Hongjun. "Savage Land: China, or U.S.A., or Chinese-U.S.A. Interpreting Maxine Hong Kingston's *The Woman Warrior: Memoirs of a Girlhood Among Ghosts* from a Chinese Perspective." Santa Barbara: UCSB unpublished typescript, 1989.

Underhill, Evelyn. *Mysticism. A Study in the Nature and Development of Man's Spiritual Consciousness.* New York: New American Library, 1974.

Williams, William Carlos. *In the American Grain.* 1925. New York: New Directions, 1956.

Wong, Sau-ling Cynthia. "Ethnic Dimensions of Postmodern Indeterminacy: Maxine Hong Kingston's *The Woman Warrior* as Avant-garde Autobiography." *Autobiographie & Avant-garde.* Eds. Alfred Hornung and Ernstpeter Ruhe. Tübingen: Gunter Narr, 1992. 273-84.

—. "Kingston's Handling of Traditional Chinese Sources." Lim 26-36.

—. "Necessity and Extravagance in Maxine Hong Kingston's *The Woman Warrior*: Art and the Ethnic Experience." *MELUS* 15.1 (1988): 4-26.

—. *Reading Asian American Literature: From Necessity to Extravagance.* Princeton: Princeton UP, 1993.

Woo, Deborah. "Maxine Hong Kingston: The Ethnic Writer and the Burden of Dual Authenticity." *Amerasia Journal* 16.1 (1990): 173-200.

Zhang Ya-jie. "A Chinese Woman's Response to Maxine Hong Kingston's *The Woman Warrior*." *MELUS* 13.3-4 (1986): 103-7.

"Adding On," Not "Giving Up":
Ceremonies of Self in Frank Chin's *Donald Duk*

Gordon O. Taylor

On May 10, 1996—among several anniversaries cited for that date during his "Writer's Almanac" segment on National Public Radio in the U.S.—Garrison Keillor took note of two seemingly unrelated events: first, the driving of the Golden Spike in 1869 at Promontory, Utah, where the Central Pacific Railroad, building from the west, met the Union Pacific Railroad, coming from the east, to complete the first rail line spanning the North American continent; and second, the birth in 1899 of Fred Austerlitz, who would later come to be better known as Fred Astaire. The connection between these two very disparate "milestones" lies only in their convergence in Frank Chin's novel of 1991, *Donald Duk*, in which the protagonist's efforts to reintegrate both sides of his Asian American identity are dramatized through a series of overlapping "ceremonies." Each of these "ceremonial" contexts—cast, for purposes of this discussion, in the categories of dance, dream, flight, and food, all connected in turn to a celebration of the Chinese New Year—is centered on the problematic relations between present and past, the United States and China, and their contending claims on Donald Duk's consciousness. Viewed retrospectively, from the vantage point of the book's conclusion, each in its way participates in, or is informed by, the rubrics of continuity, rupture, and (re)invention.

Donald Duk is the story of a young boy from San Francisco's Chinatown who is engaged in a double quest, both to resolve and to escape his conflicted sense of self. He veers in this quest between daydreams of being able to dance like Fred Astaire, thus gracefully to slip into an unambiguously American culture from the felt awkwardness of his ethnicity as embodied in his name, and increasingly compelling dreams at night of being with the Chinese laborers in the 1860s, as they build the Central Pacific eastward across the Sierra Nevada Mountains. The ritualized performance of his Fred Astaire persona—through which he seeks an inward release into a freer mode of motion from the roles he feels are imposed upon him from without—is progressively overtaken by his dreamed role in the construction of the railroad, over a century before. The dream culminates in contradictory commemorations of the mythic moment of the railroad's completion: the Golden Spike ceremony at Promontory on May

10, 1869 (the officially established celebratory image), and the inscription in Chinese, on a final wooden crosstie set down on May 8, of the names of the workers (forcibly excluded from the Golden Spike occasion after their crosstie was torn out and destroyed, and thus excluded from the official history of the event).

Donald Duk is a comic novel, at least on the surface and in its outermost layers, and if one is settling (as perhaps one should not) for a single label. Its comic exuberance and charm, however, are laced with certain poignancies and driven by ferocious ironies, suffused as well with an underlying anger which simmers throughout. Comic energy arcs back and forth between the dealings of the Duk family and the pop-culture iconography of the cartoon character Donald Duck (in *his* various family relations). Chinese American Donald Duk occasionally speaks in a quack-like approximation of cartoon Donald Duck's voice, having learned to do so in self-defense against the inevitable jokes at his expense in this vein. Conversely, as I told my students in a course called "American Culture(s): Voice(s) and Vision(s)," it may be hard—I hope it *will* be hard—for a reader of Frank Chin's novel ever again to see or hear Walt Disney's Donald Duck without a sense of that globally exported American image as now, in some irrevocable measure, Asian American.

But there are other, darker, comic-book-like (if by no means always comic) forces in play, such as those invested in a Vietnam veteran who calls himself "American Cong," an anti-superhero of sorts affected by the toxicities of the defoliant Agent Orange, a guerrilla-style witness to unresolved issues of the Vietnam war a generation later on American homeground. This character, a counterforce to officially sanctioned assumptions regarding the war and its aftermath, is associated in the novel with a figure called Lee Kuey, or the "Black Tornado," one of the 108 bandit-heroes in the Chinese folk legends of *The Water Margin*, who is also portrayed in Cantonese opera by young Donald Duk's Uncle Donald (the name reasserting the cartoon motif, even as that motif is undercut by other tonalities in the book). The arcing flashes of comic voltage, despite their often hilarious intensity, derive their brilliance in no small part from the darkness and danger of the gaps they illuminate, strobe-lit disconnections in the circuitry of U.S. culture, and in the ostensible continuity of a cultural narrative of the American past.

The tale is structured along the intersecting axes of fantasy and fact, intermittently shifting from the realm of dream to that of the interrogation of the historical record, on to that of the fictively posited "actual" present, and back again, cycling through these overlapping aspects of "reality." On the level of the emergence and progressive articulation of the 19th-century railroad-building plot, however—just a dream which unfolds in problematic relation to conventional historical accounts, but one that more and more pervades Donald's waking life—the narrative gathers a different momentum, less one of cyclical repetition and more one of cumulative intensification, acquiring in the process a different

imaginative density. On the one hand, this is the density of legend or myth, a
bicultural poetry-in-prose of triumph and tragedy, these outcomes at once commingled and mutually distinct. On the other hand, it is that of a counterhistory,
systematically as much as subversively researched, to standard American interpretations of the completion of the railroad as a watershed event in the progress
of the dominant culture, a defining step in the conquest of the frontier. In these
established historical accounts, the Chinese were essentially erased from the
"text," at least insofar as that text is represented in the novel by photographic
images of the culminating moment at Promontory, Utah, and of the wooden
crosstie inscribed in Chinese, erased even as—particularly as—the ceremonial
Golden Spike was driven. In the countertext of Donald's dreams, in which he is
both an observer and a participant, the story of this erasure itself becomes a
means toward reinscription of himself, in relation to his Chinese heritage, but
also in relation to his sense of himself as an American in America, "then" and
"now."

Ever more vivid and insistent, each involuntary "installment" awaited by
Donald (perhaps also by the reader) with a mixture of anticipation and anxiety,
the dreams are charged and directed by the disparity Donald notes between a
photograph in an old family book showing a Chinese railroad gang in the snowy
Sierras—including a boy about his own age, the same age his great-great-
grandfather would have been when working on the Central Pacific—and the
official photo in his history textbook at school of the Golden Spike ceremony, in
which not a Chinese face can be seen. The problem of relation between these
two images propels Donald—both by day in school, or in search of alternative
information in the public library, and by night in his 19th-century visions—into
the ambiguities of the space between. Neither of the two narratives implied in
the "either" and the "or" of these two pictures—whether considered in isolation
or opposition—is sufficient or complete without some reconstruction of their
relation to one another.

As the dreamscape of the railroad's construction expands in narrative time
and space, the 108 heroes of *The Water Margin*—compared at one point to
Robin Hood and his associates—and the permutations of their deeds in Chinese
opera, become entwined in Donald's imagination with the railroad history he is
investigating. Surrealistically (but convincingly enough, amid the novel's many
other mind-warps), his white friend Arnold Azalea, who is staying with the Duk
family as Donald's guest throughout the festivities that anticipate the Chinese
New Year, begins to share the same dreams, drawn into the process of historical
reinterpretation, and the self-inquiry from which it largely stems. Donald and
Arnold come into conflict even as they collaborate and conspire, with Arnold
(ironically) the more initially interested of the two in learning about China and
things Chinese, less resistant at first to the boys' common dreams of an untold
history requiring to be revealed. Thus, a framework of racial refraction is also
formed, involving the dreamers as well as those of whom they dream, however

juvenile or oblique the terms may be in which the boys learn to look at the world, and at each other, through one another's eyes.

The rail lines move inexorably toward Promontory, from the west and from the east, with reports filtering back and forth as to how much track the Chinese gang working on the Central Pacific, or the Irish working on the Union Pacific, are able to put down in a day. The record is alternatively broken and reset, and in a final push—the heroes of *The Water Margin* and the figures of Cantonese opera now inextricably infused into the documentary accounts from American books—the Chinese lay ten miles of track in ten hours, bringing the railheads within sight of each other. To commemorate the event, the Chinese workers inscribe their names and the names of those who died or came before (10,000 names—a certain suspension of disbelief is again required) on a wooden crosstie placed near the point where the ceremonial Spike is soon to be driven, a calligraphic "text" subsuming not only their individual toil on the project but also the collective history of the Chinese in America lying behind and invested in those labors.

On May 8, however, two days before the driving of the Golden Spike, this crosstie is torn out, to be split as a souvenir between the railroad barons or their representatives, Charles Crocker of the Central Pacific and T. C. Durant of the Union Pacific, and to preserve for official history a different, distinctly Anglo-Saxon sense (in Donald's words, disputing Crocker in the dream) of "who laid these crossties and spiked this track [...] and built this railroad" (129). Enraged, the Chinese tear out the unmarked crosstie which replaced theirs. A photograph of this scene on May 8 constitutes the last image in the historical record in which Donald sees clear evidence of Chinese participation in the joining of the two railheads, the last image in which, in effect, he is able to see himself, or that projection of himself re-experiencing in dreams the experience of his Chinese forebears in America. The next day Crocker assures Durant that all will be in order for the ceremony on May 10:

> I promise you [...] there will not be a heathen [a term of reference to the Chinese commonly used at the time] in sight at tomorrow's ceremonies. I will, with your permission, post riflemen up on the locomotives and the telegraph poles to warn us of the approach of any uninvited Celestials [another frequent reference to the Chinese] and keep them away, with force of arms if need be. The Golden Spike. The Last Spike will be hammered home, the telegram sent [the sledgehammer was wired to the telegraph for that purpose], our photograph made to preserve a great moment in our nation's history, without the Chinese. Admire and respect them as I do, I will show them who built the railroad. White men. White dreams. White brains and white brawn. (131)

And indeed, the photograph taken on May 10 (or that picture as it may have been cropped to become an established icon of the event, invoked through subsequent generations) is an image of the Golden Spike ceremony beyond the bor-

ders of which the Chinese workers are excluded by riflemen (who are also un-
seen, cropped out of any portion of the picture in which they may have originally appeared) positioned on top of nearby railroad boxcars.

Near the opening of the novel, Donald's history teacher had said of the Chinese in America—quoting the book written by his own professor at the University of California at Berkeley by way of acknowledging, ironically enough, the
Chinese in California as the Chinese New Year approached—that they were

> made passive and nonassertive by centuries of Confucian thought and Zen
> mysticism. They were totally unprepared for the violently individualistic and
> democratic Americans. From their first step on American soil to the middle of
> the twentieth century, the timid, introverted Chinese have been helpless against
> the relentless victimization by aggressive, highly competitive Americans. (2)

This the teacher accounts for, just as simplistically, according to the concept of
"the mandate of heaven," likening it to the European "divine right of kings." But
Donald's father later revises the meaning of this phrase, "the mandate of
heaven," into the precept that *"Kingdoms rise and fall, Nations come and go,"*
due to the ebb and flow of time, and to the inevitable perversions of power
against which Confucius warns. And he extends its meaning into more contemporary terms, telling Donald—frustrated by his failure to find the Chinese in the
usual historical accounts—that "You gotta keep the history yourself or lose it
forever, boy. *That's* the mandate of heaven" (123).

One thinks of the classroom scenes in Maxine Hong Kingston's *The Woman
Warrior*, juxtaposed moments based on episodes in the author's childhood education in both U.S. and Chinese schools. Passivity and nonassertiveness, timidity
and introversion, would seem in the passage set in the American school to characterize the prevailing behavior of the Chinese American students, not as a definition of Chinese American character but rather as a portrayal of strategic response, intuitive or otherwise, to a teacher not unlike Donald Duk's. Under the
surface of this response, quite different reactions are occurring, gathering in focus and force, not least toward Kingston's dream-visions later in the book of Fa
Mu Lan, the Woman Warrior with whom she progressively identifies. In the
passage set in Chinese school, by contrast, willful disregard for the teacher's
authority, combined with youthful resistance to parental imposition of "extra"
formal schooling in an effort to instill and sustain Chinese cultural forms, would
appear on the chaotic surface of the scene to inform the students' activity. But
beneath this rebellious, more self-confident surface, a potentially creative as well
as inevitably complex contention is taking place, between the "American" and
"Chinese" dimensions of the narrator's sense of self, as well as between those
aspects of the identities of the children more collectively depicted. So too in
Donald's case: the derivative rigidity of his teacher's attitudes and assumptions
feeds into Donald's growing fascination with the contradictions represented by

the two conflicting photographs, driving him deeper into his dreams, the crucible of his revisions of standard history, which more actively and assertively begin to spill back into waking life, indeed eventually into class and direct confrontation with his teacher.

The members of the Duk family see themselves primarily as Americans of Chinese background, rooted in the United States now for more than a single generation, rather than as Chinese still clinging to an immigrant sensibility, only transiently or "accidentally" located in the U.S., like those who came to work in the West with no intention of remaining for very long. But despite this American self-identification, "the mandate of heaven" thus defined—*"Kingdoms rise and fall, Nations come and go"*—effectively refers not only to the ebb and flow of Chinese dynasties over time, but also to the mutability of *American* myths such as Manifest Destiny, or the imperial mission of a divinely ordained Redeemer Nation. Witness the figure of "American Cong," the veteran suffering from Agent Orange, whose real name is Victor Lee, a restless "ghost" of the Vietnam era who, by "disturbing the peace" in the present (an outlaw of sorts, he is sought by the police), haunts America's conscience with respect to the past. He challenges American complacencies of presumption to moral and historical understanding, not only *vis à vis* the Vietnam era but also in connection with prior U.S. historical patterns prefiguring Vietnam. By virtue of his metamorphosis in Donald's dream both into Lee Kuey, a *Water Margin* outlaw, and into the foreman of a Chinese railroad gang, "American Cong" connects the spirit of resistance against institutionalized American authority to the same spirit latent in an immigrant minority, the Chinese railroad workers, and through them to the independence of the ancient Chinese heroes, prototypes perhaps (if not in expressly political terms) of those who resisted in Tiananmen Square.

Intermittently—in both counterpoint and complement to the 19th-century railroad plot, and in direct relation to ceremonial observances of the Chinese New Year—Frank Chin depicts the building, by Donald's father and uncle and others, of a fleet of model airplanes, faithfully reproduced as far as aircraft types and different wartime eras are concerned, but fancifully marked with symbols referring to the Water Margin figures and their counterparts in Chinese opera, rather than with regular military insignia. These planes, 108 of them corresponding to the 108 Water Margin outlaws, are delicately fashioned in paper and wood, then set aflame and flown during the culminating 15th night of the New Year celebrations. Ritually destroyed soon after they are completed, they fulfill "the mandate of heaven" as much in the beauty and skill of their creation as in their spectacular disappearance into the darkness of the old year, lighting the way, as they go, into the new.

The novel ends in an image of their flight (prevailing over the concurrent image of their fiery destruction), "all 108 aglow before they start exploding in mid-air." It also ends with the words "and food," following a final iteration of the phrasings of "the mandate of heaven." Since Donald's father is a chef of some renown in Chinatown, catering special occasions and presiding at home or in restaurants over the preparation and consumption of food, throughout the book, eating well—in the sense of proper ingredients and physical sustenance but also in that of the rituals of familial and social interaction and exchange—periodically reasserts a fundamental structure of communal continuity and coherence. The forms associated with food encompass in their recurrence, even if they cannot always cancel or contain, the forces making for discontinuity or rupture in the fabrics of family, ethnic community, society at large, or individual personality.

Donald Duk ends as well, however, in Donald's reflection on his railroad dreams, which have suddenly ceased, as if "the mandate of heaven," properly understood, has eased the pain of the loss of his own history, as represented by the railroad saga, yet has also reconfirmed his recovery of that history and thus his rediscovery of himself. It has shown him that his true ancestral name—Lee, as his father informs him, rather than Duk, like Lee Kuey or the "Black Tornado," like the true name of "American Cong," Victor Lee—was in the sense that matters most written with all the others on a railroad crosstie, which was removed and split at Promontory, Utah, on May 8, 1869, its 10,000 names thus scattered to the winds. Of all the novel's contending forms of "truth," this is perhaps the "truest," despite the evanescence of the dream in which it is inscribed, the dream itself now adrift in the winds of consciousness like the charred and splintered remnants of the model planes.

Earlier on Donald's father had said,

> I think Donald Duk may be the very last American-born Chinese American boy to believe you have to give up being Chinese to be an American. [...] These new immigrants [meaning recent arrivals in San Francisco from elsewhere in Asia] prove that. They were originally Cantonese, and did not want to be Chinese. When China conquered the south, these people went further south, into Vietnam, Laos, Cambodia, Thailand. They learned French. Now they're learning English. They still speak their Cantonese, their Chinese, their Viet or Lao or Cambodian, and French. Instead of giving anything up, they add on. They're including America in everything else they know. (42)

Donald Duk is still just a kid (Crocker, in the dream, had said "You are just a little boy. You are too young to understand how history is made" [129]). He seems to be about the age, say, of Huckleberry Finn (to whom the book at one point alludes), and is in a sense as ageless too, given (like Huck) less to intellectual system than to intuitive insight, not uninformed by error. But whether or not he analytically understands the significance of his railroad dreams, he has come to a subliminal sense of "adding on" rather than "giving up" in terms of the layerings of his own identity. He is learning to include China in everything else he already knows, rather than feeling bound by the polarized alternatives of "either" and "or." The fluidity of his Fred Astaire dance moves, and the fiercer

19th-century rhythms of blasting mountain rock and spiking railroad track, are now at novel's end—in yet another culminating ceremonial image—conjoined in his tireless dance inside a New Year's dragon, as it makes its way through the Chinatown streets. Within the dragon, hidden from those outside but reacquainted with himself, Donald is able, up to a point, to express through his part in the dragon's charge what his history teacher had called (not entirely without approval) the "violence" of U.S. individualism. But there is nothing of what the teacher had also called the "passivity" or the "nonassertiveness" of the Chinese in the way in which Donald's movements diverge from and converge with those of the other dragon-dancers. He both loses and finds himself in the spontaneous blazing of the dragon's path (an individual and a communal effort), more completely than he ever could in his desire to achieve American assimilation by dancing instead like Fred Astaire.

For Donald Duk as for Monica Sone, speaking in her Japanese American memoir *Nisei Daughter* about her release from one of the World War II "relocation" camps to which Americans of Japanese descent on the West Coast were sent after the bombing of Pearl Harbor, what she calls a "sadly split" sense of self, on either side of what she terms her "hyphenated" identity, is now more nearly at one. Sone had moved eastward to a new life (immediate return to the West Coast was forbidden) of educational opportunity and at least partial reconciliation with the society which had incarcerated her. John Okada, by contrast, had written in *No-No Boy*—a novel fraught with undischarged anger over the sheer fact of such incarcerations, as well as over the fate of those who said "no" and "no" again to U.S. military service and an oath of allegiance to the U.S. government which displaced them, suffering additional prison terms as a result—the story of one Ichiro Yamada for whom only the merest "glimmer of hope" exists at the end for resolution of such a "split."

Donald's sense of "adding on," or rather the sense espoused by his father and ascribed to Donald more as an intuitive than as a conscious acquisition, provides a context in which "hyphenations" of self, as connections *and* as disconnections or ruptures, can be accommodated without denial of conflict or complexity. Donald is perhaps by temperament more like Monica Sone, crossing bridges where he finds them (or where in his inward exploration he improvisationally builds them), without theorizing or rationalizing the process as she tends to do. Frank Chin, on the other hand, is more like John Okada or his protagonist Ichiro, feeding even in comic moments on underlying tension and unspent anger. And however sharply the distinction may be preserved in *Donald Duk* between Chin's authorial asperity and Donald's relative receptivity to change, the plausibility and effectiveness of each depends to some degree on their reciprocity. Contemplating "hyphenation" on all the levels and in all the contexts to which it pertains, one could do worse than to think of a wooden crosstie—inscribed and set down between the rails in celebration, removed in proprietary arrogance by "white brawn," its plain replacement ripped out in rage, the original crosstie then retextualized in imagination, restored to history through dream—as *itself* a "hyphen," a mark of union *and* separation, of openness *and* angry resistance, in its presence on the page or equally in its absence, an empty space enforcing the interrelated issues as to how that gap might, or might never, be filled.

The last words of the last section of Maxine Hong Kingston's *The Woman Warrior*, called "A Song for a Barbarian Reed Pipe," are "It translated well." This refers to the author's reawakened sense of the reciprocity between her own experience and the legends of her Chinese past (reciprocity rediscovered not least through her dreams of the mythic heroine Fa Mu Lan, in which the woman warrior's exploits are ceremonially retold). But it also refers to her altered sense of her "Chinese," in relation to her "American," identity in the present. She too has learned to "add on," without having to "give up," layers of experience, knowledge and cultural self-awareness durable enough to distinguish from one another, yet finely textured and translucent enough to blend and complement one another "well." In that quality of complementary communion lies a sense of translation as a ceremony of self-creation and self-expression.

So too, a final time, for Donald Duk. He "speaks," audibly or silently, publicly or privately, in various "languages"—the vocabulary of dance steps, whether based on Fred Astaire's or improvised in a New Year's dragon; his true voice or his cartoon mimicry of Donald Duck; irreconcilable iconographies of old photographs; the imagery of dreams, of building a railroad in the past or making it known more truly in the present how the railroad was built; the symbolic markings on 108 model airplanes, and the care with which the planes are sent on their final flight; the mysteries and the familiarities of food, persisting while kingdoms rise and fall, nations come and go; the idioms of childhood and impending maturity, of school and free play, not least in the sense of the widening range of self-educating consciousness, the freedom as well as the daunting challenge (in Emerson's phrase) to "build [...] your own world"; control, and the lack of control, over the actual languages, English and Chinese, in which with whatever degree of precision he thinks, feels, reads, writes, speaks or understands the speech of others.

Each of these and other such "languages" plays a part in Donald's capacity for self-awareness and awareness of the world. Each requires to be spoken, written, read, or heard in the light, and through the lens, of all the others. Each in the end, it would seem, "translates well." In such translation, thus understood, is a way of apprehending and appreciating the harmonies of ceremonial incantation or performance, resolved to whatever extent from discord, which coalesce to make up the medium of self-(re)invention in *Donald Duk*, "and food" for the ongoing insatiabilities of a (re)invented self.

Works Cited

Chin, Frank. *Donald Duk*. Minneapolis: Coffee House P, 1991.

Kingston, Maxine Hong. *The Woman Warrior. Memoirs of a Girlhood Among Ghosts*. New York: Random House (Vintage International), 1989.

Okada, John. *No-No Boy*. Seattle: U of Washington P, 1976.

Sone, Monica. *Nisei Daughter*. Boston: Little, Brown (Atlantic Monthly P), 1953.

II. Interethnic Negotiations

Funeral Rites, Ethnicity, and the Politics of Representation in Asian American Literature

Seiwoong Oh

After observing Chinese funerals in Chang Mai, the second largest city in Thailand, where Chinese immigrants have established residence since the latter half of the nineteenth century, anthropologist Anne Maxwell Hill finds that even among the Thai citizens of Chinese descent who are "highly acculturated in Thai ways," Chinese culture remains a vital aspect of their lives, "evident in the vigor, even splendor of Chinese religious life" (315). In particular, according to Hill, Chinese funeral rites, which help us see where the participants locate their social and cultural identity, "reflect the continued meaningfulness to descendants of Chinese immigrants of ancestor commemoration and links to a Chinese past" and that the rites "remain significant sources of Chinese tradition, custom, even solidarity, to contemporary generations of Chinese descendants who may equally be at home in the Thai world" (327). Although the rituals typically contain some Thai elements and are held at the sites of Thai Buddhist temples, the funerals are essentially and "unequivocally Chinese affairs," according to Hill (316).

Turning our attention to another site of Chinese diaspora, the United States, one may presume that Chinese immigrants and their American-born descendants, at least on the surface, have faithfully maintained their ceremonies and by implication, their cultural identity. Chinese funeral rites have become "exotic spectacles" readily accessible to cultural outsiders; they have also become signs of the "otherness" of the participants as well. "The gayest thing about the Chinese was their funerals," says writer Estelline Bennett, recounting her experience with the Chinese in Deadwood, South Dakota, in the early 20th century ("The Chinese in Deadwood" 2). An internet travel magazine, *Travel and Leisure,* recommends an "offbeat, quintessential tour of Chinatown" in San Francisco by following "the brass marching band that plays for Chinese funerals," where "Chinese onlookers bow and doff their hats, and the tourists stand and gawk" ("Chinatown" 2).

If we are look at Asian American literature, however, funeral rites appear to be a different affair altogether. Depending on the writer, the ritualistic details serve various aesthetic purposes, and they become a barometer of measuring how each writer negotiates the politics of cultural representation. In some works, the rites are portrayed to be eclectic and largely perfunctory in that the particulars of the ritual are often no longer meaningful to the mourners. Yet in other works, writers try to reclaim their ties to their ancestral cultures by attempting to rebuild a meaningful ritual from their dim memory. In many works, funeral scenes also demonstrate the diasporic nature of Asian American immigration as the mourners wish that the souls, especially those of the first generation immigrants, return to their native lands. This return of the soul signifies, in turn, the end of an imposed identity and the opportunity to reclaim the old, and by implication real, identity of the dead. Finally, the various ways in which Asian American writers deal with funeral rites are evidence to the diversity of sensibilities among Asian Americans in dealing with the politics of cultural representation.

Eclectic Hybridity and Perfunctory Nature

In a survey of funeral practices in the world, Robert W. Habenstein and William M. Lamers explain that Japanese funeral customs are dominantly Buddhist, whereas Korean customs show the influence of Buddhism, Taoism, and Confucianism with the added elements from Shamanism and village folkways (63). As for Chinese customs, the authors describe them as "a bewildering intermingling of Buddhism, Confucianism, Taoism, [and] Shamanism" (1). Li Shuang, in an article in *The Journal of Popular Culture*, leaves out Shamanism but offers a similar explanation:

> Chinese funerals are primarily Confucian, but they introduce Taoism as a complement. In other words, funerals contain Confucian views about the maintenance of ethics and Taoist ideas about the pursuit of immortality. Buddhist thought present in Chinese funerals should not be neglected. On the one hand, the ideas of Buddhism are opposite to those of Confucianism because Buddhism pays more attention to the next life. On the other hand, during the process of incorporation into ancient Chinese culture, Buddhism adopted some Confucian elements and formed a very close relationship with it [...].
>
> Generally speaking, Chinese funerals reveal the core of Chinese culture through their harmonious incorporation of the three Chinese religions—Confucianism, Taoism and Buddhism. (119)

If Asian funerals in general contain "bewildering" hybridity, they are depicted in Asian American literature as ever-changing, quickly adapting to the new cultural environments and yet continually bestowing meaning to the eclectic forms. Criticized by her husband for preparing a funeral too lavish for Japanese cultural standards, the great-grandmother in Julie Shigekuni's *A Bridge Between Us* takes him aside and explains to him that "things are simply different here, in

America" (11). When a Korean bachelor dies in Carol Roh-Spaulding's short story, "Waiting for Mr. Kim," the mother character is disconcerted: "'Damn,' her mother went on. 'I wish now I'd paid more attention to the shamans. But we stayed away from those women unless we needed them. My family was afraid I'd get the call because I was sickly and talked in my sleep, and we have particularly restless ancestors [...]. Was it food for every day for a month or every month for a year? What a mystery'" (268). In the end, the mother decides to do a Christian funeral because it is "simpler" and "cheaper" (268). In another example, Maxine Hong Kingston depicts in *China Men* an interesting case of eclectic hybridity. When the motor hearse stops at the Chinese cemetery, "not on a hillside in China but beside Interstate 5 on the flat San Joaquin Valley floor," Chinese men learn the process from "mortician demons," not by consulting Chinese immigrant elders or religious experts. The young narrator's mother even brings "whiskey" to be poured into the grave. When the family comes home from the burial, they do not "burn a pile of leaves and newspapers at the curb" because the family is "modern" (189). The narrator even relates another child's dream in which the grandfather appeared to say that as long as the offspring bury their parents correctly, "they would be absolved of all duties to ancestors since they were now Americans" (189). In any culture, of course, funeral customs change over time adapting to new political, social, and religious demands. In Asian American literature, funeral customs are seen to change according to the variation of cultural sites, this time as a hybrid between Asian and mainstream American cultures.

Also noticeable in the works of some Asian American writers is the fact that funeral rites are portrayed as largely perfunctory, the significance of the particulars no longer meaningful to the participants. Amy Tan, for instance, writes in *The Kitchen God's Wife*: "I guess this means Grand Auntie's funeral will be Buddhist. Although she attended the First Chinese Baptist Church for a number of years, both she and my mother stopped going right after my father died. I don't think Grand Auntie ever gave up her other beliefs, which weren't exactly Buddhist, just all the superstitious rituals concerning attracting good luck and avoiding bad" (19). The narrator, unable to read the Chinese characters in a huge banner above the casket, asks her mother to translate them. After translating, the mother adds that it is "[n]othing too special" and that it probably came from the family association to which the deceased occasionally donated (42). According to the mother, the funeral tradition is not about manifesting religious faith but showing respect for the dead (24). The narrator in the end feels "silly, taking part in a ritual that makes no sense" to her (44).

Kingston, in *China Men*, also describes the distance between immigrants and their American-born children. As old men make speeches during the funeral of Great Uncle Kau Goong, the young narrator is bewildered, unable to understand what is being said: "Perhaps on this serious occasion, they did not put things into many synonyms until they hit on one a kid could understand" (185). When adults do not bother to explain the particulars of the process, children make up theories about what is happening. When, for example, the narrator's mother instructs the children to throw paper money out the car window, they speculate that the money is probably for the deceased to spend in heaven, or "for the waif ghosts lining the street, or it was like a carrot on a stick to entice Kau Goong, who was lingering behind or hovering overhead, to the cemetery" (186-87). Also when the hearse moves through Stockton, the kids explain to one another, "We're taking him on a last look," or "We're looking for him" (187).

Similarly in Shigekuni's *A Bridge Between Us*, the mother-narrator describes her sense of alienation from the ritual: "The priest, an older Nihonzin, [...] chants something in Japanese I can't understand and drifts away. And that is how the service progresses. The priest reciting or chanting, and my not understanding [...]. I am ashamed of the blackness in my heart and of the space" (179). In Fae Myenne Ng's *Bone*, we hear about how on New Year's day Ona and her father Leon lay out a feast for the gods: one year it is the "Eight Holy Immortals"; the next, it is the "Goddess of Mercy"; another, it is "Jesus"; and then yet another, Confucius (107). When Leon wants to do a Chinese funeral for Ona, Nina "rolled her eyes and said she didn't want any of that hocus-pocus" (123).

The loss of meaningfulness of the ceremonies is also evident in John Okada's *No-No Boy*. At the funeral of Ichiro's mother, the narrator exhibits detachment from the ritualistic significance:

> As they [Ichiro and his father] took their places and glumly regarded the open casket only a few feet away, the priest sauntered across the stage with its lavish, gold-bedecked shrine and seated himself beside an urn-like gong. Without acknowledging the people present, he struck the gong several times and promptly proceeded to recite the unintelligible mumbo-jumbo revered by all the old ones present but understood by none. (191)

When the father explains the funeral procedure, which includes feeding "people who were so kind as to come" to the funeral (194), Ichiro leaves the scene, unable to handle the cultural baggage his immigrant parents brought with them. While these examples illustrate the distance between the first and second generations of Asian Americans, they also exhibit the brittle and often challenging transmission of cultural values from first generation immigrants to their American-born children.

In his *Culture and Communication: The Logic by Which Symbols Are Connected*, Edmund Leach maintains that

> the participants in a ritual are sharing communicative experiences through many different sensory channels simultaneously; they are acting out an ordered sequence of metaphoric events within a territorial space which has itself been ordered to prove a metaphoric context for the play acting. Verbal, musical, cho-

reographic, and visual-aesthetic "dimensions" are all likely to form components
of the total message. (41)

If we can accept Leach's metaphoric view of rituals, it helps explain how in
Asian American literature the metaphoric context is disconnected from the ritual, and how the verbal, musical, choreographic, and visual-aesthetic dimensions
do not help formulate the total message but rather prevent young Asian Americans from forming a synthesis of the various ritualistic details. Virtually every
movement, action, and arrangement in a funeral rite is metaphoric; however, if
the metaphor is lost to the attendees, the rite can only become pro forma.

Maxine Hong Kingston's narrator in *The Woman Warrior* blames immigrant
adults for not connecting with the younger generations: "Never explaining. How
can Chinese keep any traditions at all?" (183). Judging from the way funeral
scenes are portrayed, however, the younger generations appear to be equally
responsible, unwilling to keep the traditions, due perhaps in part to the absence
of common religious faith, to the language barrier, and also to the pressure from
the dominant culture which labels non-Christian rites as superstitious, foreign
and primitive. To call the ritualistic details "superstitious," "hocus pocus," and
"mumbo jumbo" is to deny the meaningfulness of the ritual, and is indicative of
the negation of cultural identity on the part of these young characters.

Rebuilding Meaningful Rites

In Nora Okja Keller's *Comfort Woman*, the author opens the novel with a scene
in which the mother character prepares for the fifth anniversary of her husband's
death. She places stacks of offerings to be burned after eating "the remembrance
feast" she makes ready to appease her husband's spirit (1). Later on in the novel,
the mother-narrator describes the traditional funeral rites that she performed for
her mother in Korea. Although the custom demands that the oldest son take the
coat of the deceased up to the roof and ask for the return of the spirit to "feast
and prepare for the long journey to heaven," the narrator, the youngest daughter,
fulfills the role of the eldest son by pulling out her mother's wedding dress to
climb onto the roof and calling her spirit to come back (181). After this recollection of the past, the mother prepares for the twenty-first anniversary of her
mother's death, "laying out the table" with her mother's "favorite foods, with
wine, with a set of chopsticks and spoons for the members of the family, dead
and alive, who will never eat from them" (182). There is a clear indication of her
familiarity with the ritualistic details and their meaningfulness.

When it is the daughter-character's turn to narrate, readers discern a different
perspective: although the second generation Korean American does not share the
same religious philosophy and has felt ashamed of her mother's shamanistic
rituals, she would, upon her mother's death, reclaim cultural ties to her mother

by performing a personally meaningful ritual. One generation away from the immigrant mother, the daughter-narrator refuses the Christian funeral for her mother, which has been arranged by a family friend. Instead, she decides to perform a shamanistic ritual by going over the notes and tapes her mother left for her in a box. Following the instructions, she prepares the table, saying, "Hi, Mommy, [...] I don't know if I'm doing this right" (208). Despite uncertainty, she makes it meaningful by performing a makeshift ceremony for her mother. By doing so, the daughter overcomes her early resistance to her ancestral culture and finally embraces it by performing a meaningful shamanistic funeral ceremony.

In a similar vein, Shigekuni, in *A Bridge Between Us*, draws funeral scenes with an emphasis on the meaningfulness of the ritual and on the reconfirmation of the ties between Japanese American generations. The novel opens with the great grandmother's recollection of her immigrant father's death: "The first thing I did was to lay my father's body across our kitchen table [...]. I remember the kitchen table was the only surface large and sturdy enough to hold his weight, and I chose the table where it was, in the kitchen, because that is the room with a view of San Francisco Bay where my father arrived from Tokyo with my mother back in 1898" (3-4). Since her father was a "sentimentalist," she knows he would appreciate being laid on the place with the view of the Bay; it is of secondary importance that the family could not eat their meals in the kitchen for the whole week the body is kept there. Also since her father "had been always concerned, for the sake of appearances, about hygiene," she scrubs his body that night and makes him wear his "finest silk kimono" (4). Despite the uncertainty over the correctness of the ritualistic details, her attempts to rebuild a "bridge" between her immigrant father and herself are clearly discernible.

Diaspora

No-No Boy, John Okada's only novel, portrays the death of Kenji in a way that elucidates the second-generation Japanese Americans' ambivalence about their ethnic identity, an ambivalence intensified in the wake of the military drafting during the Second World War. Kenji warns his father not to bury his body in the Japanese cemetery: "I'll come back and haunt you if you stick me in Washelli with the rest of the Japs. I've got ideas about the next place and I want to get started right" (183). Having been suffocated between a Japanese and an American identity, Kenji denies both and yearns to forge a new identity that would be uniquely his own, and not a void. In contrast, when his mother passes away, Ichiro, the protagonist in the same novel, bids her soul to return to her homeland: "Suddenly I feel sorry for you. Not sorry that you are dead, but sorry for the happiness you have not known. So, now you are free. Go back quickly. Go to the Japan you so long remembered and loved, and be happy" (186). The same diasporic, sojourner's perspective can be discerned in Shigekuni's *A Bridge Between Us*. As Reiko burns her husband's belongings following his death, she finds a note from him: "Please take a picture of Rio [their daughter] and send it with my ashes to my parents in Japan" (29). Reiko fulfills his request accordingly.

In a number of other Asian American writers, funeral scenes portray the sojourner mentality of most immigrants, who have rarely felt at home in America. Cathy Song writes in her much anthologized "Heaven":

> He thinks that when we die we'll go to China.
> Think of it—a Chinese heaven
> where, except for his blond hair,
> the part that belongs to his father,
> everyone will look like him. (77)

She further describes how her child's immigrant grandfather "never planned to stay," always meaning to go back. The poet concludes by saying that the "notion of returning" must be "in the blood" (78).

In Keller's *Comfort Woman,* the home trip of the soul is the ultimate purpose of the funeral rite: "I opened my mother's box, sprinkling her ashes over the water. I held my fingers under the slow fall of ash, sifting, letting it coat my hand. I touched my fingers to my lips. 'Your body in mine,' I told my mother, 'so you will always be with me, even when your spirit finds its way home. To Korea. To Susulham. And across the river of heaven to the Seven Sisters.'" (212). Like other mourners, Keller's narrator prays for the return of the immigrant's soul to its native land, where it would look like everyone else and be treated as such, free and real.

In Chinese American literature, the tradition of sending the bones of the deceased back to China becomes a metaphor for the sojourner mindset of early immigrants. Even in 1992, *US News & World Report* related a recent advertisement in China Daily promoting to overseas Chinese the sales of burial lots in a cemetery outside Beijing, for $500 per square meter (Bernstein 19). Reflecting this tradition, Ng writes in her first novel, *Bone*: "If Grandpa Leong had been a family man, he might have had real tears, a grieving wife [...]. Hopefully [...] when his children were grown and making their own money, they'd dig up his bones, pack them in a clay pot, send them—no, accompany them—back to the home village for a proper burial" (82). One of the main characters and the narrator's stepfather, Leon, lives with the guilt that his middle daughter's death is caused by his negligence: he promised his paper father to send his bones back to China, but even when he wanted to do so, he could not find the gravesite. After searching for the gravesite for hours in vain in the Chinese cemetery, Leon is finally informed by the Chinese Benevolent Association that unclaimed bones, presumably including those of his paper father's, were removed to an unmarked place to relieve overcrowding at the Chinese cemetery, making it impossible for Leon to keep his promise to the deceased of a proper burial.

In Chinese Canadian fiction, such as *The Jade Peony* by Wayson Choy and *Disappearing Moon Cafe* by SKY Lee, funerals also play an important role in portraying the sojourner mindset of early immigrants. In the first section of *The Jade Peony*, for example, the child narrator's best friend, Wong Suk, plans to sail back to China with the bones of the Chinese who died in Gold Mountain. The little girl does not understand the significance of the trip at the moment, but as the story unfolds, the narrator learns how in Vancouver only a small population of Chinatown ghosts could bother with the living because most of the bones in the area had been shipped back to China (157). When her grandmother's ghost haunts around the house, her father swears that "if he could ever raise enough money, the Old One's bones would be dug up and taken to the Bone House in Victoria" (163).

Also in *Disappearing Moon Cafe*, the initial scene features a main character, Wong Gwei Chang, who comes from China to take a job as a bone seeker. Chang at first does not understand why his job is important and dreads the work: "What were a few dried bones to him, except disgusting?" (12). When he touches the bones, however, he is "awed by them": the spirits in the mountains, "strong and persuasive," follow him about wherever he is and whispers to him until he knows "each one to be a hero, with yearnings from the same secret places in his own heart" (12). His job leads him to an awakening: "By then, he understood. By then, in the utter peace of the forests, he had met them all—uncles who had climbed mountain heights then fallen from them, uncles who had drowned in deep surging waters, uncles who had clawed to their deaths in the dirt of caved-in mines" (13). In short, he learns that if he lost any bones, he is "condemning human spirits to ten thousand years of aimless wandering" (17).

This yearning for the return to the ancestral land is synonymous, one would argue, with their desire to reclaim their own identity. As diasporic peoples, Asian immigrants maintained strong ties to their ancestral lands, most of them identifying themselves not as Americans but as Asians in exile ready to go back once economic and political situations improved in their native lands. Despite their centuries of history within the United States, moreover, Asian American immigrants have been mostly defined as "Other," and the return of the soul or bones to the homeland signifies the reclaiming of their old, and real, identity. Post-immigrant generations seem, according to Asian American literature, to acknowledge America as their homeland, and yet, by wishing their parents to recover their own real and free selves by returning to their country of origin, they tacitly and eloquently protest the social injustice of discrimination against their parents in America, the land of immigrants which has done little to make Asian immigrants and their descendants feel at home.

Variety of representation

Although this paper has managed to show a few similarities among certain Asian American literary pieces, it is fair to say that, judging from the way that the funeral scenes are handled, Asian American writers show a diversity of sensibilities in dealing with the politics of cultural representation. In *Fifth Chinese Daughter,* a 1945 autobiography whose "guiding theme" is to promote a "better understanding of the Chinese culture on the part of Americans," (vii) Jade Snow Wong assumes the role of a "native informant" by devoting a few pages to describing in detail a funeral procession held on a Sunday in Chinatown. Amy Tan, writing decades later, opts to present funeral customs primarily for a tourist look or at best a chance for humor over the superstitious nature of the customs. Besides the scenes from *The Kitchen God's Wife,* as introduced before, the funeral scenes in *The Hundred Secret Senses* are also invested with humor that is largely subversive of ethnic traditions. In a funeral scene, when her half-sister Kwan explains that the dead body is dressed with seven layers for her top half and five for the bottom, the narrator remembers how the ski jacket used for the seventh layer was "bought on sale at Macy's" and the price tag is still attached, "to prove the jacket isn't a hand-me-down" (240). When Kwan proudly announces that the jacket is waterproof, the narrator asks if it rains in the next world (240). Asked by the narrator why the bottom half of the body has fewer layers than the top, DuLili responds by saying, "It means that two days a week Big Ma must wander about with her bottom naked in the underworld" (241).

As in Amy Tan, *Wooden Fish Songs* by Ruthanne Lum McCunn at first appears to rely heavily on exoticization of Chinese funeral traditions. The novel opens with an extended death-bed scene in which the narrator makes the mistake of laying a stray cat on her grandfather's chest. She and her mother are convinced that his spirit is confused and has come into the young narrator's body. The first line reads: "I was marked by ghosts in my seventh winter. One ghost. My grandfather's" (3). Later in the novel, when the protagonist Gim Gong runs away from an arranged marriage, and when the family presumes him dead and pays a village priest to perform special rites to prevent Gim Gong's ghost from wandering, the author goes to great lengths to describe the "special rites": "Holding a three-sided dagger with two bells on the brass handle, the priest stabbed spirits that might wish our ghost son ill. Then he set up a ceremonial tree with candles on its four leafless branches and led us around it in a circle while he recited prayers" (275). When the ghost of the protagonist's grandmother keeps harassing her oldest son and his wife, and when her victims bring in a diviner to find out what the spirit wants from them, the author again offers a lengthy description of the diviner, "a small, chicken-breasted man in a long blue gown," and the ceremony he performs (147). In contrast, the novelist does not describe the funeral of Miss Fanny, another major character, presumably because it is a Christian funeral. Despite such descriptions of Chinese rites, however, it may be unfair to accuse McCunn of sheer exoticization. The first death-bed scene seems crucial to establishing the mindset of the mother character, Sum Jui. And the subsequent descriptions are integral to the plot, which is centered on the complicated family relationship.

If these writers have chosen to introduce elaborate funeral scenes for one reason or another, many other writers have chosen not to deal with specific funeral customs. Ng's *Bone* centers on Ona's death but the funeral itself gets no more than a few lines. The plot in Okada's *No-No Boy* includes the deaths of three major characters, but the author opts not to deal with the specifics of the rituals. Hisaye Yamamoto's "Las Vegas Charley," Kim Ronyoung's *Clay Walls* and a number of other pieces also feature major characters' deaths, but the writers leave out funeral scenes altogether. Leaving out elaborate funeral scenes may be interpreted as a political act: a refusal to submit to the role of native informants. Rather than ethnicizing and exoticizing their cultural material, and thus pandering to the taste of their mainstream audience, Ng, Kim, and Yamamoto seem to portray Asian America not as "all the same" but as filled with human beings complete with emotions, desires, and idiosyncratic individualities.

There are still other writers who use different narrative strategies to deal with funeral rites. The narrative strategy in Choy's *The Jade Peony*, for instance, is particularly interesting in the way it works counter-subversively. When the father figure neglects his funeral duties for the grandmother, the young narrator is frequently haunted by the grandmother's spirit. Only then does the father decide to pay tribute and set up a portrait and a shrine for her. Although readers may dismiss the haunting as coincidental at first, they are invited into the mind of the child narrator and are led to believe the series of hauntings to be causal. Readers, along with the father character, realize that by restoring their cultural identity, the family is able to function normally. By involving his readers in the dynamics of funeral rites, Choy, then, may be implying the importance of cultural continuity: cultural traditions, such as funeral customs, are not to done away with in favor of assimilation but to be upheld as meaningful and real.

In her *Reading Asian American Literature: From Necessity to Extravagance*, Sau-ling Cynthia Wong argues that Asian American writers bear a "sense of disequilibrium" because Asian American ethnic signs are already interpreted by the mainstream culture as foreign and other (71). Indeed, some writers seem to have compromised with the mainstream audiences' demand and expectations by staging funeral scenes as spectacles to be consumed by readers who are cultural outsiders, and also by dismissing the funeral rites as superstitious and perfunctory. In that sense, Frank Chin has a point in criticizing the practice of "cultural pornography," which panders to the taste of mainstream audiences by exploiting and exaggerating "exotic" aspects of Asian American culture.

However, as demonstrated in the paper, there are other writers who have found different ways to deal with the ethnic signs associated with funeral customs. Some writers suppress the funeral scenes presumably to avoid the danger of exoticizing. Others stage the ritual not to "sell the scene" but to reclaim their cultural identity, to find a missing link between the rituals and their meaningfulness. Still others use the funeral images as sound literary devices integral to the plot and character development. Complaining about how *The Woman Warrior* was measured against the critics' Oriental fantasy, Kingston hoped for a future with more Asian American writers to show the diversity of their sensibilities, to show that they are not "all alike." Funeral scenes in Asian American literature, with all its unique characteristics and diverse representations, show that Kingston's wish may just come true, slowly but surely.

Works Cited

Bernstein. A. *US News & World Report: Travel & Leisure.* rep. *Travel & Leisure.* January, 1997. 25 Feb. 1998.
    <http://www.pathfinder.com/travel/TL/jan/chinatown.html>.

"The Chinese in Deadwood." Adams Museum. 19 Jan, 1998. 25 Feb. 1998
    <http://www.blackhills.com/museum/chinese.htm>.

Choy, Wayson. *The Jade Peony.* New York: Picador USA, 1995.

Habenstein, Robert W. and William M. Lamers. *Funeral Customs the World Over.* Milwaukee: Bulfin Printers, 1960.

Hill, Ann Maxwell. "Chinese Funerals and Chinese Ethnicity in Chiang Mai, Thailand." *Ethnology* 31.4 (1992): 315-30.

Keller, Nora Okja. *Comfort Woman.* New York: Viking Penguin, 1997.

Kim, Ronyoung. *Clay Walls.* Seattle, WA: U of Washington P, 1990.

Kingston, Maxine Hong. *China Men.* New York: Random House, 1989.

—. "Cultural Misreadings by American Reviewers." *Asian and Western Writers in Dialogue: New Cultural Identities.* Ed. Guy Amirthanayagam. London: Macmillan, 1982. 55-65.

—. *The Woman Warrior: Memoirs of a Girlhood Among Ghosts.* New York: Knopf, 1975.

Leach, Edmund. *Culture and Communication: The Logic By Which Symbols Are Connected.* New York: Cambridge UP, 1976.

Lee, SKY. *Disappearing Moon Café.* Seattle, WA: Seal P, 1990.

McCunn, Ruthanne Lum. *Wooden Fish Songs.* New York: Penguin, 1995.

Ng, Fae Myenne. *Bone.* New York: Hyperion, 1993.

Okada, John. *No-No Boy.* Seattle, WA: U of Washington P, 1976.

Roh-Spaulding, Carol. "Waiting for Mr. Kim." *Asian American Literature: A Brief Introduction and Anthology.* Ed. Shawn Wong. New York: HarperCollins, 1996.

Shigekuni, Julie. *A Bridge Between Us.* New York: Doubleday, 1995.

Shuang, Li. "The Funeral and Chinese Culture." *Journal of Popular Culture* 27.2 (Fall 1993): 113-20.

Song, Cathy. "Heaven." *Frameless Windows, Squares of Light*. New York: Norton, 1988. 77-79.

Tan, Amy. *The Hundred Secret Senses*. New York: Putnam's, 1995.

—. *The Kitchen God's Wife*. New York: Putnam's, 1991.

Wong, Jade Snow. *Fifth Chinese Daughter*. Seattle: U of Washington P, 1945.

Wong, Sau-ling Cynthia. *Reading Asian American Literature: From Necessity to Extravagance*. Princeton: Princeton UP, 1993.

Yamamoto, Hisaye. "Las Vegas Charley." *Seventeen Syllables and Other Stories*. Latham, NY: Kitchen Table—Women of Color P, 1988. 70-85.

Mending the Sk(e)in of Memory:
Trauma, Narrative, and the Recovery of Identity in Patricia Chao, Aimee Liu and Joy Kogawa

Helena Grice

Critical attention is increasingly being accorded to fictional and autobiographical texts which are preoccupied with the varied recovery, power, and persuasiveness of memory. Memory is one place where identity is formed and various kinds of prose writing inscribe memory in differing ways. The three texts that I shall consider here mostly reject the assignation of particular generic identities and insist instead upon textual identities of their own, ones which speak to the slippery and elusive nature of recollection. Recent scholarship on ethnic texts has asserted the importance of memory for ethnic writers in the negotiation of identity. For example, Amritjit Singh, Joseph T. Skerrett, Jr., and Robert Hogan note: "Memory [...] shapes narrative forms and strategies toward reclaiming a suppressed past and helps the process of re-visioning that is essential to gaining control over one's life and future. The ethnic narrative thus becomes, in Stuart Hall's phrase, 'an act of cultural recovery,' and the emergent ethnicity embedded therein develops a new relationship to the past, which is to be recovered through both memory and narrative" (19). The personal recollections of ethnic subjects, in common with other culturally marginal subjects, may contradict "official" or culturally authoritative versions of the past. Many culturally marginalized writers foreground the workings of memory in their work, and this is also the case in much writing by Asian American women. Such an emphasis is useful for the way it allows us to read what the text does not say, as much as what it does. The insistence upon the workings of memory as incomplete, flawed, often ahistorical and subjective, may, for example, open the way to acknowledge certain textual excesses, such as silence or forgetting, which are not accounted for within conventional theories of the representation of the past. Many ethnic American writers remember the racism that WASP American culture has asked them to forget; while ethnic American women writers also remember oppressions that result from both racism and sexism. The emphasis upon and use of memory in ethnic American women's texts is partly responsible for the ways in which these writers upset the apple cart of genre. The workings of memory in a text cut across and through generic categories, touching upon and mixing the processes of officially-authorized memory (history) with personal histories (autobiography, memoir, journals) as a counter-cultural tactic. At the same time, an emphasis upon the processes of remembering acknowledges the partiality and fictiveness of that process. The workings of collective memory may also be foregrounded, as they are inscribed culturally through songs and stories.

Asian American female memory often privileges the vernacular. Myths, folklore, bedtime stories and other vernacular forms are sanctioned as valid versions of the past alongside, and often over and above, other forms like laws and written histories. Excavating the workings of memory allows us to avoid categorizing these works in reductionist ways. Many texts are self-consciously a "re-memory," to borrow Toni Morrison's phrase in *Beloved* (36), which listen to and speak the multifariousness of the past as we receive it, through both legacies of orality and textual modes of inscription.

All three novels I discuss here are specifically located within a history-memory-trauma matrix. Trauma, in Cathy Caruth's definition, "describes an overwhelming experience of sudden or catastrophic events in which the response to the event occurs in the often delayed, uncontrollable repetitive appearance of hallucinations and other intrusive phenomena" (*Unclaimed Experience* 11). All the novels also place an experience of trauma within a cross-cultural context, in which explicit parallels are drawn between parental experiences of immigration and racism, and the daughters' own suffering as a result of sexual abuse. Each narrative patterns many trauma narratives, in the sense that the plot tracks the subject's journey towards self-knowledge, catharsis, and release from a traumatic experience or experiences, which involves enacting a break with the past by confronting it in order to forge a new, more comfortable, relationship with both history and memory.[1] All the narratives also enact a process of remembering as part of a wider project of locating a more secure identity and cultural order. Much of the early part of each novel is devoted to rendering the subject's psychological confusion, instability, and inertia. Thus, each narrative enacts what Gurleen Grewal has called "ceremonial performances of memory" (140). Telling stories becomes a means of making sense of these women's place in an otherwise chaotic and alienating world. Although these stories ultimately affirm individual identity through memory, the desire to know the past, and confront it, in each case is double-edged. Release from a traumatic past can only come by confronting it, but this is always a traumatic process in itself. All of the novels place an individual experience of the trauma of sexual abuse in a wider cross-cultural context of their parents' own experiences as ethnic subjects in America. While the narratives often commemorate these experiences, and explicit parallels are drawn between ancestral/parental suffering and daughterly suffering, in

---

1   For a more extensive critical discussion of the literatures of trauma, see Kalí Tal's *Worlds of Hurt*, particularly chapter one. In addition, chapter seven contains a discussion of incest survivor narratives, which is particularly useful in the context of this piece.

each case, the parental desire to forget the past is ultimately shown to contribute to the daughters' on-going psychological problems.

These three novels share a preoccupation with how to reach and connect with memories of the past, and the dangers and pitfalls in doing so. In *Obasan*, memory is described as "a sealed vault with its cold icon" (preface). In *Monkey King*, memory is also locked up, but the central character Sally recognizes that this causes problems: "Some memory you keep underneath, so you can get on with your life. It doesn't work" (116). Maibelle, the central character in *Face*, goes further: "Memories matter. And not just for tracking time or holding an album in your hands when everyone who ever loved you is gone. Memories contain our secrets. They answer our questions. They tell us who we are and sometimes what we need" (41). This recognition of the power of memory is reinforced in each case by the nature of the traumatic memory itself. Although each woman has to uncover familial histories and traumas, these are recollected alongside a more intensely personal experience of sexual abuse, which is a particularly embodied memory. The body's capacity to forget is incomplete, even when other ways of remembering, such as through documentation, photographs, or communal/familial recollections may be absent, lost, or withheld. The workings of memory are often described using a body metaphor, with buried, often trau- matic, memories lying beneath the "skin" of consciousness. This surface/depth model of memory is one which is used in both *Monkey King* and *Face*. However, as I will later suggest, *Obasan* questions this metaphor, positing instead a conception of memory as a thread, or skein. This skein may become broken, or entangled, as the "skin" of consciousness may be damaged by the memories lying beneath. *Obasan*'s "skein" metaphor differs from the metaphor of "skin"/body, though, because it figures memory as more continuous than a surface/depth model allows.

The three texts that I have chosen to discuss are all relatively recent works by Asian American women. Obasan was published in 1981 by the Japanese Canadian writer Joy Kogawa, and has swiftly gained critical recognition as a narrative which skillfully foregrounds the workings of memory in its depiction of the traumatic experiences of its protagonist, Naomi Nakane. Naomi's story is the story of Japanese Canadians during the Second World War, a period of history which saw many Japanese Canadians persecuted and forced to leave their homes on the coast of British Columbia. In addition to this enforced relocation, Naomi suffers sexual abuse as a child at the hands of a neighbor, and also loses her mother, who is killed at Nagasaki. These three experiences constitute a traumatic history for Naomi, who must renegotiate this past in order to find peace. *Face* was published in 1994, and relates the story of a Chinese American woman's struggle to reconcile herself with a history of racism and rape in her own path towards the recovery of a secure sense of her identity. As with *Obasan*, *Face* intertwines generational conflicts and the challenges of assimilation with a traumatic experience of sexual abuse. *Monkey King*, published in 1997, is the most recent of the trauma narratives with which I am concerned here. A young Chinese American woman, twenty-eight year old Sally Wang, explores her past in order to come to terms with it. This past also includes an experience of rape as a child, and, as with *Obasan* and *Face*, occurs alongside the young girl's negotiation of her ethnic identity in a racist world.

Monkey King opens with Sally's mental breakdown, and takes place during her subsequent stay in a psychiatric hospital. During this time she reflects upon the past experiences which have resulted in her breakdown and, as the jacket cover tells us, her attempted suicide "sets her firmly on the path of memory." Sally's traumatic past is the secret of sexual abuse at the hands of an otherwise distant father during her childhood. This secret of sexual abuse is wholly enmeshed with Sally's and her parents' experiences as Chinese Americans, and the process of coming to terms with her abuse is bound up with the integration of her Chinese and American selves into a coherent selfhood.

The narrative begins with a prologue, in which Sally imaginatively reconstructs her father's immigration, his journey to the United States, from China to San Francisco. Then her memory shifts to his death, in the same place, years later. Sally envisages her father as a ghost standing before her, symbolizing his continuing haunting presence in her life. The prologue closes with Sally's initial recollection of her suicide attempt that March. This opening section firmly connects Sally's own psychological trauma with the enduring presence of her father in her imaginative, if not physical, life, as well as tying her own troubles to her father's experiences of immigration many years earlier, a connection which is continually stressed throughout the novel.

The novel's action oscillates between the present (Sally's stay in a psychiatric hospital) and her past, which she starts to revisit in her memory. Chapter One deals with her admittance to hospital, and Chapter Two explores Sally's memories of the period immediately before this, during which time she experienced the repeated and unexpected return of memories of her father: "My father was everywhere, a shock of white hair in the periphery of my vision, and then I'd turn and it would be a stranger" (20). Aware that she was suppressing something at this stage, but not sure what that was, Sally returned to the Chinatown of her childhood, where she hoped that the answers to the conundrum of her missing memories lay: "I took the bus to Chinatown and wandered around scrutinizing every single little old man on the stoops, hoping this would break the spell [...]. Walking those teeming sidewalks, I felt totally alien although the tourists thought I was part of the scenery" (21). Although at this point Sally recognizes that her traumatic memories are linked in some way to her heritage and identity as Chinese American, at this early stage of both the narrative and Sally's remembering she cannot put the pieces together, and she repeatedly questions her inability to do so: "I had killed him in my head long ago, long before he actually died. What he had done to me was horrific. Still, I'd recovered. I'd even gotten married. So what was the problem? Why was he plaguing me now?" (21).

As Cathy Caruth reminds us, trauma is an injury which can be inflicted upon both the body and the mind (*Unclaimed Experience* 3). Early in Sally's narration, the sense that her body remembers the abuse her mind has tried to forget, is very prevalent. Sally exhibits an acute self-loathing, particularly of her worth in bodily terms. She repeatedly describes herself as a "PIECE OF MEAT" (29), the capital letters of this description enforcing its potency as a label she is forced to wear. Sally's response to this troubling self-image is itself linked to the body: she chastises herself through bodily mutilation. The pain that this causes seems to provide her with a sense of bodily relief from her guilt and the burden of her memories: "It wasn't the easiest thing to do in the dark, but I knew where there was virgin skin [...]. The feeling came, not as sharp as it would have been if it hadn't been so cold, and it didn't last nearly long enough" (29).

As a child, Sally's mother tells her and her sister the Chinese folk tale of Monkey King, and this story becomes the means by which the young Sally tries to rationalize her father's abuse. The Monkey King story comes from Wu Chengen's *Hsi Yu Chi* (*The Journey to the West*, or *Monkey*, Tripitaka). The character of Monkey (Sun Wu Kong), is born of a stone egg. On a dare from the other monkeys, he enters a waterfall and discovers a new world. For this, he is rewarded as king of the monkeys and with immortality. He is a trickster figure, who is able to perform magical acts and transformations, changing his size and appearance and traveling great distances in one leap. In the best-known section of the Chinese classic, he travels with the monk Tripitaka on a journey to India in search of Buddhist scriptures. Unable to accept that the father whom she is required to respect and be affectionate towards can abuse her at night, Sally transforms the father who visits her room at night into the character of the Monkey King.

Sally's response to her abuse is secretly to draw pictures of Monkey King, which she then destroys: "I draw [...] things [...] that I don't show anyone [...]. If they were to find them and ask, I would tell them that this is Monkey King, this is his tail, this is the stake through his heart and the blood pouring out. [...]. The Monkey King is crafty, my mother said. Because he is a god, he knows everything, but he never tells it unless he has to" (123). The young Sally associates the crafty and powerful aspects of the Monkey King character with her father's behavior, as well as his emphasis upon silence. Although we are introduced to the importance of the Monkey King legend early in Sally's narration, it is not until Chapter Eleven that Sally actually remembers her first experience of abuse. She describes this incident in relation to Monkey King throughout:

> It's the smell. I open my eyes to dark and there's a change in the air, a new body in the room. The bed sagging gently as someone sits down.

In the faint light from the window I can see his outline: the long curving
torso, the bulbous head set onto a thin neck, just like pictures in the book.
There's no tail, but I imagine it curled underneath like a worm.
    "Be quiet," says Monkey King.
    [...].
    Nails as rough as crab claws between my thighs. That stick he has, that he
can make bigger or smaller when he feels like it. Or is it his tail? [...]. With one
hand he hold my wrists together over my head, with the other he covers my
mouth. He is the Monkey King, he is immortal, he cannot be stopped. Tears
wet my hair, but I do not make a sound. (137-38)

Sally's narration works retrospectively through her memory from the point of
her admittance to hospital, back through her childhood, to this first experience of
abuse. But the actual narration only reaches the story of the Monkey King two
chapters later, when we realize why Sally has connected her abuse with the story
of Monkey King. Her mother's translation of the story emphasizes his power to
abuse those less powerful than himself: "One of the stories is called Monkey
King. The Monkey King is a god and he doesn't look like a monkey at all. His
head is painted blue and red and yellow and he has the body of a man and a long
curly tail. He has a pole that he can make small to carry, big to hit people with"
(156). Sally also emphasizes the Monkey's power to masquerade in other guises,
which she associates with the dual identity that her father comes to have for the
young girl.

As a young girl, Sally thinks of herself as a very *American* girl, in opposition
to her father's constant reminders of her *Chineseness*. Her father tells her: "You
are American citizen. In your heart you are Chinese." But Sally notes: "What I
secretly know is that I am the most American kid I have ever met" (129). Sally's
reluctance to acknowledge her Chinese ancestry and heritage becomes increasingly bound up with her desire to reject a culture which she associates predominantly with her father's presence in her life. Her rejection of her father is also the
rejection of her own Chineseness, a trait she views as indelibly intertwined with
her own bodily identity as her father's daughter. We learn that throughout her
childhood Sally has been compared to her father in essentialist ways; she is repeatedly told that she shares his blood and characteristics. Her gradual path back
to her childhood in her memory thus also involves her in a confrontation with
what exactly she does share with her father. Although she remembers and relates
the stories that she has heard of her father's past, both in China and the United
States, this is a history which she ultimately disclaims in her search for a more
positive self-image of her own. She gradually comes to recognize that she need
not reject all of her family and cultural inheritances in her attempt to purge her
past. This recognition dawns as the rest of her family (her mother, aunt, and sister), each in different ways gradually admit their own knowledge of Sally's
abuse, which enables her to relinquish its continuing psychological hold upon
her.

   Despite the importance of the link between Sally's struggle with her traumatic past and her negotiation of her ethnic identity, many of the reviews of
Monkey King have stressed its un-Chinese Americanness. See noted that the
novel has "broken open the Chinese-American genre," (jacket blurb), and *Time*
magazine stressed that Sally Wang was a "universal character whose struggle for
identity anyone can identify with" (ibid). While this may be the case, this essay
argues that there is certainly a discernible tradition of writing by Asian American women in which themes of trauma, memory and the recovery of identity are
prominent, and *Monkey King* is not the first example.

Another quite recent text, which has been very successful, Aimee Liu's 1994
novel *Face*, is another notable example which tracks its female subject's struggle to come to terms with an incident of abuse, which is again linked to her
identity as Chinese American. *Face* tells the story of Amerasian character
Maibelle Chung's search for her identity in New York's Chinatown, where she
grew up, and where she finally recollects that she was raped as a child. Maibelle
is the daughter of a Chinese photojournalist and his Anglo wife. She was raised
in New York's Chinatown, but left with her family during her teenage years. As
an adult, Maibelle is haunted by an inexplicable compulsion to return to Chinatown, where she is sure that she can uncover the reasons for her on-going nightmares that hint at a suppressed traumatic past. Maibelle Chung's quest for identity is mapped by her struggle to remember and confront the incident of rape that
she has erased from her memory.
   Maibelle's relationship with the Chinatown that used to be her home continues to be characterized by ambivalence when she leaves Chinatown as a child,
but retains a psychological connection with it, partly due to her father, who is
Chinese, but also because something repeatedly draws her back. She initially
returns to undertake a photographic assignment for a friend, and it is these visits
that reawaken her contradictory feelings towards the place where she grew up.
She returns in the role of an outsider as a tourist, when she photographs her surroundings: "It's all different, I tell myself. That souvenir sign 'Tourist Welcome,' means you now" (133). Maibelle's attempts to recover her suppressed
memories involve her in utilizing another means of remembering the past, taking
photographs. During repeated returns to Chinatown in search of her past,
Maibelle photographs her surroundings in an attempt to (re)capture her past experiences. Her photography repeatedly functions in the novel as the means by
which she is able to control her surroundings and experiences, but, crucially,
when she returns to Chinatown, she loses this control. On one occasion, when
she starts photographing her surroundings, she finds herself accidentally em-
broiled in a demonstration against the kind of cultural voyeurism in which she is
involved through her photography. Maibelle significantly feels *herself* under
surveillance: "I can't shake the feeling that I'm being watched" and "I sense the

concealed faces watching," as if she is identifying with the angry sentiments of the Chinatown residents she herself has returned to photograph (133). Paradoxically, she raises her camera—the instrument of spectatorship—as a defense against appearing as a spectacle herself, by masking her face: "I hold my circle of glass to my face as if it could protect me" (138). Maibelle defends herself against the gaping boys she encounters by using her camera as a weapon, symbolized by the double meaning of "shoot," so that she turns from spectacle to spectator: "I turn quickly, raising the Leica, shoot them once, twice, three times dead on, and start running" (140). When, later in the narrative, Maibelle starts to remember her traumatic past, the process—in keeping with her profession as a photographer—is through flashbacks, a very visual (and immediate) form of memory. As Caruth notes, the "flashback, it seems, provides a form of recall that survives at the cost of willed memory or the very continuity of conscious thought" (*Trauma* 152).

Despite her paradoxical attempts to sever psychological links with Chinatown by photographing it, Maibelle's preoccupation with Chinatown as the source of her on-going psychological problems continues. As the narrative progresses, she starts to remember the childhood that she had suppressed. It emerges that her confusion over her identity and inability to relinquish Chinatown as a psychological influence upon her result from her suppression of a rape in Chinatown one night when she had returned as a fourteen year old to take photographs. The process of remembering this rape is a pivotal moment in Maibelle's quest to recover a more secure sense of identity. Towards the end of the narrative, she starts to remember this teenage visit to Chinatown, at a time when, having moved upstate, she is distanced from Chinatown both geographically and culturally and can return as a tourist to "shoot the storefronts. The ginseng and strangled ducks. The dancing chicken" (303), all the spectacles tourists are attracted to when visiting Chinatown. Psychologically, she begins to feel a part of her surroundings once more: "Chinatown wrapped around me as if I'd never left" (303). Maibelle's sense of belonging is so strong at this point that she even begins to assimilate her appearance into her environment: "Even my own reflection—taller, paler, and more out of place than ever—seemed part of the package luring me back, no longer cause to run away" (303).

Maibelle's activities as a tourist are separated from her feeling of belonging, and, armed with this new sense of security, she begins to photograph a group of boys, who obligingly pose for her. Their response is then to turn her act of violation back on her by taking her to a deserted building nearby and gang-raping her. The whole ordeal is described in a highly racially- and color-charged way. For example, Maibelle's recognition of the danger her attackers represent, is described using color coding: "So much black. Hair, eyes, clothing, sunglasses" (306). Here, for Maibelle, the black hair and eyes that she lacks, and which mark her attackers as Chinese in the dim light, function textually as a trope for threat and evil intent. Later, during the rape, her assailants taunt her in racial terms, calling her "Bai xiangku. White witch" (307). It is significant that during the rape itself, Maibelle doesn't look, she "felt rather than saw them closing in" (306). After the rape, Maibelle's defiance is to gaze at her attackers, literally facing them down, without looking away: "I stared into the flame the fat one kept waving at me. I didn't blink. Again and again, until the muscles around my eyes burned with the effort of keeping them wide" (308). Maibelle's defiance partly works by staring with the wide-eyed look that she knows occidentalizes her in the eyes of her all-Chinese rapists. The recognition that her eyes are an occidentalizing sign for her attackers allows her to use their racializing gaze as a defense, as she later says: "I retreated back into my crazy eyes" (308). Maibelle's punishment and rejection as non-Chinese, a "white witch," by the Chinatown boys, is linked here with gender violence as well. The episode works through both racial and gender tensions, and both color coding and the racializing gaze mark the distance between Maibelle and her attackers. The incident is only later linked to Maibelle through her appearance as only part-Chinese, because "the girl had red hair, was a teenager. Rumor was, she came from outside" (329).

As with *Monkey King*, the narrative of *Face* opens at a point when the central female character is undergoing the psychological anguish of a traumatic past which she has yet to exorcise. Maibelle's memories slowly return, as she herself returns to the scene of the traumatic event. Her journey into her memory tracks her concurrent research into her father's own story, as a photojournalist in China. Crucially, the two stories are linked through the use of photography as a means of recording the past; as Maibelle's father tells her, "the best photographs tell stories better than words" (286). Maibelle's father's own story is also submerged, and only emerges simultaneously with Maibelle's discovery of the truth of her own trauma. Maibelle's father witnessed a bombing in Shanghai in 1935, in which his own father was killed, an event he photographed for *Life* magazine. He tells her this story in the hope that it will help her to come to terms with her own past: "Only when the question of identity is settled can we do justice to other concerns," he tells her (292). Like her father, Maibelle had also recorded her own trauma the night of her rape, photographing her attackers before they raped her. But, like her father's photographs, those pictures were never developed and so photography as a source of memory is shown to fail in the text. Maibelle must let her body remember what the photographs did not record.

In both *Face* and *Monkey King*, the women's memories of abuse are linked to their parents' own stories of suffering. The women struggle against a shroud of familial silence about the past in order to recover their own stories. In both cases, the abuse they experienced is linked to their identity as Chinese American, and the cathartic process of remembering tracks their reconciliation with their ethnic identity. Both narratives also work retrospectively, with the protagonists travelling back through their pasts in order to forge a new future. Structurally, the narrative patterns the fragmented return of submerged memories. Each novel is episodic in structure, oscillating between past and present, and thus memory determines the form of each text. Both these novels, as well as the next I shall discuss, Kogawa's *Obasan*, also make extensive use of instruments of memory: photographs, journals, and letters, all of which provide one of the means of recall through which the subject remembers the past.

In many ways, *Obasan* works quite differently from the two narratives of trauma that I have discussed so far. Although an experience of sexual abuse is also pivotal in the central female protagonist's quest to recover her identity, this is linked far more extensively than in *Monkey King* or in *Face* to a wider story of ethnic exclusion and persecution. Kogawa's novel retells the histories of Japanese Canadian relocation and the Japanese Holocaust at Nagasaki during the Second World War. This text is also more obviously historically referential, stemming as it does from Kogawa's own childhood experiences. *Obasan* works as a cultural remembering which has as its ethical aim the eliciting of redress and apology for those atrocities. It is through the exorcism of this traumatic past that Japanese Canadian female identity is negotiated. Aspects of Japanese and Japanese Canadian history are shown to be unmanageable, traumatic, and in James Joyce's words, a "nightmare" from which the characters are trying to awake. The exorcism of the past functions as a rite of passage for Naomi Nakane, involving her in a confrontation with the ravages of both her personal and ethnic histories. These histories are seen to impinge upon Naomi's present, and memory in the text becomes a defining feature of identity.

As Kalí Tal has noted, the literature of trauma "holds at its centre the reconstruction and recuperation of the traumatic experience in question" (17). *Obasan* recounts the Japanese Canadian experience of World War II through the story of protagonist Naomi Nakane. It is loosely based upon Kogawa's own experience as a six-year old child, when she was relocated with her family to Slocan in eastern British Columbia, then subsequently to a small town in Alberta. Kogawa's preface also locates her story within the realm of history, noting that much is "based on historical events and [that] many of the persons named are real" (preface). Many of the quotations are from the Public Archives of Canada and the letters of activist Muriel Kitigawa. The effort to convey the verity of the story to the reader, indicates Kogawa's desire for her story to be taken seriously as a document of the Japanese Canadian experience at this time.

Obasan's novelistic form is characterized by textual ellipsis, rupture, and chronological disjunction. Kogawa's story demonstrates in its painful rendering of the damaging period of World War II, the struggle with a well-nigh *unmanageable* history. This narrative both shows and speaks of the self-negation which was the result of relocation. This self-negation is also evident in the almost complete *issei* silence about internment in the novel: the *issei* character Obasan's taciturnity in the text has been frequently observed, by King-kok Cheung among others (126-29). This kind of silence may be a form of cultural coping, as Kalí Tal suggests in her study, *Worlds of Hurt*; the "disappearance strategy" as she names it, whereby "a refusal to admit to the existence of a particular kind of trauma," coupled with the difficulties of speaking in spite of official silencing of the relocation story, may result in taciturnity on the subject (6). This erasure of the past is explored extensively in *Obasan*. In particular, the cyclical structure indicates Naomi's unsuccessful struggle to forget the past. In fact, *Obasan* admits the struggle with history through its formal cyclical structure. Although the time of the narrative present, in 1972, is the post-relocation life of protagonist Naomi Nakane, the continuing dominance of the past upon Naomi's present is signaled through the repeated returns to her history through her consciousness. Thus, the identity crisis engendered by the Canadian government's treatment of Japanese Canadians emerges as ongoing. Julia Kristeva has made the distinction between cyclical/monumental (as in "memorial")—or women's—time, and linear—or historical—time by asserting that cyclical time is characterized by temporal disruption and reminiscence, whereas linear time is progressive, teleological and patriarchal (445-46). The cyclical time that we find in *Obasan* results from Kogawa's representation of Naomi's subjectivity in terms of repetition, recollection, and temporal disjunction.

As in *Monkey King* and *Face*, the trauma that the central female character has experienced is shared and reflected in the experiences of other family members. Naomi Nakane, the central female character, and her elderly female relative, the eponymous Obasan, together illustrate the debilitating effects of relocation upon individual identity. Both women are depicted as stultified by their histories, unable to free themselves from the memories of relocation. Through Naomi's consciousness and Obasan's reliance upon pictures and other records, the paralysis of their current lives in the shadow of relocation is communicated. In contrast, Naomi's other older female relative, Aunt Emily, represents the desire for political reconstruction. Emily is described as a "word warrior" (39), and works ceaselessly for the redress movement. Rather than becoming trapped or controlled by her past, Emily utilizes it, through various documents of that time, such as her diary, to attain a recognition of the state's wrongdoing.

The narrative itself is governed by Naomi's memories of her and her family's past, triggered by and intertwined with present events and sensory perceptions. The oscillation in the text between Naomi's personal ruminations and recollections and the various reported accounts of that history, reflect the juxtaposition of private and public temporalities. Naomi's discontinuous narrative stresses the interplay between past and present as well as the chafing of personal and official chronologies. Naomi's and Obasan's time is private, subjective and measured by the events of their lives. In contrast, Aunt Emily's letters, reports and newspaper articles represent the public, verbalized chronology of Japanese Canadian history. Or to put it another way, Naomi's time is informal, mental time, whereas Aunt Emily's papers represent a measured and formalized temporality. Naomi's temporality, which structures the narration, is constructed by memory, so that specific events in her life measure the passing of time. In the opening pages, she notes: "In the future I will remember the details of this day, the ordinary trivia illuminated by an event that sends my mind scurrying for significance" (6).

The repeated shift into the past in Naomi's consciousness exemplifies the dominance of the past on both Naomi's and Obasan's present. Of all the characters in the text, it is these two who are least able to sever themselves from their past, and its psychological effects upon their present. As Aunt Emily tells Naomi, "You are your history" (60). As Naomi observes, Obasan's time increasingly becomes past time as the novel progresses, "the present disappears in her mind. The past hungers for her" (61). Likewise, the escalating frequency with which Naomi's own thoughts become retrospective, symbolically illuminates her awakening consciousness of both the importance of her cultural history and her desire for a return to her mother, who died at Nagasaki. She observes that "we're trapped, Obasan and I, by our memories of the dead—all our dead—those who refuse to bury themselves [... w]hen I least expect it, a memory comes skittering out of the dark [...] ready to snap me up and ensnare me" (30-31). Naomi, in fact, is repeatedly figured at the mercy of her memories: she frequently dreams of her past and struggles to leave these associations behind. She seems to almost inhabit a waking dreamworld, in which she constantly returns to moments in her past. Whereas Aunt Emily's struggle to make sense of her history leads her to turn to the causal chronology of Japanese Canadian history, Naomi's own search for answers involves her in establishing an internal self-referentiality, whereby her own mediating consciousness attempts to impose order on her present sensations and her memory.

However, Naomi's body sometimes strains her ability to remember and relate her experiences. She tells us at one point: "I cannot tell about this time [...]. The body will not tell" (235). All she wants at this point is to forget what she calls the "crimes of history" (40). Naomi's defensive maneuvers, as King-kok Cheung has noted, are suggestive of post-traumatic stress disorder, whereby her inability to "re-memory" her past, and to tell that story, due to familial and cultural prohibitions *not* to tell, defers the catharsis that accompanies that telling (143). The pain of relocation and the memories of Nagasaki are repeatedly figured in *Obasan* as bodily injuries, which must be confronted in order to be healed. Aunt Emily tells Naomi, "Health starts somewhere" (219), and that health, according to Aunt Emily, starts with memory. "You have to remember," Aunt Emily said. "You are your history. If you cut any of it off you're an amputee. Don't deny the past. Remember everything. If you're bitter, be bitter. Cry it out! Scream! Denial is gangrene" (60).

Although the story of Japanese Canadian relocation and the bombing at Nagasaki dominate Kogawa's narrative, Naomi's own psychological disquiet is also the result of an incident of abuse in her childhood. A neighbor, Old Man Gower, abused the four-year old child. Naomi has retrospectively connected the abuse she experienced with the loss of her mother, and she tells us that it was at this time that her mother disappeared. When she remembers the incident, it is interlinked with this loss:

> "Don't tell your mother," he whispers into my ear. This is what he always says. Where in the darkness has my mother gone?
> I am clinging to my mother's leg, a flesh shaft that grows from the ground, a tree trunk of which I am an offshoot—a young branch attached by right of flesh and blood [...]. But here in Mr. Gower's hands I become other [...]. If I tell my mother about Mr. Gower, the alarm will send a tremor through our bodies and I will be torn from her. But the secret has already separated us. The secret is this: I go to seek Old Man Gower in his hideaway. I clamber unbidden onto his lap. His hands are frightening and pleasurable. In the center of my body is a rift [...]. My mother is on one side of the rift. I am on the other. (77)

In common with Sally's feelings in *Monkey King*, here the young Naomi views her experience as her own fault, and this guilt serves to separate her psychologically from other members of her family. The abuse not only isolates her psychologically, it damages her in very bodily ways, and it is her body that remembers. The simultaneous disappearance of her mother and her abuse leave Naomi with a double wound, which takes her years to heal.

Many narratives of trauma figure memory as a skin stretched, painfully, across a past described as a wound. In *Obasan* we also find a slightly different metaphor for the workings of memory. Naomi tells us: "We are now no more than a few tangled skeins—the remains of what might once have been a fisherman's net. The memories that are left seem barely real. Gray shapes in the water. Fish swimming through the gaps in the net. Passing shadows" (25). In each of the novels that I have discussed, memory is a wound, but in *Obasan* it is also a thread, broken by traumatic events, which needs to be reconnected in order for the subject to heal. Kogawa uses the image of a shredded fisherman's net to describe the mess of memories. The shreds of memory which comprise each of these novels reflect this, and it is only by reconnecting these tangled skeins that each female character is able to mend the sk(e)in of her memory.

As Kalí Tal has noted, the feminist movements of the 1960s and 1970s created an atmosphere in which women were able to begin to discuss instances of sexual abuse and trauma. However, these narratives and discussions did not, as Tal observes, include the stories of women of color.[2] Tal suggests that this may

---

2 One notable exception of this is the story of the so-called Korean "comfort women," who were forced into prostitution service for the Japanese military during Japan's occupation of Korea. Due to Japan's active suppression of this history, and the cultural prohibition not to tell their stories, it has only been in recent years that the former Korean comfort women have begun to tell their stories and come to terms with their past.

be because, for a woman of color, an experience of sexual abuse is often inextricably tied up with her identity as a woman of color:

> Women of color suffer under the conditions of both sexism and racism, and for that reason they may not view sexual assault as *the* traumatic event which shaped their lives. The sexual assault of a woman of color is inextricable from her assault as a *black woman*, a *latina*, or an *Asian woman*. The refusal of women of color to focus solely, or even primarily, on sexual assault reflects an awareness of the complex and interrelated character of race, gender, and class oppression. (159)

Narratives about sexual abuse, as Tal goes on to argue, signal the beginnings of the process of change, and the three narratives I have discussed here may begin to correct the absence of stories of the kinds of abuse women of color have suffered. By connecting their narratives of abuse to narratives of the struggle to secure, claim or attain a particular ethnic identity, these writers are also united in the refusal to view sexual abuse as productive of gender oppression alone, instead making manifest the connections between different forms of racial as well as gender oppression.

Works Cited

Caruth, Cathy, ed. *Trauma: Explorations in Memory*. Baltimore: Johns Hopkins UP, 1995.

—. *Unclaimed Experience: Trauma, Narrative, and History*. Baltimore: Johns Hopkins UP, 1996.

Chao, Patricia. *Monkey King*. New York: HarperCollins, 1997.

Cheung, King-kok. *Articulate Silences: Hisaye Yamamoto, Maxine Hong Kingston, Joy Kogawa*. Ithaca: Cornell UP, 1993.

Grewal, Gurleen. "Memory and the Matrix of History: The Poetics of Loss and Recovery in Joy Kogawa's *Obasan* and Toni Morrison's *Beloved*." *Memory and Cultural Politics: New Approaches to American Ethnic Literatures*. Eds. Amritjit Singh, Joseph T. Skerrett, Jr., and Robert E. Hogan. Boston: Northeastern UP, 1996. 140-74.

Kitigawa, Muriel. *This Is My Own: Letters to Wes and Other Writings on Japanese Canadians, 1941-1948*. Vancouver: Talon Books, 1985.

Kogawa, Joy. *Obasan*. New York: Anchor, 1994.

Kristeva, Julia. "Women's Time." *Feminisms: A Reader*. Eds. Robyn R. Warhol and Diane Price Herndyl. New Brunswick: Rutgers UP, 1991. 443-62.

Liu, Aimee. *Face*. London: Headline, 1994.

Morrison, Toni. *Beloved*. London: Picador, 1987.

Singh, Amritjit, Joseph T. Skerrett, Jr., and Robert E. Hogan, eds. *Memory, Narrative, and Identity: New Essays in Ethnic American Literatures.* Boston: Northeastern UP, 1994.

Tal, Kalí. *Worlds of Hurt: Reading the Literatures of Trauma.* New York: Cambridge UP, 1996.

Wu Chengen (Wu Cheng'en). *Journey to the West.* Beijing: Beijing People's Literature Publishing House, 1955.

Ceremonies of Dialogism in Asian American Poetry

Eulalia C. Piñero-Gil

> "You're like a dead person trying to awaken, trying to see things around you with the eyes of an infant and the wisdom of a grand-mother. You are caught in the shadow like a disembodied voice. Sometimes mouthing the right words to give shape to the hidden meanings can be as satisfying as a nine-course Chinese banquet. Maybe more so." (Genny Lim, quoted in Wang and Zhao 120)

The corpus of Asian American poetry represents a rich tradition of dissenting voices. Nonetheless, it has received proportionately much less critical attention than the prose fiction. The reasons are manifold and perhaps the most important one, from my point of view, is society's inability to assimilate poetic language, followed by the critics' lack of interest in reviewing new voices, which contributes to the general assumption that it is an elitist genre for an initiated audience. In spite of the absence of public recognition, the variety of poetic creative efforts is extremely productive in the study of the Asian American community's cultural constructions. Poetry constitutes one of the most valuable artistic manifestations of this complex ethnic group as it represents diverse positions, attitudes and experiences that contrast with the generalizations that have been thematized on a limited number of well-known fetishized novels.

In this essay I will examine, through the study of five emblematic poets, Janice Mirikitani, Arthur Sze, John Yau, Amy Ling, and Nelly Wong, how dialogism constitutes an essential practice in their poetry that contributes to the multiplicity, hybridity and heterogeneity that characterizes Asian American poetry. I also contest in my analysis some critical positions that tend to classify poetic discourse according to stereotyped assumptions that only serve to reduce the poetic debates to a minimum. In this sense, Lisa Lowe draws attention to this issue when she asserts that "interpreting Asian American culture exclusively in terms of the master narratives of generational conflict and filial relation essentializes Asian American culture, obscuring the particularities and incommensurabilities of class, gender, and national diversities among Asians" (63).

Dialogism becomes a fundamental aspect in Asian American poetry as it is closely related to the reconstruction of memory and history. I take the term dialogism from Mikhail Bakhtin's study *Problems of Dostoevsky's Poetics* (1929) which addresses the question of voice and polyphony stating that all utterances are dialogic. In this manner, Bakhtin also considers the novel as the dialogic form "par excellance" because in the interaction of voices, the voice of authority is disrupted by other voices in the text. Nevertheless, I posit that a similar point may be made with reference to other literary genres, such as poetry and theatre, as they base their discourses on orality and performance.

Likewise, David Buchbinder, in his revealing essay "Poetry and History," argues that

> words are sites of conflict, since as signs they have been used not only in different, but opposed and contradictory, situations and contexts. Their meanings, therefore, lose definition and determination, and these signs become, rather, a locus in which cultural discourses and social forces are played out, in dialogue, as it were, with one another. Verbal texts, therefore, are places in which overt subscriptions to a particular doctrine or ideology are riven and disunified by the nature of the very material of which they are made. They become sites of ideological subversion. (111-12)

In my view, this analysis describes the effects most Asian American poets achieve with their dialogic poetics, in the sense that the confluence of dissenting voices generates gaps and silences that, in many instances, subvert the dominant ideology. In addition, there is a special concern with articulating voices that help to construct the past of the community. These voices arise from the various histories, discourses, fragments, and experiences that conform a sort of "culture of bricolage," as Garret Hongo has termed it (xxiii). This fragmentary poetry, that is imagined from a series of recycled voices of the past or the present, becomes, in most cases, an act of homage to the ancestors who were silenced by the dominant culture. Those stigmatized histories of oppression and marginalization were kept as family secrets that became part of a parallel culture of exclusion and margins. For the younger generations, those inherited stories were the product of many voices reconstructing them throughout generations to the point that, in some cases, the collage of voices was contradictory. The result is that, in some instances, the poets become active cultural historians that struggle to make sense out of a series of fragmentary voices (Piñero-Gil 121-34). In this light, Lisa Lowe points out, "the making of Asian American culture may be a much less stable process than unmediated vertical transmission of culture from one generation to another. The making of Asian American culture includes practices that are partly inherited, partly modified, as well as partly invented" (65).

The activist poet Janice Mirikitani constructs her poetry by incorporating voices from the past or stories that were part of her family's heritage. She liberates the hidden voices of many generations in her poem "Breaking Silence" by verbalizing her mother's testimonies on the internment camps for Japanese and American citizens of Japanese ancestry. The structure of the poem is dialogic in the sense that the poet clearly separates the mother's devastating testimony from the speaker's explanations of the historical events. The theatrical effect stresses the tension and rage of the mother's voice:

> Pride has kept my lips
> pinned by nails
> my rage confined.
> But I exhume my past
> to claim this time.
> My youth is buried in Rohwer,
>
> Obachan's ghost visits Amache Gate,
> My niece haunts Tule Lake.
> Words are better than tears,
> so I spill them.
> I kill this, the silence ... (190)

In a similar way, Mirikitani's "In Remembrance" recounts the story of her uncle in one of those internment camps—monuments of oppression and racism that were created for controlling United States citizens of Japanese ancestry whose only crime was their non-European origin. The poem is an eulogy to her Uncle Minoru in which the speaker reconstructs the memory of an honest man who was generous and a good citizen: "the wounds hiding in your throat, / the wound in your heart / pierced by unjust punishment, racism, and rejection / sharp as blades" (350). Mirikitani's voice articulates the community's views through the repetition of a "we" that demands justice for a victim of a history of oblivion. In fact, the word "silence" is repeated several times in the poem to emphasize the dangers of forgetfulness: "We will not leave your memory / as a silent rancid rose. / Our tongues become livid with history and / demands for reparations" (351).

The relocation and internment of 120,000 people of Japanese origin signified one of the most degrading and humiliating experiences for a community that had contributed to the economic development of the West Coast area. The history of Minoru is the symbol of many other voices that were obliged to repress the years behind barbed wire. Nevertheless, Mirikitani's poem is a manifesto against the dispossession of Japanese American's history:

> Our tongues are sharp like blades.
> We overturn furrows of secrecy.
>   Yes, we will harvest justice.
> And Uncle, perhaps
> your spirit will return
> alive in a horse, or a bird,
> riding free in the wind
> life surging through
> the sinews of your strong shoulders.

> And yes,
> the struggle continues on
> with our stampede of voices. (351)

Mirikitani's poetry posits a discourse based on the contrast of voices in order to represent the living accounts of the Japanese American community. This textual technique contests overtly the official versions of history, as well as the methods by which the establishment systematically discriminates against ethnic discourse.

The Chinese American translator Arthur Sze, who is also Director of the Creative Writing Program at the Institute of American Indian Arts in Santa Fe, is a poet influenced by both the Chinese poetic tradition and native American culture. Sze's poem "The Negative" articulates a series of broken images that overlap in an attempt to recreate a vision of a Chinese street. The poet's eye becomes a quick camera taking glimpses of people's lives but transcending the mere physical presence to explore the afflictions and paradoxes of human condition:

> I see a photograph of a son smiling who two years ago fell off a cliff and his
> photograph is in each room of the apartment.
> I meet a woman who had smallpox as a child, was abandoned by her mother
> but who lived, now has two daughters, a son, a son-in-law;
> [...].
> I see a woman who tried to kill herself with an acupuncture needle
> but instead hit a vital point and cured her chronic asthma. (193)

These images reflect anonymous voices of any Chinese street, where people do not control destiny but simply observe and act according to their limited possibilities. In this manner, the poet argues that personal tragedy has two distinct visions: on the one hand, the individual's experience, and on the other, the limited vision of an observer who, in this case, transforms the scenes into mere photographic negatives without the complete scope of representation. It is as if the poet could only offer a partial vision of a complex reality: "As negative reverses light and dark / these words are prose accounts of personal tragedy becoming metaphor, / an emulsion of silver salts sensitive to light" (193). Arthur Sze seeks to reconcile in his poetry the Chinese poetic tradition with his American education. In doing so, the poet contrasts both cultures from the point of view of an unknown voice from the East: "A Chinese poet argues the fundamental difference between East / and West / is that in the East an individual does not believe himself / in control of his fate but yields to it" (193).

In "The Network," Sze celebrates the story of an immigrant who left China for San Francisco, which was in fact the adventure of thousands of workers. In this case, the protagonist has a name—George Hew—but the speaker broaches the intimate intricacies of a humble life that leaves traces of its existence in the memory of a few people. Sze explores the implications of the apparently insignificant cultural journey of an immigrant. The disappearance of a man from his country implies a profound change in his life, as well as in the lives of his family and community. In fact, a single man belongs to a complex network that in many cases appears to be irrelevant for the statistics or the cold numbers announcing that the presence of a group of immigrants is changing the ethnography of a country. For Sze, memory is a powerful recourse for reconstructing the presence and absence of those who were only a number in society:

> We live
> in such a network: the world is opaque,
> translucent, or, suddenly, lucid,
> vibrant. The air is alive and hums
> then. Speech is too slow to the mind.
> And the mind's speech is so quick it breaks
> the sound barrier and shatters glass. (234)

The manner through which Sze introduces the voices of the past expresses a reflection on language, speech, memory, and the need to liberate the voices from their silence, making those private stories sound and vibrate.

In a similar way, John Yau's experimental poetry intends to depict the difficulties of formulating an identity through the uncertainties of language. As George Uba notes, "his effort primarily is to disconnect rather than connect, to project a world cut off from certitude—a world in which human beings exist in perpetual exile, their lives an amalgam of absurdity, banality, and insufficiency, and in which politics are ephemerae of a provisional reality" (43).

Yau's poetry avoids easy images and common references. He focuses on harsh contrasts and discontinuities in an attempt to portray the cruelties of modern society through a defamiliarizing use of language. In my view, though Yau does not openly center his poetic discourse on ethnic issues, the allusions to ancient China in his book *Corpse and Mirror* (1983) confirm an intertextual continuum that permeates almost all his work. The references to places, poets, names of people or simply word games are the echoes of a Chinese American identity involved with the discussion of subjectivity in postmodern urban America. In particular, his search is intimately related to other voices that are a fundamental part of his own. In relation to this, Yau has asked: "Who or what is behind the pronouns? What are the voices suspended inside any one of us? What are the voices out there, speaking to the ones in here? Does their language meet any experience I might know? Do language and experience run along parallel tracks? How to get from here to there through language, by language, and in language" (Wang and Zhao 224).

Clearly, Yau is particularly concerned with the inability to discern in what way(s) language functions to accurately describe our experiences. At the same time, the poet is aware of the impossibility of portraying a complete profile of an individual by naming or simply referring to a pronoun. He addresses all these aspects in his work by emphasizing his resistance towards accepting traditional means of representation. In addition, his profound knowledge of contemporary art has a decisive effect on his kinetic presentation of reality. The disconnected images suggest to the reader a surrealist imagination. His poem "Engines of Gloom and Affection" (1989) exemplifies Yau's disconcerting portrayal of a modern American city. He proffers images of unrelated and unknown voices in the middle of a phantasmagoric urban landscape where the protagonists have no emotional bonds and suffer in absolute isolation. He appears to highlight language's incapacity to express the protagonists' anguish, problematizing the failure of language as an epistemological tool. The speaker's voice articulates a series of dreadful images that cannot be explained nor described but expressed in a few concise words. The direct effect of juxtapositions emphasizes the impossibility of any descriptive attempt:

> The sky is green, and there is no book to tell us what it means. It has never stopped raining. Three men, four of them speaking. A woman carries a photograph of worms under her tongue. I have spoken out of turn. The proportions are awkward, the details coarse.
> The sky is green, and there is no book to tell us the names of our children. Have you noticed the dead man hugging a doll? Have you thought about why she found it necessary to laugh so loudly? And, why, for example, the heads of the statues were removed and stored in a vault beneath the hospital? (575)

The narrative stanzas of the poem, he suggests, are the only forms through which an unacceptable reality may be encompassed. Yau formulates his theories of language, voices and bodies by blurring the distinctions among them. The lack of affection makes objects and people elements of the same scenario without any visible differences apart from the disturbing effect of the shocking contrasts. In this way, Yau achieves his principal aim: to write about what is outside his subjective "I." In a revealing interview with Edward Foster, the poet claimed that "to write about one's life in terms of a subjective 'I' [...] is to fulfill the terms of the oppressor. I suppose I don't know who this 'I' would or could speak for. Myself, what for?" (48-49).

Yau's challenging assertions entail the assumption that the traditional poetical speaker or lyrical voice is, in a certain way, following specific patterns that might be easily identified by the establishment. This rejection brings into play the poet's ideological subversiveness and elucidates what Priscilla Wald has called Yau's "dis(-)orienting poetics" (133). Yau's emphasis on resisting interpretation and the conventional construction of a poetical world is essential for reading his abstruse poetry. Therefore, the reader should be aware that the poet's quest is that of illustrating the tensions of "fin du siècle" society and the impossibility of assuming it in a conventional way. In this regard, the critic Juliana Chang asserts that "poetic language is not a smooth mirror reflecting social relations or an archive of fixed cultural essence, but a rough and uneven terrain through which we may glimpse how cultures and histories are refracted, suppressed, and reimagined" (94).

Another fascinating instance of dialogism appears in Amy Ling's confessional chapbook of poems and paintings *Chinamerican Reflections* (1984). Through the emotional portrayals of her family and the cognizant discovery of her Chinese heritage, Ling recreates a lyrical speaker that explores various aspects of her bicultural identity by intertwining distinct voices of the past and the present. In order to offer a visual glimpse of her appreciation for Chinese art, Ling illustrates her poetry with a series of alluding paintings that construct an idealized vision of her Asian inheritance. In my view, *Chinamerican Reflections* is the fruit of a privileged artist and humanist that captures essential elements of both cultures through an autobiographical tone. In fact, the title of the collection suggests the author's intention to merge her bicultural legacy by the significant presence of the word "Chinamerican." In this manner, Ling expresses her idea of broaching poetry as an open genre where her personal vision on art, society, and bicultural experience may find a textual space of self-exploration. In the note to the reader the poet confesses that "deep emotion—joy, but more often pain—impels me to write. These poems, then, are the highs and lows of my life, while the paintings reflect the serenity to strive for. Welcome to [...] my inner landscapes" (1).

In "Peking," Ling reconstructs her vision of the imperial city in which she was born, through the interaction of many voices that bring images from a past she was informed about by her mother, and the fundamental link between the two worlds. The dialogical structure of the poem allows Ling to vividly reimagine her first visit to Peking forty-three years after her parents emigrated to America when she was a child:

> It was only the response I gave
> when people asked, "Where are you from?"
> "How interesting! What a long way you've come."
> I'd hasten to add, "I left at seven months."
> Occasionally one would say, "I've been there,
> What a beautiful, proud city!" (20)

The utterance of familiar voices from distant cities, like Peking, contributes to the exploration of similarities that are shared by most cultures. Furthermore, Ling blurs the cultural boundaries by the inclusion of a multiplicity of social voices and their individual expressions.

The poem "Sister" is a revealing instance of a generalized attitude that may be found among many second-generation immigrants who, under the strong pressure of cultural assimilation, choose to ignore their origins. The imposed desire of becoming truly an "American," dispossessed of history and past, is represented in a dialogue between two sisters who have opposed visions on their ethnic ancestry:

> "So what if your parents and you came from China?
> What's China to me?
> I'm American, always have been,
> born in Brooklyn—can't get more American than that.
> Never felt any prejudice,
> always had friends,
> Don't even know any Chinese,
> but you,
> Why dredge up the past?
> Forget it.
> Move on." (13)

Forgetfulness and self-denial become the most effective weapons against the recognition of an ethnic identity. In this dialogue, Ling problematizes the alienation and the acculturation that Chinese Americans who want to be accepted by the community suffer, neglecting the consequences of their attitude. The second stanza of the poem "Sister" concludes with a clear warning against the radical assumption that considers that the past can be eliminated by simply denying cultural roots: "sealing your self out, / cutting off a past / ever present / on your face" (13).

The poet and activist Nellie Wong works with voices that generate dissent, contradiction, and political awareness about the social reality of Asian Americans, but, in particular, about the world of women in their families and in their workplaces. She conceives of writing as both a political tool and a means of artistic expression that allows her to come to grips with the heritage of her ancestors who, like ghosts, haunt her past as well as her present. In her epigrammatic poem "Ironing," she constructs a typical family scene with voices that represent opposed visions about the role of women in society:

> Papa drank and ate
> while I ironed my family's clothes.
> In our silence he blurts:
> "Marriage, hmphh!"
> I did not answer Papa's words.
> I only ironed my family's clothes. (13)

The speaker dramatizes the voice of patriarchal power representing the traditional point of view, and the eloquent silence of women that accept certain tasks but silently refuse to continue with the reproduction of inherited stereotypes. I consider "Ironing" a profoundly ironic poem on the social oppression of women in the family that embodies the first and most important social institution of patriarchal education.

In "We Can Always," Wong approaches another aspect of cultural discrimination against Chinese Americans through the exploration of certain jokes which exemplify the racial stereotypes that, through common places, reinforce the misconceptions about the otherness:

> A disc jockey says.
> "You should know better
> than to rob
> a Chinese grocer
> If you do
> you will want to rob
> again in another hour"
>
> and people laugh
>
> A newspaper columnist says:
> "How come them heathen Chinee
> are always observing New Year's
> a month late? When they gonna
> get up to date?"
>
> and if we can't laugh
> at ourselves, we can always
> go back (29)

Once more, Wong uses voices from different social backgrounds to show how everyday life reproduces surreptitiously sinophobic attitudes that are even enjoyed and shared by the audiences, as in the case of the two significant instances of the poem. The dialogical construction of "We Can Always," and the opposition of utterances contribute to the creation of conflict and discussion in the text. Thus, the poem becomes a textual locus in which cultural discourses and social forces are played out in undermining dialogue.

As has been argued, the different instances of dialogism explored in this essay exemplify, as in the case of Mirikitani's poetry, how the juxtaposition of voices articulating the drama of the internment camps might serve as a communal cathartic process of speaking the historical silences. Thus, Mirikitani reclaims, through these enacting and empowering voices, historical memory. In a different way, Sze's dialogical poetry focuses on stories that belong to an indeterminate past and, at the same time, entails a significant reflection on language. Similarly, Yau articulates, in his poetry of disjunction, a dialogism based upon the fragmentation of voices that resist an authorial "I." His dialogism responds to the interest in the fragmented self as a symbol of the impossibility of depicting a univocal subjectivity. Differently, Ling's voices establish a dialogue that contributes to the building of an imaginary bridge between Chinese and American cultures. In Wong's poetry the heteroglossia discloses voices that are quoted and displayed to show the stereotypes and clichés that conform everyday language. Her transgressive dialogism uncovers how the social inertia does not contest the prototypical expressions that reinforce traditional discrimination and alienation.

In my analysis, I have highlighted the singularity of five Asian American poets as evidence of their distinctive dialogism which I view as the result of processes of inheriting, modifying and inventing an ethnopoetics of their own. I also consider that their conspicuous use of voices develops an ethnic consciousness that characterizes most Asian American poetry and confers upon it a unique idiosyncrasy. In a sense, therefore, the inherent polyphony of most Asian American poetry problematizes this ethnic discourse, and its role in society in a process of endless celebration of diversity and heterogeneity. Asian American culture is not a stable expression; on the contrary, it is constantly re-defining itself. As a result, poetry is the mirror of this discontinuity and should be considered bearing in mind the impossibility of articulating a homogeneous poetics.[1]

Works Cited

Bakhtin, M.M. *The Dialogic Imagination: Four Essays.* Ed. Michael Holquist. Trans. Caryl Emerson and Michael Holquist. Austin: U of Texas P, 1981.

—. *Problems of Dostoevksy's Poetics.* Trans. R.W. Rotsel. Ann Arbor: Ardis, 1973.

Bruchac, Joseph, ed. *Breaking Silence: An Anthology of Contemporary Asian American Poets.* New York: Greenfield Review P, 1983.

Buchbinder, David. "Poetry and History." *Contemporary Literary Theory and the Reading of Poetry.* Melbourne: MacMillan, 1991. 98-119.

Chang, Juliana. "Reading Asian American Poetry." *MELUS* 21.1 (Spring 1996): 81-98.

Foster, Edward. "An Interview with John Yau." *Talisman* 5 (Fall 1990): 43-49.

Hongo, Garrett, ed. *The Open Boat. Poems from Asian America.* New York: Anchor Books, 1993.

Lee, A. Robert. "A Western East: America's 'China' Poetry in Marilyn Chin, Russell Leong, John Yau and Wing Tek Lum." *Borderlines: Studies in American Culture* 2.4 (June 1995): 380-93.

Lim, Shirley Geok-lin. "Reconstructing Asian-American Poetry: A Case For Ethnopoetics." *MELUS* 14.2 (Summer 1987): 51-63.

Ling, Amy. *Chinamerican Reflections.* Lewiston: Great Raven P, 1984.

---

1   The author gratefully acknowledges financial support from the Spanish Ministry of Education (Project PB-98-0101 DIGICYT).

Lowe, Lisa. "Heterogeneity, Hybridity, Multiplicity: Asian American Differences." *Immigrant Acts: On Asian American Cultural Politics.* Durham: Duke UP, 1996.

Mirikitani, Janice. "In Remembrance." *Making Waves. An Anthology of Writings by and about Asian American Women.* Ed. Asian Women United of California. Boston: Beacon P, 1989. 350-51.

—. "Breaking Silence." *Breaking Silence: An Anthology of Contemporary Asian American Poets.* Ed. Joseph Bruchac. New York: Greenfield Review P, 1983. 190.

Piñero-Gil, Eulalia C. "The Anxiety of Origins: Asian American Poets as Cultural Warriors." *Hitting Critical Mass* 4.1 (Fall 1996): 121-34.

Sze, Arthur. "The Negative." *Chinese American Poetry. An Anthology.* Eds. L. Ling-chi Wang and Henry Yihenz Zhao. Seattle: U of Washington P, 1991. 193.

—. "The Network." *The Open Boat. Poems from Asian America.* Ed. Garrett Hongo. New York: Anchor Books, 1993. 234.

Uba, George. "Versions of Identity in Post-Activist Asian American Poetry." *Reading the Literatures of Asian America.* Eds. Shirley Geok-lin Lim and Amy Ling. Philadelphia: Temple UP, 1992. 33-48.

Wald, Priscilla. "'Chaos Goes Uncourted': John Yau's Dis(-)Orienting Poetics." *Cohesion and Dissent in America.* Eds. Carol Colatrella & Joseph Alkana. New York: SUNY, 1994. 133-58.

Wang, Ling-chi and Henry Yihenz Zhao, eds. *Chinese American Poetry: An Anthology.* Seattle: U of Washington P, 1991.

Wong, Nellie. *Dreams in Harrison Railroad Park.* Berkeley: Kelsey St. P, 1983.

—. *The Death of Long Steam Lady.* Los Angeles: West End P, 1986.

Yau, John. "Engines of Gloom and Affection." *Postmodern American Poetry.* Ed. Paul Hoover. New York: Norton, 1994. 575.

III. Poetic Creation

Marilyn Chin's Poetry of "Self as Nation": Transforming the "Lyric I," Reinventing Cultural Inheritance

Zhou Xiaojing

In "The End of A Beginning," the opening poem of her first volume of poetry, *Dwarf Bamboo* (1987), Marilyn Chin's persona refers to herself as "the beginning of an end, the end of a beginning" in working-class Chinese American history (3).[1] This self, claiming to be part of a collective history and identity, differs radically from the "I" in conventional Western lyric poetry as defined by Helen Vendler. At the same time, Chin's poetics, grounded in the intrinsic connections between self and others, between the present and past, and between the private and public spheres, suggests an alternative line of critical inquiry that breaks away from a dominant mode of criticism on modern and "postmodern" American poetry, which polarizes the individual and the collective, detaches the author from the text, and separates the personal from the political and historical.

It seems that this polarization, to a large extent, results from an individualist conception of the self which characterizes the conventional Western "lyric I." In defining lyric poetry, Vendler asserts that "the normal home of the 'soul' is the lyric, where the human being becomes a set of warring passions independent of time and space" (5). For Vendler, the "soul" is "the self when it is alone with itself, when its socially constructed characteristics (race, class, color, gender, sexuality) are felt to be in abeyance." Moreover, Vendler adds that the soul's utterance can construct a lyric "I" that is the opposite of its socially constructed identity: "The biological characteristics ('black like me') are of course present, but in the lyric they can be reconstructed in opposition to their socially constructed form, occasioning one of the lyric's most joyous self-proclaiming: 'I am I, am I; / All creation shivers / With that sweet cry' (Yeats)" (7). Vendler's definition of the lyric reiterates Harold Bloom's formulation of modern American poetry in terms of English Romantic lyric poetry. Bloom claims that 1744, the year in which Alexander Pope died, marked a turning point in Western poetry. Rather than dealing with "the characters and actions of men and women clearly

---

1   Marilyn Chin, "The End of A Beginning," "The Cricket," "The Narrow Roads of Oku," "Counting, Recounting," "Chinaman's Chance," and "Where We Live Now," in *Dwarf Bamboo* (Greenfield Center: The Greenfield Review P, 1987). Copyright © 1987 by Marilyn Chin. Reprinted with permission from The Greenfield Review Press.

distinct from the poet who observed them," Bloom contends, "the best poetry internalized its subject matter, particularly in the mode of Wordsworth after 1798. Wordsworth had no true subject except his own subjective nature, and very nearly all significant poetry since Wordsworth, even by American poets, has repeated Wordsworth's inward turning (*Agon* 287). The self's interiority as the sole subject matter of poetry, according to Bloom, has led to poets' anxiety of influence (*Anxiety* 11).

Bloom's exclusionist theory of poetic traditions, which is modeled on Freud's psychosexual analysis of the father-son relationship in terms of "the family romance" (8), particularly his theory of lyric poetry, has been challenged by critics such as Marjorie Perloff. By equating poetry "with lyric, with Romantic subjectivity," Perloff notes, Bloom dismisses any possibility "that poetry might deal with anything outside the enclosed self" (*Dance* 174). Contesting Bloom's formulation of modern poetry as "Wordsworthian crisis lyric," Perloff constructs an alternative "postmodern" poetic tradition of which Ezra Pound is "the pivotal figure in the transformation of the Romantic (and Modernist) lyric into what we now think of as postmodern poetry" (176, 181). She further argues that "Postmodernism in poetry [...] begins with the urge to return the material so rigidly excluded—political, ethical, historical, philosophical—to the domain of poetry, which is to say that the Romantic lyric, the poem as expression of a moment of absolute insight, of emotion crystallized into a timeless patterns [sic] give way to poetry that can, once again, accommodate narrative and didacticism, the serious and the comic, verse and prose" (180-81). Characterized by the juxtaposition of disparate materials, including prose fragments, the mode of postmodern poetics, Perloff states, "is that of collage" (183). At the same time, she asserts, the conventional "hall-marks of the late modernist lyric will become less prevalent as our conception of the relation of self to world become more closely adjusted to the phenomenology of the present. In understanding that present, a narrative that is not primarily autobiographical will once again be with us, but it will be a narrative fragmented, dislocated, and often quite literally non-sensical" (168-69). Though it is not clear what Perloff meant by the phrase "the phenomenology of the present," her remarks about postmodern poetics suggest that fragmentation and the "death of the author" are among its underlying notions. As she contends, "postmodern 'poetry' and 'theory'—say the writing of John Ashbery and Roland Barthes (#13)—are part of the same larger discourse" (Licence 12).

Perloff's definition of postmodern poetry and her construction of this poetic tradition are similar to the methodology and effects of Bloom's formulation of modern American poetry in that her location of postmodern poetics in Eurocentric cultural formations and deconstructionist discourses fails to address the social and historical conditions which give rise to contemporary poetry by women and minority American poets. Although she challenges critical approaches which treat the lyric "as if the genre were a timeless and stable product to which various theoretical paradigms can be 'applied' so as to tease out new meanings," her discussion of postmodern poetics as a mode that breaks away from the auto-biographical and emotive characteristics of the lyric ignores contemporary auto-biographal lyric poetry by women and minorities. Indeed, by emphasizing the characteristics of postmodern poetics as opposite that of Romantic and Modern-ist poetry, Perloff overlooks the changes taking place in the raced and gendered "lyric I" such as those in Marilyn Chin's poetry.

Asian American critics have pointed out the difference of Asian American subjectivity, which cannot be explained away by "postmodern" fragmentation of subject or indeterminacy of meaning. Shelley Wong, for instance, argues, that "a distinction between the lyric 'I' of mainstream American poetry and that of Asian American poetry needs to be made because of the way the assumption or maintenance of an autonomous 'I' results in different social and political ramifi-cations" (137). Responding to Norman Finkelstein's contention that recent changes in the status of the "lyric I" result from a postmodern phenome-non—"the alienation of the subject is displaced by the fragmentation of the sub-ject" (4)—Wong raises provocative questions about the status of Asian Ameri-can subjectivity: "Was the Asian American subject ever not 'fragmented'? Was, then, the lyric 'I' ever available to the Asian American writer?" (138). On a similar note, Traise Yamamoto emphasizes the difference of Asian Americans' raced subjectivity and the impact of material history and social conditions on its formation, noting that "valorizing the fragmentation of multiple subject-positions alone as a positive alternative to the unified and coherent self is an ex-ercise in absurdity when applied to a raced subject whose experiences tell him/her that to celebrate the fragmented is to celebrate his/her own dismember-ment" (76). Furthermore, Yamamoto points out that "for the raced subject, an ontology and epistemology based on fragmentation not only pose serious politi-cal problems but also tend to subvert the attempt to integrate the several and dis-parate aspects of being and bring them to bear on a sense of self" (75). Marilyn Chin's poem, "The End of a Beginning," demonstrates both the difference of Asian American subjectivity and the attempt to integrate disparate aspects of the self's identity fragmented by the difference of race, class, and culture. This dif-ference and attempt have transformed the individualist and transcendental status of the "lyric I" and have produced a new lyric mode that is emotive, didactic, autobiographical, and rooted in the specific social and historical conditions of Asian Americans.

Speaking of her poetics, Chin expresses her dissatisfaction with the mode of American lyric which is "dominated by self." As minority Americans, Chin says, "[w]e have to be greater than self." She emphasizes her belief that poetry "has to teach, to illuminate, to make the world a better place" (quoted in Tabios 281). But poetry, for Chin, is also a complex form of art that demands a great amount of hard work to realize its aesthetic and didactic potential. "Poetry is about precision," says Chin, "and I think things in a poem should snap together beautifully" (quoted in Tabios 305). At the same time, Chin wants to transform

Eurocentric and monolingual aspects of "mainstream" American poetry, and to give voice to ethnic working-class Americans in her poems. As she writes in the Introduction to an anthology of Asian American literature, *Dissident Song* (1991), which she edited with David Wong Louie: "It is our duty to usurp the canon from its monolithic, monolingual, monocultural, and henceforth monotonous fate. It is up to us 'ethnic' writers to save American literature from becoming suburban 'white noise'" (4).

While searching for new forms and styles to articulate the personal and collective experience of Chinese Americans, Chin reclaims and reinvents her Chinese cultural inheritance, and develops a voice that is uniquely her own—passionate and compelling, at times humorous, at times heartbreaking. Chin often employs a Daoist humor and a self-mocking tone in trying to break away from the traditional mode of lyric poetry, especially "the ponderous expressions of a Wordsworthian, brooding self."[2] In "The End of A Beginning," for instance, Chin escapes self-centered importance by weaving a lightly self-mocking humor into the fabric of the self's connection to and position in the history of Chinese Americans:

> The beginning is always difficult.
> The immigrant worked his knuckles to the bone
> only to die under the wheels of the railroad.
> One thousand years before him, his ancestor fell
> building yet another annex to the Great Wall—
> and was entombed within his work. And I,
> the beginning of an end, the end of a beginning,
> sit here, drink unfermented green tea,
> scrawl these paltry lines for you. Grandfather,
> on your one-hundredth birthday, I have
> the answers to your last riddles:
>
> This is why the baboon's ass is red.
> Why horses lie down only in moments of disaster.
> Why the hyena's back is forever scarred.
> Why, that one hare who was saved, splits his upper lip,
> in a fit of hysterical laughter. (*Bamboo* 3)

By connecting the Chinese immigrants who built the railroad in America to the Chinese who built the Great Wall over a thousand years ago in China, Chin is giving voice to the experience of the working-class, while inscribing their history. She achieves compression through historically charged symbolic images such as the American transcontinental railroad and the Great Wall, and through contrast between these images and the culturally symbolic images of the "unfermented green tea" Chin's persona is drinking and the poem she is writing.

---

2   Chin's telephone conversation with the author of this article, on May 12, 1998.

This contrast reinforces the speaker's claim to be "the beginning of an end, the end of a beginning"—a ruptured connection to the past which is further implied in her direct address to "Grandfather," thus rendering the historical and collective at once personal and more than personal.

Moreover, the speaker's calling upon her "Grandfather," like her "scrawl[ing] these paltry lines" for him, helps prevent her remarks about herself from becoming a self-aggrandizing claim, while smoothly propelling the transition in the poem from the past to the present, from the collective to the personal, and from quiet contemplation to inspired incantation. Following this transition, in accordance to the voice of a grandchild, the syntax and rhyme scheme of the last section become simple and rhythmic like a nursery rhyme. The resulting aural effect and the visual images in the riddles provide another contrast to the images of death "under the wheels of the railroad" and bodies "entombed" within the Great Wall, adding another cultural dimension to the historical. At the same time, a continuity is implied in the riddles which connect the speaker to her grandfather, who serves as a bridge between her and China.

Chinese Americans' historical and cultural connections to China are a major theme and subject matter in Chin's poems. The first part of *Dwarf Bamboo*, subtitled "Parent Node," consists of a series of allusions to various periods of Chinese history, from the first century B.C. to the last dynasty, from the Nationalist movement to the Communist revolution, and from the Japanese invasion to the Cultural Revolution. As she inscribes Chinese history, Chin appropriates her Chinese cultural heritage into both the content and form of her poems. In "The Cricket," for instance, the culturally distinct content is accompanied by a new composition method. Rather than progressing by logical development of argument, or simultaneous movement of observation and contemplation, as is typical of traditional Western lyric, "The Cricket" depends on imagery to motivate the movement of the poem, which jumps from one time-space to another through a loose association to the central image:

> I am sad for the cricket,
> Sadder for the late
> First century B.C. Tibetans
> Who tried to get rid of it.
>
> Billions of yellow-black
> Herbivorous villains
> Devoured the Himalayan Valley,
> Now as good as the Dead Sea,
>
> Mowed prodigiously over
> The Yangtze, desecrated
> The shrine of the Gods
> Of Fruition and Harvest.

A cricket can be a friend.
As individuals they're all right.
Before her exile, Yang Kuei Fei
Held one in her palm.

No wonder the Grand Eunuch
Of the Dowager T'zu Hsi said
Unleash it and it will kill;
Cage it, it will sing. (*Bamboo* 15)

The paradox of potentially destructive and creative forces symbolized in the cricket is developed and revealed through associations of geography, history, and historical figures. These historical details render the cricket both concrete and abstract. Thus the meanings and implications of the poem are enriched, rather than limited, by its historically and culturally specific allusions. Moreover, those historical and cultural allusions displace Eurocentricism in Bloom's formulation of the modern American lyric canon and in Perloff's construction of the postmodern American lyric tradition, while creating a kind of disjunctive temporality, which Homi Bhabha considers a central aspect of "the politics of cultural difference." For this kind of "disjunctive temporality," Bhabha contends, "creates a signifying time for the inscription of cultural incommensurability where differences cannot be sublated or totalized because 'they somehow occupy the same space'" (177).

Thus Chin's appropriation of non-European culture in her poems is not motivated simply by a nostalgic sentiment or an aesthetic consideration. Her incorporation of Chinese history and culture in "The Cricket," and other poems, enables her to intervene in the dominance of Eurocentric culture in American poetry. This impulse to inscribe cultural difference as intervention is what Homi Bhabha calls "the *effect* of discriminatory practices—the production of cultural *differentiation* as signs of authority—[which] changes its value and its rules of recognition" (114). Chin's appropriation of Chinese culture is in part generated by the exclusion, degradation, and marginalization of Chinese immigrants and their culture in American history and mainstream American culture.[3]

Chin further resists European cultural dominance in American poetry by introducing a Zen Buddhist world outlook, sensibility, and poetics through intertextual appropriation and revision of the writings by the renowned Japanese poet, Matsuo Bashō (1644-1694). The title of her poem "Narrow Roads of Oku" echoes that of Bashō's travel diary, *The Narrow Road to the Deep North*, which

---

3   Maxine Hong Kingston in *China Men* has documented the history of exclusionary laws against Chinese, and there are a few book-length studies on the representations of Asians in mainstream American literature and culture. See Kingston, "The Laws" 152-59; William Wu, *The Yellow Peril: Chinese Americans in American Fiction 1850-1940*; Gina Marchetti, *Romance and the "Yellow Peril": Race, Sex, and Discursive Strategies in Hollywood Fiction*, and Darrell Y. Hamamoto, *Monitored Peril: Asian Americans and the Politics of TV Representation.*

consists of both prose and poetry. She combines and rewrites selections from
Bashō's prose and poems, and creates something new in the voice of Bashō
while capturing the poet's perceptions and states of mind. At the beginning of
The Narrow Road to the Deep North, Bashō makes references to the ancients'
travels, and describes in prose his restlessness and urge to travel: "I myself have
been tempted for a long time by the cloud-moving wind—filled with the strong
desire to wander" (*Road* 97). Chin weaves these references seamlessly into
Bashō's monologue, rearticulating and transforming the metaphorical expression
of his restlessness into a compelling image:

> I, too, could not resist the wind.
> It bends me forward, backward
> All night long.
> By the time the cocks call
> I'll be long gone.
> [...].
> The moons are lovely at Matsushima.
> The fish are jumping at Matsushima Bay. (*Bamboo* 5)

Chin's description of the moons and the fish in the last two lines effectively
conveys Bashō's excitement about his travels. This mode of representing a state
of mind and emotions through images enacts Bashō's poetic principles which
insist that poetry issues from the oneness of the poet with the object he/she observes.

Chin continues to recreate Bashō's travel experience, and to perform his poetic principles and his philosophy about life through intertextual revision in the
rest of the poem. In this process, moreover, Chin develops a style and voice
which are uniquely her own. Her intertextual appropriation of Bashō at once
reinscribes and transforms the given text and style. *In The Narrow Road to the
Deep North*, Bashō recorded in prose that he sold his house before his journey to
the North, and wrote a linked verse of eight pieces which he hung on a wooden
pillar of the house. The starting piece reads:

> Behind this door
> now buried in deep grass,
> A different generation will celebrate
> The Festival of Dolls. (98)

In her poem, Chin alludes to what Bashō did and to his verse with such acuteness and directness that she succeeds in revealing his individuality, accentuating
his attitude toward life, and capturing what poetry meant to him:

> Stranger, I sell you this house—
> [...].

> You can have your wife, your daughter, her gewgaws
> For my name is Bashō.
> I have no wife to feed,
> No kindling to drag.
> I'll tack-tack this ricepaper on your door
> For my name is Bashō.
> Let my stanzas flap in the wind,
> My noble flags of distinction. (*Bamboo* 5)

Apart from the ideological and aesthetic functions, Chin's intertextual revision of Bashō's writings is a way of affirming her Asian cultural heritage and a process of reinventing her hybrid identity through incorporating and transforming the given in her poems.

However, the process of this reinvention is sometimes accompanied by a sense of her fragile connection to her Chinese heritage, which she is losing with the passage of time and the process of assimilation. Much of this sense and the resulting tensions are dealt with in the second part of her first volume, subtitled "American Soil." The opening poem of this part, "Counting, Recounting," captures Chin's feeling of the inevitable acculturation of Chinese Americans. It begins with the speaker talking to her little sister, remembering their drive from Boston to Long Beach "to visit grandma who sent us colored blankets / crocheted by her own hands." As the poems unfolds, we learn that Grandma is dying, "wrapped in a soft variegated blanket / dyed by her own hands." The last section of the poem summarizes:

> About death, about the long drive,
> this is what I remember:
> grandma died by her own hand.
> You slept colorfully, like a pig.
> I worried about bridges
> becoming fewer and fewer,
> by and by. (*Bamboo* 27)

Chin's masterful use of variations on the blankets and Grandma's hand generates the development in each section of the poem, while unifying the movement of the poem with Grandma's changing condition. She also deftly achieves a double meaning in the last sentence, which simultaneously suggests the speaker's fear to confront her dying grandmother and of gradually losing all the bridges between her and China through the deaths of older generations of Chinese immigrants who are the cultural bridges for American-born Chinese. "I am afraid of losing my Chinese, losing my language, which would be like losing a part of myself, losing part of my soul," says Chin in an interview with Bill Moyers, and adds, "Poetry seems a way to recapture that" (70).

For Chin, recapturing her Chinese cultural heritage in poetry involves reinventing the self and the inherited. Several of her poems explore the necessities,
conditions, and difficulties of this reinvention. In "Chinaman's Chance," Chin
suggests that historical and social conditions for Chinese immigrants have made
the survival of Chinese cultural identities difficult. The title of the poem alludes
to the racist laws aimed at disempowering Chinese immigrants economically and
politically, making it impossible for them to have a chance to fulfill their
"American dream." As the poem develops, the title begins to reveal another
layer of implication: Chinese immigrants' and their children's chase after the
materialistic "American dream." In a conversation with Maxine Hong Kingston,
Chin mentions her own dream of becoming a poet which contrasted with the
immigrants' dream of buying houses ("Writing the Other" 1). The conflict between the spiritual and the material is at the center of "Chinaman's Chance."
The opening section of the poem raises a question about the soul and the body,
and the middle section situates that question in the historical contexts of Chinese
American experience:

> If you were a Chinese born in America, who would you believe
> Plato who said what Socrates said
> Or Confucius in his bawdy way:
>> "So a male child is born to you
>> I am happy, very very happy."

>   *   *   *   *   *   *

> The railroad killed your great-grandfather.
> His arms here, his legs there . . .
> *How can we remake ourselves in his image?*

> Your father worked his knuckles black,
> So you might have pink cheeks. Your father
> Burped you on the back; why must you water his face?

> Your father was happy, he was charred by the sun,
> *Danced and sang until he died at twenty-one.*

> [...].

> Your body is growing, changing, running
> Away from your soul. Look,

> Not a sun but a gold coin on the horizon,
> *Chase after it, my friend, after it.* (*Bamboo* 29)

Responding to the question raised at the beginning, this middle section plays out,
rather than solves, the tension between the ancient Greek and Chinese philoso-

phers' beliefs. Confucius' patriarchal value that privileges males seems futile for young Chinese men who left home to die young, laboring under harsh conditions in North America. Plato's and Socrates' belief in the soul is superfluous when Chinese immigrants cannot even survive physically. These philosophers' respective doctrines are not pertinent either for a younger generation of Chinese Americans whose bodies are running away from their souls, chasing after "a gold coin at the horizon." The irony in this section accentuates the difficulties Chinese Americans face in reinventing their cultural identities.

The speaker's ironic tone gives way to a meditative mood, and a triumphant tone in the last section of the poem. Chin uses imagery and riddle-like questions to change the topic and generate a different tone, while maintaining the unity of the poem by beginning the section with a question:

> Why does the earth move backwards
> As we walk ahead. Why does mother's
> Blood stain this hand-me-down shirt?
>
> [...].
>
> We have come small and wooden, tanned brown
> As oak pillars, eyes peering straight
> Through vinyl baggage and uprooted shoes.
>
> We shall gather their leftovers: jimsons and velvets,
> Crocuses which have burst-bloomed through walks.
> We shall shatter this ancient marble, veined and glorious... (*Bamboo* 30)

Chin's poem suggests that historical forces make the transformation of culture inevitable; reclaiming cultural heritage is an on-going process of renegotiating values and reinventing identities.

However, the process of change, especially assimilation, is not without loss and pain. In "Where We Live Now (II)," Chin explores the consequences of assimilation for her family. The poem begins with the speaker looking at family snapshots. Her gaze pauses on a family photo taken at Easter, without the father, who sends them a photo "of himself and an unnamed woman" with "the cryptic message, / 'business as busy as usual, / and the woman is only temporary.'" The poem ends with Chin's ironic comment:

> Such a typical American story,
> but it wouldn't hurt to recognize—
> she was white and very beautiful. (*Bamboo* 41)

According to Chin, the poem is based on her own life experience. Her father had an affair with a white woman, and talked to her on the phone in front of her mother, who did not speak English. Eventually the father left the family for the white woman. In Chin's poem, the white woman functions on both personal and symbolic levels. She is the person who has led to the family's fragmentation; she is also symbolic of the privilege of whiteness and the dangerous allure of the American dream. In her other poems, especially her later ones, Chin further explores women's experiences, "hoping to be a conduit for her mother's voice and the voices of other Asian women" (Moyers 75). She also continues to investigate the various consequences of assimilation and negotiate her hybrid cultural identity.

While exploring the anxieties, fears, and possibilities of resistance in the process of assimilation, Chin searches for new poetic styles and forms to articulate these complex emotions, including her awareness of a raced and gendered subjectivity. In "The Barbarians Are Coming," collected in her second volume *The Phoenix Gone, The Terrace Empty*,[4] she incorporates and revises the modern Greek poet C.P. Cavafy's poem, "Waiting for the Barbarians," and a passage from the ancient Chinese text Lao Tzu to express in different voices and images immigrants' psychological and emotional states in the process of assimilation. Cavafy's poem is written in the form of a dramatized dialogue, through which a scene and its meaning are revealed:

What are we waiting for, assembled in the forum?

The barbarians are due here today.

Why isn't anything happening in the senate?
Why do the senators sit there without legislating?

Because the barbarians are coming today.

[...].

Why this sudden restlessness, this confusion?
(How serious people's faces have become.)

[...].

Because night has fallen and the barbarians have not come.
And some who have just returned from the borders say
there are no barbarians any longer.

And now, what's going to happen to us without barbarians?
They were, those people, a kind of solution. (20-21)

---

4   Marilyn Chin, "The Barbarians Are Coming," "Barbarian Suite," "How I Got That Name,"
     "The Phoenix Gone, The Terrace Empty," and "The Gilded Cangue," in *The Phoenix Gone,
     The Terrace Empty* (Minneapolis: Milkweed Editions, 1994). Copyright © 1994 by Marilyn
     Chin. Reprinted with permission from Milkweed Editions.

The last two lines, set off from the dialogue, indicate that the whole political regime, from the emperor to the senate, from the consuls to the praetors are acting under an illusion—"the barbarians are coming today." The "barbarians" are used as a delusive solution to the state's problems. According to Cavafy's comment on the poem, the "barbarians" are "a symbol" (59).

Chin borrows Cavafy's symbolic use of the "barbarians" and his technical strategy of revealing a state of mind through dramatization, but she changes both the meaning of the symbol and the dramatization in her own poem. Through vivid imagery and a compelling voice, Chin creates a sense of urgency and crisis by opening the poem with a description of the barbarians' approaching cavalry:

> War chariots thunder, horses neigh, *the barbarians are coming.*
> What are we waiting for, young nubile women pointing at the wall,
>   *the barbarians are coming.*
> They have heard about a weakened link in the wall. *So the*
>   *barbarians have ears among us.*
> So deceive yourself with illusions: you are only one woman, holding one
>   broken brick in the wall.
> So deceive yourself with illusions: as if you matter, that brick and that wall.
> *The barbarians are coming*: they have red beards or beardless with a top knot.
> *The barbarians are coming*: they are your fathers, brothers, teachers, lovers;
>   and they are clearly an other. (*Phoenix* 19)

Rather than an eagerly expected presence as in Cavafy's poem, the "barbarians" in Chin's poem are an invading force that threatens to destroy people's illusion of maintaining their racial and cultural purity. The image of the brick wall evokes the Great Wall of China, built to stop the invasion of "barbarians." As the poem unfolds, it becomes clear that it is an illusion that the "barbarians" can be barred by the wall; "they are your fathers, brothers, teachers, lovers," though they are "clearly an other."

The poem dramatizes Chinese immigrants' anxiety about and resistance to assimilation, and their illusion that individuals can preserve cultural and racial purity. Chin confesses in an interview that she fears losing her Chinese language, "which would be like losing a part of myself, losing part of my soul," but that "assimilation *must* happen. There's *no way* I can force my children to speak Chinese. There is *no way* that the pure yellow seed, as my grandmother called it, will continue." Moreover, Chin points out, "Just as I think it's impossible to keep Chineseness pure, I think it's also impossible to keep whiteness pure. I think *everything* must merge, and I'm willing to have it merge within me, in my poetry" (Moyers 70, 73).

The merging of different cultures and its implications for white Americans are also part of the dramatization of anxiety and illusion in Chin's poem, as implied in the difference of the "barbarians," who are both Caucasian ("they have red beards") and Asian ("or beardless with a top knot"). Chin enhances the double meaning of the illusion about "the barbarians" by appropriating and revising one passage from the ancient Chinese text *Lao Tzu* in the last half of the poem. In the passage, Lao Tzu is called "ill-bred" by a visitor who sees him being frugal with food, but Lao Tzu is indifferent to the name-calling. When asked why he remained indifferent, Lao Tzu said:

> "The titles of clever, wise, divine, holy are things that I have long ago cast aside, as a snake sheds its skin. Yesterday if you had called me an ox, I should have accepted the name of ox; if you had called me a horse, I should have accepted the name of horse. Wherever there is a substance and men give it a name, it would do well to accept that name; for it will in any case be subject to the prejudice that attaches to the name." (quoted in Waley 17)

Chin incorporates Lao Tzu's attitude toward naming and names in her poem, thus producing a transition from the fear of the "barbarians" and illusion about the self, to the attitudes of the barbarians:

> If you call me a horse, I must be a horse.
> If you call me a bison, I am equally guilty.

> When a thing is true and is correctly described, one doubles the blame by
>   not admitting it: so, Chuangtzu, himself, was a barbarian king!
> Horse, horse, bison, bison, *the barbarians are coming*—
> and how they love to come.
> The smells of the great frontier exult in them.

> *after Cavafy* (*Phoenix* 19)

With this shift of perspective from those who feel threatened by the "barbarians" to the "barbarians" themselves, Chin exposes the prejudice that accompanies the names one gives to the other. Despite the degrading names, "the barbarians" keep coming, but their arrival stimulates excitement about the unknown rather than simply anxiety. By drawing from different literary and cultural traditions, Chin achieves a rare combination of psychological complexity and emotional intensity in her poem.

She further explores the consequences of Chinese Americans' assimilation in another poem, "Barbarian Suite." The poem consists of six passages, each articulating a particular aspect of the inevitability of change, and the resulting loss and fragmentation in the process of a second-generation Chinese American's acculturation:

> The Ming will be over to make way for the Ch'ing.
> The Ch'ing will be over to make way for eternity.
> The East is red and the sun is rising.
> All bleeds into the ocean in the Califia west.

> My loss is your loss, a dialect here, a memory there—
> if my left hand is dying will my right hand cut it off?
> We shall all be vestigial organs, the gift of democracy.
> The pale faces, the wan conformity,
> the price we pay for comfort is our mother tongue. (*Phoenix* 22)

While asserting her sense of fragmentation, the speaker indicates with irony that assimilation into the American mainstream culture is a process of losing one's ethnic cultural heritage while conforming to the dominant culture.

Passage II illustrates the departure of the younger generation of Chinese Americans from their cultural background through descriptions of a generation gap between the grandchildren and their grandmother, who serves as "the bridge" between China and America. The difference between them signifies a cultural and economic transformation:

> We can no longer dress her and improve her accent.
> We can no longer toil in her restaurant "Double Happiness,"
> oiling woks, peeling shrimp.
> [...].
> We study Western philosophy and explore our raison d'être.
> All is well in the suburbs when we are in love with poetry. (*Phoenix* 22)

Rather than a sequential development from this second passage, Passage III, consisting of a series of rhetorical questions, challenges the speakers' sentiments over the loss of her Chinese cultural heritage and undercuts her satisfaction with her Western bourgeois lifestyle, from a different subject position signified by the switch from the first-person to second-person pronoun. The switch is enhanced by the speaker's colloquial diction and the use of slang:

> What did ya think, the emperor will come to your grave?
> [...].
> What did ya expect, old peasant, old fool,
> one day out of the woods and the dirt will eject
> from your nostrils? (*Phoenix* 22)

In response to these challenges, Passage IV acknowledges the difficulty of assimilation and its creative, transformative possibilities. Rather than being passively assimilated, Chin's persona appropriates and transforms the dominant culture, as the speaker declares defiantly by alluding to T.S. Eliot: "We dare to eat peaches and discuss the classics" (*Phoenix* 23).

Developing the theme of assimilation further, Chin, in Passage V, introduces a new cross-cultural subject who is completely at home with different cultures despite the disapproval of her Chinese ancestors:

> One day they came to me, my dead ancestors.

They whispered *sse-sse-sse*, homophonous with "death."
I was under the covers with my barbarian boyfriend,
blowing smoke rings, talking jazz—"Posterity"
in yet another "compromising position,"
addenda to the Kama Sutra.
I was playing Goddess/Dominatress
and kept a piece of his ear as offering. (*Phoenix* 23)

This new cross-cultural subject is "the beginning of an end, the end of a beginning" as Chin emphasizes in Passage VI, which returns to Grandmother's generation, who "believed in the restaurant called 'Double Happiness,'" where "[t]he cash register rang its daily prayer wheels" for the "dying" old generation and the young "saved" Chinese Americans. The ironic tone of Chin's poem belies the apparently peaceful assimilation of "AmerAsia so harmonious under a canopy of stars" (*Phoenix* 23).

Chin also further problematizes Asian American assimilation by exposing racial stereotypes of Asian Americans and the perpetual marginalization of their social status. In "How I Got That Name," subtitled "an essay on assimilation," Chin reveals that her father, "obsessed with a bombshell blond" changed her name from "Mei Ling" to "Marilyn" (*Phoenix* 16). Despite the desires and efforts of immigrants like her father to assimilate and become white, Asian Americans are marked as Other and stereotyped as "Model Minority" in the racial politics of United States. Chin employs self-mockery to expose the naturalized stereotypes of Asian Americans:

Oh, how trustworthy our daughters,
how thrifty our sons!
How we've managed to fool the experts
in education, statistics and demography—
We're not very creative but not adverse to rote-learning.
Indeed, they can *use* us.
But the "Model Minority" is a tease.
We know you are watching now,
so we refuse to give you any!
Oh, bamboo shoots, bamboo shoots!
The further west we go, we'll hit east;
the deeper down we dig, we'll find China. (*Phoenix* 17)

The switch of the voice from "I" to "we" is one of Chin's characteristic strategies for giving many levels to the self, making the personal part of the collective. Even though Chin has appropriated the mode of American "confessional" poetry by using autobiographical materials as subject matter, and family members as characters, the self and the personal are always connected to collective histories and experiences.

Chin is especially preoccupied with women's experiences and their positions in the social and familial structures, and in their personal relationships. In several poems, she attempts to resolve the "deep pain and guilt" she feels for her mother as a result of her father's betrayal and her mother's cultural dislocation (Moyers 75). While dealing with her mother's suffering in the title poem "The Phoenix Gone, The Terrace Empty," Chin locates it in history and connects it to other women's experiences. "My feminism is born out of personal and familial experiences," says Chin. Having read feminist writers such as Hélène Cixous and Adrienne Rich, "The Phoenix Gone, The Terrace Empty," Chin notes, "is a softly-feminist poem" (quoted in Tabios 280). Artistically, the poem, which took her four years to perfect, could be said to be Chin's masterpiece. The title of the poem is a line from Li Bai (701-762), a poet of the Tang Dynasty (618-907). The poem is in part inspired by Chin's reading of some notes by an Imperial Gardener about the imperial consorts in the Ming Dynasty (1368-1644), while visiting the Tai-Chung University library in Taiwan, where Chin studied classical Chinese.

While the title of the poem, "The Phoenix Gone, The Terrace Empty," evokes the ancient history of China, its images suggest its irretrievable past and historical changes. Under the title, Chin adds an epigraph in four Chinese characters, translated into English as "the river flows without ceasing." The sense of continuity implied in the epigraph counterpoises the sense of loss in the title, creating ambivalence and tension, which help Chin achieve compactness and intensity. At the same time, the poem's structure and line arrangement are modeled on the visual aspect of the flowing water of a river, as captured by the three irregular vertical lines of the Chinese character for river. The poem begins with an imperial consort walking down the stairs in a garden cautiously because of her bound feet:

> Shallow river, shallow river,
> these stairs are steep,
> one foot, another,
> I gather the hem
> of my terry-cloth robe.
> Quietly,
> gingerly,
> [...]
> past the courtyard,
> past the mulberries,
> [...]
> softly,
> gingerly,
> [...].
> "Who in the netherworld walks on my soles
> as I walk?

And opens her black mouth
when I cry?
Whose lutestrings
play my sorrow?
Whose silence
undulates
a millennium
of bells,
in which
all of history
shall wallow?" (*Phoenix* 46-47)

The consort's questions help connect her suffering to those of other women; they are also questions Chin attempts to respond to by giving voice to the consort's and other women's experiences in her poem.

In addition, these questions serve as a transition from the first passage to the third, in which Chin gives voice to her parents and grandparents. Her comparison of her parents to "water bison" (*Phoenix* 47), and her reference to her grandmother's "oiling her shuttle" and grandfather's "massive bellows" as an "itinerant tinker" (*Phoenix* 48), shift the focus of her poem from the imperial court to the village, from the aristocracy to the working class, and from ancient history to a comparatively recent past. At the center of this passage is the mother, whose youth and past happiness Chin tries to recapture:

I think of
love
or the warm blur,
my mother—
I remember hate,
the hard shape,
my father.
[...].
Do you remember
the shanty towns
on the hills of Wanchai,
tin roofs
crying into the sun?
Do you remember
mother's first lover,
hurling
a kerosene
into a hovel?
Ooooh, I can smell
the charred sweetness
in his raven hair.
The hills ablaze

> with mayflies
> and night-blooming jasmine. (*Phoenix* 48)

In contrast to this idyllic world of the mother's youth in China, the next passage is about the father's money-obsessed world. With an abrupt change of imagery, the poem moves from China to America as its focus shifts to the father:

> Open the gate,
> open,
> the gilded facade
> of restaurant "Double Happiness."
> The man crouched
> on the dirty linoleum
> fingering dice
> is my father.
> He says:
> "Mei Ling, child,
> Mei Ling, don't cry,
> I can change our lives
> with one strike." (*Phoenix* 48-49)

The sense of urgency and determination in the speaker's tone seems to suggest that Chin's persona is bracing herself in order to confront the unpleasant sight of her father. However, by giving voice to the father, Chin reveals a gentle side to him. The next passage continues to focus on the father, revealing more about him from the perspective of the speaker's aunt. Moreover, this passage contains three interwoven voices, which not only bring different perspectives on the father's situation, but also introduce history and generate variations of tone and rhythm within the passage. It is worthwhile to quote it in whole to illustrate Chin's masterful skills of smooth transitions, and her capacity for a range of voices and tones. One can also get a better sense of how she breaks the lines in such a way that their movement emulates a flowing river:

> Do you know the stare
> of a dead man?
> My father the ox,
> without his yoke,
> sitting on a ridge
> of the quay.
> Auntie Jade
> remembers:
> "Hunger
> had spooned
> the flesh
> from his cheeks.
> His tuft

of black hair
was his only movement.
That Chinaman
had no ideals,
no beliefs,
his dreams
were robbed
by the Japanese,
his fortune
was plundered
by the Nationalists,
the Communists
seared his home.
Misery had propped
him there.
When you pray to your ancestors
you are praying
to his hollowness."
Amaduofu, amaduofu—
child, child
they cried,
"Ten thousand years of history and you have come to this.
Four thousand years of tutelage and you have come to this!" (*Phoenix* 49-50)

With the question "Do you know the stare / of a dead man?" Chin turns away
from the father's perspective to the daughter's by replacing his voice with hers,
while continuing to keep the focus of the poem on him. Her description of the
father in terms of "the ox, / without his yoke, / sitting on a ridge / of the quay"
vividly portrays the father's dislocation. At the same time, the image of "the
ox"—"a toiling animal, a beast of burden"—helps Chin foreground the working-
class experience, which shifts her reference from "the courtesan image towards
village vignettes with my family as characters." As she explains, "Ox is my Chinese lexicon for working class Chinese which is my people, my family" (quoted
in Tabios 298). By associating the father with the ox, Chin provides a social
context for the father's actions. She also allows Auntie Jade's voice to intervene
to provide a historical perspective on the father's situation, and explains with
sympathy to the judgmental daughter: "Misery had propped / him there." In response to the aunt's remarks about the father's hollowness and about the daughter's prayer to her ancestors, Chin inserts a phrase of Buddhist chanting:
"*Amaduofu, amaduofu*," which is followed by the ancestors' chastising comments. The couplet form of these comments, with their long, incantatory rhythm,
breaks down the swift tempo of the poem, thus enhancing its function of sum-
ming up the father's life, with which Chin has reached some sort of absolution.
By the end of this passage, the father is no longer simply a hateful "hard shape,"
a despicable gambler, to the daughter.

Following the ancestor's remarks of disappointment about the father, the poem moves to the daughter's life. Again, Chin generates the transition with a question that simultaneously connects to the preceding passage and looks to the next:

> Shall I walk
> into the new world
> in last year's pinafore?
> Chanel says:
> black, black
> is our century's color.
> Proper and elegant,
> slim silhouette... (*Phoenix* 50)

References to the speaker's walking "into the new world," her "last year's pinafore," and "our century's color" all resonate with the imperial consort's walk and her "terry-cloth robe," thus relating Chin's persona to the imperial consort, and to the mother and other Chinese women of the past, while generating another transition in narrative and time, motivating yet another movement from the past to the present.

With the above transitional segment, the poem begins to focus on the daughter's life in the following passage, in which her choices in life are judged by the mother with disapproval:

> "So, you've come home
> finally
> with your new boyfriend.
> What is his name?
> Ezekiel!
> Odd name for a boy.
> Your mother can't pronounce it.
> And she doesn't like
> his demeanor.
> Too thin, too sallow,
> he does not eat beef
> in a country
> where beef is possible.
> He cannot play the violin
> in a country
> where rapture is possible.
> He beams a tawdry smile,
> [...].
> And that Moon
> which accompanied his arrival,
> that Moon won't drink
> and is shaped naughtily

like a woman's severed ear." (*Phoenix* 50-51)

The mother's reference to "that Moon" and drinking evokes the Tang poet Li Bai who constantly drinks to and with the moon in real life and in his poems. For the mother, the absence of companionship and harmony between the moon and the man is a bad sign for the daughter's boyfriend. Her reference to the shape of the moon's phase as a sign of disharmony also serves to shift the reference from the American culture to the Chinese, enabling the rest of the poem to return to allusions to ancient Chinese history and culture.

In juxtaposition to the mother's interpretation of the shape of the moon, the next short passage evokes a traditional Chinese sign of the snake biting her own tail, "meaning harmony at the year's end." But Chin immediately inserts a different interpretation of the sign: "Or does it mean / she is eating herself / into extinction?" (*Phoenix* 51). The implication of female self-annihilation in the sign helps Chin to refocus the poem on women's suffering and subjugation, by referring to Chinese women's bound feet again in the next passage:

> Oh dead prince, Oh hateful love,
> shall we meet again
> on the bridge of magpies?
> Will you kiss me tenderly
> where arch meets toe meets ankle,
> where dried blood warbles? (*Phoenix* 51)

The "bridge of magpies" alludes to a Chinese myth in which once a year magpies flow together to make a bridge over the Silver River (the Milky Way) to allow the starcrossed lovers to meet. Chin uses this allusion ironically to expose the fact that women were forced to bind their feet in order to please men. With the line "Will you kiss me tenderly," Chin echoes the imperial consort's words about the "flagstones" which "caress my feet, / kiss them tenderly" (*Phoenix* 46), an indirect way of expressing the pain she endures in her bound feet.

But the poem ends with a change of voice and tone, and a shift away from bound feet, moving from magpies to "little bird," and then to the phoenix. At the same time, the speaking voice switches back to that of the mother after another incantatory transitional segment:

> *Little bird, little bird,*
> *something escaping,*
> *something escaping...*
>
> *The phoenix gone, the terrace empty.*
> *Look, Mei Ling,*
> *yellow crowfoot in the pond,*
> *not lotus, not lily.* (*Phoenix* 51)

While the images in the last lines echo those in the opening passage of the poem, the line from Li Bai's poem evokes a sense of change with the passage of time. In accordance with this sense of an irretrievable past, the mother reminds the daughter that she is at a different time and place, where the pond has "yellow crowfoot" rather than "lotus" and "lily," which allude to metaphors for Chinese women's bound feet that meet the aesthetic standard size for female beauty. But these metaphors also suggest women's oppression and suffering, which Chin attempts to give voice to in the poem. By directing the daughter's attention to "the yellow crowfoot in the pond," the mother articulates her point of view, which is different from the daughter's. By ending the poem with the mother's voice and viewpoint, Chin raises questions about her attempts to speak for other women. As she says, "It was a moment of questioning the poem's role as a con-duit of other women's voices" (quoted in Tabios 307).

In "The Gilded Cangue" subtitled "(*Phoenix* series #2/3)," Chin further ex-plores the necessity of speaking for other women through her poetry, and the consequences of keeping silent about women's lives. For Chin, these questions also concern the relations between art and life, as the speaker in the poem asks: "What is poetry if it could forget / the meaning of her life?" (*Phoenix* 56). She continues to investigate the possibilities of using her poetry as a conduit for other women's voices in the final poem of her second volume, "A Portrait of the Self As Nation, 1990-1991." As the title indicates, the female speaker in the poem integrates the personal and collective identities of race, gender, national-ity, and culture. She locates personal identities and relationships in the contexts of racism, colonialism, and imperialism. Her exposure of "the power of exclu-sion" exercised against the Other (*Phoenix* 96) and her ironic comments on Eurocentricism—"Why save Babylonia or Cathay, / when we can always have Paris?" (*Phoenix* 97)—help explain her insistence on exploring the self's con-nections to history and ideologies of race, gender, and nation, an insistence which is also a resistance to the mode of American lyric "dominated by self."

The reasons for Chin's insistence on integrating the personal and the collec-tive in her poems also underlie her impulse to reclaim and reinvent her Chinese cultural heritage. In attempting to recapture Chinese culture, history, and literary traditions in her poems, Chin is not simply resisting, but also intervening in the dominance of Eurocentric culture and literary traditions, particularly the con-ventions of lyric poetry as defined by Bloom and Vendler. Yet, in opening the poetic to the political and historical, and in making narrative and didacticism an integral part of her poetry, Chin does not renounce the emotive and autobio-graphical in order to enact the postmodern collage mode of "a narrative frag-mented, dislocated, and often quite literally non-sensical" as Perloff puts it. In-deed, her poetics resists identification with the modern lyric tradition that can be traced back to Wordsworth, or with the postmodern tradition that has Pound as its precursor. Rather than a transcendental soul, the soul of Chin's lyric is part of a socially and historically specific self. This self and its particular time and place are precisely the sources of the "warring passions" of her "lyric I." Although resolutely political, her poems possess the lyric values Vendler singles out—"spontaneity, circumstantiality; a sudden freeze-frame of disturbance, awakening, pang; an urgent and inviting rhythm," and "compression" (4). Chin's poetry moves, disturbs, and illuminates, realizing its lyricism and didacticism through poetic forms invented to embody the undulations of consciousness with emotional intensity and linguistic precision. Commenting on Chin's second volume, Adrienne Rich says that "reading her, our sense of the possibilities of poetry is opened further, and we feel again what an active, powerful art it can be."[5] Marilyn Chin's poetry unsettles established notions of poetic genres, and challenges conventional assumptions about the possibilities of poetry.

Works Cited

Bashō, Matsuo. *The Narrow Road to the Deep North and Other Travel Sketches.* Intro. and trans. Nobuyuki Yuasa. New York: Penguin Books, 1983.

Bhabha, Homi K. *The Location of Culture.* London: Routledge, 1994.

Bloom, Harold. *Agon: Towards a Theory of Revision.* Oxford: Oxford UP, 1982.

—. *The Anxiety of Influence: A Theory of Poetry.* London: Oxford UP, 1975.

Cavafy, C.P. *The Essential Cavafy.* Intro. Edmund Keeley. Trans. Edmund Keeley and Philip Sherrard. Hopewell: The Ecco P, 1995.

Chin, Marilyn. *Dwarf Bamboo.* Greenfield Center: The Greenfield Review P, 1987.

—. *The Phoenix Gone, The Terrace Empty.* Minneapolis: Milkweed Editions, 1994.

—. "Introduction." *Dissident Song: A Contemporary Asian American Anthology.* Eds. Marilyn Chin and David Wong Louie. Santa Cruz, CA: Quarry West, 1991. 3-4.

—. "Writing the Other: A Conversation with Maxine Hong Kingston." *Poetry Flash* 198 (September 1989): 1, 4, 7-8.

Finkelstein, Norman. "The Problem of Self in Recent American Poetry." *Poetics Journal* 9 (June 1991): 3-10.

Hamamoto, Darrell Y. *Monitored Peril: Asian Americans and the Politics of TV Representation.* Minneapolis: U of Minnesota P, 1994.

Kingston, Maxine Hong. *China Men.* New York: Knopf, 1980.

Marchetti, Gina. *Romance and the "Yellow Peril": Race, Sex, and Discursive Strategies in Hollywood Fiction.* Berkeley: U of California P, 1993.

Moyers, Bill. Interview with Marilyn Chin. *The Language of Life: A Festival of Poets.* New York: Doubleday, 1995. 67-79.

---

5   See Adrienne Rich's blurb on the back-cover of Marilyn Chin's *The Phoenix Gone, The Terrace Empty.*

Perloff, Marjorie. *The Dance of the Intellect: Studies in the Poetry of the Pound Tradition.* Cambridge: Cambridge UP, 1985.

—. *Poetic License: Essays on Modernist and Postmodernist Lyric.* Evanston, IL: Northwestern UP, 1990.

Rich, Adrienne. Back-Cover Blurb of Marilyn Chin's *The Phoenix Gone, The Terrace Empty.* Minneapolis: Milkweed Editions, 1994.

Tabios, Eileen. "Marilyn Chin's Feminist Muse Addresses Women, 'The Grand Victims of History.'" *Black Lightning: Poetry-In-Progress.* New York: The Asian American Writers' Workshop, 1998. 280-312.

Vendler, Helen. *Soul Says: On Recent Poetry.* Cambridge: The Belknap P of Harvard UP, 1995.

Waley, Arthur. *Three Ways of Thought in Ancient China.* Stanford: Stanford UP, 1995.

Wong, Shelley Sunn. "Unnaming the Same: Theresa Hak Kyung Cha's *Dictée.*" *Writing Self and Nation: A Collection on* DICTEE *by Theresa Hak Kyung Cha.* Eds. Elaine H. Kim and Norma Alarcón. Berkeley: Third Women's P, 1994. 103-43.

Yamamoto, Traise. *Masking Selves, Making Subjects: Japanese American Women, Identity and the Body.* Berkeley: U of California P, 1999.

Undercover Asian:
John Yau and the Politics of Ethnic Self-Identification

Dorothy J. Wang

Film noir, Jasper Johns, Anna May Wong, Eugene Delacroix, Dashiell Ham-mett, X-rated movies, German expressionist writers. Upon encountering the po-etry of John Yau, many readers find their expectations and preconceptions about "Asian American poetry" unsettled. Not only the paucity of the "usual (signify-ing) suspects" but also his experimental style, prolific output (a dozen volumes of poetry, two books of short stories, half a dozen art monographs, countless art reviews and contributions to artist's catalogs) and his choice of career (art critic) give Yau a distinct profile in the field of Asian American poetry, one that chal-lenges our very notion of that category. What to make of an Asian American narrator who asks, "Could I use 'beloved' when I didn't love them [his parents] and hardly knew them?" (*Hawaiian Cowboys* 11). Or an Asian American critic who declares, "[t]he mind's capacity to remember can interfere with the body's ability to experience, [...] this is the polar situation which must be avoided"? (Yau, *The United States* 53).[1] The reader is thrown off by the lack of explicit ethnic markers, the absence of an unproblematic autobiographical "I" and/or a clearly delineated political voice, and the irreverent de-privileging of family and memory.

Because Yau's poetry has not easily fit into any category—cultural national-ist, "ethnic," multiculturalist, L=A=N=G=U=A=G=E, modernist, postmodernist, New York School—and because he tends to relish the role of iconoclast, critics' interpretations of Yau's work often focus narrowly on those angles that reflect their particular interests. For example, those interested in experimental poetry focus on formal innovation while almost completely eliding the cultural and po-litical signification of certain markers, while others interested in Asian American literature often overlook the profound influence of Western avant-garde/experimental writers and artists on his work, especially as it manifests

---

1 Yau is writing on Jasper Johns's work here, but his concurrence with this statement can be verified in numerous other declarations and in his poetry.

itself formally. Criticism that acknowledges the multiple influences on Yau's work and the full range and complexity of his oeuvre is still scant.[2]

His association with John Ashbery, a former teacher who selected Yau's *Corpse and Mirror* (1983) as a National Poetry Series selection, has proven, says Yau, "both beneficial to me and [has] worked against me" (Wang, Interview). The Ashbery connection and the perception that his work did not fit narrow definitions of "ethnic poetry" meant that most mainstream and experimental poetry critics neglected (and continue to neglect) Yau's subject position as an Asian American writer when reviewing his work. Yau himself felt that Richard Elman's 1983 review of *Corpse and Mirror* in *The New York Times Book Review* was "racist" for this oversight (particularly inexplicable given Yau's photo on the back cover) (Wang, Interview). In a 1997 review of his latest poetry volume, *Forbidden Entries*, Marjorie Perloff alludes to his earlier book of poems *Sometimes* (1979) and comments, "[t]here was no indication, at this stage of Yau's career, that the poet is in fact Chinese-American" (39), a baffling statement given another photo on the back cover; three poems entitled "Marco Polo," "From the Chinese," "Chinese Villanelle," and "Their Shadows," an autobiographical poem on his grandparents; and the numerous poems about New York City Chinatown in his first book, *Crossing Canal Street* (a title which provides a clue to the perceptive reader). It was as if an experimental Asian American poet were such a contradiction in terms that (white) critics, both mainstream and "avant-garde," could not register the fact.

Yau speaks of the late 1970s and the 1980s, the period before he became included in anthologies of Asian American writing (in the early 1990s),[3] as one in which "there was literally nobody sympathetic to me. Nobody. They couldn't see what I was getting at because they didn't perceive me as being an Asian American poet" (Wang "Noir of the Self" 61; Interview). At the same time, Asian American writers—many of whom, like the men comprising the editorial collective of *Aiiieeeee!* (Frank Chin et al.), had cultural nationalist leanings—rejected his work, says Yau, because they thought it was "not Asian enough." Thus, "there was this feeling 'Well, who am I related to or identified with? I'm identified with the New York School but I don't feel a part of it'" (Wang, Interview).

---

2   Priscilla Wald's "'Chaos Goes Uncourted': John Yau's Dis(-)Orienting Poetics" does the best job of accounting for both the formal and political significance of Yau's poetry.

3   For example, Yau is included in Ling-chi Wang's and Henry Yiheng Zhao's *Chinese American Poetry: An Anthology* and in the first Asian American anthology published by a major New York publisher, Garrett Hongo's *The Open Boat: Poems From Asian America*, but not in Joseph Bruchac's ground-breaking 1983 anthology *Breaking Silence: An Anthology of Contemporary Asian American Poets*. He does, however, appear in the poetry section of the Winter 1983 (8.4) literary issue of *Bridge*, an Asian American community magazine published in New York City, through the efforts of the poetry co-editors Walter Lew and Kimiko Hahn; Lew remembers consciously trying to solicit more experimental Asian American poetry for that issue (personal e-mail).

Being part of no group—by necessity or by choice—can sometimes look suspiciously like trying to be all things to all groups. The acrimonious (and by now infamous) 1994 exchange between Yau and Eliot Weinberger in the pages of *The American Poetry Review* in 1994 ignited charges and counter-charges of white liberal racism, career opportunism, ethnic posing, disingenuous denials, and self-loathing. The truths of Yau's relationship to his ethnicity and his career trajectory, of course, lie somewhere in between the accusations and denials, truths as complex and contradictory as those constituting the Asian American subject/poet: "*Je* [sic] *un autre*, wrote Rimbaud. I am the Other—the chink, the lazy son, the surrealist, the uptight East Coast Banana, the poet who is too post-modern for the modernists and too modern for the postmodernists. You have your labels, their falsifying categories, but I have words. I—the I writes—will not be spoken for" (Yau, "Neither Us" 40). "Might it not be possible," he asks later in the same essay, "that the self is made up of many selves, incomplete and fragmented?" (41).

As evidenced by the somewhat defensive tone of Yau's list—"the chink, the lazy son," etc.—a Chinese American poet acknowledging these "many selves" on the explicit thematic level, runs the risk of being called, variously, an ethnic opportunist, "militant," self-hater, or a yellow Uncle Tom (Charlie Chan). In his poetry, Yau often chooses to tap into these fragmented multiple selves through formal, rather than solely thematic, means: by use of repetition, circularity, narrative fragmentation, parataxis, interruption, substitution (of letter and/or word), framing issues, and various other techniques.

In this essay, I argue against those who claim that Yau's early poetry showed no evidence of his ethnicity and subject position and that it was only in the last decade that his Asian American identity became manifested in poems explicitly marked by ethnic and racial themes. I also argue against those critics who, though they noted Yau's Chinese ethnicity, did so mainly by characterizing his poetry in Orientalist terms and overlooking the more political implications of his writing. Indeed, Yau's characteristically parodic—some might say cynical—tone in his poems and his analysis of the split self can be said to be directly influenced by his experiences as a minoritized subject who had an ambivalent relationship to both "Asia" and "America" growing up in New England. Those who insist on seeing him as another "experimental" writer because his work taps explicitly into "avant-garde" American and European traditions[4] and overtly foregrounds technique have been oblivious to the effects of his social, political and cultural positioning as an Asian American subject/writer and the manner in which his poetry confronts the issues of assimilation, history, racism, and linguistic displacement–not thematically, straight on, but by means of mirrors.

---

4   Yau shares the "avant-garde" label with a handful of other Asian American poets, such as Mei-mei Berssenbrugge, Theresa Cha, Myung-mi Kim, and Tan Lin (a former student).

But before turning to Yau's early books, I would like to examine more closely the vitriolic debate in which the first explicit charges of Yau's ethnic opportunism were launched. In the July/August 1994 issue of *The American Poetry Review*, Eliot Weinberger accused Yau of "creat[ing] a remarkable new persona for himself: that of the angry outsider 'person of color'" (43).[5] Weinberger was writing in response to Yau's negative review of his 1993 anthology *American Poetry Since 1950: Innovators & Outsiders* in that journal two months earlier. In that piece, "Neither Us Nor Them," Yau criticizes Weinberger for the "logic and didactic reasoning he uses to bring them [the poets] together in a single volume"—namely Weinberger's criteria that the poet be born before the end of World War II and publish work of importance after 1950—primarily because these criteria allow Weinberger, argues Yau, to justify which poets, or which types of poets, to exclude:

> Weinberger's need to construct hierarchies and either/or constructs prevents him from responding to the changing complexity of post-war American poetry, its various traditions.
> *American Poetry Since 1950: Innovators & Outsiders* begins with William Carlos Williams (1883-1963) and ends with Michael Palmer (b.1943). There are thirty-five poets in all, five of whom are women. Denise Levertov (b. 1923) and Susan Howe (b. 1937) are the only women among the nineteen active poets Weinberger has judged important enough to include. Langston Hughes (1902-1967) and Amiri Baraka (Leroi Jones) (b. 1934) are the only African-American poets. As to other *Others*, forget it. (45-46, original italics)

In the Letters section, Weinberger and five of his supporters[6] respond to Yau's accusations by lambasting him for his "nervous breakdown in print," his "rant," "crazed invective," "sick race-mongering," "repellent race-baiting," "idiotic conclusions," and "opportunism" (43-47).[7] To back up his charge that Yau has expediently taken on the "remarkable new persona" of "angry outsider 'person of color,'" Weinberger cites his own multi-cultural credentials and discredits Yau's:

> [Yau] has probably never written a topical social-protest poem in his adult life [...]. I spent years studying Chinese—which John barely speaks and cannot read [...]. John has never, before this, written on any minority writers [...]. This is demagoguery, pure and simple—coming from a man who has never publicly, before this, shown any interest in black writers at all. I will not dignify his scum-bag race-baiting with a point-by-point response, or a defensive white lib-

---

5   Marjorie Perloff echoes this accusation when she writes in her 1997 *Boston Review* review of *Forbidden Entries*: "John Yau has always cultivated the image of Angry Young Man."

6   In the Letters section, there are no letters by Yau's supporters, only letters by Yau rebutting letters by Weinberger and his supporters, Esther Allen, David Hinton, Forrest Gander, Roberto Tejada, and Cecilia Vicuna.

7   The first six accusations are made by Weinberger, the last by Roberto Tejada.

eral list of the things I've written and the publishing projects I've been involved
with [...] (43)

But a "defensive white liberal" list is precisely what Weinberger spends most of
his letter enumerating. The African-American poet and critic Aldon Nielsen
points out, "[Weinberger's] only real response to Yau's central charge is to deny
it" (24). Yau himself makes the same charge ("Mr. Weinberger makes many
points, but he fails to address the primary and simple issue I raised in my essay")
and adds in response to Weinberger's charge of "his new persona": "One's color
is neither something you can put on and take off, like a coat, nor an ideology you
announce one moment and ignore at another" (Letters 44).

The heatedness of the accusations and counter-accusations—of racial opportunism, of veiled white liberal racism—gives some indication that whatever raw
nerves were being touched had less to do with feelings of anger towards the at-
tacker than perhaps feelings (of guilt, insecurity) about oneself. Nevertheless, a
reader might still be left wondering, "So how accurate is Weinberger's charge
that '*John knows he is lying*' (original italics)?" Was Yau, up until the early
nineties, a whitewashed avant-garde poet running with the New York school and
SoHo artists—an "uptight East Coast banana"? Or has he always been, as he
claims, interested in issues of autobiography and racial identity—"I've thought
of myself as a poet who wanted to write about things 'autobiographical' but am
always trying to figure out how to do it" (Wang, "A Noir of the Self" 61)—but
chose to deal with these issues unconventionally?

The truth, of course, lies somewhere in between. One can certainly make the
case that in the first 10 years of his career, Yau *did* seem less than eager to identify with other Asian American writers—whether a result of, as he claims, aesthetic and/or ideological differences or his own feelings of denial/self-hatred
(most likely a combination of those feelings and others). Speaking with Edward
Foster in 1990, Yau admitted to feelings of "anger and self-hatred" as a young
man and having "had trouble accepting who I was or what I was. You know,
being Chinese-American and living in, but not belonging to, this homogeneous
community" (40, 50). Yet, whatever the lack of Yau's public identification as a
Chinese American poet, both Weinberger and Perloff are mistaken when they
imply that ethnic identity has never concerned Yau and that he "took it on" only
late in his career and for purely opportunistic reasons. As the Asian American
critic George Uba says, "His identity formation involves the dissolving of the
more apparent devices of the 'ethnic' but not a denial that such evidences, on
some level, persist" (46).

In various interviews, Yau's own statements about his Chinese American
background and identity are often modulated by the interview's context and who
is doing the questioning. In his interview with the editor of *Talisman: A Journal
of Contemporary Poetry and Poetics*, Edward Foster, who ran a special issue on

Yau (Fall 1990), Yau alludes to his being Chinese American in the following
manner:

> You know, who you are is simply an accident of birth. You know, you're born
> through this thing you didn't decide on, but then you're imprinted in all sorts of
> ways. A Boston Brahmin or a first-generation child of an immigrant. You can
> make a bigger case about that, or you can try to use it without making a giant
> case about it. You know, it doesn't entitle you to anything. It just simply is
> what happened. And I don't want to deal with the accident of my birth as a
> right or entitlement. But I don't want to ignore it either, and so it becomes to
> me an interesting dilemma: how do I deal with it? How do I write about it? (48-
> 49)

In that interview, Yau names writers who influenced him, some of whose poetry
he imitated: Ezra Pound, Harry Matthews, Raymond Roussel, John Gould
Fletcher, H.D., T.E. Hulme, John Ashbery, Clark Coolidge, Michael Palmer,
Barbara Guest, Jack Spicer, Laura Riding, John Weiners, the Beats, Robert
Creeley—predominantly white writers from what *From the Other Side of the
Century*, a recent experimental poetry anthology, dubs "the other side of the
century"—i.e., that "other" "avant-garde" poetic tradition which runs counter to
that posited by *The Norton Anthology of Modern Poetry*. Yau also mentions to
Foster that he was reading Yukio Mishima in high school but does not go into
detail about the significance of this fact. By contrast, in his interview with me in
1993, he told me that, because he was "definitely looking" for Asian American
role models while growing up in Brookline, Massachusetts, he looked to
Mishima and the artist Isamu Noguchi. Also, in his interview with Eileen
Tabios, Yau mentions having been interested, as a child, in the paintings of the
Chinese abstract painter Zao Wou ki, who lived in Paris (382).

   Perhaps the best way to gauge the extent to which Yau's ethnicity and subjectivity as an Asian American poet expresses itself in his work is to examine the
trajectory of his career, particularly the books preceding the appearance of the
clearly ethnically marked Genghis Chan, or what Marjorie Perloff calls, in reviewing *Forbidden Entries*, "more overt representations of racial oppression"
(39)—poems that, not surprisingly, she finds the "least successful." Are there
ways in which ethnicity operates "covertly" in Yau's poems, not unlike the
movements of the undercover Genghis Chan?

   A quick glance at Yau's first seven books—*Crossing Canal Street* (1976);
The Reading of An Ever-Changing Tale (1977); *Sometimes* (1979); *The Sleepless Night of Eugene Delacroix* (1980), a collection of prose pieces; *Notarikon*
(1981), which was subsequently incorporated into *Broken Off by the Music*
(1981); and the 1983 National Poetry Selection *Corpse and Mirror*
(1983)—preceding Genghis Chan's first appearance in *Radiant Silhouette: New
and Selected Work 1974-1988* (1989) reveals that, even from the beginning,
Yau's poems bear the impress of his experiences as an Asian American sub-

ject/poet, though not in the expected formulations. His books yield plenty of contradictory layers—traces of the "self [that] is made up of many selves, incomplete and fragmented" (Yau, "Between the Forest" 41).

Yau's first publication, the chapbook *Crossing Canal Street*, inaugurates the representation of this fragmented self: Canal Street separates Chinatown from SoHo, the art gallery district in Manhattan, functioning as both a literal and a metaphorical marker of two "sites" of Yau's identity (to simplify: white/downtown/artsy and Chinese/Chinese American). Of the 13 poems in the book, seven deal explicitly with Chinese or Chinese American themes, with titles such as "Suggested By A Chinese Woman Eating Alone On Mott Street," "An Old Chinese Gentleman Drops In To See His Cronies In A Coffeeshop (Mott Street)," and "Kuo Min Tang Chinese Nationalist Party." As is evident from the titles, the poems suggest classical Chinese poetry, not only in their content but in their forms too. However, unlike the poems of Marilyn Chin, Yau's do not read as direct imitations of Tu Fu or Li Bai but as imitations of Poundian imitations (filtered through Ernest Fenollosa) of classical Chinese poetry. Indeed, in *Crossing Canal Street*, Yau observes these old Chinese men and women from a Poundian Imagiste perspective that is both distanced and somewhat coy.

In his interview with Edward Foster, Yau said, "Pound's Chinese poems were very, very meaningful to me then. I just read them over and over again. For me, they were about being Chinese, about some kind of identity" (43). This statement acknowledges that for Yau, as for many Asian Americans, the formation of an ethnic identity and perceptions of Asian culture was and is largely determined by white (high and low) culture's refracted depictions.[8] In this light, T.S. Eliot's unironic declaration that, "Pound is the inventor of Chinese poetry for our time" in his introduction to *Ezra Pound: Selected Poems* might be extended to include "inventor of Chinese American poetic subjectivity" for those poets coming of age before the "Yellow Power" movements of the 1960s.

The poems in *Crossing Canal Street*, many of them imitations of haiku and the "pictographic" Chinese style Pound praised so highly, strike one as if they

---

8   I do not want to imply that Asian Americans can have a purely unmediated relationship to Asian culture—as the poetry of Li-Young Lee shows, this fantasy is an impossibility—but simply to emphasize the force with which dominant discourses write the Asian American subject and how what seems a "direct" relation to some essential "Chineseness" is really filtered through multiple scrims. As with Li-Young Lee's and Marilyn Chin's, some reviewers (mis)read Yau's work as descending directly from Chinese poetry—this is the case even with non-mainstream critics, such as those in the experimental journal *Talisman*. For example, David Chaloner writes, "I suspect that the mysterious and potent resistance to complete exposure lies in an inheritance from the more ancient culture of China"; he later adds, "What now appears as an intricate and symbolic manifestation of the writer's past, alluded to in early, more autobiographical work, is the curiously timeless presence of an ancient sensibility" (113). In that same issue of *Talisman*, Kris Hemensley writes in "A Further Note on John Yau": "His writing is as funny as Wang Wei's, Tu Fu's, Li Po's" (118).

could have been written by a white poet, not only because of their Imagiste forms but also their Orientalist references to brocade, pearl and silk ("Suggested By A Waitress In YEE'S") and the chapbook's exotifying preface by Robert Kelly, who refers to Yau as a "far kin" of the "Crimean Tatars" (rumblings of Genghis Khan). At this early stage, one sees little evidence of Yau's characteristic parodic distance from his subject matter. These imitations lack parody's critical edge or what Bakhtin describes as parody's "nature": "transcrib[ing] the values of the parodied style" (75). Yau has yet to learn what he himself admonishes Asian American readers 18 years later: "You are spoken for when you learn to mimic your master's voice, when you accept the limits of his or her poems as if they were your own" ("Between the Forest" 38).

It is perhaps inevitable that a young Chinese American poet would imitate the style of white poets—after all, these are his dominant poetic influences—but what is discomfiting in *Crossing Canal Street* is the distance and disdain—at moments, disgust—with which Yau observes the inhabitants of Chinatown. In his portrayals, Chinese men and women and their body parts are likened to animals and objects: an egg, moon, bird of prey ("Suggested By A Chinese Woman Eating Alone On Mott Street"); sides of meat, pigeons, locusts ("Suggested By Men At The Lunch Counter (Mott St.)"); almond petals, black drops of oil ("The Waiter"); dried fruit ("An Old Chinese Gentleman Drops In To See His Cronies In A Coffeeshop (Mott Street)"; pigeons, squirrels, and vultures ("A Recent Saturday Night").

Perhaps not unintentionally, Yau includes no overt ethnic signifiers in his second book, *The Reading of an Ever-Changing Tale* (hereafter *Reading*), but, again, a close reading reveals the effects of Yau's subject position, though disguised: in a poem title ("The Yellow Window") and in certain lines—"They were impostors / 'But so are you'" ("The Loop" lines 41-42) and "[c]ertain colors got lodged under / the fingernails before their names / came to grace our speech" ("The Reading of an Ever-Changing Tale" 1-3). The voice in *Reading* is more wry, knowing and cynical than that in *Crossing Canal Street*—all of his books to come will include variations of this ironic/parodic voice, one in which the self steps outside of the self and provides commentary on itself: the "I" split into subject and object.

In his next book of poems, *Sometimes*, a more accomplished volume than his previous two (though it includes some poems from the appropriately named *The Reading of an Ever-Changing Tale*), ethnic signifiers are suggested by the section and poem title "Marco Polo," a stray line ("As an ancient Chinese poet wrote...," from "Shimmering Pediment"), and in particular three poems in the last section: "Their Shadows," an autobiographical poem about his Chinese paternal grandfather and English paternal grandmother,[9] and two imitations of classical Chinese poems: "From the Chinese" and "Chinese Villanelle." It is also in *Sometimes* that Yau first publishes his overtly "experimental" combinatory poems (with puns, letter- and word- substitutions)—what Edward Foster calls "word salad" poems—which are by now, a trademark of his poetry. Here is "Ten Songs" in its entirety:

> Trying to find a way to say something that would make it
>   make its sense
> Trying to find a way to weigh something that would make
>   its own lense
> Finding it trying to say something they would
>   make a lense of
> Finding the saying of something weighing the sense
>   of it trying
> Making the trying something that would find its sense
> Sensing the making trying to find something it says
> Saying the finding is there to find is making it make sense
> Making it make sense is finding something to say
> Something to say is finding a lense to sense the making
> Something making the making something something else

In the interview with Foster, Yau explains that he started writing these types of poems in the mid-seventies, having been directly influenced by the artist Richard Artschwager's drawings (and indirectly influenced by the OULIPO writers Raymond Roussel and Harry Matthews): "At a certain point I realized that my poems were so dependent on the visual image that I wanted to react against that [...]. And so I thought, why not just use words as physical things in some way, literally cut them up and play around with them" (43-44). The form of this poem embodies the act of the poet's "[t]rying to find a way to say something that would make it make its sense" (line 1). That Yau does not say, "something that would make sense," but instead, "something that would make *its* sense" (emphasis added) suggests that it is the "say[ing] something"—i.e., language or words themselves—that make the sense, not the "content" of the intended idea. And these words have a materiality ("Trying to find a way to weigh something"); the poem gives the sense that individual words have been cut out and re-glued in different sentences. At the same time, the sentences do not become total nonsense: syntax is kept intact, though semantic meaning and grammar have been torqued.[10] The word "lense" suggests that Yau has not left the visual altogether (after all, it is a visual artist's work who inspires him), but it is now the mind's

---

9   Yau frequently mentions his grandmother's having been English so as to emphasize the fact that he is one-quarter English (in my personal interview with him and in Tabios' and Foster's interviews as well).
10   Thanks to Craig Dworkin for this observation.

"lense"—language—that primarily concerns him, not the image: in other words, *how* one sees more than *what* one sees. The poem also implicitly mocks conventional "logical" narrative approaches to "find[ing] a way to say something" that would "make sense" and the assumption that words arranged in an orderly linear manner actually do make sense.

Like his two later volumes of prose, *Hawaiian Cowboys* (1995) and *My Symptoms* (1998), his fourth book, *The Sleepless Night of Eugene Delacroix* (1980), contains pieces that are much more explicitly autobiographical than his poems. Yau's prose pieces (stories and prose poems) have a fluidity and unflinching autobiographical honesty that not infrequently make them more compelling than his rule-constrained or self-consciously "postmodern" poetry. Two pieces in *Sleepless Night* offer explicit portraits of his parents: "Electric Drills" (23-25) and "Toy Trucks and Fried Rice" (33-36); the latter, a description of the "Chinese Benevolent Association's Annual Christmas Party," provides one of the most explicit portrayals of the poet-speaker's parents, their background, and the poet-speaker's relationship to his ethnicity: "He had come to the party with his parents. He had been told ever since he could remember that he was Chinese [...]. He sat in a metal folding chair and listened to a language neither he nor his parents could understand" (34, 36).[11]

But in these autobiographical sketches, Yau expresses no emotional attachment to his parents. Unlike Li-Young Lee, Yau has an aversion to sentiment and to the romanticization of memory, whose trope is metaphor. Nor does he believe that one can have direct access to the past. Writing in his book on Jasper Johns, *The United States of Jasper Johns*, Yau asks, "[H]ow can one be a painter whose yearning for knowledge isn't satisfied by evoking the unmediated, insisting on the literal, or believing in metaphor?" (3).A few pages later, he writes that "looking supersedes memory and an engagement with reality can begin [...] memory and habit prevent us from looking at the world" (7).[12]

In *Broken Off by the Music*, his sixth book, Yau's style becomes much more experimental. Many of the poems feel surreal. The middle section, "Late Night Movies," comprises his first series of punning letter- and word-substitution/combination poems begun in *Sometimes*; this four-poem series prefigures in theme and style his later Genghis Chan and "Hollywood Asians" series. *Broken Off by the Music* contains virtually no signs of ethnicity (except in the title of one poem, "Shanghai Shenanigans"), leading one to conjecture that, at this stage in Yau's career, there is an inverse correlation between formal experimentation and his ability to write autobiographically about his family and

---

11   "The people at the party [...] spoke Cantonese and were, according to his mother, only farmers anyway," writes Yau; the speaker-poet's parents spoke Shanghainese and Mandarin. See Priscilla Wald's reading of this story in "Chaos Goes Uncourted: John Yau's Dis(-)Orienting Poetics" (142-45).

12   One could question what Yau means by "reality," a word, like "actual" and "nature," that he uses frequently in the Johns book.

ethnicity. It is as if joining this avant-garde "camp"—one from which most minority poets were or felt alienated—precluded one from talking about ethnicity. One is reminded of Yau's recollection of when he first began to encounter a New York art world: "I remember I started reading *Art in America, Artforum,* and *Art News* when I was in Boston University. And I remember thinking when I was young that I could never write in *Artforum* because I didn't understand what anybody said in that magazine. It seemed to be speaking to an incredibly intelligent audience, and I wasn't part of it" (Foster 42). What is unspoken but implied is that this avant-garde literary and art "in-circle" is not only "incredibly intelligent" but also coded white and middle-class; these are coteries not likely to consider a son of immigrants for membership. Yau's awareness of this exclusivity is made explicit when he repeatedly emphasizes Andy Warhol's outsider son-of-immigrants status in his book *In the Realm of Appearances: The Art of Andy Warhol*:

> Whereas by the 1960s Wyeth's family was considered an American institution, and was celebrated in the press, Warhol's family were impoverished immigrants. His father was a coal miner and his mother a housewife; neither of them ever spoke English with ease. (4)

> In each phase of his career Warhol was an assimilationist, someone who did what he thought would get him accepted by those he believed were more successful or, if not that, more wealthy and more powerful than he. He was good at targeting his market. He was someone who couldn't forget that he was the son of immigrants and had to prove himself. This need was the job he never knew how to leave. (64)

> [...] he hated the fact that he was an outsider. (77)

> The youngest son of a poor working-class family, Warhol desperately wanted to gain admittance to bourgeois society. (97)

> The language Warhol would in his lifetime master, the one his parents never learned to express, is one that tries to disguise its rage and obsequiousness. It is the language of someone who is desperate to belong. (126)

Yau's insistence on the fact of Warhol's immigrant background, one that other critics tend to gloss over, reveals the extent to which—despite his criticisms of Warhol—Yau intimately understands Warhol's outsider status and desire to belong. In other words, even in art criticism that reveals nothing overtly "ethnic" or autobiographical, Yau's experiences and position as an ethnically marked subject exert a subterranean pressure.

Yau hit the poetry big leagues in 1983, when his *Corpse and Mirror* was chosen by John Ashbery as a National Poetry Series selection and published by a major publisher, Holt, Rinehart and Winston. On the back cover, a photo of

black-clad Yau sitting next to an African primitive sculpture appears beside a
bio blurb informing the reader that Yau's "art reviews and essays have been
published in *Art in America, Artforum, Artsmagazine, Portfolio,* and *Vogue.*" He
had arrived—or so it seemed. *Corpse and Mirror,* a mixture of poetry and prose
pieces, includes selections from three previous volumes (*The Reading of an
Ever-Changing Tale, Notarikon,* and *Broken Off by the Music*) and shows Yau's
talents to their advantage.

   There is a maturity and haunting seriousness to the writing in *Corpse and
Mirror*—images of death and disembodiment float above desolate de Chirico-
like landscapes suspended in a surreal (and unreal) sense of time; the speaker is
often figured as an outsider, solitary. *Corpse and Mirror* maintains a balance
between pieces that address autobiography and questions of ethnicity directly
and those that treat Yau's experiences as an Asian American subject in more
transmuted form. For example, "Missing Pages," a fable-like tale about a tourist
island whose "jeweled towers" rise from the bay, ends with a local host explaining to the tourists how the legend of the towers comes about:

> Anyone can add whatever they like to the story, or take some chunk of it away,
> if in their opinion, it impedes the narrative flow. At the beginning of summer
> (or the tourist season) the story, by then refined into its smoothest chapters, is
> written down by the mayor. A vote is taken by the council. If it passes approval,
> which it always does after a few revisions are made, the story is sealed away in
> a vault.
>   In the fall, when school begins, the children of the island are taught the story
> in their classes. It becomes the basis for the entire curriculum: literature,
> mathematics, even biology and the other natural sciences. In this way the chil-
> dren learn what must be forgotten, if they are to continue sleeping in their
> whitewashed cottages by the sea. (34)

This parable about an "official" history crafted to have a "narrative flow," made
to seem inevitable and natural, and learned by schoolchildren resonates with
Yau's own experiences growing up as a Chinese American in Boston and being
taught a hegemonic version of history. In an interview, he recalls that during his
teen years, while looking for Asian American role models, he realized that:

> information wasn't free in this country [...]. These people are withholding in-
> formation. And for me—I probably took it fairly personally—I just felt like
> when you're growing up, you want to find role models, and if this society de-
> prives you or prevents you from identifying with somebody, then they're actu-
> ally operating under a rubric that says, "These things don't matter." But the fact
> is, they *do* matter. They're using that rubric of universality, but they're incredi-
> bly racist. (Wang, Interview)

This intermeshing of personal and social histories was also brought home to Yau
as a child when his father would read to him "over and over and over" stories

about Native Americans and tell him that "nobody in America was truly American except for the Indians." His father would say, "'We're all foreigners. Don't
believe those people—they don't know anything'"—statements which, laughs
Yau, "definitely did not help when I took American history classes" (Wang, Interview).[13]

The end of "Missing Pages" lends itself to ambiguous and contradictory interpretations: the confusion comes with the placement of the conditional phrase
"if they are to continue sleeping in their whitewashed cottages" right after the
word "forgotten." The normal reading of the syntax suggests that, in order to
keep sleeping peacefully in their "whitewashed" (or Americanized) homes, the
children must forget the official version—a reading which would seem to contradict the logic of what is demanded (and happens) under assimilation. An al-
ternate reading of the parable would be that the legends taught by the locals are
what must be forgotten when the children encounter white tourists—in other
words, that Asian Americans might be taught one version of history at home
(e.g., that of Yau's father) and in their ethnic communities but that this version
must be forgotten in the wider (white) world. The only problem with this second
reading is that it elides the fable's depiction of the legend's institutionalization
("In the fall, when school begins, the children of the island are taught the story in
their classes.")

A third reading that would account for these apparent contradictions might
go like this: the phrase "what must be forgotten" signals a shift in tonal register
from the rest of the sentence–more specifically, an authorial intrusion. This second voice is an example of what Bakhtin calls a "hybrid construction": "an utterance that belongs, by its grammatical (syntactic) and compositional markers,
to a single speaker, but that actually contains mixed within it two utterances, two
speech manners, two styles, two 'languages,' two semantic and axiological belief systems" (304). In this reading, yes, the children must learn these stories in
order to continue sleeping in their whitewashed cottages, but, as the more pre-
scient author reminds us (in a voice that ruptures the univocal fabric of the fable's language), it is crucial that these stories "be forgotten." Here, "must" is
read as an imperative, a warning to those who might become sucked in and assimilated.

Yau writes constantly of the choice facing minority writers and artists: "The
bind every hybrid American artist must deal with is this: Should he or she investigate the constantly changing polymorphous conditions affecting identity, tradition, and reality? Or should he or she choose to assimilate into the mainstream
art world by focusing on the approved aesthetic issues?" ("Please Wait" 59).
Likewise, the children when they grow up must make a similar choice. As a
whole, "Missing Pages" parodies legends and fables that purport to teach a les-

---

13 Yau writes of his father's telling him this alternative version of history in "Toy Trucks and
    Fried Rice" (*Radiant Silhouette* 69).

son. He rips off the ideological mask to show that the bases of these legends are not founded in "dream[s] from heaven" but made by men "in daylight and desire."

In the last two sections of *Corpse and Mirror* ("The Lost Colony" and "Carp and Goldfish"), the markers of "Chineseness" become increasingly overt. In Section V, "The Lost Colony," three previously published poems—"Chinese Villanelle," "Three Poems for Li Shang-yin," and "Shanghai Shenanigans"—allude in their tone and imagery to classical Chinese poetry. There is nothing explicitly autobiographical here though the section's title and the poems' titles hint at something more than passing interest in things Chinese. But in Section VI, "Carp and Goldfish," Yau takes up once more the topic of his parents and his childhood, begun in "Electric Drills" and "Toy Trucks and Fried Rice" (*Sleepless Night*), in "Two Kinds of Story-Telling," "After the War (I)," "After the War (II)," "After the War (III)," "After the War (IV)," "Two Kinds of Language," and "Carp and Goldfish." Perhaps it is not coincidental that these pieces are some of Yau's most powerful—it is as if, freed from the a-historical non-material atmosphere of the volume's other poems, he taps into a fluency.

Yau explains how he came to write the poem "Carp and Goldfish," whose title he "heard in my head as a pun on 'Corpse and Mirror'":

> [T]his pun encouraged me to think of a way out of the "Corpse and Mirror" poems, because I didn't like the time in those poems, the mythical time—it seemed too removed or too removed to be actual. And I had this memory of something that happened to me as a child that I [...] was trying to figure out a way to write about, and I kept circling it [...]. And so one thing led to another, and I thought, could I make a diptych out of this piece of prose? Could I get an echo going back and forth between two narratives? [...]. I didn't want to focus on one event but to bounce it off something else without diminishing it [...]. Maybe I was reacting against, you know, having grown up and having read Robert Lowell and disliking the subjective excesses of his work. So the question became, how do you use autobiography [...]? (Foster 45)

To turn to the autobiographical is not, in Yau's case, to turn confessional or even personal. He struggles to find a way to deal with autobiographical material without either resorting to prescribed autobiographical narrative modes or completely erasing the subject. His description of the work of Jasper Johns, one of his favorite artists, could aptly be applied to his own: "Johns makes a sculpture that is neither an expression of the 'I' nor a pure work of art" (*In the Realm of Appearances* 40).

The privilege of writing self-indulgently about one's personal problems assumes, Yau implies, that one's own experience is interesting or generalizable in some way—a privilege denied to writers of color in this country: "[A]lmost from the beginning I wanted to get away from that 'I.' It was something I associated with Robert Lowell and Sylvia Plath: the 'I' as victim. There seemed to be something wrong with it, something privileged [...]. O'Hara believed his life was immensely interesting [...]. But I didn't see my life as that immensely interesting" (Tabios 386). In his 1994 essay "Between the Forest and the Trees," Yau asks, "Might not this I be a false mirror?" (38). Mirrors are a recurrent image in Yau's work–but his mirrors do not reflect clearly and straightforwardly; they distort and refract the subject in much the same way that language does.

"Carp and Goldfish" is a diptych comprised of two counterpointed sections. The first tells a fable-like story of a five-year prince in old China, who watches the carp in a garden pond while the narrator presages the fall of the kingdom and the coming of "succeeding reigns of tyrants." The tone of the piece is vaguely "Chinese"—thus, parodic of moralizing Chinese parables or, more likely, of Orientalist imitations/parodies of Chinese parables (for example, in its references to "clouds [that] turn into dragons," the "moon trembl[ing] against the sky"). The piece ends, "Meanwhile, the carp burrow into a book by someone whose ability to remember facts circumscribes his desire to tell stories" (84).

The other half of the diptych is an autobiographical account of a young boy's decision, while his father sleeps nearby, to make his new goldfish feel "comfortable in their new home" by adding salt to their bowl—an act which, of course, kills them. Goldfish are native to China, where they were first domesticated centuries ago from the wild form, a carplike fish.[14] For "Americanized" Chinese Americans, as for the "domesticated" goldfish, this notion of return is "both an impossibility and a repressive illusion" (Foster 39). One reason the boy is able to arrogate to himself the task of doing what is best for the fish is that he distances himself from them, viewing them as utterly "alien and indifferent" ("he had not been able to find any that he liked.").

Yau's concern with the autobiographical in *Corpse and Mirror* coincides with, and may have been influenced by a similar turn, in the career of Jasper Johns (the title "Corpse and Mirror" comes from one of Johns' diptychs). In *The United States of Jasper Johns*, Yau writes about Johns' *Racing Thoughts* paintings of 1983 and 1984: "Since Johns has spent much of his career deliberately refusing to make any overt autobiographical references, the changes he made in the early 1980s must be regarded as significant [...]. However, the subject was the artist's life rather than personal memories. After all, memory, as Johns's *Flag* made clear, is not to be trusted; it interferes with one's experience of reality" (103). Yau also uses materials from his own life without turning them into "personal memories": at no point does he attempt to retroactively interpret or comment sentimentally on these childhood incidents. Like his hero Johns, who "knew that he could not succumb to the power of memory and personal associations, that he had to be as rigorous in his examination of his thoughts as he was of the flag" (90), Yau refuses nostalgia: he too must "ensure that any reference

---

14 A real goldfish, however, "reverts to this [carp] type when it escapes from domestication and has been known to hybridize with the carp" (*Columbia Encyclopedia* 1103).

to the past is connected to the present [...]. Otherwise, the paintings will seem nostalgic in their intent" (107). In this respect, Yau and Li-Young Lee are similar—"I *don't feel nostalgic because I don't know what to feel nostalgic for*," says Lee (quoted in Moyers 258)—though Lee, unlike Yau, does not mistrust sentiment as well.

Yau also borrows from Johns the idea of the diptych, which Yau goes on to use in several poems. This "split" form not only allows two ways of telling a story but also materially embodies the "double consciousness" or double perspective of the Chinese American poet. It allows Yau to juxtapose—*without synthesizing*—various ways of being and seeing: the historical and the personal, the past and the present, the mythic and the prosaic, the "Chinese" and the "American." At the same time, a tenuous connection is suggested, like the hinge joining two panels of a painted diptych. The two sides "mirror" each other but with a difference.

Likewise, the carp and the goldfish are kin (biologically and symbolically; not coincidentally, both figure as symbols of prosperity in Chinese culture), but, with the passage of time and dissimilar environments, they become very different. In trying to identify with the goldfish, the boy has an amniotic memory of salt water: "He remembered the stinging taste of the sea as they knocked him over, his mother beside him so he would not be afraid" (85). But this misguided memory of "home" (goldfish are freshwater fish) that the boy imposes onto the fish—an act of identification that erases the singularity of the fish, much in the same way that assimilation is posited on likeness, not difference—is as erroneous and impossible as a memory of China as "home" would be for a Chinese American. For the goldfish, of course, the error proves to be fatal.

The diptych form also allows the two story "panels" to comment on one another meta-textually: "Meanwhile, the carp burrows into a book by someone whose ability to remember facts circumscribes his desire to tell stories" (84). The two halves of the diptych in effect parody the word of the other by presenting something similar but not quite. The chance operations of memory, the sense of the foldedness of time and the materiality of writing—the carp "burrow[ing]" into the book—find parallel in the Surrealist game of *cadavre exquis* ("exquisite corpse"), in which sentences would be produced by players taking turns writing a word on a piece of paper, folding the sheet to conceal the word, and passing the paper on to the next player.[15]

In two other diptychs, "Two Kinds of Story-Telling" (72) and "Two Kinds of Language"—themselves pieces that mirror and refract one another—Yau provides explicitly autobiographical details about his mother and father, respectively. In "Two Kinds of Story-Telling," the mother figure is characterized in the

---

15 A major reason Yau was drawn to Surrealism, a movement he labels "politically and socially radical," is that, in his opinion, "[a]mong modernist movements, surrealism is the only one who openly accepted people of color" (Tabios 390).

first half as telling fairy tales about her past in China and in the second, symbolic narratives of change about her life in America:

> Her childhood was composed of fairy tales. The places she described existed in a world accessible only to the words: "Once upon a time." China was a kind of Eden she could never return to, and he [the narrator] would never know, except by hearsay. [...]. What was awful about the past is mentioned only to reveal how the present is better, and how the future will be better still [...]. The inspiration behind them [such symbolic narratives] is the passage of the *Mayflower* to the New World [...]. She was lulled into believing these narratives of change were a necessary accomplishment. What was curious about these attempts was she remembered almost nothing of American history. In her mind the names—*Mayflower, Pilgrim,* and *Plymouth Rock*—were associated with businesses; one on a moving van, the other two in insurance ads. (72)

In these passages, one hears resonances with "Missing Pages" (fairy tales and symbolic narratives, the forgetting of actual history) and "Carp and Goldfish" (the impossibility of return). The first half of "Two Kind of Story-Telling" parodies the fairy tale form and its supposed "happily ever after" endings and neat lessons by resolutely not providing a happy ending or lesson. The second half parodies moralistic tales (it begins "People who think they are no longer imprisoned by their poverty always try to glamorize the past") by not providing a pat moral but, instead, ending ambiguously: an ironic, comic commentary on what American myths really come down to.

In the first half of "Two Kinds of Language," a boy listens to

> his parents talking the language they brought from China. Often he began squirming, trying to understand what was being said amidst the smells and sounds of cooking. Usually they began talking this way when they didn't want him to understand what was being discussed. Sometimes it was him. He couldn't always tell. If he listened hard enough, what he thought he understood was the intonation and the voice, rather than what was being said. (73)

Again, language is understood as materially located—"amidst the smells and sounds of cooking"—and as a code the Chinese American son cannot decipher. What is important is not so much the content of words ("what was being said") but how they are being spoken ("the intonation and voice"), just as in Yau's poems, "form" decisively determines the reception of "content."

In the second half of "Two Kinds of Language," a now-adult son sits with his parents in a silent car driving on the back roads of North Carolina:

> Neither of them spoke, as song after song [from the radio] filled the car [...]. All the songs seemed to tell a similar story, and yet the words and music never quite seemed to fit together [...]. Inside the car it felt the same to him as it did before, when he was a child.

>   In the other room someone was speaking a language he could barely under-
>   stand. (82)

Silence and mis-communication characterize the Chinese American family, surrounded by the volubleness of American songs. For Yau, "communication occurs with many layers and is always on the brink of not arriving, not being wel-
comed" (Tabios 387). And yet, even in the supposedly "normal" American cultural transmissions, there is a split between signifier and signified: "the words
and the music never quite seemed to fit together." Songs played on the radio
have as an assumption shared popular culture—here, American and mainstream.
There are "repertoires of favorite tunes" ("Missing Pages" 33) that get played
over and over again, (re-)writing the minority subject into being. Frank Chin
captures the power of the radio, what Yau calls "an electric heart," in his short
story "Sons of Chan," when the Chinese American actor who plays Charlie
Chan's son recalls radio shows and hit songs from his childhood:

>   The electricity of a thousand old radio shows loud with the voices of dead stars
>   shuddered in my antenna bone from pole to pole, like ancestors, put my blood
>   and me on like clothing, kept me company [...].
>   *A fiery horse with the speed of light, a cloud of dust and a hearty HI YO SILVER.
>   I know many things for I walk by night. I have seen the men and women who
>   have dared step into the shadows. Listen! [...] while traveling in the Orient I
>   learned the mysterious power to cloud men's minds.* (*Chinaman Pacific* 154-
>   55, original italics)

>   My flesh throbs from the beat of every radio show I'd ever heard inside out
>   pole to pole blasting again. (157)

>   Even now I seem a creature out of an old hit tune. (161)

The hybrid conqueror/detective figure[16] of Genghis Chan is born as a hybrid out
of such popular genres. As Bakhtin writes, "The ideological becoming of a human being [...] is the process of selectively assimilating the words of others"
(341), though in the case of Asian Americans, it is they who are assimilated by
others.
    As can be seen from the above readings of various poems in Yau's seven
books preceding the appearance of the overtly "ethnic" Genghis Chan, even
those poems and passages unmarked by explicit (autobiographical) references to
ethnicity and self manifest the effect of Yau's history and subject position as a
Chinese American poet. While Yau's deconstructing of a traditional lyric
"I"—"the single modulating voice that names itself and others in an easily con-
sumable narrative—writing in a language that is transparent, a window overlooking a world we all have in common" ("Between the Forest" 40)—has been

---

16   See Brian Kim Stefans.

cast by some white critics as generic postmodern erasure of the subject, Yau makes clear, in the interview with the Asian American Writers' Workshop's Eileen Tabios, that this desire to get away from a certain confessional autobiographical "I" had much to do with growing up Chinese American:

> Maybe it's part of being Asian American, that is, that my family spent hours talking about the importance of family versus the individual [...]. My family was dysfunctional, traumatized by the Second World War and by having to emigrate to American [sic] in 1949, penniless and largely without friends. They had to start over, but they could not let go of the past, about which they were unrealistic. So I didn't believe in the family, but I also didn't believe in the "I"—particularly the "I" as victim. (Tabios 386)

Unlike Weinberger, who from his unacknowledged (white liberal) position of privilege can uncritically declare, "I believe that, in this society, all poets are Others" ("Letter" 43), Yau sees that social and ethnic context of his family upbringing, as much as the eccentricities particular to any family, "shows up in my poetry as me being slightly disenfranchised, isolated, trying to communicate, and thinking communication is largely impossible" (Tabios 387).

Like Ashbery, O'Hara, and Weiners, poets he admires, "who were gay but used an 'I' that's not necessarily gay" (Tabios 384), Yau has chosen to express his subjectivity in a manner that neither denies subjectivity nor renders it solipsistic. His interest in art also helped him to "shift it [the 'I'] to a different plane": "I think of abstract expressionism where the 'I' is the subject versus minimalism where the 'I' is the object. Is there an 'I' that is both object and subject, an 'I' seen in different profiles?" Yau asks (Tabios 384-85).

From his first book, John Yau has, knowingly or not, explored the (self-) delusions and delirium, the perils and pleasures, of crossing an internalized Canal Street, and his entire oeuvre—with its interest in the divided subject, estrangement from language and family, the undercover self—while an ever-changing tale, has been undergirded by the immutable fact that, in his words, "[o]ne's color is neither something you can put on and take off, like a coat, nor an ideology you announce one moment and ignore at another" (Letter to *American Poetry Review* 44).

Works Cited

Bakhtin, M.M. *The Dialogic Imagination.* Ed. Michael Holquist. Trans. Carly Emerson and Michael Holquist. Austin: U of Texas P, 1981.

Bruchac, Joseph, ed. *Breaking Silence: An Anthology of Contemporary Asian American Poets.* Greenfield Center, NY: The Greenfield Review P, 1983.

Chaloner, David. "On John Yau." *Talisman: A Journal of Contemporary Poetry and Poetics* 5 (Fall 1990): 113-14.

Chin, Frank. *The Chinaman Pacific and Frisco R.R. Co.* Minneapolis: Coffee House P, 1988.

—, et al, eds. *Aiiieeeee!: An Anthology of Asian American Writers.* 1974. 1983. New York: Mentor, 1991.

The Columbia Encyclopedia, 5th ed. Eds. Barbara A. Chernow and George A. Vallesi. New York: Columbia UP. 1993.

Eliot, T.S. "Introduction." *Ezra Pound: Selected Poems.* London: Faber and Faber, 1928.

Elman, Richard. "Three American Poets (Review of *Corpse and Mirror*)." *New York Times Book Review* (September 18, 1983): 36.

Foster, Edward. "An Interview with John Yau." *Talisman: A Journal of Contemporary Poetry and Poetics* 5 (Fall 1990): 31-50.

Hemensley, Kris. "A Further Note on John Yau." *Talisman: A Journal of Contemporary Poetry and Poetics* 5 (Fall 1990): 118 .

Hongo, Garrett, ed. *The Open Boat: Poems from Asian America.* New York: Anchor Books, 1993.

Messerli, Douglas, ed. *The Other Side of the Century: A New American Poetry 1960-1990.* Los Angeles: Sun and Moon P, 1994.

Moyers, Bill. *The Language of Life: A Festival of Poets.* Ed. James Haba. New York: Doubleday, 1995.

Nielsen, Aldon. *Blank Chant: Languages of African-American Postmodernism.* Cambridge: Cambridge UP, 1997.

Perloff, Marjorie. Rev. of *Forbidden Entries. Boston Review* (Summer 1997): 39.

Stefans, Brian Kim. "Private Eye." Rev. of *Edificio Sayonara* by John Yau. *A. Magazine* 2.3 (1993): 60-61.

Tabios, Eileen. "Approximating Midnight: A Conversation with John Yau." *Black Lightning: Poetry-in-Progress.* Ed. Eileen Tabios. New York: The Asian American Writers Workshop, 1998. 379-402.

Uba, George. "Versions of Identity in Post-Activist Asian American Poetry. *Reading the Literatures of Asian America.* Eds. Shirley Geok-lin Lim and Amy Ling. Philadelphia: Temple UP, 1992. 33-48.

Wald, Priscilla. "'Chaos Goes Uncourted': John Yau's Dis(-)Orienting Poetics." *Cohesion and Dissent in America.* Eds. Carol Colatrella and Joseph Alkana. Albany: State U of New York P, 1994. 133-58.

Walter, Lew. *"A New Decade of Singular Poetry." Bridge: Asian American Perspectives* ("Literary Issue") 8.4 (Winter 1983)**.**

—. Email. July 21st, 1998.

Wang, Dorothy. "Noir of the Self: A Talk with John Yau." *A. Magazine* 2.3 (1993): 61.

Wang, Dorothy. Personal Interview with John Yau. New York City, May 13, 1993.

Wang, Ling-chi and Henry Yiheng Zhao, eds. *Chinese American Poetry: An Anthology*. Santa Barbara: Asian American Voices, 1991.

Weinberger, Eliot. "Letter to the Editor." *American Poetry Review* (July-August 1994): 43.

—, ed. *American Poetry Since 1950: Innovators and Outsiders*. New York: Marsilio Publishers, 1993.

Yau, John. "Between the Forest and Its Trees." *Amerasia Journal* 20.3 (1994): 37-43.

—. *Broken Off by the Music*. Providence: Burning Deck, 1981.

—. *Corpse and Mirror*. New York: Holt, Rinehart and Winston, 1983.

—. *Crossing Canal Street*. Binghamton, NY: The Bellevue P, 1976.

—. *Forbidden Entries*. Santa Rosa, CA: Black Sparrow P, 1996.

—. *Hawaiian Cowboys*. Santa Rosa CA: Black Sparrow P, 1995.

—. *In the Realm of Appearances: The Art of Andy Warhol*. Hopewell, NJ: The Ecco P, 1993.

—. Letters to the Editor. *American Poetry Review* (July-Aug. 1994): 44-47.

—. *My Symptoms*. Santa Rosa, CA: Black Sparrow P, 1998.

—. "Neither Us Nor Them (Review of *American Poetry Since 1950: Innovators and Outsiders*)." *American Poetry Review* (March-April 1994): 45-54.

—. "Please Wait by the Coatroom: Wifredo Lam in the Museum of Modern Art." *Arts Magazine* 63.4 (Dec. 1988): 59. Revised version published as "Please Wait By the Coatroom," *Out There: Marginalization and Contemporary Cultures*. Eds. Russell Ferguson, Martha Gever, Trinh T. Minh-ha, Cornel West. Cambridge: MIT P, 1990. 132-39.

—. *Radiant Silhouette: New and Selected Work 1974-1988*. Santa Rosa, CA: Black Sparrow P, 1989.

—. *The Reading of an Ever-Changing Tale*. Clinton, NY: Nobodaddy P, 1977.

—. *The Sleepless Night of Eugene Delacroix*. Brooklyn: Release P, 1980.

—. *Sometimes*. New York: The Sheep Meadow P, 1979.

—. *The United States of Jasper Johns*. Cambridge: Zoland Books, 1996.

The Way a Calendar Dissolves:
A Refugee's Sense of Time in the Work of Li-Young Lee[1]

Johnny Lorenz

Facing the past from the vantage point of Walter Benjamin's angel of history, we are witness to "one single catastrophe which keeps piling wreckage upon wreckage" (257). In his autobiographical work *The Winged Seed*, Li-Young Lee echoes the angel's sad assessment:

> Entire days, even years, stand like ruins which permit no clue as to what once stood, and to try to enter those precincts is to cast myself down unlit avenues, where here half of a face appears, and there a voice comes out of a mouth, and up ahead the living and the dead are eating impossibly at the same table. It's mathematical, distance and time add up to shadow. (88)

The shadow does not extend back in time, but towards us. The daunting length of this shadow provokes Lee's assertion: "It has been late a long time" (97). This history of ruins—of wreckage and absences—informs Lee's preoccupation with ancestry and identity-formation. Benjamin's angel is doomed to look backward, but his fate suggests a false dilemma; the tragedy of this angel is not simply that he is trapped in his backward-looking gaze and cannot see what lies ahead but rather that his existence is defined by a split between two incommensurable ways of looking.

If distance and time add up to shadow, Lee's work nevertheless encourages an imaginative shift away from this calculation of loss. In his attempt to create meaning among the ruins, Lee reconstructs the past—through language and memory—in order to transform these ruins into the haunted structures of a living poetry. Benjamin sought to undermine his angel and proposed an approach to history that would "fight for the oppressed past" by "blast[ing] a specific area out of the homogenous course of history—blasting a specific life out of the era or a specific work out of the lifework" (262-63). William Carlos Williams identified the unassuming past tense—the *was*—as the problem of history. He says

---

1   While the title of this essay arises from my reading of Lee's treatment of dislocation and haunting, I am reminded of Richard Hugo's poem, "The Way a Ghost Dissolves," the title of which lingered in the backroom of my imagination.

of History, "It is concerned only with the one thing: to say everything is dead" (188). Lee's work—full of echoes, heavy with ritual, stitched with the broken threads of memory—creates intimacies across chronological distances. History is more than the wreckage that sits across vast and discrete temporal distances. The ghosts that we discover in Lee's books give evidence of the past's refusal to keep still, to remain wreckage. And the shadows, the missing pieces, the vacancies—these inform the beautiful, enduring and damaged frameworks of our haunted memories.

A face—its architecture of skin and bone—is a palimpsest of ancestry; it is a complicated repetition, a reconstruction of faces, faces we have known and faces unfamiliar. Our faces are, in a sense, versions of a text, but versions that suggest the impossibility of exact origins:

> my face my mother's face.
> My hair is also hers.
> She inherited it from the horses
> who recovered it from the night. (*Rose* 39)

In these lines, Lee reads his own face as a recurrence, and he re-imagines the shadowy ruins of origin through a private myth-making: his ancestors are horses; his black hair comes from the night sky. While a face reproduces itself, never exactly, as a family inheritance, it is also the returning mark and cause of otherness. When Lee's persona in "The Cleaving" describes the local butcher, he suggests a mirroring. Lee begins the poem with a description of the butcher's face, a reflected image: "this man with my face" (*City* 77); he also ends the poem with this reflection: "This immigrant, this man with my own face" (87). And while one might argue that a face is not sufficient material with which to build a community, a face works nevertheless as a sign, a sign of shared dislocations and re-locations, a sign of probable empathy. This design that is not of our own making, this face that we discover in mirrors and photographs, suggests, too, our own helplessness and the limits of our power, for our faces are circulating texts that others read and to which they assign their own meanings, meanings generated with the interpretative tools of desire, resentment, recognition, or racist reductions. The Native American poet James Welch, in his poem "Plea to Those Who Matter," reveals with anger and painful irony the degree to which members of American minority groups are forced to look at themselves through a removed and oppressive gaze:

> See my nose? I smash it
> straight for you. These teeth? I scrub my teeth
> away with stones. I know you help me now I matter. (23)

This self-directed violence is motivated by a mock desire, perhaps even a sincere desire, to refashion a face, but the realization of that desire is impossible. Responding to an unimaginative and unjust hermeneutics of race, the speaker cannot change his audience so he dreams of changing the structure of his face. In Lee's "The Cleaving," the poem offers similar irony; once again the center of a face, the nose, receives the brunt of a violent gaze—and once again this gaze is transformed into an ironic, self-directed disgust:

> Brothers and sisters by blood and design [...]
> that jut jaw
> to gnash tendon;
> that wide nose to meet the blows
> a face like that invites (*City* 81)

These poems offer a disturbing articulation of W.E.B. DuBois's theory of double-consciousness, the juxtaposition of two competing lenses, the adoption by necessity of a self-negating gaze, the gaze of your oppressors.[2] Your face constitutes a text that is yours, a text, however, that you did not write. Individuals who belong to communities discriminated against by virtue of the recognizable, repeated text of a face—a text whose meaning has been prescribed by social imaginings of the other—must reckon with the haunting in their blood, the recurrences dictated by genetics, but, more accurately, they must reckon with the recurrent, vicious and narrow readings of "race" that refuse to die. The text of an "Oriental" face is another draft of the other: a race, as Elaine H. Kim explains, "supposedly obedient, docile, efficient at carrying out the mandates of the decision makers" (148-49); a race, as Lee's poem quotes from Emerson, that "managed to preserve to a hair for three or four thousand years the ugliest features in the world" (*City* 83).

   The sense of being an outsider—of not belonging, of being one of the many who are "lost in America" (*Winged Seed* 76)—saturates the poetry of Li-Young Lee. He claims an American city as his home, but nevertheless his American experience is charged with a feeling of homelessness: "city I call home, in which I am a guest" (*City* 51). In an interview with Bill Moyers, Lee is asked to explain where he is from; his response reveals an interesting problem: "I say Chicago, then I tell them I was born in Indonesia, but I'm adamant about insisting that, although I was born in Indonesia, I'm Chinese. I don't want them to think that I'm Indonesian—my people were persecuted by the Indonesians" (257). The face of the other requires an explanation: where are you from? Though Lee is Chinese, he does not know China; it is an imagined homeland. In his feeling of exile, in the reality of being a refugee, Lee nevertheless cannot remember his lost home. In that same interview, Lee asserts: "I don't feel nostalgic because I don't know what to feel nostalgic *for*. It's simply a feeling of disconnection and

---

2   DuBois defines double-consciousness as a "sense of always looking at one's self through the eyes of others, of measuring one's soul by the tape of a world that looks on in amused contempt and pity" (5).

dislocation" (258). But this imagined China is not an illusion nor is it fantasy; it becomes real through its imagining. In his poem "I Ask My Mother to Sing," Lee reveals how China exists for him in language:

> I've never been in Peking, or the Summer Palace,
> nor stood on the great Stone Boat to watch
> the rain begin on Kuen Ming Lake, the picnickers
> running away in the grass.
>
> But I love to hear it sung:
> how the waterlilies fill with rain until
> they overturn, spilling water into water,
> then rock back, and fill with more. (*Rose* 50)

Lee travels to a homeland made of words, a China that is sung. His poem serves as a space in which a mother's memory—the very geography of her stories—can be committed to paper and subsequently re-visited by a son or by a reader.

In *The Winged Seed*, Lee shares with us the story of his father's paper model, an exact reproduction of Solomon's Temple. This paper temple could be dismantled and reconstructed and thereafter augmented every time Lee's family relocated. The temple itself mirrors Lee's life, a refugee's life, a life repeatedly rebuilt. But the temple is lost: "And where is it this day? One must not ask. Where is that magnificent temple? For it lives only in the sentences of its description, and only inside the imagination of the reader of those sentences" (*Winged Seed* 37). It is lost, and yet it endures; it is another place made of words. In this refugee's re-telling of dislocation and homelessness, Lee's language is a means by which he resurrects histories and gives them location: the page itself. He makes a home for himself in language. This sense of home, created through the act of telling, is an argument for language as a tool for survival.

> But I own a human story,
> whose very telling
> remarks loss.
> The characters survive through the telling,
> the teller survives
> by his telling; by his voice
> brinking silence does he survive. (*City* 26)

And by locating a personal China in language—in the songs of his mother and in his own poetry—Lee reaffirms the imagined nature of culture. Zhou Xiaojing's "Inheritance and Invention in Li-Young Lee's Poetry" approaches Chinese American culture as an organic framework: "The difference between the speaker's feeling of disconnectedness and his mother's and grandmother's feeling of dislocation and nostalgia shows a generational disparity which is characteristic of immigrants' experiences. This difference indicates discontinuity and

fragmentation in the speaker's inherited Chinese history, culture, and identity"
(116). Lee's expression of, and participation within, Chinese American culture is
like one of his "furious versions of the here and now" that operate as "drafts toward a future form" (*City* 19) only because that imagined form remains forever
in the future. Ethnographer James Clifford argues that culture is not "a unified
corpus of symbols and meanings that can be definitively interpreted" but rather
it is "contested, temporal, and emergent" (19). This emergent aspect suggests
that culture—hyphenated or not, Chinese or Chinese American—is re-invented
by necessity. The inevitability of this re-invention shows itself in Lee's "Persimmons," in the poem's play with Chinese and English.

> Donna undresses, her stomach is white.
> In the yard, dewy and shivering
> with crickets, we lie naked,
> face-up, face-down.
> I teach her Chinese.
> Crickets: *chiu chiu*. Dew: I've forgotten.
> Naked: I've forgotten.
> *Ni, wo*: you and me. (*Rose* 17)

"Persimmons" offers translations and telling silences; words forgotten do not
disappear but enter Lee's linguistic inventory of memory and loss. *Dew ... Naked* ... not everything can be remembered. But one silence always differs from
another by that which is not said. We discover the way a shadow traces a figure
of loss, but nevertheless a figure remains. If Lee's Chinese has been damaged, or
informed, by time and distance, by his location in the United States, so has his
English been corrupted, beautifully, by his other tongue. Of his experience in an
American elementary school, Lee recalls confusing the word *persimmons* with
precision:

> Other words
> that got me into trouble were
> *fight* and *fright*, *wren* and *yarn*.
> Fight was what I did when I was frightened,
> fright was what I felt when I was fighting.
> Wrens are small, plain birds,
> yarn is what one knits with.
> Wrens are soft as yarn.
> My mother made birds out of yarn. (*Rose* 17-18)

His mistakes became an occasion for violence: "Mrs. Walker / slapped the back
of my head / and made me stand in the corner" (*Rose* 17). Where Lee's tongue
erred, his imagination later would fashion a defense. The boy's mistake provides
an opportunity for the man's later insight, a meaningful confusion, an imaginative weaving that suggests how *fight* and *fright*, and *wren* and *yarn*, have every-

thing to do with each other. Lee's poem is, in a sense, a gift to his younger self, a more tender response to a boy's unruly tongue. The poem is also a measure of the poet's own success, for his "error" is published, and his corrupted words are anthologized and celebrated in classrooms.

In "Furious Versions," Lee returns, again, to his childhood. He suggests that his own voice realized itself the very moment he became a refugee:

> He did not utter a sound his first three years,
> and his parents frowned.
> Then, on the first night of their first exile,
> he spoke out in complete sentences,
> a Malaysian so lovely it was true song. (*City* 27)

In this self-directed mythmaking, Lee's voice, from its first articulation, always has been the exile's voice. "I'm like my landlocked poplars: far from water, I'm full of the sound of water" (25). He is an exile of place but also of time. In the latter sense, Lee's homelessness is also part of a more general existential condition; he suggests in his interview with Bill Moyers that the refugee experience "may be no more than an outward manifestation of a homelessness that people in general feel. It seems to me that anybody who thinks about our position in the universe cannot help but feel a little disconnected and homeless" (258). Certainly, the refugee experience cannot be reduced to a poeticized "outward manifestation" of a universal condition,[3] but Lee's comment sheds light on his own self-imagining. The damage inflicted by time—specifically, the passing of loved ones—compounds Lee's sense of disconnection. The figure of his father, a teacher imprisoned and tortured in Sukarno's prisons in Indonesia, appears again

---

3   It should be noted that while coercive displacement is not a universal condition, it informed the character of the last century. Refugees have traveled across human history, but the 21st century inherits a wide geography of massive dislocations. In 2000, there were approximately 22.3 million refugees worldwide, or one out of every 269 people on earth (United Nations High Commissioner on Refugees, *Refugees by Numbers: 2000 Edition*, 4). U.S. policy toward refugees and immigrants in general has been, throughout the last century, inconsistent and, very often, cruel. The Gold Mountain Poems etched by Chinese immigrants onto the walls of the Angel Island detention center in San Francisco give testimony of how, in early 20th century America, the Chinese were criminalized as a race. But the criminalization of immigrants and asylum-seekers continues to this day. According to a Human Rights Watch Report of 1998, *Locked Away: Immigration Detainees in Jails in the United States*, "The U.S. Immigration and Naturalization Service (INS) is currently housing more than 60 percent of its 15,000 detainees in local jails throughout the country. Faced with an overwhelming, immediate demand for detention space, the agency has handed over control of its detainees to local sheriffs and other jail officials without ensuring that basic international and national standards requiring humane treatment and adequate conditions are met. INS detainees-including asylum seekers-are being held in jails entirely inappropriate to their non-criminal status where they may be mixed with accused and convicted criminal inmates, and where they are sometimes subjected to physical mistreatment and grossly inadequate conditions of confinement" (section *I. Summary and Recommendations*).

and again in Lee's work. Lee's father subsequently escaped with his family, became a preacher, and spread the gospel in all parts of Southeast Asia and, eventually, in a small American blue-collar town. Lee's poetry is, among other things, a remembrance of his father:

> And always a rose for one I love
> exiled from one republic and daily defeated in another,
> who was shunned by brothers and stunned by God [...]
> who taught me to love the rose, and fed me roses, under whose windows
> I planted roses, for whose tables I harvested roses (*Rose* 41)

This private symbolism of the rose echoes the familiar Christian fascination with the rose as a symbol of wounded beauty, of the passion of self-sacrifice: the rose bears the color of Christ's blood. Lee's rose, too, suggests the beauty that can be located in suffering, in loss. The death of Lee's father creates a more profound sense of exile; the son recognizes with heartbreaking certainty that time makes exiles of us all:

> Love, how the hours accumulate. Uncountable.
> The trees grow tall, some people walk away
> and diminish forever. (*Rose* 58)

They diminish; they do not disappear. As suggested earlier, they "survive through the telling." Nevertheless, we are banished from the days that recede behind us. We might envision another angel of history, a biblical angel with flaming sword, ushering us into exile. We are banished not from a garden but from days. Lee uses poetry to undermine this exile by suggesting the poem itself as both a location and a moment in which intimacies are re-established.

Lee's family fled Indonesia as refugees, but their final destination, the United States, has its own troubled history of persecution against the Chinese, the race that completed the transcontinental railroad—the steel backbone of the American nation—in the latter half of the 1860s. Less than twenty years after the construction of the railroad, the Chinese, scapegoated for socio-economic ills across the West Coast, would be targeted by exclusionary anti-immigrant legislation at the local and federal levels. As the language of the Chinese Exclusion Act of 1882 argues in thinly disguised racist rhetoric, "the coming of Chinese laborers to this country endangers the good order of certain localities within the territory thereof" (The Chinese Exclusion Act, May 6, 1882, Chapter 126). Lee inherits a long history of struggle, the struggle to make a home for oneself against both informal as well as institutional efforts to deny the Chinese any space. Within this history of struggle, and against a history of displacement and homelessness, Lee's poetry becomes a home, fashioned with pain and tenderness, a space inhabited by lovers, parents, ghosts ... voices of the living and the "dead," the dead who eat at the same table as the living, the dead who do not need bodies to continue to inform the imaginations of the living.

In Lee's autobiographical *The Winged Seed*, we hear the voice of someone lost, the voice of a ghost, of someone who seems to be both absent and present. The anonymous ghost who haunted Lee's childhood home in Java, the child-ghost whose weeping could be heard but not seen, is described by the servants as one who "got lost and now is trapped between two worlds" (120). Ghosts appear again and again in Lee's poems—not anonymous ghosts, but ghosts of loved ones: a brother's ghost "opening and closing doors" (*City*, 35); a father's ghost "waving to me" (*Rose* 33) from the garden. The poem "My Indigo" reveals a ghostly flower: "You live a while in two worlds at once" (*Rose* 31). This flower represents Lee, as Zhou suggests, in that it "expresses Lee's own feelings resulting from his experience of life in exile, wandering from country to country" (114). The flower's two worlds can be read as that definitive, albeit imagined, split between East and West. The flower, in its short-lived beauty, may reside, too, in a liminal or phantasmal space between life and death.

If a ghost is one who wanders between two worlds, Lee implicates himself as a ghostly presence. And in his attempt to undermine the logic of linear time, Lee's ghostly walking allows him to move through the clock that stands between him and the past. Take for example Lee's poem "Ash, Snow, or Moonlight":

> Am I stricken by memory or forgetfulness?
> Is this the first half of the century or the last?
> Is this my father's life or mine? (*Rose* 52)

Lee's speaker, his own ghostly persona, blurs the distinction between father and son, between one era and the next. This confusion of time—and of identity—continues in the poem "Furious Versions":

> But if I waken to a jailer
> rousting me to meet my wife and son,
> come to see me in my cell
> where I eat the chocolate
> and smoke the cigarettes they smuggle,
> what name do I answer to? (*City* 14)

Lee re-imagines himself as his imprisoned father. In these passages, time exists not beyond but within memory; in such a reality, one moves through unfamiliar decades as though they were rooms. Lee becomes his father by moving into him, by donning a distant era, a distant face. Lee is his father again; he is a recurrence, a repetition of someone lost in time. Lee consistently undermines the logic of chronology as if to suggest that, while we may organize our reality with clocks and calendars, we do not experience time as a fixed line. In *The Winged Seed*, Lee once again complicates this linearity:

Didn't I one day kneel in the mud and snow, halfway up a hillside, halfway to
my father's grave, and hold my wrist to an icy cataract, and see the shriveled
vine and the gold seed pods?
  Or was that last night on the stairs? (34-35)

By playing with the logic of linear time, Lee transfigures himself into a ghost
among ghosts. The division between the living and the dead is blurred, and
ghosts seem to be both haunted and haunting.

  Within the rich context of exile, Lee's complication of time also manifests itself through his motif of rain, for rain—specifically in Lee's *Rose* collection—bears the aspect of another ghostly presence. Rain travels back and forth,
wandering across geographical and temporal distances. Consider the example of
"Rain Diary":

Where did the rain go? Across the fields? Out to sea?
Straight down
to my father
in his boat, with a lamp. Last night
I found the red book the world lost,
the one which contains the address of the rain,
all the names of the beloved dead, and how
and where they can be reached. (*Rose* 59)

In these poems, the rain is another homeless presence. It moves across our maps.
Rain needs no passport. It comes and goes, and these travels occur across both
space and time. The rain finds Lee's father somewhere in the distance, but also
somewhere in the past. Rain is the recurring presence of water, "water we
crossed to come to America, water I'll cross to go back, water which will kill my
father" (27); so the very element of water comes to signify homelessness, in
terms of both displacement as well as death. But water is also "my father's life
sign" (26). If water is the sign of Lee's father, the rain becomes Lee's own sign,
whether by choice or by haunting; it is another inheritance: "between my eyes is
always the rain, the migrant rain" (69). Rain is that unique natural phenomenon
that dissolves the distinction between earth and sky; it blurs the horizon and
touches everything. And in this dissolution, time itself seems to melt:

thus the rain
marks its passage through time, steadily
darkening what it touches,
and makes indistinguishable the moments
by narration in a monotonous voice (55)

This rain that complicates the certain measures of a clock, this rain that confuses
the sequence of moments by its steady falling of water, must be counted among

the ghostly presences in Lee's work. Neither earth nor sky, the falling rain exists
between two worlds.

The rain becomes a surrogate for the figure of Lee's father, and it suggests
that one does not need a ghost's face to be haunted. In her book *Ghostly Matters: Haunting and the Sociological Imagination*, Avery Gordon argues that a
ghost is merely a sign; it is not the haunting itself.[4] Haunting is a "particular way
of knowing" (8), an attitude towards history that acknowledges the agency of the
past, an agency with which we must negotiate. Haunting complicates the safe
distances assumed by our chronologies. Lee's books are inhabited by ghostly
figures—especially the ghost of his father, a father homeless in death as he was
in life. The ghostly aspect of rain, the water between two worlds, is heightened
when the rain and Lee's dead father merge into a single haunting figure, an
anatomy of water: "I remember my father of rain" (*Rose* 60); and elsewhere:
"my father, arriving on legs of rain, arriving, this dream, the rain, my father"
(62). Lee admits ghosts into his verse, or rather they gain entrance, as though
they had been waiting outside, waiting to be acknowledged. They come to signify the paradoxical presence of a lack, an absence that overwhelms the heart of
a son who can only locate that which is not there: "Rain knocks at my door and I
open. No one is there, and the rain marching in place" (62).

The theme of haunting suggests the sorrow woven throughout Lee's poetry,
but we might consider, too, the ways in which haunting is a blessing, for Lee's
work is a celebration of remembrance in the rich and complicated project of
identity-formation. Tender moments in the "now" appear to Lee's mind as reflections of moments in his past. Take, for example, Lee's poem "The Gift"; the
poet removes a splinter from his wife's hand, and the moment becomes a mirroring of another act of love: once, as a child, Lee felt a splinter in his hand. His
father took care of the child's injury:

> Had you entered that afternoon
> you would have thought you saw a man
> planting something in a boy's palm,
> a silver tear, a tiny flame. (*Rose* 15)

This metaphor of planting a seed suggests a teleology of love, an act of kindness
that will later reproduce itself. But the poem also thinly veils the reversal of this

---

4   Gordon differentiates haunting from the presence of a ghost in the passage below (the idea of a
     "structure of feeling" is borrowed from Raymond Williams' *Marxism and Literature*):
     If haunting describes how that which appears to be not there is often a seething pres-
     ence, acting on and often meddling with taken-for-granted realities, the ghost is just the
     sign, or the empirical evidence if you like, that tells you a haunting is taking place [...]
     haunting is a very particular way of knowing what has happened or is happening. Being
     haunted draws us affectively, sometimes against our will and always a bit magically,
     into the structure of feeling of a reality we come to experience, not as cold knowledge,
     but as a transformative recognition. (8)

chronology, for a seed is located, too, in the hand of his wife, and the blossoming that occurs is the flower of remembrance.

Lee suggests love as a resurrection of the past. In his motif of hair, woven through his first book of poems, *Rose*, Lee re-imagines the hair of his wife, Donna, as the hair of his mother. He transforms his father's gaze into his own gaze. In the poem "Dreaming of Hair," Lee sleeps beside his wife, tangled in her hair: "In the morning I remove it from my tongue and sleep again" (*Rose* 22). Lee's speaker then recalls his childhood—how he would sleep beside his mother and wake with her hair in his mouth (23). He imagines hair, like language, as the fabric of love. This motif develops in the poem "Early in the Morning," in which the speaker describes how his mother keeps her hair rolled tightly in a bun:

My father likes to see it like this.
He says it is kempt.

But I know
it is because of the way
my mother's hair falls
when he pulls the pins out. (25)

The subtle implication is that Lee's knowledge arises here from his own erotic desire while looking at his wife's hair. The poem presents the act of removing hairpins as a sensual movement, and a prelude, for Lee's mother's hair falls "[e]asily, like the curtains when they untie them in the evening" (25). The poem concludes at this very moment, with the falling of hair, the closing of curtains, the arrival of night and the implied consummation of desire. A woman's hair mirrors the hair of another in her youth, and a father's desire is the precedent for his son's own response to extravagant beauty.

This motif of hair extends to the poem "Braiding," in which Lee borrows from his parents their own rituals of love. The braiding is a re-enactment, a performance that establishes a link to the past:

We two sit on our bed, you
between my legs, your back to me, your head
slightly bowed, that I may brush and braid
your hair. My father did this for my mother,
just as I do for you. (*Rose* 57)

Through this small ritual of braiding hair, Lee weaves love between himself and his wife, but he also weaves love between generations, for it is familial love that motivates Lee's impulse to preserve his parents' ritual, a ritual constituted by his mother's gift of hair "heavy and black as calligrapher's ink" (25) and his father's gift of hands, hands like Lee's hands, hands that work "within and against time" (*Rose* 58). The work of braiding makes a beautiful order of hair, as a poet makes a beautiful order of language. This braiding measures time not with calendars but with a repeated act of affection, with recurring measures of love that "cross over one year and one year" (58). With the vocabulary of physics, Albert Einstein argued that time is not a rigid structure. Gravity—the relationship of large bodies responding to each other—informs time, changes time, drags and quickens it. Lee's language suggests, too, that our human bodies make time, that the braiding of hair makes time—a sensual time that is not the measure of our actions but rather *is* our actions. Time exists in our movements and in our hands.

But for a calendar to dissolve, it must first exist. We organize our lives with days and years. And while we may be prisoners of a time we invent, Lee reveals that the past does not stand at exact distances from the mind. Informed by the ghosts that keep him company, Lee weaves days with language, dismantling chronologies. And through this weaving, it is not the moments in time that die, but rather the distances between them.

Works Cited

Benjamin, Walter. *Illuminations*. Trans. Harry Zohn. Ed. Hannah Arendt. New York: Shocken, 1968.

Clifford, James. "Introduction." *Writing Culture: The Poetics and Politics of Ethnography*. Eds. James Clifford and George E. Marcus. Berkeley: U of California P, 1986.

DuBois, W.E.B. *The Souls of Black Folk*. 1903. New York: Penguin, 1989.

Gordon, Avery. *Ghostly Matters: Haunting and the Sociological Imagination*. Minneapolis: U of Minnesota P, 1997.

Hugo, Richard. "The Way a Ghost Dissolves." *The Norton Anthology of Modern Poetry*. 2nd Edition. Eds. Richard Ellmann and Robert O'Clair. New York: W.W. Norton & Company, 1988. 1121-22.

Human Rights Watch. *Locked Away: Immigration Detainees in Jails in the United States* 10.1 (September 1998): 1-84. (www.hrw.org)

Kim, Elaine H. "Defining Asian American Realities Through Literature." *The Nature and Context of Minority Discourse*. Eds. Abdul R. JanMohamed and David Lloyd. New York: Oxford UP, 1990. 146-70.

Lee, Li-Young. *The City in Which I Love You*. New York: Boa Editions, 1990.

—. *Rose*. New York: Boa Editions, 1986.

—. *The Winged Seed: A Remembrance*. New York: Simon & Schuster, 1995.

Moyers, Bill. *The Language of Life: A Festival of Poets*. New York: Doubleday, 1995.

United Nations High Commissioner on Refugees. *Refugees by Numbers: 2000 Edition*. 1-14. (www.unhcr.ch)

Welch, James. *Riding the Earthboy 40*. New York: The World Publishing Company, 1971.

Williams, William Carlos. *In the American Grain*. New York: New Directions Publishing Corporation, 1925.

Zhou, Xiaojing. "Inheritance and Invention in Li-Young Lee's Poetry." *MELUS* 21.1 (Spring 1996): 113-20.

IV. Narrative Experiments

Everyone's Story:
Narrative *You* in Chitra Bannerjee Divakaruni's "The Word Love"

Rocío G. Davis

Chitra Bannerjee Divakaruni, born in India and presently living in the United States, first received critical attention with her award-winning poetry characterized by its "powerfully authentic language" (Sen-Bagchee 77). Her first collection of short stories, *Arranged Marriage*, chronicles the lives of Indian women who struggle to translate the traditions of the old world to a new world setting. Many of the stories depict tragic lives and desperate situations; others tell of compromises made or open defiance to tradition; all articulate the dramas of women caught between cultures, struggling to formulate individual subjectivities as they hover between duty and personal fulfillment. Her representations of the choices, rebellions, and decisions of these women are portrayed through the narrative skills of a poet with the gift of imaginatively entering the psyche of her female characters in order to articulate tensions and correlative emotions. Among the most powerful tools Divakaruni appropriates in her fiction is the narrative technique she employs in the story "The Word Love." The opening line of this story immediately situates the reader at the center of the drama: "You practice them out loud for days in front of the bathroom mirror, the words with which you'll tell your mother you're living with a man" (57). The poignancy of the rite of passage is heightened by the writer's choice of narrative perspective, the second person point of view, a rhetorical strategy utilized for perhaps the first time in writing by an Asian American, opening up new possibilities for theoretical and narrative development as well as creative expression.

Divakaruni's manipulation of point of view in this story through the use of the narrative *you* illustrates one of the directions critics are signaling as the renewed course for the development of Asian American literature and criticism. King-kok Cheung explains in the introduction to *An Interethnic Companion to Asian American Literature*:

> as this literature—along with the theory and criticism accompanying it—expands, original parameters are modified and contested; paralleling the explosion in volume is a proliferation of perspectives [...]. A significant switch in emphasis has also occurred in Asian American literary studies. Whereas identity politics—with its stress on cultural nationalism and American nativ-

ity—governed earlier theoretical and critical formulations, the stress is now on heterogeneity and diaspora. The shift has been from seeking to 'claim America' to forging a connection between Asia and Asian America; from centering on race and on masculinity to revolving around the multiple axes of ethnicity, gender, class and sexuality; from being concerned primarily with social history and communal responsibility to being caught in the quandaries and possibilities of postmodernism and multiculturalism. (1)

Many Asian American writers appear to have arrived at the consensus that the exercise of renewed, even experimental, narrative forms, will lead to more relevant creative inscriptions of increasingly multi-layered subjectivities. Notably, from Maxine Hong Kingston to the present, the most important Asian American works have challenged generic constraints by using innovative narrative perspectives, a phenomenon that Patricia Lin Blinde attributes to "the richness of bi-cultural life experience [which] cannot be contained within the limits of literary dictates" (53). In the same vein, Garrett Hongo warns that if writers neglect to produce "new critical approaches and widen parochial perspectives regarding literary style" the modes of critical thinking will be limited to three approaches: the assumption that what is *essentially* Asian American depends on "overt political stance and conformity to sociological models," the notion that "a writer writes from a primary loyalty to coherent communities," and "categorical dismissal for literary qualities deemed 'assimilationist' or 'commercial'" (4-5). The process of establishing Asian American identities from within, independently of hegemonic definitions, has reached a turning point clearly resonant with the phenomenological reality of the Asian American. Experimentation with genre and structure as a strategy of authorship manifests how these writers have "moved beyond the conventional dichotomous, binary construction of white and Asian-national to a positioning of ethnic identity as interrogative, shifting, unstable, and heuristic" (Lim 160). The diversity of narrative composition takes on many forms: from the short story cycles of writers like Sigrid Nunez and Lois-Ann Yamanaka to the episodic and regressive narration used by Fae Myenne Ng in *Bone* and Aimee Liu in *Face*; from the multi-layered collage of Theresa Cha's *Dictée*, to the magic realism of Amy Tan's *The Hundred Secret Senses*. These are among the more conspicuous examples of the narrative and theoretical challenges contemporary Asian American writers pose to their readers and to the larger body of literary theory that seeks to define it.

In the light of these developments, Chitra Divakaruni's innovative use of narrative perspective, more than solely challenging traditionalist fiction instructors' admonitions that "second person point of view doesn't exist," widens the range of referentiality of the text itself. When we discuss the literary meditations of ethnicity's necessary intersection with the processes of identity, we refer, in the first place, to the story as a means of contextualizing the lives of an individual or a community within the conditions and circumstances that are created by or that shape, in different or similar ways, the lives of Others. But secondly, and more importantly for our purpose, we must take into account and read these texts as

> theoretically informed and informing rather than as transparently referential human documents over which we place a grid of sophisticated Euro-American theory in order to extract meaning. This theory-as-grid model repeats the colonizing or imperialistic strategy of containment and domination of the 'other' as inferior and dependent (on external theory to construct meaning), the very strategy we must seek to escape if Asian American literature is to speak to us in its own theoretically informed voice. (Goellnicht 340)

No longer are the texts to be read as mere ethnography; the growing sophistication of the writers leads them to engage, within the creative work itself, with the theoretical questions plaguing postmodern and multicultural writers. This observation highlights the importance of Divakaruni's assay into the narrative *you* within the context of developing theories and practice of the Asian American experience in and with literature. Her technique opens up possibilities on both a thematic level—as it offers a new way of dealing with the process of subjectivity and immigrant positionality, interrogating notions of identity and choice—and on a textual level, as it challenges the traditionally accepted border between narrator and narratee, between text and reader. More importantly for an Asian American text, it subverts established notions of reader identity, widening the terrain for possibilities of the classification of the reader and hegemonic assumptions on his or her identity.

The second person point of view, transgressive and illuminating, "simultaneously opens up new possibilities for representing consciousness and provides a site for the contestation of constricting discursive practices" (Richardson 319). As a tool within which to enact the process of achieving selfhood through an intense reworking of questions such as oppositionality, marginality, boundaries, displacement, and authenticity, this manner of narration draws attention to the object of the drama by subverting traditional patterns of discourse. "The Word Love" tells of a young Indian woman, the only daughter of an absorbing widowed mother in India, who falls in love and moves in with an American she meets while studying at Berkeley. At the center of the story lies her obsession with her mother's reaction to the fact that she is living in sin with a foreigner. Her anxiety centers on the question of love as a reason and excuse: she ponders definitions, recollects cautionary tales, seeks outlets, analyzes positions. The story offers diverse definitions of the complex term at its center, interrogating the nature of relationships and transcultural beliefs and experiences. The question of cultural formation, personal contingencies, and choices invests the story with its multi-dimensional drama: life in Berkeley cannot be more different from life in India. Nonetheless, as Francine Prose points out, the chasms Divakaruni's protagonist straddles have "less to do with the ground beneath [her] feet than with the gap between past and future" (20). Divakaruni's choice of narrative mode conditions the story's entire structure and greatly determines both the receptive stance and the aesthetic involvement of the reader.

The narrator of "The Word Love," the voice that says "you," unidentified and unnamed, invisible but omniscient, is the center of consciousness in the story. Bruce Morrisette argues that the use of the narrative *you* "holds a strong implication of judgment, of moral or didactic address [... the voice that says *you*] is the person *par excellence* of interrogation and imperative" (16-17). The narrating voice in this short story accuses, questions, raises doubts, and forces the protagonist to look closely at every one of her actions and rethink every one of her decisions. The opening line sets the tone for the account, the protagonist's painful journey through the consequences of her actions, her inability to take control of her own life, and her ultimate arrival at a resolution. A justification of the narrative use of *you* may lie in that something is to be revealed to the character which she or he does not know, at least on the level of language (Morrisette 16). Unnamed throughout the story, the protagonist is represented as extremely insecure and indecisive, which makes the second person narration more urgent; as the main character cannot seem to speak for herself, a voice must be found to speak her story. The narrator, therefore, serves to formulate what the narratee is unable to or may be unaware of, converting this technique into a powerful tool for the articulation of the drama of disjunction. The protagonist's reworking, reevaluation, and revisioning of herself, led by the narrating voice, illustrates Stuart Hall's claim that we should think of identity "as a 'production' which is never complete, always in process, and always constituted within, not outside, representation" (222). Goellnicht points out that "rather than thinking in binary terms of inside/outside, we should perhaps think of hybrid positions as a web of multiply intersecting and shifting strands in which the precise location of the subject is extremely difficult to map [...] subject positions are not the result of essential determinants but are culturally produced (in relation to other positions) and socially learned, a complex and continuous process" (340). The narrator of "The Word Love" inscribes the unnamed protagonist's dialogue with being and belonging as a result of hastily made decisions and disregard for the possible consequences of one's actions.

Interrogating choices and future plans while evoking the past, the narrative *you* exposes the process of the protagonist's desperate attempts to find her bearings in the midst of overwhelming personal and cultural influences and imperatives. The personal dilemma becomes a metaphor for the subtext of the immigrant's cultural drama of choices and decisions, for the option between preservation or assimilation, and a reminder that, very often, much must be given up before something may be gained. Before leaving India, obedience to her mother was unquestioned and the only transgressive episode in her past ended in tearful remorse and the promise to be faithful. In Berkeley, her acquiescence to live with a man appears to be more a result of passive acceptance of his needs and his desires than a rational decision based on her own convictions and wants. The accusing tone of the narrator brings into focus the sequence of events and insights that the protagonist seems to prefer to ignore, under guise of not being aware of possible consequences. Her position in her own story is difficult to map as she has been manipulated as a pawn to serve the varied interests of other players: mother, lover, societal expectations and demands, possibilities and invitations. The narrative *you* becomes the means through which Divakaruni scrutinizes and transcribes the trajectory of the protagonist's bitter journey towards self-awareness and the awakening to the possibility of self-determination.

This form of narrative perspective enhances the articulation of a mind in flux, journeying smoothly back and forth in time and place, through the workings of the protagonist's memory and obsession with relationships: "Outside a wino shouts something. Crash of broken glass and, later, police sirens. But you're hearing the street vendor call out *momphali, momphali fresh and hot*, and she's smiling, handing you a coin, saying, *yes, baby, you can have some*. The salty crunch of roasted peanuts fills your mouth, the bathroom water runs and runs" (60). The narrating voice has the power to transport her back to where her mother speaks to her on the phone, the place where the "old *ayah* (she has been there from before you were born) stands behind her, combing out her long hair which lifts a little in the breeze from the fan, the silver in it glimmering like a smile. It is the most beautiful hair in the world" (63-64). It is also a voice that dramatically conveys the anxiety of deception:

> The first month you moved in with him, your head pounded with fear and guilt every time the phone rang. You'd rush across the room to pick it up while he watched you from his tilted-back chair, raising an eyebrow. (You'd made him promise never to pick up the phone). At night you slept next to the bedside extension. You picked it up on the very first ring, struggling out of layers of sleep heavy as water to whisper a breathless hello, the next word held in readiness, *mother*. (63)

But later, the narrator explains, "you grew careless. Sometimes you'd call out from the shower for him to answer the phone [...]. At night [...] you didn't care which side of the bed it was as long as you had him to hold on to. *Or was it that you wanted her, somehow, to find out?*" (64).

Monika Fludernik, discussing Joyce Carol Oates's story "You," argues in favor the suitability of second person fiction for the expression and description of certain types of relationships: "Since address combines a distancing factor (foregrounding the non-identity of the *I* and the *you*) with the presupposition of an acquaintance with the person thus addressed, it proves to be a fictional mode adaptable to detailing the jig-saw structure of the mother-daughter relationship" ("Second Person" 239). By analogy and extension, Divakaruni's appropriation of this narrative strategy in a story that centers on two relations of complex intimacy, widens the elaborate implications of devotion and obligation: "You tried to tell him about your mother, how she'd seen her husband's face for the first time at her wedding. How, when he died (you were two years old then), she had taken off her jewelry and put on widow's white and dedicated the rest of her life to bringing you up. *We only have each other*, she often told you" (58). The word *love* is the refuge the protagonist hides behind in the midst of the storm building around and within her. When she practices aloud how she will tell her mother what she is doing, "[s]ometimes they are words of confession and repentance. Sometimes they are angry, defiant. Sometimes they melt into a single, sighing sound. *Love*" (57). This is also how she accounts for her torment at the idea of hurting her mother: "You wanted him to know that when you conjured up her face, the stern angles of it softening into a rare smile, the silver at her temples catching the afternoon sun in the backyard under the pomegranate tree, love made you breathless, as though someone had punched a hole in your chest" (58).

Interestingly, there is another voice in the story that speaks to the main character, a "whispery voice that lives behind the ache in your eyes, the one that started when you said yes and he kissed you, hard. *Mistake*, the voice said, whispering in your mother's tones" (59). This voice is easier to recognize and identify as that of her conscience—formed by her mother—and the narrator tries to placate it with the same excuse: "Sometimes, the voice sounds different, not hers. It is a rushed intake of air, as just before someone asks a question that might change your life. You don't want to hear the question, which might be *how did you get yourself into this mess*, or perhaps, *why*, so you leap in with that magical word. *Love*, you tell yourself, *lovelovelove*. But you know, deep down, that words solve nothing" (59). When her mother learns the truth and the daughter is cut off completely, the latter remembers the character in a cautionary tale her mother had told her, a tragic suicide because of the shame of an illicit love: "you dream of a beautiful girl knotting stones into her *palloo* and swimming out into the middle of the dark lake. The water is cool on her heaving breasts, her growing belly. It ripples and parts for her. Before she goes under, she turns towards you. Sometimes her face is a blank oval, featureless. Sometimes it is your face" (66).

The urgency of the narrative voice prompts the imperative to identify it, a chore complicated by the possibilities offered by this perspective. As Monika Fludernik argues, "[i]f there is address, there must be an addresser, an *I* (implicit or explicit), and hence a narrator, and this narrator can be a mere enunciator or also a protagonist sharing the *you*'s fictional existence in the story level. This implies that second person fiction radicalizes and complicates the well-worn dichotomy of homodiegetic and heterodiegetic fiction—the coincidence and non-coincidence of the realms of existence between the narrator and narratee on the one hand and the protagonists of the fiction on the other" ("Second Person" 219). A close reading suggests four possibilities. First, the narrator may be the alliance of the chorus of the characters who demand the protagonist's attention, converting it into a multi-layered cry for attention: both her mother and her lover seek to claim her, the narration of her story may be viewed as their means of doing so. Both coexist even in the same physical space, because "[t]he first thing you did when you moved into his apartment was to put up the batik hanging, deep red flowers winding around a black circle" (61). The presence of this going away present from her mother, a "talisman," in the apartment highlights simultaneous urgency of the two conflicting forces of her life. Secondly, on a more abstract level, the narrative voice may embody a cultural accusation—a reminder of the price one must pay for rejecting traditions and forms of the past in favor of the immediacy of the pleasures and distractions of the present. *"What will you remember of him when it is all over?* whispers the papery voice inside your skull" (63), and the narrating voice makes the internal query reverberate.

Another prospect is that, because second-person fiction is "'open' on the scale between narration and interior monologue, where the text's address function can frequently be read as an instance of self-address" (Fludernik, "Introduction" 289), the voice may actually be the protagonist's own. On the level of discourse, this incorporation of the *you* articulates the unstable nature and intersubjective constitution of the self. This suggests the possibility of a consciousness working on two levels, so that the protagonist is both player and critic of her own drama, making the narrative voice, in Divakaruni's words, "a split of many [possible] entities [...] most closely the internal self of the main character" (Letter, April 7, 1998). This is evident, for instance when, in the middle of her trauma of deception, the voice declares: "You'd watched the upside-down titles of his books splayed across the table. *Control Systems Engineering. Boiler Operations Guide. Handbook of Shock and Vibration.* Cryptic as tarot cards, they seem to be telling you something. If only you could decipher it" (58). Furthermore, the recurrent use of the mirror, as a way of reflecting back to the protagonist images of herself and as a sounding board against which to practice what she has to tell her mother, for instance, supports this idea. In the final scene, her decision to leave is taken when, walking out into the rain, she takes part in the following scene: "Coming toward you is a young woman with an umbrella. Shoulders bunched, she tiptoes through puddles, trying hard to stay dry. But a gust snaps the umbrella back and soaks her. She is shocked for a moment, angry. Then she begins to laugh. You are laughing too, because you know just how it feels" (71). This episode, and the description of the young woman, re-presents the main character's own story and way of living. It appears that she must see, in a bathroom mirror or by observing someone else enact her itinerary, the circumstances of her life before she can actually take control of it.

Finally, we must consider, as Divakaruni suggests, that the narrative voice is "ultimately [...] the author's voice" (Letter, April 7, 1998). As an Asian American writer aware of her role in the development of literature's dialogue with a growing consciousness of a transcultural individual identity, Divakaruni may actually be formulating a dialogue with the process of Asian American subjectivity. The choice of second person narration radically alters the tone of the story and provides a unique speaking situation for the author, one that does not occur in other types of narratives and that continuously defamiliarizes the narrative act. Clearly, one of the more prominent emotional effects of second-person narration is, according to Fludernik, its "decidedly involving quality, which provokes much greater initial empathy with second-person protagonists than with first- or third-person characters" ("Introduction" 285-86). From her position as scholar and writer, therefore, Divakaruni may be revising, through the intermingling of creative imagination and literary theory, the boundaries of that subjectivity, recognizing its contingencies and therefore sustaining its validity and authenticity. Moreover, the use of the narrative present in the story—as in much second-person fiction—eliminates the duality between the time of narration and that of the story narrated, making the tragedy both individual and communal, granting it both singularity and recurrence. The protagonist is an individual, but her story is shared by many.

This aspect, which radically modifies the traditional relationships among writer, character, and reader, is reinforced by the use of the narrative *you* because the form is, according to Helmut Bonheim, "potentially more ambiguous in its functions than are the other pronouns" and he uses the term "referential slither" to denote the second person narrative's inherent capacity for addressing both the actual reader and a narratee as well as denoting a fictional protagonist (76). Critics unanimously highlight this possibility of the form. Mary Frances Hopkins and Leon Perkins characterize the narrative *you* as "an actant by definition" and therefore "internal to the story" but they go on to note that "the relationships of this *you* to the external reader may vary within the text, providing a source of complexity in the texture of the story" (121). Its usage can engender a heightened engagement between reader and protagonist, because "we may oppose identification with a *you* we resist, or we may sympathize more fully with a central character" (Richardson 319). The manner of characterization in the story requires analysis in the light of these ideas. The protagonist finds herself torn between characters who are types more than individuals, unequivocal metaphors of cultural forces: the Indian mother—representing tradition and a stable family life—and the WASP boyfriend who embodies a world of more ambiguous relationships. Each makes radical demands on the main character; no compromise is possible.

Throughout most of the story, the main character remains indecisive, cringing under the demands of both mother and lover, allowing herself to be led by circumstances rather than imposing her own ideas or choices. At no point does she take responsibility for her situation, the word *love* serving as an excuse for her growing sense of insecurity and instability. She will be led to the absolute limit, including the contemplation of suicide as a way of escaping the consequences of her mother's rejection and the man's foreseen abandonment. After her mother has cut her off, she finds that he too has become estranged: "Sometimes when he is talking, the words make no sense. You watch him move his mouth as though he were a character in a foreign film someone has forgotten to dub. He asks you a question. By the raised tone of his voice you know that's what it is, but you have no idea what he wants from you" (67). At the end of the story, caught in a rainstorm, her memory flashes back to the past and she makes her decision to leave and begin again:

> Thunder and lightning. It's going to be quite a storm. You remember the monsoons of your childhood. There are no people in this memory, only the sky, rippling with exhilarating light. You know then that when you return to the apartment you will pack your belongings. A few clothes, some music, a favorite book, the hanging. No, not that. You will not need it in your new life, the one you're going to live for yourself. And a word comes to you out of the opening sky. The word love. You see that you had never understood it before. It is like rain, and when you lift your face up to it, like rain it washes away inessentials, leaving you hollow, clean, ready to begin. (71)

The conclusion to "The Word Love," arguably abrupt and problematic on the level of story for its unexpectedness and deviation from character, offers valid suggestions at the level of cultural discourse. The resolution of the renewed subjectivity often implies, more than choosing between two radically opposed polarities, the stripping away of essentials and starting all over again. Furthermore, opening up a possibility for the protagonist, the second person point of view also opens up a possibility for the reader. The use of the narrative *you* becomes one of the more interesting facets of contemporary ethnic literary theory and criticism because, while in standard fiction the protagonist/narratee is quite distinct from the actual or implied reader, nevertheless, "one of the more unsettling features of this mode of narration is that this distinction can be collapsed whenever the *you* could refer to the reader as well" (Richardson 312). As Divakaruni points out, "[t]he *you* is the main character, but also the reader, as it were. What I like so much about the second person view is how it brings together the character and the reader into one seamless experience" (Letter, April 7, 1998). In the manner of Greek tragedy, where catharsis was achieved by inspiring pity for the hero and fear for oneself, Divakaruni's short story obliges the reader to face the experience of cultural imperatives and choices in the manner that implicates the reader most directly, drawing him or her into the narrative and suggesting that this is, more than just the protagonist's story and dilemma, ours as well. Interestingly, Helmut Bonheim points out that "[t]he person addressed is not only the supposed reader: he is also the person the story is about. We think of the person spoken *about* in most stories as fictive. The persons spoken *to* as real, namely ourselves, the readers. In the *you*-story the two are conflated" (69). This suggests that the world the story refers to is much larger than the one literally portrayed: while it obviously is someone's story, by extension, it becomes everyone's story. Nonetheless, because the protagonist is addressed directly as *you* by other characters in the story, Divakaruni impedes a total identification of the world of the text with that of the reader.

Considering the urgency and implications of the Asian American cultural politics that Divakaruni works within, and her awareness of the dynamics of the culturally diverse audience of her story, her innovative use of narrative perspective further challenges, in Brian Richardson's terms, "the monolithic *you* that implies a universal, deracinated, ideal construct" (323). This critic explains that ethnic writers who use the second person address tend to be "painfully aware of antithetical communities of reception, as well as the ideological codes that typically encase notions like the model reader. The assumptions that white middle and upper class audiences bring to the act of reading are thus foregrounded and exposed—particularly the insidious assumption that they are, 'naturally', the universal *you* addressed by the text" (323-24). Divakaruni, by identifying and contesting the assumed *you*, generates a widening of discursive space, where more and more diverse voices may be heard and similarly plural subjectivities may be addressed. She thus appropriates and modifies the rich ideological possibilities of the second person narration which "invites a rewriting of commercial discourses intended to exploit their readers through the illusion of identification, [and] helps dramatize the mental battles of an individual struggling against the internalized discourse of an oppressive authority, and it is a useful vehicle for minority writers to foreground a subjectivity typically excluded from common, unexamined notions of *you* and *us*" (Richardson 327).

"The Word Love," as a discourse on immigrant self-definition through negotiation with the demands of the past and of the present, demonstrates the strong collective impulse that has characterized much ethnic fiction. Using the paradigms of monologue but extending the range and possibilities of speaker and listener to embody the dramatic negotiations of immigrant subjectivity, Chitra Divakaruni weaves together the sources of meaning to see if there is a way to ensure the survival of the individuals and the group. The second person narrative that articulates the contingencies of individual and communal story interrogates assumptions on self-representation, creating and maintaining subjectivity through literary discourse. The manner in which Divakaruni manipulates the narrative *you* as a metaphor for the fragmentation and multiplicity of ethnic lives becomes an exposition of the between-culture position and the complex process towards self-identification. As such, the impressionistic perspective and fragmentation of consciousness emphasizes the subjectivity of experience and understanding. The subsequent narrative, a reflection of a tendency towards the openness and hybridity specific to recent Asian American writing, provides enriching glimpses of societies in the process of transformation.

Works Cited

Blinde, Patricia Lin. "An Icicle in the Desert: Perspective and Form in the Works of Two Chinese-American Women." *MELUS* 6.3 (Fall 1979): 51-71.

Bonheim, Helmut. "Narration in the Second Person." *Recherches Anglaises et Americaines* 16 (1983): 69-80.

Cheung, King-Kok. "Reviewing Asian American Literary Studies." *An Interethnic Companion to Asian American Literature.* Ed. King-kok Cheung. New York: Cambridge UP, 1997. 1-36.

Divakaruni, Chitra Bannerjee. "The Word Love." *Arranged Marriage.* New York: Anchor Books, 1995. 57-71.

Divakaruni, Chitra. Letter to Rocío G. Davis. April 7, 1998.

Fludernik, Monika. "Introduction: Second-Person Narrative and Related Issues." *Style* 28.3 (Fall 1994): 281-311.

—. "Second Person Fiction: Narrative *You* as Addressee And/Or Protagonist." *AAA-Arbeiten aus Anglistik und Amerikanistik* 18.2 (1993): 217-47.

Goellnicht, Donald C. "Blurring Boundaries: Asian American Literature as Theory." *An Interethnic Companion to Asian American Literature.* Ed. King-Kok Cheung. New York: Cambridge UP, 1997. 338-365.

Hall, Stuart. "Cultural Identity and Diaspora." *Identity: Community, Culture, Difference.* Ed. J. Rutherford. London: Lawrence and Wishart, 1990. 222-37.

Hongo, Garrett. "Asian American Literature: Questions of Identity." *Amerasia Journal* 20.3 (1994): 1-8.

Hopkins, Mary Frances, and Leon Perkins. "Second Person Point of View in Narrative." *Critical Survey of Short Fiction.* Ed. Frank N. Magill. New Jersey: Salem, 1981. 119-32.

Lim, Shirley Geok-lin. "Assaying the Gold; or, Contesting the Ground of Asian American." *New Literary History* 24 (1993): 147-69.

Morrisette, Bruce. "Narrative 'You' in Contemporary Literature." *Comparative Literature Studies* 2.1 (1965): 1-24.

Prose, Francine. "Life in the Global Village." *Women's Review of Fiction* XII.6 (March 1996): 20.

Richardson, Brian. "The Poetics and Politics of Second Person Narrative." *Genre* XXIV (Fall 1991): 309-30.

Sen-Bagchee, Sumana. "'Mericans, Eh?" (Review of *Arranged Marriage*). *The Toronto Review of Contemporary Writing Abroad* 14.3 (Spring 1996): 72-77.

Otherness as Reading Process: Theresa Hak Kyung Cha's *DICTEE*

Kirsten Twelbeck

> Why resurrect it all now. From the Past. History, the old wound.
> The past emotions all over again. To confess to relieve the same folly.
> To name it now so as not to repeat history in oblivion. To extract each
> fragment from the word from the image another word another image
> the reply that will not repeat history in oblivion. (*DICTEE* 33)

When in 1982 the Korean American performance- and short-film artist Theresa Hak Kyung Cha published *DICTEE*, no one in the Asian American Studies departments took notice of this multilingual text whose visual structure is characterized by different forms of writing and images. More than a decade later, pioneering Asian American critic and community activist Elaine Kim confesses that she was originally "put off by the book" (3). Laura Hyun Yi Kang, too, admits to an original preference for "homogenous definitions of Korean/American identity and collective experience" (76).[1] These confessions can be found in *Writing Self Writing Nation*, co-edited by former sceptic Elaine Kim herself. Although the collection offers some of the most insightful analysis to date (I especially admire how this book combines five different approaches to the text, reaching from the personal to the theoretical and the artistic), its overall *gesture* is irritating in the sense that it is represented as *the* legitimate interpretation of *DICTEE*: by means of cover-design, the organization and chronology of the texts, a very emotional preface which points to a connection between the political concern which manifests itself in *DICTEE* and the *sa-i-ku* crisis of 1992, and an introductory essay which embraces *DICTEE* as a kind of personal secret told forth. *Writing Self Writing Nation* implies a claim to cultural ownership. Appropriating the same red cover, equipped with a frontispiece taken from *DICTEE*, and illustrated with a "visual essay," the collection is staged as a kind of "by-text" to the reprint of *DICTEE*, published one year later by the same press. In the preface, Kim declares herself a spokesperson for *DICTEE* by labeling *Writing Self Writing Nation* an "intervention" in contemporary debates that "largely ignored or sidelined Korea

---

1   For a similar confession see Kim 3-4: "What *Dictée* suggested [...] seemed far afield from the identity I was after: a congealed essence defined by exclusionary attributes, closed, ready-made, and easy to quantify."

and Korean America in their discussions of the book" (ix).[2] In her highly autobiographical and certainly illuminating "reflection" on *DICTEE*, Kim takes the
role of a cultural insider, and thus authorizes herself to explain the cultural
meanings implicit in the text.[3] In the course of her essay, the immigrant-artist
Cha, American-born critic Kim, and the "struggling women" of Korea and Korean America (22) become one: "We are linked to nation by the blood our ancestors spilled and used to sign their protests against colonial erasure and the ink
we use to make them and ourselves visible" (23). In order to justify this connection, Kim reads *DICTEE* in a largely associative and selective manner, identifying parallels between the text and her own experience as a member of a minority
group. In itself, this method is absolutely legitimate. Reading oneself "into" this
open and fragmented structure is precisely what *DICTEE* invites the reader to
do.[4] However, it also stresses its singularity, reminding the reader of her status
of "guest" to the personal account which is *DICTEE*: "Then you as a viewer and
guest, enter the house. It is you who are entering to see her. Her portrait is seen
through her things, that are hers" (98). Herself a highly self-reflective reader of
"her" life, the writing "subject"[5] of *DICTEE* continuously reminds every one of
us of our "own" modes of perception, of our different conventions and codes of
understanding. It is this gesture of respectful distance that the introductory essay
misses, thus not speaking *with* but *for DICTEE*.

My second objection to *Writing Self Writing Nation* concerns its status within
the academy. It is the second book that has been dedicated to a single Asian
American literary text.[6] With its help, *DICTEE* has become the central text of the
Asian American anti-canon and thus the book that best represents the contempo-

---

2   This assertion cannot bear close examination. When we look at earlier contributions, almost all
     of them read the aesthetics of *DICTEE* as specifically "Asian" or even "deeply Korean." The
     name of the author, the Korean history referred to, and numerous images from an Asian/Korean
     background without a doubt helped to identify the "mysteriousness" of *DICTEE* as a specifically
     "Asian" trait. Thus, early analyses largely led to satisfy "orientalist" desires (Edward Said).
     However, this is not at stake in Kim's complaints. In both her preface and her introductory es-
     say to the collection, she clearly focuses on ethnicity, not interpretive quality. For a summary of
     the "orientalist" fantasies employed regarding *DICTEE,* see my essay "Reading the Literatures
     of Korean America."
3   Gayatri Chakravorty Spivak problematizes this figure in "How to Read a 'Culturally Different'
     Book" 135. Although Kim in her contribution takes a clearly personal stance, the subtitle ("A
     Korean American's Reflection") posits her (and Cha) as representative of a seemingly homoge-
     nous ethnic identity. As the first essay in the collection and the only contribution which offers a
     personal account, "Poised in the In-Between" does hold a position of authority.
4   In "Reading the Literatures of Korean America" I have developed this thought in more detail.
     What is meant here in general is an "implied reader" who, according to Wolfgang Iser, is al-
     ways driven by a wish for closure. Mechanically speaking, the more "open" a text, the more
     will the reader "invest" herself in it. For a definition of the "implied reader," see Iser 50-67.
5   Because *DICTEE* is also a deconstruction of the notion of an autonomous, unified and fixed self,
     the "subject" needs to be understood in quotation marks.
6   The first one is *Approaches to Teaching Kingston's* The Woman Warrior (Lim 1991).

rary experience of Korean Americans, especially of women.[7] However, its readership is largely limited to the academy.[8] Virtually in the shadow of the celebration of *DICTEE*, there is a growing body of contemporary Korean American works that remains largely unnoticed. Most of them are highly conventional autobiographies like Peter Hyun's *In the New World*, Mary Paik Lee's *Quiet Odyssey: A Pioneer Korean Woman in America* or K. Connie Kang's *Home Was the Land of Morning Calm*.

As an attentive reader of Korean American literature, I want to first "de-canonize" *DICTEE* by positing it within the broader context of Korean American immigrant literature, and then "re-canonize" it as a unique text that makes it possible to experience "otherness" in a "cultural" sense. The overall goal of this double move is to loosen the text from the grip of contemporary discussions without denying its partaking in a specifically Korean American literary discourse. I locate the difference between these two texts not so much in the identity constructions themselves, but in their strategic effects employed towards an implied reader. As Donald Richie has rightfully noticed (unfortunately not without employing "orientalist" imagery), "[t]he Korean story belongs to all of us, and it is this which the diseuse, shaman-like forces speaking through her, tells us" (11). My essay self-consciously embraces the perspective of a European reader of Korean American literature. It is a reader who has been following contemporary debates within the field of Asian American Studies for several years. Of course, being overall dependent on texts written by or about Korean Americans, on the internet and on the opinions of Korean German "ethnic insiders," one comes up against limiting factors. However, this detachment might just as well be understood as a "culturally different" approach since it allows for a perspective in which the formative influence of contemporary American debates

---

7   As Shelley Sunn Wong points out, the mind-change concerning *DICTEE* stands in direct relation to the "changing frameworks of reception within the Asian American community [!], changes that are a result not of transitory literary fashions but, rather, the conjunction of several historical developments in the 1970s and 1980s" (103-4). Guillory rightfully states, that it "is only *as* canonical works that certain texts can be said to represent hegemonic social groups. Conversely, it is only *as* non-canonical works that certain other texts can truly represent socially subordinated groups" (9).

8   *DICTEE* self-consciously affirms its intellectual profile by introducing a figure called "Elitere." In her excellent analysis of Cha's subversive use of invocation of the muses, Shelley Wong interprets this re-naming (of the muse associated with music, Euterpe) as an ironic commentary on the high status of epic literature: "With its resonant play on 'elite' and 'literare', Elitere emerges to critique the privileged place of epic as high literature. As an oppositional gesture, Cha assigns to Elitere the office of lyric poetry" (115). My comment should be seen as additional, not contrary. Also, the readership of *DICTEE* is limited to the English-speaking. When I interviewed two Korean American booksellers in the Los Angeles "Koreatown" in 1996, they had never heard about *DICTEE* nor about any other Korean American books written in English. The only Korean American text they could offer me was a success-story from the American Mid-West, written in *hangul*. Thus, there is a real problem of accessibility for the immigrant generation, a reason why Chang-Rae Lee wanted *Native Speaker* to be translated into Korean in the first place. See Belluck 20.

concerning the institutional status of Asian American Studies or the Canon is less prevalent. Contextualized thus, my analysis should not be seen in opposition to the contributions in *Writing Self Writing Nation* but as an objection to the impression of exclusive "ownership" asserted by that publication.

The first part of my essay juxtaposes *DICTEE* with a far more conventional work, Peter Hyun's *In the New World*, an almost classical "immigrant autobiography".[9] As Heike Paul has demonstrated in her dissertation, works like this are often relegated into the realm of "non-fiction" and thereby escape the attention of the literary critic, while sociologists and historians read them as authentic sources.[10] This division not only along the lines of genre but also of discipline is fatal, since it leads us to overlook the exceptional situation in the history of this body of works: most Korean American texts have been written in the 1980s and 1990s, but their authors are a significantly heterogeneous group. Historically, they stem from different generations, class backgrounds, and community histories. Due to the multilayered history of Korea, the dramatic changes of geography that took place in this century (due to colonization, division, urbanization and globalization)—the country left by early immigrants like Peter Hyun was very different from the one experienced by those who came in the aftermath of the Korean War like Theresa Cha.[11] Gender, of course, becomes a crucial category both in terms of experience and in regard to the texts. All written in the last quarter of the century, these texts engage in a literary conversation about the things that have changed and about the ones that have not. As this brief comparison will show, *DICTEE* in fact shares an interest in the very same "basic" questions, which are pronouncedly Korean American.

I could hardly have chosen two authors, whose (auto-)biographies differed more radically. The male author of *In the New World* (1995) died aged 87, before writing the final draft of the book. The edited text is a highly conventional life-story. As one of the first non-white directors in the American theater, Hyun enjoyed considerable success. However, his artistic ideal of integrating elements

---

9   In "The Necessary Ruse: Immigrant Autobiography and the Sovereign American Self," William Boelhower sketches the immigrant as a person who has experienced two different societies, a circumstance that puts her or him into a position to compare two cultural systems. Nobody else but the immigrant, he argues, sees the American "new home" as much as "an experiment, if not indeed an asylum" (307). Boelhower develops a formula for the genre of the immigrant autobiography (see also 197). For a criticism of this generalizing theory, see Sau-ling Wong 152.

10 Referring to Sucheng Chan's editing of Lee's *Quiet Odyssey*, Paul states: "Mary Paik Lee is turned into an object of 'acquaintance', and thus is robbed of her agency as a literary immigrant: first, as 'historical specimen' she is subsumed into a global historical context of Korean American history, second, she is silenced as a historical subject" (230).

11 These two authors cannot represent the community of Korean American writers as such. I would like to mention other widely neglected authors like Mary Paik Lee, who writes from a working-class point of view, or Ty Pak, whose short stories link the Korean American experience to the Korean War. Today, a younger generation emerges, with writers like Chang-Rae Lee and Nora Okja Keller.

from Asian art into experimental modernist theater was not appreciated. After years of discrimination, isolation, and exclusion, he gave up. Depicting himself as a man of considerable self-confidence, Hyun managed to restart his career as a major in the American army. In 1945, the U.S. military sent him to Korea on a diplomatic mission. He was sent back to the United States for being too critical of the activities of the U.S. military there and too sympathetic to the communist opposition in Korea. A perpetual victim of a racist society, the protagonist is increasingly marginalized and driven into the ethnic ghetto he originally wished to escape from. In the end, he joins the civil rights movement. Shocking in its overall development, this heroic life-story can also be read as an effort to compensate for the endless chain of biographical ups and downs. *DICTEE* is of a totally different nature. When it was completed in 1982, Cha was only 31. Unlike Hyun, whose experiences in modern theater were not incorporated into the formal structure of his very didactic, and genre-conformist text, Cha's early involvement in performance art and film has deeply influenced the "experimental" nature of her book. *DICTEE* has been described as a multilayered, multilingual, and multimedia work that merges different styles of writing and visual forms. As indicated by its use of several Asian and European languages, this work contains not only a variety of literary conventions but also feeds on several cultural contexts.

However different in terms of form and focus, both authors write about and from an immigrant's experience. In order to analyze the similarities and differences between these two books, I have selected three interrelated topics which are, although treated differently, central to both texts (and to many other works by immigrants as well). They are, first, the struggle for a place to call "home;" second, language as a site for identity production; and third, gender as a culturally constructed limitation.

Home

Both Hyun and Cha moved to the United States while they were in their teens. Both of them temporarily returned to Korea. Hyun was sent there in 1945 to promote the U.S. military policy among the Koreans. I consider this episode the central turning point in his autobiography. While the first part of the book resonates with the wish of the subject to "Americanize," with all the connotations this carries, Hyun now accuses the U.S. military of being an insult to the Korean people. The protagonist finds a new identity among political leaders in the Korean educated classes instead. For the first time the author reclaims his formerly rejected identity as a "Korean":

> What startled them most was the sight of me in a U.S. Army officer's
> uniform. I could hear them speculating:

"Is he American or Korean?"
"Can't you see? He's an American officer."
"Yeah, but he looks like a Korean!"
I spoke to them politely. "Nyee, na nun Hangukin im ni da." ("Yes, I am Korean.") (212)

Here and elsewhere, the author takes the role of a translator, a position problematized in *DICTEE*, whose author would rather reject national identity and cultural translatability as an overall concept.[12] However, even in *In the New World*, there is something ambivalent about this code-switching. The "Koreanness" Hyun is struggling to formulate is an almost paradoxical construction, since it is described as an inborn "Americanness" originating in Korea. In his view, the Christian faith, which his family like many Korean immigrants understood as a religion of resistance, makes them predestined to Americanization. A historically inherited "mentality" of adaptability and stubborn willpower makes "the Korean"—unlike immigrants from Japan and China—the "better American," without denying his roots.[13] Throughout the book, Korea is depicted as *the* Asian country culturally closest to the United States. While Hyun criticizes the imperialistic conduct of the U.S. troops in Korea, he also highlights positive aspects of the American "way of life," which the country has organically incorporated: "most of the men wore smart Western suits, and the swagger in their walks was also new [...]. The women [...] did not yield the right of way to men on the sidewalks, they kept walking in straight lines" (208). Obviously, Hyun reinforces the orientalist dichotomy between a progressive and enlightened West and the traditional and patriarchal societies of the East. On the other hand, the society he describes has not suffered "cultural colonization," but has self-consciously selected some of the progressive "American" notions of equality.

When in 1981, almost forty years later, the protagonist/narrator of *DICTEE* returns to Korea, she experiences a country which is not "Western by will," but "Westernized", controlled by a "machine that purports to employ democracy but rather causes the successive refraction of *her* none other than her own" (89). One year after the massacre of Kwangju, where thousands of peaceful demonstrators lost their lives, the southern part of the divided country is ruled by an oppressive militaristic government supported by the United States. Unlike Hyun, who was celebrated as a liberator from a long period of colonialization by Japan, Cha is distrusted and scorned. Even her body bears the mark of traitor, not of liberator:

---

12   For a problematization of the discourse of translation, see Niranjana.
13   There are numerous examples of this attitude in the text. The narrator tends to take a paternalistic attitude towards colleagues from Japan and China. In an episode about hitchhiking in America, Hyun writes: "I soon discovered no one would or could give all of us a ride. I explained this to the two students from Japan, gave them a map, and at the first opportunity put them in a car heading to Pittsburgh. My last words to them were, 'Don't be afraid.' Not too long afterward, I, too, got a ride" (71).

> You return and you are not one of them, they treat you with indifference. All the time you understand what they are saying. But the papers give you away. Every ten feet. They ask you [sic] identity. They comment upon your inability or ability to speak. Whether you are telling the truth or not about your nationality. They say you look other than you say. As if you didn't know who you were. You say who you are but you begin to doubt. (56-57)

While the liberator Hyun claims to have easily abolished public doubts about his national identity by speaking Korean, the returning "subject" of *DICTEE* experiences a crisis of representation, that prevents her from speaking at all: "You open your mouth half way. Near tears, nearly saying, I know you I know you, I have waited to see you for long this long" (58). Cha's Korea of the 1980s is neither the "better America" Hyun was creating, nor an alternative to the United States, nor their product. Her migrating, marginalized, and female "subject" cannot "choose" her identity. She does not feel fully represented either in the United States or in Korea. Instead, the marginalized "subject" is confusedly "beginning to doubt" the overall notion of a fixed identity. Going beyond the "dictation" by Korean nationalism and the Catholicism implicit in her name, the "subject" of *DICTEE* opposes the idea of a primary home and celebrates a "perpetual exile" (81).

Language

Much has been said about how Cha displaces any idea of origin by her subversive and ironic use of language and languages, like Korean, English, French, Latin, and Chinese. Evolving from a history of colonization, exile, migration, and several intellectual and religious traditions, the female speaker of *DICTEE* constantly moves across cultural and linguistic barriers. "Cha rejects any romantic insistence on a fixed, essential identity through language," writes Laura Hyun Yi Kang (85). *DICTEE* itself insists that "our destination is fixed on the perpetual motion of search" (81). There is camouflage involved, when the foreign language student "mimics the speaking" of her new country, when "she takes on their punctuation" (4). However, she "takes the pause" too (5), she stutters, breaks the words, replaces the (native) sound with (her own foreign) voice (158). As Elaine Kim has argued, the speaker is "poised in the in-between" in terms of place and identity. *DICTEE* itself resists any discourse of wholeness: "Almost a name. Half a name. Almost a place" (159).

Itself "stuttering," grammatically "incorrect" and linguistically hybrid, *DICTEE* self-consciously shifts the responsibility of being understood from the "speaker" to the one who listens. It is in the beginning of the text that her foreign speaker "gives birth" to the text, deciding that "the pain not to say" is greater "than is the pain to say" (3). As self-consciously as it claims its right to speak,

DICTEE takes the risk of being misunderstood as a text. Indicated by the shifting meanings implicit in its language (which approaches the reader as a "diseuse's" prophesy, a threatening "disease" and as linguistic "dis-use"), the text accepts that communication, especially across various kinds of imaginary or real borders, involves frustration and embarrassment. This is a motive also found in *In the New World*. When its protagonist learned English at 17, he suffered exclusion:

> "It was a strange fino-menom," I said rather proudly.
> Dead silence.
> "What did you say, Peter?" the teacher asked.
> "It was a strange fino-menon," I repeated.
> "How do you spell it?" The teacher appeared puzzled.
> "P-h-e-n-o-m-e-n-o-n." I remembered the spelling, fortunately.
> "Oh," the teacher smiled, "you mean "phe-nom-e-non"." The class burst into roaring laughter. (17)

When Cha formulates the process of acquiring language, she uses metaphors of pain and deprivation such as raw flesh, rape, cancer, suffocation, and the violence of giving birth. When he tries to speak English, the protagonist of Hyun's autobiography also suffers physically:

> Such a way of speaking completely violated all the proper speaking manners I had learned in Korea: keep your face expressionless, don't reveal your emotions when you speak, and so on, until one could cultivate the perfectly immobile face of a cultured person. Now I had to forsake all the discipline and training and learn to speak in a different form; with a wide-open mouth, bare teeth, and flipping tongue—in general, with a contorted face. It was embarrassing even to try. (17-18)[14]

However, a former exile in Shanghai's Korean community, and used to the racial slurs directed to him there, the protagonist of Hyun's autobiography overcomes initial shame and masters English, just as he formally learned to speak Chinese. As a metaphor of successful assimilation, language acquisition in *In the New World* not only "americanizes" the protagonist but also the person of author. By mastering the conventional code of the American autobiography Hyun has, at least symbolically, inscribed himself into "America." In contrast to Hyun, Cha refuses this one-sided move "into" the linguistic mainstream. Her text prefers to settle on the outskirts of genres and languages thus positing its "subject" on the margins of cultures and nations.

---

14 In Monica Sone's *Nisei Daughter,* Kazuko, the second-generation Japanese American narrator, rebels against the body-related etiquette promoted by Japanese immigrants in her neighborhood. Here too, differences in the cultural construction of the body are used to highlight one's relationship to "America".

Gender

Unlike Cha's speaker, the protagonist of *In the New World* is eager to overcome any trace of foreignness and is "determined to master the art of placing the accent over the right syllable" (17). He embraces English as "not only a language" but "a way of life" (28). Hyun describes language acquisition as an initiation of himself as an Asian boy into a new life as a Western man. He emphasizes not having succumbed to the "polite and shy" Western stereotype of Asian men, but having resisted any humiliation by being "bold," "daring," and "self-confident" (18). In the text, language control functions as the first step into Western masculinity, which is further signified by access to money, women, and cars. However, this dream of "melting in" shatters in real life. Although his experiences follow a downward curve, the text does not admit failure but insists on the "male" law of the American genre of success. The author employs the image of the *American Phoenix*, who, once destroyed, rises above his former gains. As a youth, he is characterized as a fighter. Grown up, he is repeatedly described as a pioneer and self-made man. The author embraces the image of the tough guy when he recalls his years as a soldier. Referring to his married life he labels himself the "breadwinner." *In the New World* can be read as a compensatory success story and fictional masculinization by what autobiography-critic Abbott has called a "crack-up," his description of someone who has suffered too many failures in life.[15] However, this is only one level on which the text can be read. Being overwhelmingly a masculine self-authorizing text, *In the New World* also seeks to formulate a speaking position from which to launch a bitter criticism of a racist society, which repeatedly hindered Hyun from obtaining what he thought was his mission in life, be it as a director or a diplomat.

DICTEE also refers to culturally constructed gender norms as obstacles, central for "her" self-positioning. In the case of the female subject, however, "she" can only destabilize the dichotomy (in which "the Asian woman" functions as "super-feminine") as such. In *DICTEE*'s description of Korea and of the United States, gender is constructed as a fixed hierarchical, binary opposition: "He is the husband, and she is the wife. He is the man. She is the wife. It is a given" (102). On the one side, the speaker ironically recalls a country deeply influenced by Confucianism and Korean nationalism. Here, a woman's place in historiography is limited to that of martyrdom. However, it is Catholicism that marks her name. *DICTEE* excessively mimics the prayers of Thérèse de Lisieux, the female saint who submitted herself to "the Name of the Father."[16] Emptying Catholic

---

15 "It is certainly possible for a person to undergo several major transformations in his or her life, but it is also possible that these repeated conversions are desperate attempts to avoid realization of the crack-up" (Abbott 192).

16 *DICTEE*'s treatment of Thérèse is much more complex than I can discuss here. As my dissertation shows in detail, *DICTEE* is also about taking possession of the "dictated" discourses that "occupy" the postcolonial subject. In my view, Cha not only mocks the prayers of Thérèse, but

female sainthood of its pathos by integrating prayers into translation exercises, and stripping Korean martyrdom of its sublime heroism by reducing it to the untimely death of a young woman, Cha points to the oppressive, nationalist functions of this image. However, she doesn't construct "positive" counter-images like Hyun does, when he challenges stereotypes with his version of a truer self. In *DICTEE* there is no authentic self, only an invitation to "lift the immobile silence" (see 179) imposed by deteriorated patterns of speech and nationalist rituals.

Though the "male" text Hyun left for later generations of Korean Americans is definitely not the kind of cultural memory promoted by Cha, and although *DICTEE* refuses to represent the kind of didactic information Hyun assumed to be politically useful, I do see a central political issue shared by both: their urgent call to exercise what we might call "cultural perspectivism." In the last page of his autobiography, after having demonstrated his efforts to assimilate, Hyun finally dares to challenge the unshaken ideological foundation of American pluralism, both in terms of culture and language: "Why must the world's people come and adopt the American way of life? Can't American people, too, learn and understand the cultures and languages of other lands?" (179). Having traveled far and experienced the hospitality of "Third World-peoples" who "love to practice their English" and "are so much friendlier, when you know how to say 'thanks' and 'good bye' in their native tongue," the imaginary liberal reader will easily support that claim. *DICTEE*, however, puts her/him to the test. More than just pointing to the necessity of intercultural understanding and the pain involved, Cha's text challenges any reader to question the usefulness of learned patterns of understanding and makes her or him question any notion of what is "given," therefore reminding all of us who are willing to submit to the "dictation" of its "foreign" sound, of an "other" within ourselves.

---

also shows her as a historical figure beyond martyrdom, who practiced a powerful "discourse of her own." The authors of *Writing Self Writing Nation* repeatedly point to the fact that Cha attended a Catholic school in United States as a pivotal event. Although I readily agree that this experience may have been deeply influential, this information is not found in the text. It is interesting to note, however, how *DICTEE* works towards activating personal memories concerning early experiences with the faith of the dominant society. Thus, in a conversation about the Catholicism referred to in *DICTEE*, a Korean German friend told me that in the 1960s and 70s, the only schools that accepted Korean school diplomas in Southern Germany were Catholic. Korean children, who often came there because their mothers worked as nurses, had to consent to be baptized and take on a biblical name in order to gain access to those schools. The official reason for this re-naming was the "difficulty" implicit in Korean names. Ironically, most of the Korean pupils chose Christian names that could easily be pronounced and transcribed into Korean.

Experiencing "Otherness"

This hypothesis owes much to the work of Gabriele Schwab, who has written extensively on the aesthetic effects experienced by the reader of modernist or postmodern fiction. Referring to developmental psychology (Winnicott, Ehrenzweig, Bateson) Schwab defines the experience of reading as a sort of training towards accepting "Otherness," a category she understands both as psychological and cultural. Like the play of children, she argues, reading functions on an "intermediary level." "Lost" in reading/playing, the loss of the mother/the imaginary is temporarily compensated by a creative symbolic act, which is closely connected to the imaginary. Put differently, the division of the symbolic and the imaginary is temporarily blurred, thus enabling the individual temporarily to loosen and suspend the limits of its subjectivity and thus expand through a kind of contact with its "own" Other (Schwab, *Entgrenzungen* 42).

According to Schwab, this experience is facilitated by texts that dispense with narrative closure, like the ones modernism and postmodernism have produced. The *language* most suitable for enabling this process is the poetic, with its inclination towards the "other" qualities of speech, such as sound and rhythm (Schwab, *Mirror* 71-99)[17] Such a text cannot unfold its creative potential, when the reader expects to communicate with it on a predominantly informative, "secondary" level. This attitude will be disappointed even when the texts—in a postmodern manner—follow a strategy of radical self-reflection. As this essay will later show in more detail, *DICTEE* is just such a self-reflective and "musical" text. Its resistance to narrative closure and linearity, the radical breakdown of the semantic, and the constant shifting between the visual and the oral alienate the reader from her conventional reading habits. I have actually found myself listening to *DICTEE*, reading it aloud, experimenting with accents on the words, putting in commas since there are only a few. Virtually "overwhelmed" by a growing accumulation of contradictory information, a growing network of inner-textual links, a constant shifting between contexts and categories of knowledge, languages and genres, the reader creates her or his own system of orientation by finding new modes of understanding. As Schwab suggests, a "successful" reading of such a text involves a kind of "letting go," an approach of "unfocused attention," including submission to the more body-oriented "musical" qualities of a text (*Entgrenzungen* 52). Readers who have learned to enjoy texts like that,

---

17 Julia Kristeva, who is an important source for Schwab, has also located "revolution" in poetic language. Clearly Cha's use of language resonates with ideas we might summarize as "écriture féminine." Although this "theoretical practice" is absolutely central for an understanding of Cha's use of language, it is, after all, "just" another discourse, "inhabited" by the parasitical "subject" of *DICTEE*. The feminine connotation of the "Other" is clearly marked as a cultural construction, since the title of the book always reminds the reader of the ideological nature of *all* discourses—including its own.

according to Schwab practice a new "openness" necessary for intercultural contact:

> This training also means attuning us to a radical otherness. Unfocused attention is decidedly "noncentric" in the most encompassing sense: it precludes focusing on the centrisms that still haunts our global world—be they ethnocentrism, sexism, racism, nationalism, or religious fundamentalism. (*Mirror* 87)

This generalizing parallel she draws does not seem convincing when we think of the authors Schwab concentrates on, such as Beckett or Pynchon. However, its truth-value is elevated when applied to texts like *DICTEE* that explicitly deal with the notion of (a plural, shifting, hybrid) *cultural* otherness. "Marked" by a constant breakdown of the categories implicit in the schooling genres of translation, "History," or religious prayer, *DICTEE* constantly reminds the reader that the categories problematized are always also (multi-)cultural. Reaching to its smallest "unit," its "broken tongue" (75), this text leaves no possible doubt about its (multi-)cultural nature. The musical qualities resulting from the semantic breakdown are always *also* allusions to the colonized Korean, who, denied a "language of her own," "speaks in the dark" (45), to the "broken tongue" of the Korean American immigrant, the "other speech" (132) of the woman who, according to Lacanian psychoanalysis, is "speaking" the other, being spoken, "cannot speak" (106). Interspersed with the "cultural" languages "dictated" by Western and Korean nationalism, Western and Korean religion, Western and Eastern colonialism, Western and Eastern philosophy, Western and Eastern gender norms, the textual subject of *DICTEE* (and the reader) "remain[s] apart from the congregation" (155), a "transplant to dispel upon" (20), "fixed on the perpetual motion of search. Fixed in its perpetual exile" (81). Thus, the destabilizing effect of this overwhelmingly hybrid text is never "just" an attack on conventional norms of reading (which, of course, are always cultural and historical). In the process of reading *DICTEE*, we are led to realize that the "stable ground" we lose is that of our own cultural norms and beliefs. In that sense, we may understand *DICTEE*'s metaphors borrowed from tectonics and archeology as indicative of the process of reading *DICTEE*: "Earth is made porous. Earth heeds. Inward. Inception in darkness. In the blue-black body commences lument. Like firefly, a slow rhythmic relume to yet another and another opening" (160). Here, *DICTEE* quite narrowly analyzes what happens when we read, or rather "delve into" *DICTEE*. The "pleasure" of the text lies not so much on the cognitive level—although it is indispensable for the overall understanding of *DICTEE*—but in the capacity of the reader to give her- or himself up to it, to become the "firefly," which, constantly filling itself with new energy, dances along its way from "opening" to "opening."

As Schwab makes clear in her analysis of the aesthetic effect implicit in John Cage's "noise-music," this "crazy dance" follows a composition (an alternative "dictation") which is explicitly experienced as non-chaotic (*Mirror* 71-99). There are, in fact, ways to integrate the multiple and broken voices of the text. The first one predominantly relies on an interpretative system, schooled in feminist-poststructuralist and postcolonial theory. Accordingly, most contemporary critics tend to analyze the "broken language(s)" of *DICTEE* within a theory of resistance through and thus in language. Shelley Sunn Wong, for example, celebrates the text as a specifically Asian American "contest" against the Western "ideology of wholeness" (109).[18] However, it is only on the predominantly "secondary" level of "meaning," that *DICTEE* attempts "to inscribe a very fluid and heterogeneous Korean feminist subjectivity" (98) by subverting the English language. The second unifying "strange attractor" in the text is much more bound to the "imaginary." It is through an *emotional* impact that *DICTEE* "inscribes" "fluidity" and heterogeneity into its reader, whatever her cultural and linguistic background may be. In fact, *DICTEE* has never been described as "chaotic" but rather as "beautiful" (Wolf 11) or "offending" (Kang 75).[19] Towards the end of the text,[20] *DICTEE* itself indicates that we in fact do dispose of a capacity to experience its polyvocal "slipperiness" (Kang 76) and disruptive structure as meaningful and enjoyable: "All rise. At once. One by one. Voices absorbed into the bowl of sound" (162). It is disruption itself that becomes the ordering principle, the absorbing "bowl" of the reader that enables this mixture of voices to resonate. Integrated into a common rhythm that makes change of the temporal its very own element, the mixture of literary genres, the constant change of grammatical person, the abrupt introduction of "other" languages and a constant shifting between visual and audial reception can all "flow" together and create the "different sound" *DICTEE* is aiming at: "Same word. Slight mutation of the same. Undefinable. Shift. Shift slightly. Into a different sound. The difference" (157). Interestingly, this "sound" clearly carries the discernable traces of a Korean (American) woman's history of domination as well as it heralds from "another epic another history" (81). However, this "other" memory, like all other "truths," remains hidden by the only instrument able to give notice of it: Lan-

---

18 In the same volume, Elaine Kim links the unreliability and fluidity of Cha's language to the feminine colonial subject's perception of the inadequacy of language to represent "her" (19). Lisa Lowe interprets it as an elaboration of the writing subject as "hybrid and multilingual" (36). Laura Hyun Yi Kang, who is at the same time very much aware of the mutual relationship between text and reader, states that *DICTEE* "expresses the desire for self-expression and agency in language" (78).

19 Kang states that, when she first read *DICTEE*, she found herself "literally yelling at the book" (75).

20 This spatial category is bound to the time implicit while we read a text "from the first to the last page." However, what we actually do while reading *DICTEE* is best described as a spiraling movement, reaching back and forth throughout the text, always following the variety of "traces" transmitted to the reader. After having "gone" through some of the paths laid out, the reader's understanding of *DICTEE* will be "completed" with every new reading. Thus, *DICTEE* is actually a text without an ending.

guage, the element of dictation/ *DICTEE.* Allowing oneself to be "caught in [its] threading" (4), the reader of *DICTEE,* while being constantly made aware of the "deadness" of words (133), at the same time casts aside doubts about the representative function of language. Conscious of our *irrational* desire for a language-as-representation and communication, text and reader conspire in a shared hope: "If words are to be uttered, they would be from behind the partition [...]. If words are to be sounded, impress though the partition in ever slight measure to the other side the other signature the other hearing the other speech the other grasp" (132).

Clearly written from an immigrant's experience, the "subjects" of *DICTEE* and *In the New World* turn to code-switching as a means of survival. As their protagonists have both suffered exclusion from a self-acclaimed norm, they share a common concern with the widespread obsession with "centrisms," resulting in an inability to change viewpoints. Although they both speak from the margin(s), the textual "subjects" locate their speaking "position" quite differently. *In the New World* makes us witness a Korean American man's almost desperate effort to justify his ability to be accepted as a part of the mainstream. Stressing his superiority both as a man and a Korean American (in contrast to Japanese and Chinese immigrants) he follows a deeply contradictory strategy. Reading *In the New World* can serve as a highly instructive exercise regarding the pitfalls inherent in "claiming America" through the conventional means of the American dream of individual success.

Going far beyond genre conventions (by pitting them against each other), Cha has instead decided to go precisely against those conventions. Creating a text that is virtually "insinuated" by the "blood/ink" of cultural, national, religious, and linguistic hybridity, *DICTEE* "gives birth"[21] to an un-fixed subject beyond a self. A subversive inscription of a multiple self, this counter-narrative *also* causes the reader to lose control over her cultural belief-systems. Thus, on the "intermediary level" of the text we witness an interweaving of reader and the hybrid "subject" of the text.

This mechanism is best described as a process. The initial "fascination" of the Western reader, who may feel "invited" into the text by an "exotic" imagery (the calligraphy is just an example of this gesture),[22] quickly comes to an end.[23] Encountering the "other" within herself, the reader will go through a phase of

---

21   One of the many beginnings of *DICTEE* describes a birth-scene (see 3-5).

22   In my opinion, *DICTEE* uses a repetitive technique of "gazing back," labeled "mimicry" by Homi Bhabha (85-92 and 102-22). I have decided not to elaborate on this thought, since it would lead away from the central interest of this essay.

23   With its references to the "great" and "original" cultures of the West (*DICTEE* incorporates Greek mythology and photographs of "mysterious" Egyptian statues), the effect on non-Western readers should be quite similar.

frustration, comparable to the "dis-ease" experienced by tourist and immigrant alike, when confronted with their own inadequacy and inappropriateness. Like the immigrant/tourist, the patient reader will then try to understand and invent new codes to facilitate orientation. The first one heavily practiced by any "professional" reader of *DICTEE* (including myself) is a practice of association and comparison. Thus, while for Kim, reading *DICTEE* meant remembering her childhood as a member of a minority, Cha's discussion of the Korean division gained importance to me when I ambivalently watched the former "class enemy" crossing the "iron curtain" between the German East and West. The second approach involves research, translation, and communication with "cultural insiders."[24] Another possibility lies within the exercises integrated in the text. Like a student of a foreign language, I "écrivais en francais" as I was told by a translation exercise, which forms a part of the text. Struggling with my French I expected to find a clue to a phrase like: "The people of this country are less happy than the people of yours" (8). In some instances, the translations and my experiments in pronunciation did give new meaning to the text, but most of the time I was betrayed. Luckily, nobody witnessed these embarrassing language-games, and they remained on the level of playful riddles. As Hyun insists, immigrants (and, on a different scale, tourists) tend to be less lucky.

Although all of these "techniques" broaden the overall perception of *DICTEE* (and ourselves), "[e]ach observance" is merely a "prisoner of yet another observance, the illusion of variation hidden in yet another odor yet another shrouding, disguised, superimposed upon" (145). Always aware of the specifically female Korean (American) context of the speaking "subject," the reader is overwhelmed and disintegrated by the multiplication of meanings and languages, until she opens up to the "other" dimension of language. Operating on an "intermediary" level, text and reader engage in an exercise that includes being "inhabited" by a *Gestalt*, that differs in form as well as in temporality. Allowing oneself to submit to the sound and rhythm of *DICTEE* involves a readiness to doubt and "forget" internalized cultural norms and truths. Again, this is reminiscent of the new immigrant/tourist strategies of "committed wait-and-see." Of course, the difference between "immigrant" and "tourist" is crucial. While for the migrating and marginalized subject implicit in *DICTEE* disintegration and "otherness" are permanent, the experience of the reader resembles the one of the (individual) tourist: as a playful, textual experience, "homelessness" is limited in time and devoid of risk. "Outside" of the text, both reader and immigrant alike usually prefer to be same, not Other.

---

24 As I have argued elsewhere, this "unveiling" of a highly "veiled" text forms one of its primary strategies. That is why I think that "explaining" *DICTEE* from an "insider's" viewpoint is not consistent with the imaginative author's intent. By introducing her text through a frontispiece showing Korean calligraphy, Cha virtually "sends" the reader *outside* of the text, to the library, the dictionary, the native speaker. See also my "Reading the Literatures of Korean America."

Works Cited

Abbott, Philip. *States of Perfect Freedom: Autobiography and American Political Thought*. Amherst: U of Massachussetts P, 1987.

Belluck, Pam. "Living Between 2 Cultures: Pain of Assimilation." *International Herald Tribune* 18 July 1995: 20.

Bhabha, Homi. *The Location of Culture*. London: Routledge, 1994.

Boelhower, William. "The Necessary Ruse: Immigrant Autobiography and the Sovereign American Self." *Amerikastudien* 35.3 (1990): 297-319.

Cha, Theresa Hak Kyung. *DICTEE*. 1982. Berkeley: Third Woman P, 1995.

Guillory, John. *Cultural Capital: The Problem of Literary Canon Formation*. Chicago and London: U of Chicago P, 1993.

Hyun, Peter. *In the New World*. Honolulu: U of Hawai'i P, 1995.

Iser, Wolfgang. *Der Akt des Lesens: Theorie ästhetischer Wirkung*. München: Wilhelm Fink, 1976.

Kang, K. Connie. *Home Was the Land of Morning Calm*. Reading, MA: Addison-Wesley, 1995.

Kang, Laura Hyun Yi. "The 'Liberatory Voice' Of Theresa Hak Kyung Cha's *DICTEE*." Kim and Alarcón, eds. 73-99.

Kim, Elaine H. "Poised on the In-between: A Korean American's Reflections on Theresa Hak Kyung Cha's *Dictée*." Kim and Alarcón, eds. 3-30.

Kim, Elaine and Norma Alarcón, eds. *Writing Self and Nation: A Collection on* DICTEE *by Theresa Hak Kyung Cha*. Berkeley: Third Woman P, 1994.

Kristeva, Julia. *The Kristeva Reader*. Ed. Toril Moi. New York: Columbia UP, 1987.

Lee, Mary Paik. *Quiet Odyssey: A Pioneer Korean Woman in America*. Seattle and London: U of Washington P, 1990.

Lim, Shirley Geok-lin. *Approaches to Teaching Kingston's* The Woman Warrior. New York: Modern Language Association, 1991.

Lowe, Lisa. *Immigrant Acts: On Asian American Cultural Politics*. Durham and London: Duke UP, 1996.

—. "Unfaithful to the Original: The Subject of *Dictée*." Kim and Alarcón, eds. 35-69.

Niranjana, Tejaswini. *Siting Translation: History, Poststructuralism, and the Colonial Context*. Berkeley: U of California P, 1991.

Paul, Heike. *Mapping Migration*. Heidelberg: Universitätsverlag, 1999.

Richie, Donald. "The Asian Bookshelf." *The Japan Times* 27 July 1983: 11.

Said, Edward. *Orientalism*. New York: Random House, 1978.

Schwab, Gabriele. *Entgrenzungen und Entgrenzungsmythen: Zur Subjektivität im modernen Roman*. Stuttgart: Franz Steiner Verlag, 1987. Published in English as *Subjects without Selves: Transitional Texts in Modern Fiction*. Cambridge: Harvard UP, 1994.

—. *The Mirror and the Killer-Queen: Otherness in Literary Language.* Bloomington: Indiana UP, 1996.

Sone, Monica. *Nisei Daughter.* Boston: Little, Brown & Co., 1953.

Spivak, Gayatri Chakravorty. "How to Read a 'Culturally Different' Book." *Colonial Discourse / Postcolonial Theory.* Eds. Francis Barker et al. Manchester and New York: Manchester UP, 1994.

Twelbeck, Kirsten. "Reading the Literatures of Korean America." *Postcolonialism and Asian American Literature.* Eds. Seiwoong Oh and Amritjit Singh (forthcoming).

Wolf, Susan. "Theresa Cha: Recalling Telling ReTelling." *Afterimage* (Summer 1986): 11-13.

Wong, Sau-ling Cynthia. "Immigrant Autobiography: Some Questions on Definition and Approach." *American Autobiography.* Ed. Paul John Eakin. Madison: U of Wisconsin P, 1991. 142-70.

Wong, Shelley Sunn. "Unnaming the Same: Theresa Hak Kyung Cha's *Dictée.*" Kim and Alarcón, eds. 103-40.

The "American" Voice in Asian American Male Autoperformance

Robert H. Vorlicky

Asian American performance art—and in particular, the rise of Asian American male autoperformance in the 1990s—is grounded in both Asian *and* (Western European-) American traditions.[1] Regarding the latter, one can cite several (among many) public, historic figures who contributed to the creation of an "American" character, and hence to the idea of "America" and a distinct "American" voice. In origin, the American voice is performative, whether on page or stage. Its continuity is heard most clearly and consistently through its self-reflexive and nationalistic refrains. Yet it is a voice not unfamiliar with rupture; for centuries it has either dismissed or submerged disruptive cadences, only to find within these last decades that the otherwise conventional (i.e., white-inflected) tune is actually changing and diversifying. What is perhaps most threatening to the foundational, originating voice of continuity has been the emergence, in the latter half of the 20th century, of a "reinvented," or emerging voice, one that is, in fact, many voices capable of an impressive range of harmony and dissonance.

In 17th- and 18th-century American autobiographical writing, the authorial male "I" characterized not only a literary genre but a nation and its citizens. This voice emerged as early as 1608 in Captain John Smith's narration of his travels and adventures, and it is traceable in a variety of prose from Jonathan Edwards's diary and correspondence to John Woolman's *Journal* and Ben Franklin's *Autobiography*. It is, what Robert Sayre calls, "the preeminent kind of American expression" (147). This distinctly sexed and gendered "American expression" aggressively sought to clarify an otherwise complicated (if not contradictory) relationship between the "I"-voice and the community. The tension between the individual and the group continued to evolve as a vital, necessary topic in the

---

1   Portions of this essay were delivered on April 5, 1998, at the European Association for American Studies Conference, Lisbon, Portugal. The panel, "Asian American Ceremonies: Continuity, Rupture, or Invention," was organized and chaired by Rocío Davis and Sämi Ludwig; I want to thank them for their continued interest in Asian American male autoperformance. A more comprehensive analysis of Spalding Gray's autoperformances and their comparison to the works of Dan Kwong (some of which is excerpted, revised, or updated in this essay) has appeared in the author's "Marking Change, Marking America: Contemporary Performance and Men's Autobiographical Selves."

autobiographies, personal essays, poetry, and journals of such 18th- and 19th-century Anglo American luminaries as Thomas Jefferson, Ralph Waldo Emerson, Walt Whitman, and Henry David Thoreau. Addressing the connection between autobiography and the making of the United States, Sayre concludes, "Commencing before the Revolution and continuing into our own time, America and autobiography have been peculiarly linked" (147). Expressed differently, the United States and the autobiographical "I"-voice have been thought of, historically, as one and the same, and they have been perpetually linked as such in Anglo American men's writings.

The earliest Anglo American male subject voices severely restricted the range of *topics* they engaged, moving from often mundane observations and catalogues of daily experience to vivid comparisons and contrasts between the New and the Old Worlds. Nonetheless, this voice presented itself as foundational. Upon it rested the challenges set forth by issues of personal identity, citizenship, and nationalism which were untangled, constructed, and set forth as the "ideal," the "universal," and the "representative." The solution offered by the voice was relatively simple: one demonstrated trust in the present voice through, as Sayre argues, either mimicry or emulation (152). Through this action one built upon the virtues of the voice in order to create a shared sense of (national) character with all others. After all, the singular, autobiographical voice presumably spoke for the nation, and the author's experiences were presumably the experiences of other Americans. His story was to be read and to be heard as the life of an American and of America as a new nation with its (allegedly) indigenous culture. From this perspective, male autobiography functioned early on as a literary equivalent to the budding myth of America—a myth that, as Jeffrey D. Mason argues, is "exceptionally powerful because it creates and wields fictions in an attempt to transcend the personal and particular and to convey the experience of an entire culture" (11). Central to most myths of the United States is the influential, albeit problematic American masculine ethos.

Recent attention to previously marginalized autobiographical writing has effectively disrupted conventional notions of what constitutes works of personal, literary, and even national worth. Gender, race, ethnicity, and sexuality are among the features valued today when the specificity of the "I"-voice is ascertained and located. Indebted to the path-breaking scholarship in autobiography theory from the mid-1950s through the 1970s, critics since the 1980s have once again altered the landscape of autobiography studies.[2] Focusing their research in areas of gender, race, ethnicity, and colonialism, contemporary critics are unearthing, reclaiming and recognizing hitherto undervalued or absent autobio-

---

2   Among the major scholars working in the area of autobiography theory from the 1950s through the 1970s are Georges Gusdorf, James Olney, Stephen Butterfield, and Philippe Lejeune; theoreticians since the 1980s include Mary Mason, Albert E. Stone, Sidonie Smith, Nancy K. Miller, G. Thomas Couser, Susan Stanford Friedman, and William L. Andrews.

graphical texts written by women, lesbians and gays, and heterosexual men of color. These texts have been positioned within and against the dominant auto-biographical paradigms that conflate American identity and white male identity. Quite dramatically, therefore, the stories of the "American" and of "America" captured in the first person singular have changed astonishingly in the last third of the 20th century. It is at this juncture in American history—and specifically in American theatre history—that the voice of Asian Americans (as well as other previously marginalized peoples) begins to take center stage. And quite often it does so in the form of autoperformance.

In terms of theatre practice, autoperformance derives from the convergence of autobiographical material, the physical presence of the "individual," and the authorial "I"-voice of the speaker. Richard Schechner draws a significant distinction in relation to autoperformance: "I don't mean monologues in the traditional sense of a one-person show, but in the more radical sense of using the person who is performing as the source of the material being performed. Compressed into a single presence is author-director-performer" (44). Deborah Geis locates the source of America's interest in monologue in the experimental theater of the 1960s and 70s. Its "postmodern revisioning of subjectivity," argues Geis, "inspired new approaches to the portrayal of characters' 'inner lives', and this obviously had a significant impact upon the role of monologue" (37). This same experimental theatre contributed to the development of performance art and, in particular, of autoperformance. According to Peggy Phelan, "Performance Art's most radical and innovative work often involves a thrillingly difficult investigation of autobiography. By rejuvenating the possible ways of presenting and representing the self, Performance Art has changed the notion of theatrical presence and widened the methods by and through which the self can be narrated, parodied, held in contempt, and/or made to be the source of revelatory vision and thought" (28). Autoperformance, I believe, remains a flexible, engaging dramatic genre that will serve as a structural and contextual bridge between the 20th and 21st centuries in American theatre. It is a form that is malleable with its myriad options for storytelling; also, its content erases neither the actor's body (and all its markings) nor his freely chosen topic selections.

In the introductory chapter to her invaluable book, *Performing Asian America*, Josephine Lee astutely presents the history of Asians in America as necessary background to understanding the varied and changing *representations* of Asians on stage that would occur throughout the 20th century. Tracing the discrimination of Asians by America's institutional structures of immigration and naturalization, Lee highlights the Chinese Exclusion Act of 1882 (which was repealed in 1943), the 1929 National Origins Act, the McCarran-Walter Act of 1952, and the more liberating Hart-Cellar Act of 1965, which abolished the quota system. In 1989, for example, over a quarter million Asians immigrated to the United States. Filipinos, Chinese (from China, Taiwan, and Hong Kong),

Asian Indians, Koreans, and Vietnamese were among the largest groups at that time (Lee 2-3).

Lee marks the 1970s as the "real" rise in the presence of Asian American theatre and performance in the United States. But she also problematizes this dating by noting the extent to which Chinese and Japanese American experiences, unfortunately, have often been taken to represent the idea of and the work of "Asian America" at the exclusion of dramatic works by Asian Indians, Pacific Islanders, and Southeast Asians. Confronting this situation that there is no "us" that exists "in terms of a homogeneous community of ordinary Asian Americans," Lee suggests "then at the very least," Asian Americans can connect through "an intensely imagined commonality shared by a number of diverse individuals and social groups" linked by "a continuing emphasis on 'pan-ethnicity'" (9-10).

Contemporary Asian American male autoperformance has helped tremendously to respond—to create—a counter-tradition to the traditional theatrical (and also filmic) representations of Asian American men (historically portrayed by Anglo actors) as castrated, self-effacing, asexual, contemptible individuals. While Lee, in general, confines her analysis to the study of plays, she does not include monodramas among them. In very striking ways, therefore, the rise of Asian American autoperformance (which is a specialized form of monodrama) has been—and remains—at the cutting edge of Asian American drama and performance.[3] Its roots are not to be found in the continuity of a race-specific historical and theatrical past, as much as in a rupture of *theatrical tradition*—through which the autoperformer's original (i.e., ancestral) culture and the invention (or discovery) of his *hybridic self in "American" culture* is performed through his language and body. One strand of his roots reside in the early American autobiographical writings mentioned earlier while another more recent strand—in the traditional art of Asian storytelling (i.e., the aesthetics of detailed, nuanced narrative)—is firmly grounded in American women's performance art from the 1960s to present time.

From the late 1970s through much of the 1980s, American male autoperformance was dominated by the work of Anglo American performance artist Spalding Gray. By the late 1980s and early 1990s, however, heterosexual men of color and gay male autoperformers presented their work around the United States—generally in large urban centers such as New York, Los Angeles, and Chicago. Asian Americans artists such as Lane Nishikawa, Han Ong, and Dan Kwong, to name but a few, were performing monodramas to critical acclaim in local, community-centered productions.

---

3   Among the prominent Asian American solo performers, some of whom are autoperformers, are Amy Hill, Nobuko Miyamoto, Lane Nishikawa, Jude Narita, Nicky Paraiso, Canyon Sam, Denise Uyehara, Han Ong, Alec Mapa, and Dan Kwong.

Whereas early Anglo American writers valorized a kind of self-made individualism that helped to establish them as representative men among men, contemporary male autoperformers transform—or invent—a kind of self-identified individualism, or personalization, that recognizes a man's public articulated perception of what Una Chaudhuri calls his "difference within" (199). In turn, this individualized self connects to a range of outer "communities," which may include those that provide a sense of cultural past.

One of the most compelling Asian American autoperformers in the United States today is Dan Kwong, a third generation Japanese American. Kwong often premieres his work at Highways Performance Space, a not-for-profit alternative theatre in Santa Monica, California. From his earliest full-length monodrama, *Secrets of the Samurai Centerfielder* (1989) to his latest, *The Night the Moon Landed on 39th Street* (1999), Kwong focuses his narratives on what it means to be a racial and cultural "hybrid" (his mother is Japanese and his father Chinese)—as well as an Asian American, a heterosexual, and a man. His stories take him across the vast terrain of racism, sexism, homophobia, violence, abuse, disease, crime, and sexual compulsion. Enlivening his narratives in performance, Kwong employs a range of multimedia, theatrical techniques and simple, symbolic props: hand puppets, shadow play, suggestive costuming, pre-recorded musical scores (from American rock to European classical and Asian traditional folk), energetic movement (from tai chi to erotic dancing and child's horseplay), film, interactive video, projected photographs, and voice-overs.

While these theatrical elements enhance the vitality of Kwong's narrative, they do not detract from the performer's main objective: to present selected personal stories that convey the complexities and contradictions inherent in both his uniqueness from and his sameness to others, and to explore artistically the way in which his experiences are and are not grounded in conventional notions of "America." Perhaps his greatest link, besides physical theatricality, to other male autoperformers—from ground-breakers Tim Miller and Keith Antar Mason to Luis Alfaro and Han Ong—is a deliberate foregrounding of relationships to men, to masculinity, to what it means to be a man in the United States, which remains a hotly contested issue in American culture.

An early full-length work, *Tales from the Fractured Tao with Master Nice Guy* (1991) captures the presence of continuity, rupture, and invention in Kwong's autoperformance. Thirteen sections constitute *Tales*, which Kwong summarizes as the story of his "dysfunctional family, Asian American style."[4] Mapping out the early innocence of his childhood as a hybrid member of an over-achieving Asian American family, Kwong moves to the traumatic family rupture caused by his parents', Sam and Momo's, divorce. Interacting with a wizened apparition called "Master Nice Guy" (the performer himself in a beard

---

4   All subsequent page references to *Tales from the Fractured Tao with Master Nice Guy* the are from the playwright's unpublished manuscript.

and projected on a pre-recorded video), Kwong hears the fatherly advice that he must not allow his "secret" pain to be "locked up inside too long." "It's bad for you, makes you crazy," warns Master Nice Guy. "That's old-country stuff, boy. You're an *American* Asian. Might as well take advantage of it!" (4). Not only is the confessional perceived as an "American" trait, but the United States itself is framed as a geographical *place* and a psychological *location* for release.

The majority of the remaining sections either allude to or directly address Kwong's secret: the depth of the pain and dislocation created by the absent father that Kwong had not hitherto expressed in words. Announcing in Brechtian fashion a section toward the end of the performance, "To Myself," where Kwong recalls a dream in which his dad humiliates him, the overhead text sign ("This is our silence, between father and son—the history of Asian men") is countered by Kwong's angry shouts at his father. In order to break that silence and thereby to have the chance *not* to repeat the father's story of domestic violence, isolation, and eventual loneliness, Kwong moves through anger to recognition, and finally to compassion toward his dad. Within the final sections, Kwong recalls, in snippets of dialogue, a phone call he had with his father, after he had moved to Chicago when he was nineteen years old. Sam, after nearly a decade, was breaking the silence that had suffocated his own past as well as his relationship with his son: "I'm sorry," the father repeats several times, words that "spoke for many years." Crying, which he had never done in front of his son, Sam "went on as if he had to finish emptying his heart" (18); finally, Asian American father and son were able to express their love to each other—something that continuity had previously frustrated, which resulted in unavoidable rupture and yet offered the possibility of invention, here between a father and his son, a microcosm of a much larger cultural issue. Later that night after their phone conversation, Kwong says with much relief at the end of the monodrama that he "cried for the first time in eight years [...] like a young child whose broken heart had finally been seen" (19).

Topical issues of note arise in two other critically noteworthy monodramas by Kwong. *Monkhood in 3 Easy Lessons* (1993) highlights his relationship to his maternal and paternal grandfathers amid his exploration of Asian American male identity, the absence of Asian American heroes from "American" history, current violent racial bashings in Los Angeles, the World War II internment camps, and the author's wish to be a stud and not "some WHIMPY CHINK." This latter issue echoes the earlier work of Frank Chin, who linked Anglo American "masculinist" culture to a desirable stage image for Asian American men; Kwong, however, eventually deconstructs this racial, gendered paradigm through his autoperformance. In his 1996 monodrama, *The Dodo Vaccine*, Kwong internalizes the power of the generational "song of life"—a recognition of the value of one's differences within and without that was passed on to him by his grandfather—in order to "invent" a space within which he could freely move between himself as an individual and as part of various communities. In this piece, provocative questions related to sexuality and sexual behavior intersect with those centered on Asian American identity as the story teller confronts issues of HIV status and AIDS in the heterosexual community. As a straight man, Kwong releases his own guilt over his lingering homophobia, only to come to recognize the commonality between the racist oppression he experiences as an Asian American and the homophobic injustices endured by his "gay brothers and lesbian sisters" (*Dodo*).

As part of an informal, email interview in March 1998, I asked Dan Kwong to address the current state of Asian American drama and performance. A well-known and respected performer on the United States's West Coast who is increasingly gaining fans throughout America and Great Britain as his work is produced, Kwong celebrates the reality that the Asian American performance scene has grown exponentially since the mid-1980s. Workshops and classes are held regularly throughout the country, he acknowledges, during which younger Asian Americans find encouragement and accessibility to using performance as a form of creative expression.

According to Kwong, a

> strong body of work is emerging which deals primarily with issues OTHER than race and ethnicity, mainly around gender, sexuality, and class. These subjects are usually framed within an Asian American's perspective, but the artist's Asian-ness may or may not be in the foreground of the work. To me, this is a logical progression. There will always be a need for work which addresses cultural identity as long as we have racism and cultural chauvinism. This is often the entry point for people of color who are exploring their identity through performance, because racism is such a monumental factor in the lives of people of color growing up and/or living in the United States. (Interview)

"What I see now," Kwong continues,

> is work that talks about issues *within* the Asian American community, whether it be the classisism, sexism, domestic violence, gay oppression, or internalized racism acted out toward other Asians or other people of color. I now see Asian American artists trying to challenge their own communities on where we have our own shit to clean up, aside from (but not totally unrelated to) the external racism we face living in the U.S. [...].

Finally, there is also a new aspect which includes Asian American artists who are tackling issues of Asian American communities other than their own. For example, Jude Narita, a pioneer Japanese American writer/performer has created a new piece *Walk the Mountain*, which deals with the legacy of the Vietnam War for the Vietnamese and Cambodian people [...]. It is a notable step forward when people make the effort to speak out for the liberation issues of other groups. In this era of cultural identifying and (re)claiming one's heritage in the face of racism, alliance building across groups requires us to step outside of victim identity, and perhaps to recognize that we all play a part in the cycle of oppression, as targets and as agents of oppression. If you ain't part of the solution, you're part of the problem. (Interview)

Central to Kwong's identification as an artist is the sheer "celebration" he finds in

the act of performing [since it] is an act of joy, even if the subject matter is painful or difficult [...]. Tradition is sometimes very subtly present, sometimes more obvious. When I incorporate martial arts forms such as iaido (Japanese sword) or tai chi, it is obvious that I'm drawing upon traditional forms. Or in the manner I choose to tell a story. There is a strong tradition of the enjoyment of irony and paradox in both Japanese and Chinese culture, and even if it may not always be obvious, I draw upon this tradition in my work. (Interview)

As is evident in the artistry of Dan Kwong, a new generation of Asian American theatre practitioners is alive and thriving in the United States—within workshops, on the stages within local communities, and increasingly more visible in the not-for-profit and commercial theatres. Most importantly, their silence is now broken and their voices celebrated—and the theatre has become a crucial location for their bodies to be seen and for their voices to be heard. With deep passion and vision, Kwong frames his own performances by noting that "celebration is inherent to the form of my art; standing in front of people and telling a story I care about, or dancing like a wild man, or hitting baseballs into a net" (Interview).[5]

Works Cited

Chaudhuri, Una. "The Future of the Hyphen: Interculturalism, Textuality, and the Difference Within." *Interculturalism and Performance*. Eds. Bonnie Marranca and Gautam Dasgupta. New York: Performing Arts Journal Publications, 1991. 191-207.

Geis, Deborah. *Postmodern Theatric[k]s: Monologue in Contemporary American Drama*. Ann Arbor: U of Michigan P, 1993.

Kwong, Dan. *The Dodo Vaccine*. Unpublished manuscript, 1994. Spitalfields Market Art Project, London. April 1994.

—. E-Mail interview with Robert Vorlicky. 24 March 1998.

—. *Monkhood in 3 Easy Lessons*. Unpublished manuscript, 1993. Japan American Theater, Los Angeles. June 1993.

—. *The Night the Moon Landed on 39th Street*, Unpublished manuscript, 1999. Highways Performance Space, Santa Monica. June 1999.

---

5   A collection of Dan Kwong's monodramas, *From Inner Worlds to Outer Space: The Multimedia Solo Performances of Dan Kwong*, edited with commentaries by the author, is forthcoming (Cassell P, 2002).

—. *Secrets of the Samurai Centerfielder*. Unpublished manuscript, 1989. Highways Performance Space, Santa Monica. September 1989.

—. *Tales from the Fractured Tao with Master Nice Guy*. Unpublished manuscript, 1991. Highways Performance Space, Santa Monica. January 1991.

Lee, Josephine. *Performing Asian America: Race and Ethnicity on the Contemporary Stage*. Philadelphia: Temple UP, 1997.

Mason, Jeffrey D. *Melodrama and the Myth of America*. Bloomington: Indiana UP, 1993.

Phelan, Peggy. "Spalding Gray's *Swimming to Cambodia*: The Article." *Critical Texts* 5.1 (1988): 27-30.

Sayre, Robert F. "Autobiography and the Making of America." *Autobiography: Essays Theoretical and Critical*. Ed. James Olney. Princeton: Princeton UP, 1980. 146-68.

Schechner, Richard. *The End of Humanism: Writing on Performance*. New York: Performing Arts Journal Publications, 1982.

Vorlicky, Robert H. "Marking Change, Marking America: Contemporary Performance and Men's Autobiographical Selves." *Performing America: Cultural Nationalism in American Theatre*. Eds. J. Ellen Gainor and Jeffrey D. Mason. Ann Arbor: U of Michigan P, 1999. 193-209.

V. (Re)Constructing Self

Rituals of Mothering:
Food and Intercultural Identity in Gus Lee's *China Boy*

Alicia Otano

Gus Lee, in his first novel, *China Boy*, deals with the clash of two worlds as experienced by a child, and demonstrates how the child manages to reconcile these conflicting forces and finds a place for himself in his multicultural setting. The use of the child perspective, the description of the apprehension of sensations and the attempt to make sense of the world, is a powerful tool in the communication of the developing subjectivities in Asian American literature. The appropriateness of the theme of childhood and the use of the child narrator in immigrant texts is self-evident. Peter Coveney's seminal work, *The Image of Childhood*, emphasizes the advantages of the child as a literary theme in texts that center on the consequences of cultural transfer in the modern world: "In childhood lay the perfect image of insecurity and isolation, of fear and bewilderment, of vulnerability and potential violation" (32). The repetitive use of the child as a metaphor for the experience of immigrant adaptation to a new environment invites the examination of childhood narratives and the specific advantages they offer for the presentation of these issues.

The point of view employed in the articulation of immigrant narratives is of central concern to both writers and critics because to identify the voice of the narrator is to examine the creative process of narration. Interest is heightened when the prism, the perspective through which the story is presented, is the voice of a child. In contemporary literary criticism, *voice* has come to mean both the act of narrating and the aspects of a story that help identify and situate the narrator. It has become, in short, "identity," defined to include the narrator's point of view, perspective, focus, and stance (Otten 3). The question of who looks and who sees is crucial to the study of the presentation of childhood in literary texts where the writer is almost always an adult. The interplay of two focal points—that of the experiencing child and that of the observing or reminiscing adult—engages a double vision: the child's experience, and the adult narrator's use of that experience. Moreover, as Richard Coe has pointed out, childhood constitutes an alternative dimension, one which cannot be conveyed by the utilitarian logic of the responsible adult; not "accuracy" but "truth"—an inner, symbolic truth—becomes the only acceptable criterion (2). Therefore, the adult narrator often takes advantage of the imagining, the creating, the remembering, the retelling of these "truths" from the child's perspective to focus the experience of personal and communal identity from the very beginning. The voice of the child becomes pivotal to two fundamental concerns in the presentation of the Chinese American subject: how the self is constituted and how meaning is established.

In the fiction of Chinese American writers like Gus Lee, the search for a valid beginning to the telling frequently mirrors the narrators' own search for the stage at which they become the individuals they now feel themselves to be. Consequently, this search for an opening, the act of recapturing the first memory, or isolating the moment when the child first becomes aware of its identity, is crucial. The element of interest here is not so much in the child character *per se* as in a state of awareness, a point of new and conscious beginning, for which childhood is the most obvious analogy. If, as Laurie Ricou asserts, "rebeginnings" insist on being a framework for understanding, it follows that the narrating memory is continually searching childhood for the defining incident (35-36). In Lee's novel, the voice and experiences of the child are introduced by and filtered through the adult narrator, who focuses on the experience through his memories of life after his mother's death. The question of the child's adapting to personal and cultural circumstances and the emotional responses these arouse becomes a critical juncture in the employment of this type of point of view. Specifically, the idea of food and the ceremonies associated with it, act as a prism in *China Boy* through which to view both culture and familial affiliation, unifying narrative concerns.

A child's definition of happiness is one of the major exercises in the novel. The process of the young Chinese American Kai Ting's emotional and cultural development may be mapped by analyzing the role that food plays in his life. As Sau-ling Wong explains, quoting James W. Brown: "[E]ating is one of the most biologically deterministic and, at the same time, socially adaptable human acts—a meal can be a simple prelinguistic phenomenon or a multivalent sign coded in language, manners and rites—alimentary images pose particularly intriguing challenges in the interpretation of nonmainstream literature" (18). Food in cross-cultural literature may thus be examined as a code that expresses a "pattern of social relations," reading the contents and sequencing of meals as texts with their corresponding form and thematic content (Douglas 61). Moreover, the description of food and meals plays a fundamental role in Asian American literature, as Wong has shown in *Reading Asian American Literature: From Necessity to Extravagance*. Just as "the novel of manners could not eschew the depiction of meals without doing irreparable damage to the very aesthetic and social criteria on which it was based" (Brown 6), Chinese American fiction must necessarily deal with the role of food and meals if it wishes to present a coherent and realistic portrait of the evolving culture it describes. The focus, in many cases, is on "how eating and drinking constitute an elaborate and complex sign language which metonymically brackets and informs all aspects of discourse and human experience" (Hinz v). In the case of the novel in question, personal and cultural self-affirmation is directly associated with food and to the provider of meals. Affection is measured by degrees of culinary generosity experienced by the young boy. As Coe points out, for a child, there is no "better" world—the child only knows that it is happy or not happy (233). My analysis of the novel will therefore center on the diverse mechanisms through which happiness—or the absence of it—are conveyed in *China Boy*.

Food, and all the ceremony associated with it, plays a central role in the process of self-awareness and the Asian American's evolving subjectivity be-cause of the emotional impact the culinary dimension of life has on young Kai, specifically through the strong presence of the mother figure, a central touch-stone in his development. For the boy, his mother and the food she prepares for him are the prime constituents of the Chinese world that is their emotional, and therefore "real," home. Despite being born in the United States, Kai literally lives and functions in a parallel Chinese world, protected from everything alien to the traditional Old World way of life. What happens when this parallel world is shattered because of the mother's untimely death, leading to the loss of all that represents and embodies the culture of the heart, is a beautifully documented account on what and how the child perceives. There is no attempt by the narrator to "judge" the events in those young, formative years: there is only a need to transmit immediate feeling and emotional responses. Moreover, the specificity of this Chinese American text lies in the recounting of the boy's growing notions of self-within-family that parallels his cultural development, his increasing con-sciousness of self-within-place: the end of childhood implies the rupture of the "pure" Chinese identity his mother encouraged. Kai's status as a foreign child resembles a stage in development similar to childhood and ensures that the American acceptance is tied to his realization of manhood (So 149).

Psychologists generally agree that the most important formative events take place before the child reaches the age of five. Yet, if memory can be situated with reasonable accuracy at the age of three in many human beings, there is no question that, in the case of *China Boy*, its status is highly significant. Kai's per-ceptions and the primarily sensual recollections he has of them are key to the process of forging a sense of identity. The identification between food and Kai's mother is highlighted in the early chapters of the book. The mother provides the meals and the meaning behind them: "Eat, my son, eat!" she would encourage, as she "carefully extracted and then placed the valued fish's cheek on my plate. I smiled, for this meant she loved me" (41). Caught eating a peanut one day, Kai remembers being picked up by his mother, whisked to the bathroom and made to throw up while she wailed: "Please, please, Only Son! NO, NO PEANUTS! It weakens your shigong, your vital spirit! Here! Take some Chiing chun bao, the liquids of life! [...]. I did not wait my entire life to finally have a son, here, in this remote world, to have you die of peanuts!" (21). Her panic arose from the experience of a first cousin's only male son dying from eating peanuts in China. Kai's recollection of the event, apart from emphasizing his mother's concern for his well-being, will mark his life: "Eating peanuts became the equivalent for me of spitting on an ancestor's grave" (21).

In terms of social psychology, the table symbolizes maternal affection and physical contact with the environment. The mother figure therefore serves as the first introduction to the world and the table becomes the locus of initiation into society (Brown 16). Thus, Kai's mother arranges to hold the traditional Red Egg Ginger Party in order to celebrate the male baby and her own survival of child-birth. Bowing to America and its circumstances, the party is not held one month after birth as is customary in China, but four years later: "It was flouting tradi-tion. He [Kai's father] was a proud iconoclast. Meeting the rigidity of the past with equal fervor" (28). This is precisely what the child's mother could not do. She contrived to make the Red Egg Ginger Party as traditional as possible:

> Red paper reflecting good fortune with bright gold calligraphy hung in the kitchen. The largest banner bore the name of her father, Na-Gung, and she pre-pared a special seat for him at the other end of the table from her husband [...]. Jennifer and Megan made the special Mother's chicken soup. It brewed inside the brown earthenware vessel with the nipplelike lid handle emblazoned with the characters for double happiness. Dozens of eggs were boiled in bright red dye. The soup was medicinal for the mother's recovery; the shape of the bowl was suggestive of reality, and the eggs spoke for themselves. (28)

All these scenes related to food and eating with the family demonstrate how the narrator privileges these rituals as a vital part of the negotiation of identity and self-affirmation. Alimentary detail supports and validates the epistemological process: it is a supplement to cultural meaning. Moral values and meals are complexly interwoven: the giving, receiving, eating, and serving of food become means of signifying. Moreover, it appears that something about the immigrant situation—perhaps the shock of permanent relocation to a white dominated soci-ety and the daily trials of adjustment—caused the first generation to value effi-cient eating unquestioningly, "almost as a measure of spiritual stamina" (Wong 25). This highlights James Brown's idea that, in any given culture, the structure of the meal reflects social organization to such an extent that it may be consid-ered a microcosm of a particular society at a specific moment in its history (4).

The manner in which the family celebrated this feast articulates some of the peculiarities of the Chinese in America in the 1950s. For Kai, the table repre-sents the mother country and the meals he ate when his mother lived were an act of identification with his heritage culture and an adherence to its values. At the same time, the manner in which the celebration was held demonstrates that the family had—consciously or not—made concessions to the ways of the land they had moved to. This illustrates the extent to which food categories encode social and cultural events by expressing hierarchy, inclusion and exclusion, boundaries and transactions (Mennell et al. 10). In *China Boy*, the serving of meals establishes and communicates love, pride, familial and social standing, and gratitude, as the meals are carefully positioned and structured to highlight and explain motivation and development. The child is naturally part and parcel of the ceremony and its significance: "So we ate for hours, laughing and full of the joy of family" (28).

References to the pivotal role that meals play in Chinese culture are made throughout the novel:

> The Chinese eat with the joy of abandonment, the relish of a pride of lions. The object of a Chinese meal is eating. It is not a spectator sport, and the theme of the exercise is free pleasure after a long day's work. Chinese food is complex artistry in preparation and simple unrestrained celebration in eating. People talk, shout, laugh [...] and permit the child within us all to romp freely with happy little chopsticks at dinnertime. (78-79)

Furthermore, the descriptions of the food that the Chinese community so revel in stress much of their culture-specific delight in culinary matters: "'This,' [Father] said, pointing, 'is called sea cucumbers.' But they are not vej-ah-tables. They are ocean slugs. Yes, yes. It's terrible. See there. Chicken heads. Not cut off, since that's bad luck [...]. So we have the head, looking back at us. Cutting fish head is okay, since cheek is special" (133). What unites the immigrants in many Asian American texts that describe food, asserts Wong, "is an ability to eat uncompromising substances and to extract sustenance, even a sort of willed enjoyment from them; to put it symbolically, it is the ability to cope with the constraints and persecutions Asian Americans have had to endure as immigrants and racial minorities" (25). This manner of eating by the Chinese in the United States becomes an extremely effective form of cultural affirmation and emotional gratification—a continuity with a past—while the white American revulsion towards these customs emphasize the chasm between the communities. For this reason, Kai's trials begin when his mother passes away and his world is transformed. The culture-specific way of eating and considering food are among the first things that change when his father remarries a white American and brings her home to be a mother for his children. Edna's arrival implies rupture on various levels: the child stands to lose even the memory of his mother, and the culture she embodied and re-created in the home, most vividly portrayed through food. The adult narrator, looking back, recalls at one point that "Edna must have viewed her first meal in our home in nauseous dismay, a rapid descent into Dante's kitchen. The snuffling, the talking with food in the mouth, the elbows on the table, the unknown taxonomy of the strange things on people's plates probably had the same effect on her as a Milk of Magnesia and mustard-based emetic" (79).

The arbitrary working of memory leads to the question of authenticity in the recollection and representation of early childhood. Coe argues that where the symbolism is unmistakable, one may suspect the shaping influence of the mature artist's sense of value and form (98). In *China Boy* the adult narrator always looms in the background, guiding the reader (and maybe himself) towards the discovery of patterns, the analysis of motives and the interpretation of events. Nonetheless, the author's use of sensory perceptions reminds us how the acuteness of these senses influences the process of memory. Kai is only six when his mother dies, an event comprehended in fragments. In the traditional Chinese way, the boy is not informed directly, and must come to the conclusion almost by himself. Consequently, Kai mourns through his relationship with food: "I ate less, performing an unconscious, immature child's ching ming by offering my food to my lost and missing parent" (52). The child is literally consumed by guilt, and by his incomprehension of the situation. Food, his mother's principal way of showing her love, will now symbolize his loss. This supports Sau-ling Wong's contention that alimentary images, juxtaposed and read as a group, symbolize Necessity—"all the hardships, deprivations, restrictions, disenfranchisements, and dislocations that Asian Americans have collectively suffered as immigrants and minorities in a white-dominated world" (20). The personal and cultural self-esteem that the mother's Chinese food contributed to the boy's life will be effaced by the introduction of new food—the most vivid symbol of a new way of life—as a WASP stepmother enters the household.

The relationship established between food and the child's sense of security occupies a central position in the novel. Kai seeks solace in food in times of deepest confusion or sorrow. The emotional charge he receives keeps him going, be it from the greasy fries in the panhandle restaurant or from the coveted baked dumplings and steamed cakes from Chinatown. When a certain food is imposed, as often happened with Edna, it becomes another tool for torture. Meals become "fresh breadsticks, boiled cabbage, flinty lima beans, hardy brussel sprouts, and undercooked hamburger stew" (82). Though the narrator recognizes that Edna did not do any of these things to make them suffer "but that she merely wanted to improve the home" (83), the emotional toll will be high. She tells Janie, for instance, that "when you learn to enjoy brussel sprouts, I will allow you to buy that dress at Sears," not realizing, as Janie informs her, that the "sale ended months ago, and it's not on the rack" (83). The saying "you are what you eat" takes on frightening connotations in the case of Edna: her food implies manipulation and forced change.

The arrival of a stepmother is a crucial and determining factor in Kai's life. There is no room for compromise in their relationship and this is the cruelest means of punishment for a child like Kai. The only sister living at home and closest to him in age is aware of this. Physical abuse in the house and violence outside—where he is forced to remain after school—shadow Kai's world after his mother's death. Slaps on the face (not very Chinese, according to his sister,

Janie), the destruction of his toys, and all the delicious, familiar food vanished from their table constitute the new world order. But the first Mrs. Ting's presence continues to be very palpable for the little boy. Though her portrait no longer hangs where it once did, to him it is still there. The bedspread where she once sat is still there for him to rub his hand against, and—ironically—the smell of burnt toast brings her back immediately.

The psychological warfare through food persists. The adult narrator recalls:

> Edna knew that we, like the soldiers of Bonaparte, lived on our stomachs. The heart of the matter, in a Chinese household, is food [...]. Her cultural offenses were launched when our defenses were weakest—at dinner. Communication to Janie and me arrived with the boiled squash in the presence of our father [...]. "We are only to speak English henceforth," she announced. "Absolutely no Chinese in any form. The removal of this foreign food will help, since I understand that no proper words exist to describe it." (76-77)

At another moment in the narrative, the voice of the adult Kai explains the place of food and eating in his stepmother's home, undercutting pathos with humor:

> The purpose of a meal with Edna was protocol. We learned an elaborate preparatory procedure that made scrubbing for brain surgery seem dilatory. No talking, no grinning, Death to laughers. Food to a fascist is somber business [...]. Chairs just so. No wrinkles in the tablecloth. Without funds, we purchased silver and glassware [...]. Salad forks on the outside! We never saw a salad and had little soup [...]. The marks of childhood endure. Today, when I see silverware improperly aligned, I feel a jab of fright, a small tender sliver of pain, a threat of disorder and possible doom. (79)

Fittingly, the chapter entitled "Banquet" illustrates the chasm between this new world order and the traditional one that the boy Kai and his sisters long for. The entire family attends the Ting Hui Family Association banquet where Kai's father makes a triumphant entry because he has married an American. Edna's presence is an eye-opener: she is attractive and she is foreign. Nonetheless, her inappropriate behavior highlights some of the consequences of their marriage in relation to the rest of the Chinese American community. Edna does not fit in and unknowingly trespasses her bounds as the wife of a Chinese man. She is made a fool of and leaves the party with the rest of the family before dinner is over. Kai's long-awaited family reunion, with the promise of a magnificent meal laden with all the familiar smells and tastes ends tragically: "I chewed faster, stuffing my mouth until Megan hustled me to my feet and escorted me away" (137).

This major turning point in his young life sets the stage for a more dramatic one: being set loose on a San Francisco panhandle neighborhood. Kai's father decides to send him to the Y.M.C.A. in order to make Kai learn how to defend himself—something essential in their area. The first day, the Y.M.C.A. takes on mythic proportions: "I recognized the Y.M.C.A. for what it was: a place of torture, a palace of pain, a formal school where street horrors were enacted under adult supervision and children lined up for lessons like prisoners in front of firing squads" (145). Confusion, fear and insecurity color Kai Ting's world until he begins to fit into the microcosm that is the brotherhood at the Y.M.C.A. "Fitting in" takes place through the help of Tony Barraza, the coach who has much in common with the lonely boy: "He missed his son and looked for him on crowded streets" (153). Barraza's wife had left him almost as Kai's mother had left: with no explanations and without giving him a second chance. The child's obsession with food and family are familiar and understandable to Tony Barraza and Angelina Costello, the manager of the Y.M.C.A. cafeteria, who will not only feed Kai but make him feel wanted. They understand the child's deep-seated need to be fed, and to be cared for. For Tony Barraza this behavior becomes an act of charity towards Kai: "Angelina. This here kid, this kid, he needs a meal. He needs ten meals. So I'm ordering as many as he can eat [...]. This is charity. God's work, fer God's sake" (157). Once again, food and caregiving become interrelated for the little boy.

Angelina Costello, the narrator recalls, reminded everyone at the Y.M.C.A. of the mother unlucky ones should have had. She smiled like she meant it, as if she liked everything around her. The boy begins to idolize her because of this motherliness and her generosity with the cafeteria food:

> She controlled food. I was in love. She looked at me. She saw an empty stomach, her cause for existence [...]. I inhaled food at Angie's café the way a whale does plankton [...]. I loved the routine of the café which existed to produce food. The sound of silverware being washed, the griddles sizzling, the smell of fries, the pickle relish and mustard, the cheeriness of Mrs. Costello, the availability of her food [...]. Looking at her I had the religious experience that churches seek to inspire in their parishioners. (162-63)

Tony Barraza's efforts to feed him and make him feel special will not pass unnoticed by the sensitive boy: "I was in Tony Barraza the Hook's home, eating egg sandwiches that he had made, without a schedule to meet, a fist to avoid, or a care in the world. A dog sat at my feet and ate crumbs from my sandwich. 'I happy, Mister B'laza,' I said" (225-26). In this manner, the Y.M.C.A. provides a substitute mother as well as substitute father and brother figures who feed and form him, and a repertoire of sounds and smells that replace the smells and sounds of a home that was becoming increasingly unfamiliar.

In her obsession to make Kai a real American, Edna forces him to look for affection elsewhere: the Y.M.C.A. provides it through its own community. Christine So notes that Gus Lee argues in favor of traditional and community-based institutions in *China Boy* because they offer the possibility of unity within diversity through a common goal (145). Interestingly, the relationships that develop in the novel tend to be across different minority groups, most often with African Americans. Kai finds he must go beyond trying to assimilate into white

America and instead win acceptance from a group that seems opposite his own. To survive in the neighborhood, he attempts "to become an accepted black male youth in the 1950s—a competitive, dangerous, and harshly won objective. This was all the more difficult because I was Chinese. I was ignorant of the culture, clumsy in the language, and blessed with a body that made Tinker Bell look ruthless. I was guileless and awkward in sports. I faced an uphill challenge with a downhill set of assets" (4). Toussaint, his African American friend from the neighborhood, and his mother and the Y.M.C.A. gang give him a sense of belonging to a wider, multiethnic community. This transcends Edna's vision of America but it is authentic. More importantly, it is the one that will make the difference to a child.

Yet there is another world that draws the child home. Chinatown attracts Kai because of the smells, and the familiarity. Chinatown, the boy observes, "was like its host city—small and compressed in physical dimensions, boundless and ephemeral in spirit" (242). The description is just as aptly applied to Kai Ting himself, as a strategy of reconnection between his cultural heritage and his present world—his manner of emphasizing a struggle between continuity and renewal. Here he comes across his Uncle Shim, an important family friend from when his mother was alive, who then decides to buy him clothes to look like a Chinese scholar. When the boy visits the elders in Uncle Shim's circle of friends, he is greeted as the hope of a new China. These old men remind him of Tony Barraza, good talented men stunted by mistakes and limitations in their past. A boxing demonstration for the elders brings a round of applause. This ambiance, the same one his mother created around him, poses no problems for Kai—he fits in and knows his place among the Chinese: "I looked at these old men and loved them" (251). Once again, food—Chinese food, with all its implications for the boy—is crucial in his incursions into Chinatown, and descriptions of those meals are charged with emotional associations:

> For fifty cents I got a huge cauldron of rice overlaid with oyster-beef sauce, finely chopped scallions and onions, and a raw egg. The rice and beef were so hot that stirring the egg with the other ingredients cooked it. I inhaled food. It was my addiction, my habit, my love. Chinese food brought more than splendid sauces, delightful flavors, wonderful textures, and all the pleasures of a child's innocent tastes. It carried a spiritual message of the past and suggested hope for tomorrow through the survival of continuity. My mother's spirit lay within the wafting aromas. (242)

The novel repeatedly substantiates how the most profound revelations of essentials and of deepest needs are inspired by activities associated with the consumption of food. Because even in its solitary form eating represents a communicative act (Brown 13), the boy's recurring search for this particular kind of food emphasizes his desire for continuity, his struggle to reconnect with a personal and cultural past lost to him.

Such observations made by the adult looking back justify the young boy's hounding compulsion to eat. The reader recognizes what social psychologists call an eating complex: repetition, regularity, stability, solidarity, and uniformity (Brown 16). All these qualities present in the mealtime experience have been lost and missed by the young boy since his mother's death. His strategy for reconnection includes his friendships at the Y.M.C.A. and his encounters with Uncle Shim. The existence of characters like Uncle Shim and Tony Barraza is fundamental to this character's journey of self-awareness and his nascent self-esteem. Kai can communicate much more easily with them than with his own father. These men, from worlds radically apart, have something in common—their loneliness and desire for sons. Their concern for Kai and the way they care for him—feeding the boy and educating him for the world as they see it—unites them. Moreover, Kai fills a void both men have in their lives. The underlying message of *China Boy* transcends racial differences: people need to feel that they are loved, that they belong. Kai does resolve the clash of the two cultures of which he is, by accident, a part. Acceptance does not involve turning his back radically on his heritage, nor does it imply conversion into an African American, like Toussaint or the other boxers. The child develops his necessarily multi-layered self within his personal and communal terrain of action, moving away from the adoration of his mother to the emulation of role models at the Y.M.C.A., a multicultural America in miniature.

The transformation of the young boy into a more self-confident human being suffers a setback when one of the neighborhood bashers gives him a beating. His budding self-assurance disappears and he even begins to lose interest in the food that had once made him feel so secure. The loneliness he felt when his mother died begins to overwhelm him again. The concern of the coach Mr. Lewis and the other characters at the Y.M.C.A. will cause the child to finally break down and cry. The built-up tensions had been too much for someone so young. The accumulation of tensions, fears, and loneliness weighing down on the child for so long finally find release in tears. The characters and events in his life's drama—Big Willie Mack the basher, Edna the stepmother, the futile search for his mother, and a growing fear of death—combine to create a situation beyond the boy's control and understanding. Most importantly, he realizes that, because all his mother's portraits had been removed, he was in danger of not remembering her face: "I had lost her face and I felt my own features fall apart like an old brick hotel in a Frisco earthquake" (288). Ultimately, Barney Lewis's belief in Kai and in his ability to fight Goliath restores his confidence. Mr. Lewis reminds the child that his mother's spirit is not lost and that he can be strengthened by her presence. There is absolute trust on the part of the boy: "If coach, if Mr. Lewis, really believed I could do this..." (289).

The humor that pervades the adult narration of childhood memories tempers the drama in Lee's novel. As Christine So explains, ethnic Americans have often used humor to offer resistance to processes of non-assimilation: "Frequently, a satire of prevailing power structures, ethnic humor has been read traditionally as a means of exposing a variety of American myths of belonging and of revealing an anxiety of assimilation" (142). The exaggerations in the representation of the American stepmother, for instance, illustrate this point. Edna corresponds to the stereotype of the wicked stepmother, yet her cruelty centers on rejecting her stepson's biculturality, forcing him to adhere to the model she means to establish. This way, *China Boy* utilizes humor to mitigate the alien status of a Chinese boy, revisioning him as an American, even as it questions the myth of unconditional American acceptance (So 143). Lee uses comedy to make American sense of Kai's foreign "nonsense" and a national understanding of his confusion. This is quite true: in retrospect, incidents are told from a Chinese American adult's point of view even though those incidents were experienced by him as a Chinese child. That these episodes are being recollected is testimony to a coming to terms. Also, the fact that much of the humor arises from confusion in Kai's apprehension of the world stresses the appropriateness of the child's point of view in the narration of immigrant texts. So argues that Lee succeeds in "conflating Kai's disorientation as a Chinese-American boy with the bafflement of childhood" (149). Since it is unclear exactly where the confusion stems from—either the boy's youth or his foreign background—that ambiguity reinforces the notion that assimilation and growing up might be two sides of the same coin.

When carefully scrutinized, however, there is a sense of sadness very often present as a final note to all the humorous situations lived by Kai. For instance, when the child wolfs down food in one of his escapes to Chinatown, the sight of him closing his eyes with the dreaminess of the Lop Chong he is consuming as he walks directly into a tall stack of wooden produce crates is a funny one. But the humor is lost when the reader witnesses how Kai runs away embarrassed by his inability to apologize in the language he could once speak (244). Further, Lee elicits many laughs from his reproduction of the Chinese American child's struggles with the English language, as well as from the puzzlement the boy experiences because of a lack of cultural introductions to many typical American things or habits. As So affirms:

> That Kai overcomes ethnic pain while maintaining ties to his ethnic heritage makes his experiences even more attractive, and Lee fulfills our desire for Kai's triumph and relief of his misery. Especially within a post-Vietnam context, a narrative about an American hero whose morality prevails, whose faith in American institutions endures, and whose ethnicity stands as a testimony to his strength but not as a barrier to his success demonstrates a national need to recover from wounds recently inflicted. (153)

Kai Ting has been successful: his mother gone, he has been "adopted" through the caring and nurturing of many "mothers" that have crossed his path. Two worlds have been reconciled in the mind of the child: we have witnessed how through genuine care—food and acceptance—a transcultural child begins to find himself, and a process of invention begins.

Works Cited

Brown, James W. *Fictional Meals and Their Function in the French Novel 1789-1848*. Toronto: U of Toronto P, 1984.

Coe, Richard N. *When the Grass was Taller: Autobiography and the Experience of Childhood*. New Haven: Yale UP, 1984.

Coveney, Peter. *The Image of Childhood*. London: Penguin, 1967.

Douglas, Mary. "Deciphering a Meal." *Daedalus* 101. 1 (1972): 61-81.

Hinz, Evelyn J. "Introduction: Diet Consciousness and Current Literary Trends." *Mosaic* 24. 3/4 (Summer/Fall 1991): v-xiii.

Lee, Gus. *China Boy*. New York: Penguin, 1994.

Mennell, Stephen, Anne Murcott and Anneke Van Otterloo. *The Sociology of Food: Eating, Diet and Culture*. London: Sage Publications, 1992.

Otten, Charlotte F. and Gary D. Schmidt, eds. *The Voice of the Narrator in Children's Literature: Insights from Writers and Critics*. Westport, CT: Greenwood P, 1989.

Ricou, Laurie. *Everyday Magic: Child Languages in Canadian Literature*. Vancouver: U of British Columbia P, 1987.

So, Christine. "Delivering the Punch Line: Racial Combat as Comedy in Gus Lee's *China Boy*." *MELUS* 21.4 (Winter 1996): 142-54.

Wong, Sau-ling Cynthia. *Reading Asian American Literature: From Necessity to Extravagance*. Princeton: Princeton UP, 1993.

Cultural Cross-Dressing in *Mona in the Promised Land*

Amy Ling

Article I of the Amendments to the U.S. Constitution guarantees five freedoms to all U.S. citizens: freedom of religion, speech, the press, peaceable assembly, and the right to petition. Gish Jen, in her latest novel, *Mona in the Promised Land*, adds a sixth to this list: freedom of cultural choice. Nearly all the characters in this brilliant, hilarious novel defy the boundaries that humankind has always liked to draw in order to differentiate same from other—to keep those who are in, in and those who are out, out. Gish Jen makes a mockery of these boundary lines though she fully, and playfully, acknowledges the distinguishing traits themselves. By showing that such traits can be assumed like clothing, or embraced through conversion, consumed like food and culture, and practiced by choice, she riddles with ridicule nationalist and fascist ideas of "blood," "birth," "racial or national purity" and even gives ethnic studies, where it embraces these notions, its comeuppance. In fact, the thesis of *Mona in the Promised Land* seems to be: if one does not cross these traditional but arbitrary boundaries, one stagnates. The world is in constant flux and people must be open to change as well. Cultural crossings are not just amusing aberrations or frivolities: they are evidence of adaptation and are essential aspects of growth.

Identity is a complex intersection of many aspects. The first seven aspects: race, sex, class, age, familial birth order, nationality, culture have been generally considered immutable while the latter two—personal relations and professional roles—are a matter of personal choice. In an earlier time, before emigration/immigration and sex-change operations, everyone would have agreed that the first seven items on this list were pre-determined, but in the modern era, where space travel is almost commonplace and "aliens" for the most part are now extra-terrestrials, nationality and culture have switched from the predetermined and immutable *prix-fixe* column of the identity factors menu to the *à la carte* column. And in the United States, the nation of immigrants, this à la carte section is very long, the choices varied.

The United States was first described by Hector St. Jean de Crèvecoeur in the 18th century and later by Israel Zangwill in the 19th century, as a great Melting Pot, a term now out of favor because of its homogenizing and amalgamating qualities and its Anglo-centric connotations. The preferred metaphor in Canada has been *mosaic* or *salad*, with each element retaining its separate flavor or color. But some have objected that *mosaic* implies a separation too rigidly maintained. For these people, *stew*, or perhaps *paella*, would be the more accurate comparison: each ingredient sends out its own juices—chicken, scallop, shrimp, garlic—and retains something of its own flavor and shape but also cannot help but absorb some of the juices of the other ingredients in the large general pot. However, this image does not allow for a piece of chicken to decide to become a scallop. Nonetheless—to continue the food analogy—as anyone who has ever eaten in a Buddhist vegetarian restaurant well knows, the versatile soy bean, as tofu, can be transformed into an almost infinite variety of imitation meat dishes with texture, appearance and even taste so close to the real thing that the two can barely be told apart. So, too, some people may be capable of total metamorphosis, while others may not.

Mona Chang, Jen's adolescent Chinese American heroine, decides to convert to Judaism. Her family has recently moved to a predominantly Jewish neighborhood north of New York City, and as she explains to her astounded mother, "American means being whatever you want, and I happened to pick being Jewish" (49). She is simply asserting her American Freedom of Cultural Choice. After a period of religious instruction with Rabbi Horowitz, she undergoes the requisite ceremonies: taking the ritual bath or mikvah, chanting her Shema Israel, burning her special four-stranded candle, having three witnesses sign her certificate. And "in this way, she becomes Mona-also-known-as-Ruth, a more or less genuine Catholic Chinese Jew" (44). Of course, her outward form still bespeaks her Chinese racial ancestry, (the chicken cannot look like a scallop) but her chosen identity and religion is Jewish (however, she can taste like one).

To Mona, this choice seems no stranger than her having once been Catholic, but everyone around her is incredulous. Helen, her mother, is the most insulted and distressed, "How can you be Jewish? Chinese people don't do such things" (45). When Mona concludes then that she must not be Chinese, Helen cannot fathom this since Mona is her daughter and Helen is Chinese. Rabbi Horowitz thinks Mona's desire to convert to Judaism is simply adolescent rebellion—wanting to be like her friends and unlike her parents. Although he undertakes her instruction and makes possible her conversion, later, Jen implies, he is fired by the conservative elements in the temple for such overly liberal actions. Mona's Jewish schoolmates and friends are bemused and teasingly dub her Changowitz.

What is unusual about Mona's choice is that it goes counter the dominant social hierarchy. Helen claims that she would not have found Mona's becoming "American" strange, for when she and her husband Ralph immigrated to the United States, they expected that their children would grow up no longer "purely Chinese." But for Helen, Jewish is not American. That Helen, educated by French missionary nuns in Shanghai, became Catholic was perfectly understandable because the conversion took her one step up, closer to those in power. But

Mona's matching steps with a world-persecuted minority is a step down in Helen's opinion and therefore incomprehensible. Helen asserted a freedom of action for herself and the possibility to be many things simultaneously, for as she explains, "Oh, well, we are still Buddhist after we are baptized [...]. We are Buddhist, and Taoist, and Catholic. We do however we want" (42). But though Helen the adolescent did however she wanted, now as a controlling Chinese mother, she is unwilling to allow the same freedom to her child.

In *Racechanges,* Susan Gubar notes that "a culture that systematically devalues blackness and establishes whiteness as the norm effectively endorses, even enforces, black to white racechange" (11). When whites put on blackface, they are often posing, temporarily, as the Other in order to understand or mock the black experience, but when blacks pass as white, they tend to leave behind permanently, or as long as their actual racial designation remains successfully hidden, the devaluation associated with being black. Simone de Beauvoir's *The Second Sex* compares the position of the woman with that of the Negro and the Jew—universally persecuted and devalued groups (Gubar 44). Thus, Mona's choice not only makes visible this conventional value judgment but rejects and defies it.

As Rabbi Horowitz explains to Mona, "your parents want to be Wasps. They [WASPs] are the only ones who do not have to make themselves heard. That is because they do the hearing." But Mona's reasoning is perfectly logical: "We are a minority, like it or not, and if you want to know how to be a minority, there's nobody better at it than the Jews" (53). To this, her mother replies that Mona has too big a mouth. But what attracts Mona to Judaism is precisely its encouragement of the big mouth, the inquiring critical stance—"ask, ask instead of just obey, obey." "I like it that you tell people to make a pain in the neck of themselves" (34), she explains to Rabbi Horowitz.

Helen, however, worries about the slippery slope. If today Mona wants to be Jewish, tomorrow she may want to be black, next a boy, or even a tree! In other words, if you disregard one boundary, then no boundary is firm, no difference is sacred. (Mona does not tell her mother that in Ovid, a young woman is indeed transformed into a tree.) Boundaries give Helen a sense of security. She knows what and who she is because of the existence of these boundaries. If they can be so easily crossed, then she fears chaos will result. For Mona, however, growing up in a multiracial, multiethnic community, boundaries are barriers set up by bigots who feel superior to others unlike themselves. To cross these boundaries is to demonstrate that you do not accept the hierarchical values associated with their erection: that you believe in the equality of all peoples, in a just, classless society.

Mona's conversion to Judaism is the most elaborated example but only one of many cases of cultural cross-dressing in this novel. In fact, nearly all of the sympathetic characters are busily engaged in crossing boundaries. Cultures may be distinguished by formal ceremonies and ritual, but more often they are characterized by more mundane and informal markers like clothing, food, and language. Mona's boyfriend, Seth Mandel buys a dashiki, "his first new clothes in years," to show solidarity with the African Americans who are part of Camp Gugelstein, a brief aborted experiment in utopia. Callie, Mona's older sister, and Naomi, Callie's roommate at Harvard, wear kilts while waitressing in a New England resort. Customers regularly ask them, "What part of Scotland are you from?" to which Chinese American Callie replies, "the Far Eastern part" and African American Naomi retorts, "From deepest, darkest Wales" (170).

Naomi, perhaps even more than Mona, is the ultimate cultural-crosser, a woman with an omnivorous cultural appetite. An African American from Chicago, Naomi shows Callie, a Chinese American from Scarshill, what it means to be Chinese. Naomi reads Lao Tzu, practices *tai qi*, "does meditation and yoga, chants, drinks tea and makes kites." Naomi even knows how to make "authentic tea-smoked duck that involves burning tea leaves in a wok and smoking the duck in it for sixteen hours" when even Helen has now begun to make "Peking duck, Westchester style," by "soaking it overnight in Pepsi Cola" (186). Yet Naomi also likes sweet potato pie, knows all about jazz and can "tease cool jazz from free jazz, bebop from hard bop [...] she scarfs down her collard greens with as much gusto as anybody, maybe more" and "she also likes Chinese dumplings and diet soda, not to say Scrabble, film noir, star gazing, soccer. [Naomi] is, in short, a statistical outlier and overcompensator, a Renaissance woman" (169). What's more, liberated Naomi believes that our ancestors do not have to be related to us by blood; we can choose them, as she has chosen Harriet Tubman and Sojourner Truth, also Roberta Flack. "Forget your parents," she tells Mona and Callie (129), a novel and subversive idea, but easier said than done.

The line between identifying cultural markers and negative cultural and racial stereotyping is often uncomfortably thin, distinguishable primarily by the intent and purpose of the speaker or writer. In the description of Naomi above, Jen is not putting down Naomi for liking sweet potato pie and collard greens: she is simply asserting that Naomi is equally comfortable and knowledgeable about the African American culture into which she was born as she is about Chinese culture which she has chosen to acquire. Unlike Mona, who knows only three Chinese words of the Shanghai dialect: *byeh fa-foon* (stop acting crazy), *shee-veh* (rice gruel) and *ji-nu* (soy sauce), Naomi's accent and vocabulary in Mandarin Chinese is extensive and excellent.

Authenticity, ethnic and cultural, is a vexed and complex issue which Gish Jen also explores and explodes because it, too, creates undesirable hierarchies of superiority and inferiority. Authenticity harks back to what Werner Sollors has designated as European notions of "descent" rather than American ideas of "consent." Seth Mandel explains with a grin, "I am afraid I am an authentic inauthentic Jew [...]. More ethnic than religious [...] in the process of becoming an inauthentic inauthentic Jew" (112). For her part, Mona is an inauthentic Chinese. Because of her Chinese features, others assume that she is Chinese and knows all about Chinese culture. Friends' mothers ask her to taste-test their Chinese cooking, not realizing that Mona knows almost nothing about Chinese cuisine. "'Very authentic.' She tries to be reassuring. After all, they're nice people, she likes them. 'De-lish.' She has seconds" (6). She simply doesn't want to hurt anyone's feelings. She tells her new friend Barbara Gugelstein that she can make her hands hard as steel simply by thinking them hard, that if she can't break bricks she can break arms—then, realizing, that she had seen these things on TV at Barbara's house the previous evening, she thinks up something original and confides to Barbara that she knows how to get pregnant with tea because "that's how they do it in China" (5).

Mona is playing at being Chinese, posing because she looks the part, but an impostor nonetheless. She is not passing, because Chinese-ness is not something she aspires to, but she exploits accepted ideas of the Chinese as exotic, inventive and strange, and what could be more exotic, inventive, and strange than getting pregnant with tea? Granted, Gish Jen is playing for laughs, but she is also making a serious point. She is asserting that culture is acquired, not innate. A Chinese American girl brought up in the U.S. with an American education will naturally be more American than Chinese, more familiar with Thanksgiving Day celebrations than with the Lantern Festival or Dragon Boat Races. Thus, Mona's own physical appearance is a kind of built-in, inadvertent racial and cultural cross-dressing. (She may be beef who just happens to look like chicken wanting to be a scallop.)

So common are U.S. racial minorities whose physical appearance belies their cultural identity that food-related slang expressions, negative in connotation, have arisen to describe them: *oreo cookies* for African Americans who are black on the outside and white on the inside; *apples* for overly assimilated Native Americans and *bananas* for Asian Americans. Callie, a sometime banana, works to bridge the discrepancy between her physical appearance and her cultural identity by studying Chinese language and culture at Harvard. By the epilogue of the novel, she is wearing Chinese padded jackets and cloth shoes and calling herself Kailan. In fact she has become "so Chinese that Ralph and Helen think there is something wrong with her" (301). But how "authentic" is a Chinese who must study the Chinese language (in my case, from a Jewish teacher) and who assumes Chinese clothing as an afterthought? On the other hand, how significant, after all, is "authenticity?" How does it really matter?

This sunny, funny novel, however, is not without dark shadows. Mona and her friends constitute an idealistic, socially-conscious group of young people who seek to live their beliefs in a more equitable world. Realizing that African Americans have suffered more than any minority group, Mona offers Alfred, an African American cook in her father's pancake house whose girlfriend has just kicked him out, a temporary home in Barbara Gugelstein's parents' house while Mr. and Mrs. Gugelstein are away for the summer. However, she and Barbara begin, disturbingly, by offering him the servant's quarters above the garage, and only gradually allow him access into the main house, and then with many restrictions, which he blithely ignores. Eventually and only for a short period, Alfred and his buddies, Barbara and her cousin, Mona and Seth create a utopia of racial harmony, which they call Camp Gugelstein. But the snake in the garden rears its ugly head when Barbara discovers that her father's silver hip flask has disappeared. Insulted that he and his friends could be suspected of theft, Alfred not only moves out but uses information Mona has disclosed about her father to begin a lawsuit against Ralph Chang for racial discrimination. (In the democratic United States, power shifts are possible and the economically disadvantaged are not without recourse.) Although the lawsuit is eventually avoided when the flask is found, and Mona makes Alfred a formal apology, social and class barriers have again been erected. As Luther the Race Man puts it,

> "Who own the flask? Who keep picking it up, you got to tell us to put it down? Who like to steal the flask, who don't got no flask like that at home? [...]. I think that flask would look just fine on my fireplace mantel."
> "Cut the shit," says Alfred, beside him, "You ain't got no fireplace." (204)

As owners of the pancake house, and as a family who owns things like silver hip flasks, the Changs and Gugelsteins, although minorities, belong to a different social class than Alfred and his friends. Despite the generosity and equitable impulses of the younger generation, the gulf between haves and have-nots is wide and deep, and perhaps, unbridgeable. Fear and suspicion on the one side and resentment and anger on the other are inevitably conflicting emotions which make long-term harmonious co-existence impossible as long as major economic inequities exist.

In the inequitable reality of the United States, two types of cultural cross-dressing occur: one we might call "lateral"—from minority to minority, the other "vertical"—from minority to majority. Jen apparently approves of the first type: Mona (a Chinese American) converts to Judaism, Seth (a Jew) wears a dashiki, Naomi (an African American) is fluent in Chinese. These "lateral" crossings are significant because they have been less common than what had previously been considered "vertical" crossings—from minority to majority: Helen becomes Catholic, Barbara Gugelstein has a nose operation, Naomi and Callie wear kilts. The vertical crossings like Barbara's nose job, which implies shame and denial of the self, can only have a detrimental effect while the lateral crossings, which involve the layering of other cultural traits onto those one already possesses, express solidarity with other groups who share a history of persecution and enhance/enrich the self. Thus, in Jen's worldview, loss is less, while more is better.

The one exception to all this fluidity is the Ingles family, who find it unnecessary to cross any cultural boundaries. WASP and uppercrust, they are already at the apex of the social pyramid; from commanding heights, they look down on everyone else. Their table in the resort dining room is on a special raised platform with a view of the sunset; their family shirt is Lacoste, their family shoe is the scuffed-up Top-Sider without socks—no love beads, bell-bottoms and water-buffalo sandals for them—too ethnic. They never order seconds at dinner and never raise their voices; as Naomi explains, "They are the oppressors. We are the expressers" (184). They play croquet ("A game Mona did not think was played outside of *Alice in Wonderland*" [174]) and they monopolize the resort's tennis courts.

Only Eloise Ingles, the stepdaughter, makes brief attempts to cross-over when she discovers, to her dismay, that her dead mother was Jewish. Being half Jewish, she sometimes raises her voice and is "a bit [...] expressive" (183). But her attempt to learn about the Jewish faith, in comparison to Mona's effort, is half-hearted and short-lived. After an argument with her stepmother, she intends to spend the night in the worker's quarters at the resort where her friends are employees and her family are paying guests, but her father quickly and effortlessly reclaims her and returns her to her rightful place. For Eloise, there may be a modicum of hope for tolerance and change, but the rest of her family are charming snobs and heartless cads.

The Ingles have the confidence of being singularly "at home" in the U.S. while bicultural minorities are often torn between two "homelands." "Just because a place is your homeland doesn't mean you would feel at home there," says Barbara Gugelstein about Israel. Though she may be proud to proclaim herself a Jew, her home is where her family and friends are—in the United States. Nonetheless, the fact that she must make the assertion that America is home attests to the tenuousness of her claim. When immigrants or children of immigrants "return home" to their ancestral lands, they experience the exhilarating novelty of finding themselves physically in the majority. However, at the same time, such visitors lack the comfort and familiarity levels necessary for feeling "at home." Physically relocated from others of their kind, minorities in the U.S. have been psychologically dislocated, and all experience what W.E.B. DuBois has called a "double-consciousness," an awareness of self at odds with the negating and alienating regard of others, so that even while "at home" in the United States, minorities, particularly Asian Americans, are made to feel like foreigners.

When the Ingles family invites Mona to dine with them, their manner of *noblesse oblige* and kind tolerance makes their actual condescension palpable. While totally "at home" themselves, they make Mona feel like a displaced person. When one of the Ingles boys asks Mona if she speaks Chinese, another retorts, "Of course she speaks it. Open your eyes" (182). In saying this, they deny Mona her American birthright. "'That must be so weird,' says Andrew. 'I mean, to never get a chance to see your own home.'" They also deny Mona her home. It is inconceivable to them that a person with Chinese features can be at home in America. The Ingles's boundary walls are high and distinct. Their logic is exclusive and excluding: they are the real Americans and all real Americans look like them. Mona doesn't look like them; therefore, she is not American. For them, descent is all important.

Mona's distance from the Ingles, marked by race and class, is comparable to Alfred's distance from the Gugelsteins and Changs, creating a fluidity of position dependent on situation and perspective. Although African Americans, the "majority minority" (270), unlike more recent immigrant groups, have established a cross-over presence in the dominant culture through music and dance, and a physical dominance in many sports; nonetheless, as social researcher Jerome Miller has pointed out in his book *Search and Destroy: African American Males in the Criminal Justice System*, statistics show that alarming large numbers of black men between the ages of 18 and 35 are in prison, "In Baltimore on an average day, 56% of all its African American males were in jail, on probation/parole, or bail or being sought on arrest warrants" (Ruffino 98). If *criminal* is defined as having an arrest record, more than 75% of black men in California will soon fall into that category since 625,000 black men aged sixteen and over (1/6th of the black male population) are arrested each year. 92% arrested on drug charges are subsequently released for lack of evidence but all acquire a police record making it harder to get a job, and giving evidence of police racism. Certainly, the 1992 Rodney King beating graphically illustrated the unchanged power differential between blacks and whites.

Luther the Race Man, who puts his buddy Alfred down for sleeping with a white woman, Helen who cuts off Mona for her sexual involvement with Seth, Mrs. Gugelstein who pushed her daughter Barbara to have a nose operation—all display moments of blindness, of rigidity, of misguided social values. But Mr. Ingles has the power to fire Mr. Gugelstein, Barbara's father, and does so without any qualms, cutting off the Gugelstein family income with one telephone call. His three grown sons and daughter hog the tennis court, playing beyond their time by convincing the couple that comes to claim the court that they mistook tomorrow's sign-up sheet for today's. Their father has always told them that the great lesson of life is: "You've got to know how the game is played." The Ingles family not only knows the rules, they have all the assurance of power brokers who made those rules up in the first place, and they certainly know how to bend them. "Sumner [one of the brothers] with the silver glasses [...] calls balls out when they're in; everyone would like to assume it's a matter of his prescription" (176). But his excusers are simply being polite.

Mona in the Promised Land ends on a happy note of reconciliation between Mona and her estranged mother. Helen, who had given Mona such a hard time at the beginning of the novel over Mona's purchase of a down jacket, is now herself wearing one by the novel's epilogue. Helen, who had not spoken to Mona after Mona left home and began living with Seth, now attends Mona and Seth's belated wedding. The tensions between this Chinese mother and American daughter, unlike those in Amy Tan's *The Joy Luck Club*, can be resolved because Helen is capable of change. This mother may be slow to accept new ways and she may complain vociferously, but she eventually comes around. In fact, she has come so far around that she can't understand Callie and now complains about her hitherto model daughter:

> So much trouble to find her a nice English name, why does she have to call her-self something no one can spell? She says she's proud to be Asian American [...] but what in the world is an Asian American? That's what Ralph and Helen want to know. And how can she lump herself with the Japanese? [...]. After what they did during the war! [...]. And what, friends with the Koreans too? And the Indians? [...]. Better to turn Jewish than Asian American, that's their opinion these days. At least Jews don't walk around with their midriffs show-ing! (301-2)

Helen's pettiness, short-sightedness, and self-righteousness are meant to be laughed at; however, similar attitudes have contributed to the race and class dif-ferential, manifested in Barbara's accusation of theft and Mr. Ingles's power over the livelihood and welfare of the Gugelsteins.

Race and class differentials cast a shadow on this novel as they do on life in the United States. Wealth and power seem to remain, with perhaps a few excep-tions, fundamentally unchanged in the hands of whites at the top of the pyramid. Power and privilege are still largely a matter of descent. However, with its rol-licking humor and good-natured irreverence, *Mona in the Promised Land* offers cultural cross-dressing as the means for the various peoples of the U.S. to grow in solidarity and mutual understanding. With fluidity, acceptance of difference and rejection of hierarchy, open-hearted people can shake the foundations of the old closed pyramid and replace it with a level field on which no single group will have monopoly of the center and no one will be permanently shunted to the periphery. As Michel Foucault put it twenty years ago: "We must not imagine a world of discourse divided between accepted discourse and excluded discourse, or between the dominant discourse and the dominated one; but as a multiplicity of discursive elements that can come into play in various strategies" (100). The United States, living up to its expressed ideals, would then be a cultural smor-gasbord to which all the peoples of the world would be invited to partake of whatever catches their eye and pleases their palate. In this truly utopian state, power would no longer be monopolized in a few hands on the basis of descent and color but would be flexible and shared, depending on consent and justice.

Works Cited

DuBois. W.E.B. *The Souls of Black Folk*. 1903. New York: Signet, 1969.

Foucault, Michel. *The History of Sexuality: An Introduction (Vol. 1)*. New York: Random House, 1978.

Gubar, Susan. *Racechanges: White Skin, Black Face in American Culture.* New York: Oxford UP, 1997.
Jen, Gish. *Mona in the Promised Land.* New York: Alfred A. Knopf, 1996.
Ruffino, Paul. "The Color of Justice." *The Washington Post* (22 Sept. 1996): 98.
Sollors, Werner. *Beyond Ethnicity: Consent and Descent in American Culture.* New York: Oxford UP, 1986.

Rupture as Continuity: Migrant Identity and "Unsettled" Perspective in Bapsi Sidhwa's *An American Brat*

Geoffrey Kain

In one of his classic works in behavioral psychology, *Beyond Freedom and Dignity*, B.F. Skinner investigates the nature of self from his established and anticipated vantage point of environmental determinism. Skinner describes the self as "a repertoire of behavior appropriate to a given set of contingencies" (199). Behaviors (personalities) are cultivated, he contends, by the formative power of our particular "verbal communities." And those behaviors reinforced (or selected), over time, by verbal communities serve to define cultures and cultural differences ("culture" he describes as "a gigantic exercise in self-control"). For Skinner, then, when an individual physically separates from one verbal community and becomes immersed in another (and another, and another, ...), at least some of the individual's behavioral responses (the very stuff of self) necessarily shift when the individual's environment changes,[1] while other behaviors will remain as "stored" response to what one has already learned and encountered.

While I am not eager to sidle up to Skinner's interpretations of self/personality ("man is very much like a machine"), there is something to be said for the way in which his behavioral theory anticipates and partially informs more recent theories of identity, specifically as they relate to immigrant or diasporic identity—notions forwarded, particularly, by Homi Bhabha in his investigation of cultural conflict (both in the general sense of culture and within the individual), and Shirley Geok-lin Lim, as well, in her illuminating discussions of diasporic identity. Lim usefully cautions against generalized or essentialized representations of immigrant or diasporic experience, reminding us of the various ways in which this experience has been represented or constructed in Asian

---

1   In a passage that further expands on this notion—and that will strike a chord with readers as they consider the conflict between/among Feroza, Zareen, and David in *An American Brat*, once they are all together in Denver—Skinner writes: "Two or more repertoires generated by different sets of contingencies compose two or more selves. A person possesses one repertoire appropriate to his life with his friends and another appropriate to his life with his family, and a friend may find him a very different person if he sees him with his family or his family if they see him with his friends. The problem of identity arises when situations are intermingled ..." (199).

American fiction, from the "between worlds" narrative, to the assimilationist narrative, to the exilic narrative:

> Indeed, the intersecting discontinuous trajectories of immigrant and diasporic constructions of race, class, and gender identities call into question any hegemonizing theoretization or orthodoxies, suggesting instead that these works need to be interpreted as *individually negotiating* the contestations and the co-operations of the filiative and the affiliative in the historicized context of the subjects' particular diasporic/ethnic cultures. (307)

Theories of dynamic or turbulent identity are foregrounded when approaching a text like, most classically, Bapsi Sidhwa's *An American Brat* (1993), in which we encounter the increasingly familiar (though no less intriguing) narrative of "someone from out there" who comes "here," of a spirited character who, despite her strength of resolve and youthful vigor, is fundamentally and inevitably changed by her exchanging "verbal communities." As such, she helps us to see not only the power of culture to "select" behaviors and values, but also invites us to ponder the struggle of immigrants to retain their hold on what they value of their native (and—over time—increasingly distant) culture and, simultaneously, to relinquish those values and behaviors that are not reinforced by their present environment. We observe such characters in a realm or process that Homi Bhabha described in a recent lecture as "unsettled jurisdiction" or "unsettled negotiation." In this sense, I would argue that rupture with native tradition, rupture between parents in one place and children in another very different place, rupture between generations (as the United States of one generation is not the United States of the next) seem inevitable and have certainly become a defining element of the American experience; in fact, in this dynamic society of mobile individuals, tenuous relationships, changing careers, and variegated and merging cultural groups, ruptures of all kinds have become a source of American continuity and tradition: who *hasn't* experienced some significant dislocation? Who isn't in a process of redefinition when the fiber of culture with which we interact in knowing both it and ourselves is redefining itself? Further, I would argue that rupture, or dislocation, has become such a mainstay of Asian American fiction as (in the classical sense of "holding a mirror up to life") to be a defining element in its continuity as a "body" of literature. Pangs of separation and angst over one's inability to "connect" satisfactorily or satisfyingly with one's migrant parents, one's ethnic tradition, or elements of one's adopted locale inform the larger corpus of Asian American fiction, from Maxine Hong Kingston's *The Woman Warrior* to Amy Tan's *The Joy Luck Club* to Fae Myenne Ng's *Bone* to Joy Kogawa's *Obasan* to Louis Chu's *Eat A Bowl of Tea* to Bharati Muhkerjee's *Jasmine.*[2]

---

2   Yuan Yuan, in "The Semiotics of China Narrative in the (Con)Texts of Kingston and Tan," has
    explored in detail, for example, the inevitable/unavoidable separation of experience and under-

Exceptions to the rule that physical displacement will yield significant change in values, behaviors, pursuits, etc. exist, of course, as Earl Waugh reminds us in discussing cultural continuity among South Asian Muslims relocated to North America:

> [F]amilies that are highly integrated into the endogamous, kinship-based units of a stratified society make it a social priority to proceed to build analogous social units in North America. Muslims from South Asia [...] reach out extensively to the homeland for many kinds of social and cultural reinforcements. This very pervasive control over the individual is a powerful defense against the potentially destructuring effects of their exposure to the non-Muslim host society. (xiii)

But how long and to what extent can such control actually serve to maintain an insular cultural stasis?

In *An American Brat*, this parental control over the individual child is already lost, or relinquished, as sixteen-year-old Feroza Ginwalla is sent by her Parsee parents from her native Pakistan to the United States for a three month visit with her slightly older uncle, Manek, in Boston—an uncle who does not live in a "transplant" community, as described by Waugh. Feroza's mother, Zareen, is deeply disturbed by what she perceives to be the increasing influence of Islamic fundamentalism at home over her Parsee daughter (especially significant particulars of historicized context, as Shirley Lim might identify them): "Instead of moving forward, we are moving backward. What I could do in '59 and '60, my daughter can't do in 1978! Our Parsee children in Lahore won't know how to mix with Parsee kids in Karachi or Bombay" (11). Fearing rupture or dislocation within the extended but relatively small Parsee community—rupture, apparently, accelerated by environmental influences—the parents (oddly)[3] move to "loosen up" their daughter a bit, to "broaden her outlook, get this puritanical rubbish out of her head" (14). But the mother's urge to counteract the influence of one environment by selecting another is met by the concerns of their extended family over the reputedly ubiquitous destructive forces of the American cultural environment, particularly sexual promiscuity and drug abuse ("Don't accept anything to eat or drink from strangers. It may be drugged. God knows what they will do to you" [50]).

Feroza's stay of a few days in New York is exhilarating, as she experiences emotional extremes brought on by the harassment from customs and immigra-

---

standing between parent who has emigrated to this country and child born into this country, a separation inherent in the very *language* of the stories told by the parents to their children—stories intended to connect the child to the "root" of the parent's native/original culture.

3   In an *IndiaStar* review of *An American Brat*, Manorama Mathai notes the improbability of "conservative Indian/Pak parents of sending a teenage daughter to the States to stay with an uncle some three years older and not known for his maturity," but then remarks that, despite this, "Manek's behaviour [is] plausible and Feroza's response appealing" (2).

tion officials as she enters the United States; the overwhelming bulk of goods available in endless numbers of shops; the crisp but cold efficiency of fast-food restaurants and subway trains; the "shimmering glass and steel embankments of the Manhattan skyline" (72); and her fearful brushes with drug addicts and darkened stairwells. The ominous but seductive power of the City sets the stage for Feroza's initiation into and deepening attachment to the American landscape. And as her curiosity and youthful tolerance bring her greater exposure to an array of characters, lifestyles, and personal perspectives, the distance from her embeddedness in family security increases simultaneously.

The more comical moments of Feroza's foray into the great American wilderness—sniffing at her armpits (during the early weeks of her stay) for ambient evidence of her foreignness, viewing with shock her uncle's audacious way of "working the system" by gaining a free meal at an upscale restaurant, her roommate Jo's swaggering toughness in the face of violation and abuse—are, together with the many sad and touching situations to which she is exposed, designed to illustrate the specific accumulation of incidents that, in fact, compose her extended environment over what becomes in the novel several years rather than the three months originally designed by her parents. And one cannot really avoid, as Feroza becomes more deeply entwined in American culture, the sense that she, like the characters Bharati Mukherjee has given us, is meant to be understood as one of the "new pioneers" Mukherjee alludes to (St.Andrews 57). In fact, should we somehow miss the pioneer motif, Feroza—like Mukherjee's Jasmine—moves during the narrative from east to west, beginning in New York and Boston, and ending in Idaho and Colorado, en route to Arizona.[4]

In classic/mythic American fashion, the lessons Feroza Ginwalla learns during her American sojourn "on the road" enlarge her sense of independence and individualism: "[T]he call involved not only Feroza's education and the development of her personality but also her induction into the self-sufficient, industrious, and independent way of American life" (119). From Manek's "You've got to skim what you can off the system, or the system will skin you" (144) to the rapturous exhortations of Father Fibs in Boston: "You are protected innocents, secure in your chrysalises. When you leave [...] you will test your wings. You will fly and fall, fly and fall [...]. Your wings will become stronger" (116),[5] to

---

4   As Frederick Jackson Turner observed over one hundred years ago in his landmark paper "The Significance of the Frontier in American History," "American social development has been continually begun over and over again on the frontier. This perennial rebirth [...] this expansion westward with its new opportunities [...] furnish[es] the forces dominating American character" (10).

5   Prior to writing *An American Brat*, Bapsi Sidhwa said in an interview with Feroza Jussawalla that "I don't know the Americans well enough to write of purely American characters. I will use people from my part of the world in America—the expatriate, the immigrant experience, if you like, how they interact here with the Americans [...]. I thought it would be marvelous if a Jerbanoo or a person like her could be brought here. And the way she could take off on America would be fabulous" (219).

the street-wise insights of Jo—"You don't always have to tell the truth, y'know! [...]. They'll stomp all over you" (151)—Feroza's new "verbal community" of zealous individualists largely displaces her earlier commitment to her place within the extended family and, by extension, the diasporic Parsee community.

Not entirely, however. Stuart Hall points out in "Cultural Identity and Diaspora" that diasporic identities are "'framed' by two axes or vectors, simultaneously operative: the vector of similarity and continuity; and the vector of difference and rupture; diasporic identity is a dialogue between these two axes" (226-27). As Feroza determinedly commits herself to an increasingly longer time in the States, she measures her actions and the advice of others against advice received from parents or other family members. As she becomes more deeply involved with David, the young golden-haired, blue-eyed Jewish man in Denver who becomes her fiancee, she knows that this marriage will mean defying the Parsee ban on interfaith marriages, expulsion from sacred Parsee ceremonies and temples, exclusion from important rites, and great social difficulties for her family. But she persists. And, anyway, "as for her religion, no one could take it away from her; she carried its fire in her heart" (317). Feroza finds herself steeped in the classic dilemma of (semi)consciously selecting what appears to her to be personally "favorable variations" (to use Darwin's phrase). And as Lisa Lowe has remarked on the transition from Asian to Asian American, "the making of Asian American culture may be a much less stable process than unmediated vertical transmission of culture from one generation to another. The making of Asian American culture includes practices that are partly inherited, partly modified, as well as partly invented; Asian American culture also includes the practices that emerge in relation to the dominant representations that deny or subordinate Asian and Asian American cultures as 'other'" (65). Yet Feroza's resistance involves denying dominant ideological constructs from *both* her Parsee heritage and contemporary American culture. She perceives herself as "other" from either/both of these vantage points, and thus must contend with the turbulence of an unsettled cultural jurisdiction.

The problem of sifting one's traditions and retaining some (even if only as mental image or construct) while allowing others to be dissolved or replaced by newly adopted values and behaviors emerges as a central conflict of *An American Brat*, as it is often central to the diasporic experience generally. As a recent article in *Little India* remarks on this "great divide":

> Which culture [for South Asian immigrants] is their own and how do they balance the two? [...]. Even though they will probably live out their years [in the U.S.], emotionally their bags are always packed and [South Asia] is the [South Asia] remembered, bathed in nostalgia. As [Subodh] Chandra puts it, "They are trapped in a world which they left behind and which doesn't exist any more." ("Times Apart" 21)

Nonetheless, Chandra, a political consultant for the Democratic party, also points out that members of his "new" generation "really are balancing two cultures and succeeding, though it's not without difficulties" (22). This "balancing" act, or experience of conflict, is precisely what Homi Bhabha means by his much discussed notion of hybridity. He clarifies this concept in his interview with Jonathan Rutherford: "Hybridity to me is the 'third space' which enables other positions to emerge. This third space displaces the histories that constitute it, and sets up new structures of authority [...] which are inadequately understood through received wisdom" (211).

While Feroza asserts her independence from family and traditional expectations, as she prepares for her next move (to Arizona), displaying her choice in favor of dislocation from familial/cultural expectations, we nonetheless see her struggle to "balance two cultures" to carry a cultural center with her, internally, while also resisting it at times as she adopts ideas and practices from her new environment:

> The first evening on her return to Denver, Feroza dug out her *sudra* and *kusti*. They had been hibernating for the longest time. Before going to bed, she said her *kusti* prayers and stood, hands joined, invoking Ahura Mazda's blessings and favor. All at once the image of the holy *atash* in the fire temple in Lahore, pure and incandescent on its bed of ashes, formed behind her shut lids. Its glow suffused her with its tranquillity and strength. (317)

Anthropologist Loren Eiseley has written at length on this attachment to images that, associated with what one regards as "home," may in themselves actually become a sort of home; in fact, he notes: "This feeling runs deep in life; it brings stray cats running over endless miles, and birds homing from the ends of the earth. It is as though all living creatures, and particularly the more intelligent, can survive only by fixing or transforming a bit of time into space or by securing a bit of space with its objects immortalized and made permanent in time" (229). Similarly, in my recent interview with author and painter Prafulla Mohanti, a villager born in Orissa, India, but long-time resident of London (though part-time resident of his village), he said that "there is a saying in India that you hold your world in your body. So you carry it around in you. Actually, I have never left the village, either physically or emotionally or spiritually because for me the two worlds, the physical and the spiritual, are one. Wherever I go, I carry my village inside of me" (1).

For Feroza, the abstraction of "home" is made poignantly concrete when her mother travels from Lahore to Denver armed with family members' arguments and "bribe money" for Feroza's fiancee to stop the wedding. From the family's point of view, Feroza has turned her back on what is most important (family, traditions, religious precepts) and sadly succumbed to the evils of American culture. When Feroza had first sent a photograph of David (a lover of cycling, the outdoors, etc.) to her parents, they are horrified "[t]hat Feroza should have chosen to send this photograph, of a man with his legs bared almost to his balls, was significant. Surely she must be aware of the assault on their parental sensibility [...] a terrible fear entered Zareen's mind [...]. She was confronting the 'unknown,' and she felt helpless in the face of it" (265). Zareen believes that her forcefully reminding Feroza of who she *really* is and where/what she has come from will be enough to stop the wedding and end Feroza's ridiculous drifting into the treacherous entanglement of value-free American culture. Wasting little time, Zareen makes her appeal to Feroza shortly after arriving in Denver: "It is not just a matter of your marrying a non-Parsee boy. The entire family is involved—all our relationships matter [...]. You are robbing us of a dimension of joy we have a right to expect. What will you bring to the family if you marry this David? [...]. Just husband, wife, and maybe a child rattling like loose stones in this huge America!" (278-79). Feroza responds that her mother will need to change her perspective, because this is a "different culture"—and Zareen counters that "you'll have to look at it our way. It's not your culture! You can't just toss your heritage away like that. It's in your bones!" (279).[6]

Interestingly, however, Zareen's perspective begins to change as the new environment exerts its influence over her, and she too begins to soften and drift from the cultural vantage point she has been sent from Pakistan to represent. During the first few nights she is disoriented by the silence, the lack of familiar street clatter—and (just as Loren Eiseley suggests) she finds it necessary to cover her ears and eyes and summon "the imagined presences of her caring kinsfolk and [fill] the emptiness [...] with their resolute and reassuring chatter. '[...]. Be brave. Be firm. We must not lose our child'" (282). Nonetheless, "the New World beckoned irresistibly," and her joyous adventures and shopping sprees about the city leave her "happy as a captive seal suddenly released into the ocean" (286).[7] Her commitment to her purpose weakens considerably; in fact, "the plotted course was forgotten" (286). Zareen's change of place influences her to such an extent that she "found herself seriously questioning the ban on interfaith marriages for the first time [...]. Till now these issues had not affected

---

6   Testimonials along similar lines are numerous. For example, in *Passage from India: Post-1965 Indian Immigrants and Their Children*, Agarwal describes the case of a woman named Usha who seems a prototype of the Zareen-Feroza relationship: "American society scares Usha [...]. Pre-marital sex, drug and alcohol abuse, and her perception of general American promiscuity frighten her [...]. Usha is especially proud of her daughter Shilpa, but her fierce independence leaves Usha frustrated. Usha repeatedly asks Shilpa in their many heated arguments, 'Why be so set in your ways? Why not accept the advice of people who have experienced life?' If she loses [Shilpa] to the dark forces of American society, she does not know where she would go. 'Why do our children act so American?' she asks" (11).

7   Ironically, Zareen realizes in her own experience/actions what Mickey Tan, a staff writer for the *Asian Community Times*, observes about Asian parents in general: "Asian parents need to give their children more breathing room. Living in such a pressure filled environment will cause the crushing of the human spirit and invoke the rebellious nature in anyone" (15).

her [...]. How could a religion whose Prophet urged his followers to spread the Truth of his message in the holy *Gathas*—the songs of Zarathustra—prohibit conversion and throw her daughter out of the faith?" (287). Zareen becomes critical of fundamentalism in *all* of its guises, and even visits the Unitarian church David and Feroza attend—and finds its doctrines reasonable.

However, Zareen's drift toward accepting David and Feroza's union is interrupted by dreams of "outraged kin pointing long, rebuking fingers," and she abruptly returns to her hard-line stand, insisting on the dire consequences to family of this "mixed" marriage. The intensity of her efforts—together with some of her "bizarre" (from David's perspective) ritual behavior—proves sufficient to stop the marriage. The relationship is ended by Zareen's adamant insistence that the couple be "married properly"—that is, in Pakistan, in the Parsee way which she describes for David at length, and which she maintains she can arrange, despite the unusual and unfortunate circumstances, because of her connections. The force of culture alienates David:

> He realized Zareen's offensive was not personal but communal. He knew that a Jewish wedding would be an equally elaborate affair, and though he didn't want to go through that either, he felt compelled to defend his position. "My parents aren't happy about the marriage either. Lucky they're Reform Jews, otherwise they'd go into mourning and pretend I was dead. We have Jewish customs, you know. My family will miss my getting married under a canopy by our rabbi [...]. I belong to an old tradition, too." (298)

Ultimately, it is continuity within traditions that forces the rupture between the two young people preparing for marriage; the strengthening continuity between the lovers is broken by the (fear of) power of older traditions. Again, as Bhabha has argued, "It is actually very difficult, even impossible and counterproductive, to try and fit together different forms of culture and to pretend that they can co-exist" (Rutherford 209). David "had not realized before how much Feroza's leaving her faith entailed. It was such a final break, not something she could change her mind about later and go back to for sustenance" (309). Importantly, though, Feroza does not return to her Parsee community in Lahore, but remains in the U.S., pushing on (independently) toward new adventures, and involvement with another non-Parsee remains distinctly plausible.[8]

The power of the culture in which she finds herself continues to absorb her, and she proceeds to distance herself from the potency of immediate ties to family and native culture. From one perspective—something of a traditional, mythically American perspective—Feroza's continuity with the archetypal America of

---

8   During a recent telephone interview, I asked Bapsi Sidhwa whether she intended for the power of tradition or for the attraction of the new to exert a stronger force over Feroza. She replied that Parsees have always been known for their adaptability, as well as for their ability to retain their heritage and sense of identity.

independence, individualism, open vistas, and energetic improvisation becomes stronger as the novel progresses. *An American Brat* is a tale of continuity. From another perspective, Feroza is almost altogether lost to extended family, to her religion, to modes of traditional behavior, to native place and culture as she is "swallowed" by the seductive giant of America. *An American Brat* is a tale of rupture. It is a very American tale.

Works Cited

Agarwal, Priya. *Passage from India: Post-1965 Indian Immigrants and Their Children.* Palos Verdes, CA: Yuvati Publications, 1991.

Bhabha, Homi. "One of Us." Lecture, School of Oriental and African Studies, University of London, 15 July 1998.

Eiseley, Loren. *The Night Country.* New York: Charles Scribner's Sons, 1971.

Hall, Stuart. "Cultural Identity and Diaspora." *Identity: Community, Culture, Difference.* Ed. Jonathan Rutherford. London: Lawrence and Wishart, 1990. 392-403.

Jussawalla, Feroza and Reed Way Dasenbrock. "Bapsi Sidhwa." *Interviews with Writers of the Post-Colonial World.* Jackson and London: UP of Mississippi, 1991. 198-221.

Kain, Geoffrey. "An Interview with Prafulla Mohanti." *Journal of Commonwealth and Postcolonial Studies* 6.2 (Fall 1999): 1-18.

Lim, Shirley Geok-lin. "Immigration and Diaspora." *An Interethnic Companion to Asian American Literature.* Ed. King-kok Cheung. Cambridge: Cambridge UP, 1997. 289-311.

Lowe, Lisa. *Immigrant Acts: On Asian American Cultural Politics.* Durham and London: Duke UP, 1996.

Mathai, Manorama. "*IndiaStar* Book Review: Bapsi Sidhwa's *An American Brat.*" *IndiaStar: A Literary-ArtMagazine.*
http://www.indiastar.com/sidhwa.html

Mohanti, Prafulla. Personal interview. London, 30 July, 1998.

Mukherjee, Bharati. *Jasmine.* 1989. New York: Fawcett Crest, 1991.

Rutherford, Jonathan. "Interview with Homi Bhabha: 'The Third Space.'" *Identity: Community, Culture, Difference.* Ed. Jonathan Rutherford. London: Lawrence and Wishart, 1990. 207-21.

St.Andrews, B.A. "Co-Wanderers Kogawa and Mukherjee: New Immigrant Writers." *World Literature Today* 66.1 (1992 Winter): 56-58.

Sidhwa, Bapsi. *An American Brat.* Minneapolis: Milkweed Editions, 1993.

—. Telephone interview. 5 August, 1998.

Skinner, B.F. *Beyond Freedom and Dignity.* New York: Knopf, 1971.

Tan, Mickey. "The Asian Parent: Motivator or Tyrant?" *Asian Community Times* (Winter 1994): 15.

"Times Apart: Growing Up in America." *Little India* Dec. 1993: 12-22.

Turner, Frederick Jackson. "The Significance of the Frontier in American History." *The Frontier in American Literature.* Eds. Phillip Durham and Everett L. Jones. Indianapolis: Bobbs Merrill, 1969. 9-19.

Waugh, Earle H., et al., eds. *Muslim Families in North America.* Edmonton: U of Alberta P, 1991.

Yuan Yuan. "The Semiotics of 'China Narrative' in the Con/Texts of Kingston and Tan." *Ideas of Home: Literature of Asian Migration.* Ed. Geoffrey Kain. East Lansing: Michigan State UP, 1997. 157-70.

South Asian American Women Writers' Cultural Dialogue with the Mythical West

Carmen Faymonville

> "... the West is a territory of the imagination, in a recurring drama of the American character shaped by exigencies of place, then reshaped by subsequent generations who have had to rub the strangeness about the past from their eyes to be sure who they were." (Huseboe and Geyer 9)

> "As a matter of fact, we, the people of the United States, are cousins, far removed, of the Hindus of the northwestern provinces, but our forefathers pressed to the west, in the everlasting march of conquest, progress, and civilization. The forefathers of the Hindus went east and became enslaved, effeminate, caste-ridden and degraded, until today we have the spectacle of the Western Aryan, the 'Lords of Creation,' if we may use the simile, while on the other hand, the East Aryans have become the 'slaves of Creation' to carry the comparison to its logical conclusion.
> And now we the people of the United States are asked to receive these members of a degraded race on terms of equality. Or if they came under the law they may become citizens, and what would be the condition in California if this horde of fanatics should be received in our midst." (*Proceedings of the Asiatic Exclusion League*, April, 1910: 8)

Frederick Jackson Turner, the historian of American expansion, declared the American frontier finally closed at the end of the nineteenth century. Yet those who see the frontier as closed and American culture clearly defined by Western pioneer values and heritage are assuming that Turner's hypothesis is accurate, that the frontier really is closed, and that the West is finally settled. Contemporary writers of the Asian postcolonial diaspora, employing the myth of the American West and its supposedly emancipatory promise in terms of a "Mythical America," however, seem to prove otherwise. Because U.S. demographics are rapidly changing, the "West" has become more and more "East" as Asians stake their claims to the now transnational American West.

For South Asian diaspora writers, such as Bharati Mukherjee and Bapsi Sidhwa, this changing, but still legendary American West presents a suitable locale to present a dialogue between their own cultural heritages and that of mainstream America. Within the last three decades, the western U.S. states have become the final destination of many Asian postcolonial migrants, thus changing not only the demographics of the United States, but also changing representations of the West as the mythical receptacle of American national identity. As the effect of decades of postcolonial migration, mainstream American self-definitions are challenged by the arrival of new Westerners. Both in Mukherjee's *Jasmine* and Sidhwa's *An American Brat*, the Asian emigrant protagonists are actively involved in the reshaping of American identities in the location of the American West. Yet Mukherjee and Sidhwa present their protagonists not as Huseboe and Geyer's "subsequent generations who have had to rub the strangeness about the past from their eyes to be sure who they were," but as travelers who bring their own baggage and who don't rub their eyes too hard. To both writers, the American West offers a literary landscape that represents a unique ideological space for cultural clashes and transformations. In choosing the American West as a setting for their characters' responses to the migration process, Mukherjee and Sidhwa test the validity of their original cultural assets and the survival of philosophical, political, and linguistic attributes after emigration. The exact role of the mythical American West in these two writers' fiction, however, deserves further exploration. Where and when does the West, as that "territory of the imagination," so central to both writers' political imagination, begin and where does it end? For contemporary Asian migrants the term "West" does not, as it does for American ears, resonate only with the geographical western territories of the United States. For writers of Asian heritage, the American West appears as a doubly western location, namely that imagined place in which the West shows its most western face. If the West, as Huseboe and Geyer indicate, really has no specifically localized beginning, ending, or specific space and place, precisely how do Mukherjee and Sidhwa's Asian characters reshape that West? These questions are still of burning interest to contemporary Cultural Studies and speak directly to the effects of the transnationalization of world literatures, particularly those that thematize the re-territorialization of cultures and people.

While urban Asian communities on the West Coast have been publicly recognized as diaspora enclaves and been given names such as "Little Saigon" and "Koreatown," few Asian diaspora writers have attended to the currently unfolding dispersion of South Asians into the rural American West. It is the rural, open space of the Wild West frontier that evokes the mythical dimensions of rugged individualism and pioneer mentality. Most South-Asian immigrants still settle in the traditional Asian enclaves of Hawai'i, California, and other Western coastal states.[1] But in contrast to East Asians, subcontinental migrants seem to live increasingly in suburban and non-ethnic areas.[2] Thus, an increasing number of

---

1   Pyong Gap Min reports that in 1970, 70.4% of Asian Americans lived in the West while only 17.1% of the rest of the U.S. population did. In 1990, the proportion of Asian Americans in the West decreased to 55.7% in 1990 due to an eastward movement. Thus, paradoxically the "move West" is now a "move East" for Asians with similar historical and socio-political effects and cultural ramifications for assimilation and absorption into the national cultural economy (Pyong 19). Yet California, with a 22.5% Indian population among Asian Immigrant Groups, is still one of the major states of destination for Indians, closely followed by New York and New Jersey (see Immigration and Naturalization Service, 1992 and Pyong 20). New York City now has the largest diaspora community of Indians in the U.S. with a population of over 100,000 (Pyong 22).

2   Pyong explains that this centripetal pattern is a result of cultural and linguistic heterogeneity

South Asians move outside the metropolitan areas into non-urban western spaces. Both Sidhwa and Mukherjee take cognizance of that novel migration pattern and weave their tales about young women emigrants around western and midwestern locales outside the traditional ethnic Asian enclaves.[3] While it would be an overstatement to claim that the West is the "real America," the ever-expanding frontier, and the conspicuous history of the majority culture's dominant white/Anglo interaction with ethnic groups and minorities were played out in the West. The West is recognized by Mukherjee and Sidhwa, though distinctively, as the testing ground that has historically severed previous generations of immigrants in America from their cultural origins and turned them into assimilated Americans. But recent immigration from non-European world regions has, in fact, so altered presumptions about American identity and its formative myth-subjects of rugged individualism on the frontier that the Western frontier seems to be wide open again, both in its positive and in its destructive dimensions. For now, the terms "West" and "Western" take on a non-geographical hue and echo wider philosophical concerns with colonial versus postcolonial locales.

As a result of anti-Asian immigration legislation at the beginning of this century, the United States hosted only a very small Asian, and an even smaller Indian and Pakistani population.[4] Most of the Indian immigrants were from the Punjab and took up residence on the Pacific Coast. The Immigration Act of 1965, however, abolished the discrimination based on national origin in effect for almost half of the century, resulting in a new influx of postcolonial Asian migrants, mostly from urban, middle-class backgrounds who settled in the metropolitan centers (unlike the very few railroad workers, traders, foreign students, and subsistence farmers who had come in before the Exclusion acts in the 1920s).[5] India, in fact, was among the ten major emigrant countries to the United

---

and higher educational and occupational backgrounds (23).

3 In 1993, according to the U.S. Bureau of the Census, 1993a, Table 3, 90.6% of all Indian residents (out of a total of 95.3% recorded) in the United States lived inside urbanized areas, whereas only 4.7% lived outside urbanized areas. These statistics include, however, larger cities with small but significant ethnic Indian communities such as Iowa City and Des Moines, Iowa, Madison, Wisconsin, Denver, Colorado, and other larger cities in Arizona, Idaho, New Mexico, Nevada, Nebraska, and so forth. According to Sheth, 23% of Indian Americans and Indian residents live in the American West, mostly in California. The Northeast and eastern seaboard states host more than 35% of all Indians in the U.S. (174-75).

4 Before partition in 1947, India comprised also Bapsi Sidhwa's home country, Pakistan. Separate figures for Pakistani immigrants have become available only after 1949. In 1990, 72% of South Asian immigrants in the United States were from India, compared to 22.8% from Pakistan (see Immigration and Naturalization Service, *Statistical Yearbook*, 1990). After partition, the United States government gave Pakistan an annual quota of one hundred immigrant visas. Between 1958 and 1965, according to the Annual Report of the Immigration and Naturalization Service (Washington, 1967, 62), 1,224 Pakistanis immigrated, increasing to six times that number by 1972.

5 Asian immigration increased from 9% in 1960 to 25% in 1970 and 44% in 1980 (Pyong 12). According to statistics from the Immigration and Naturalization Service, the number of immigrants from India has grown by 10 times between 1970 and 1992. Asian Indian Americans rep-

States in the 1980s. Recent Indian and Pakistani migrants are mostly economic migrants who relocated to enjoy a higher standard of living in the western definition.[6] Despite the preponderance of educated, middle class, "brain-drain" migrants from the subcontinent, increasingly poor and less educated emigrants also come to the United States due to complex world-structural factors such as political, economic, and cultural transnational ties between the West and the subcontinent.

For many Third World and postcolonial immigrants, including South Asians, the "West" is at first the northern hemisphere, Anglo-Saxon and Eurocentric culture, and only secondarily the American "Wild West." Just as western America stands for certain ideological, philosophical, and mythical concepts such as "freedom" and "individualism" and "freedom of speech," so does (justifiably or not) the Western hemisphere in general. It is thus disturbing to notice that the westward expansion of nineteenth century America is now a global westward expansion. Although America's ethnic and racial minorities have been consistently marginalized in the dominant representations of American national history, subcontinental Asians now become visible and begin to take on pioneering roles. They, too, want to see the "frontier before it's gone." This desire places those who experience that expansion into their original places and who migrate into America and its mythic spaces in a difficult location vis-à-vis the new immigrants. While native populations are banned to reservations, new settlers further displace the American Indians' original claims to the land. As the new "Indians" are coming in, the older indigenous peoples are further displaced. How is that displacement recognized, if at all, in Mukherjee's and Sidhwa's fiction?

The West, more than other American locales, is a place where "Americanism" is strictly enforced, an ideological space that has played a large role in the development of the American collective self-imagination. Acknowledging that "as America's most formative myth-subject, the West has altered the presumptions of Americans about their place in both the poetical world and the moral universe" (Gurian 127), Mukherjee and Sidhwa seemingly problematize these presumptions by positioning non-white, "Third World" pioneers on homesteads and under the western sun. [7] Although they do not seem to endorse the West as

---

resent the fourth-largest Asian American population group (Sheth 169-72). The Asian population is statistically projected to expand to 12 million by the year 2000, 17 million by 2010, and 41 million by 2050 such that Asians will account for nearly 10% of the American population by 2050 (1990 census).

6   The per capita income in U.S. dollars for India in 1988 was $300, whereas in the United States it was $13,123 in the same year (World Almanac and Imprint of Pharos Books, 1991, 743). The standard of living, measured by per capita income, was thus 12 times higher in the United States than in India (Pyong 14). In 1990, Asians comprised 2.9% of the U.S. population after growing 200% from 1.5 million in 1970, to 3.5 million in 1980, and 7.3 million in 1990.

7   As Juanita Tamayo Lott points out in *Asian Americans: From Racial Category to Multiple Identities*, Asian Americans initially denoted neither a racial category nor an ethnic group but a

what many mainstream Americans consider their "greatest experience," or "their voyage of discovery into the last unknown," in fact, "man's only true adventure," because of its obvious gendered and racial exclusions, they nevertheless exhibit a deep fascination with the United States' most enduring cultural narrative. Their novels, *Jasmine* and *An American Brat*, acknowledge, while revaluing the structural oppositions that determine mythical Western America, "the good versus the bad," "the strong against the weak," "wilderness in competition with civilization" and the individual hero/heroine "inside or outside society." For both authors the West appears as a contested space: the question is not simply deciding who belongs there, but the much profounder issue of who gets to tell the story of postcolonial migration to the heart of empires. In Mukherjee's *Jasmine*, for instance, the protagonist's encounter with the West and its ideological messages leads her to separate herself from her original culture and from ethnic enclaves on the East Coast of the United States. As Jasmine "reincarnates" in different guises from Jyoti (her Indian childhood first name) to Jase, Jazzy, Jane, and the—from an American point of view—"exotic" Jasmine, she denies her past and her national origin in favor of American certitudes and promises of emancipation. Sidhwa's protagonist, Feroza, on the contrary, finds some continuity between her Pakistani past and her American existence and evolves a more hybridized self.

To establish the relationship of these two Asian diaspora/migrant women writers' protagonists to the mythical and geographical American West, and thus to analyze the West as a locale for the invention of cultural/national selves borne of continuity or rupture with national origins, I focus in the following on Sidwha's protagonist, a foreign student named Feroza, and Bharati Mukherjee's illegal immigrant, Jasmine, who comes to the United States from India to commit Sati when her husband is murdered in India. Both Mukherjee and Sidhwa evoke the trope of the American West in their writings as a powerful metaphor for the postcolonial migrant experience and the cultural dialogue that informs most immigrant writing in terms of cultural mediation. Sixteen-year-old Feroza,

---

legal status (87). Only later in the twentieth century did minority membership become synonymous with racial categories as Americans stressed skin color and blood as defining characteristics of people. The term "Asian American," of course, is now regarded as a misnomer since it includes a variety of pan-ethnic groups which share some cultural and political bonds but have developed quite separate ethnic and national characteristics. I use the term "Asian American" as a relative rather than as an absolute term and in order to circumvent the nationalistic inscription of migrants in terms of their countries of origin. Using this pan-ethnic and pan-racial category does not mean that it should be replacing or substituting self-defined labels for specific ethnic groups such as Indian diasporan or Pakistani-American, and so forth. Although not all Asian immigrants identify with pan-Asian categories in an American context, Sidhwa and Mukherjee certainly do. This does not exclude the incorporation of Asian Americans into a much larger transnational framework which would supersede a narrow American context of minority discourse which I advocate elsewhere. The term "Asian American" can thus linguistically function to represent connections to other Americans, both majority and minority, and relationships to other Asians throughout the world outside the limitations of that majority-minority discourse.

a Pakistani belle, brought up in the Parsee community in Lahore, travels to the United States to spend time with her uncle, Manek. After acquainting herself with the East Coast, Feroza sets out on her own and moves West as she becomes more and more fascinated with American myths and cultural prescriptions. The First World, and, in particular the American West, as Sidhwa's narrator remarks, promises "the sheer physical space the vast country allowed each individual, each child, almost as a birthright" (312). Thus, the West is a playground for expansion and self-realization depicted no longer as the last frontier, long closed, but as a new testing ground for postcolonial and "third world" migrants eager to discover the promised land and the American dreams exemplified not only by modern technology but also by pioneering treks into the unknown signifying the escape from societal and kinship restraints.

Although both Sidhwa and Mukherjee treat the West as more than a mere frontier zone between settlements and raw wilderness, and although both acknowledge the West's encompassing mythical and ideological appeal for migrants, they deal with the implications of the West's force, moral and otherwise, quite differently. In *Jasmine*, the West, at the very least, holds the promise of transformation and renewal as the immigrant's imagination is gripped by American ideology. As in earlier American literature, Mukherjee portrays the West as a locale towards which immigrants are directed because it is a place to test human strength. Sidhwa, on the other hand, uses the slogans of the West, such as "You can't rely on anyone but yourself if you want to live in this country" (135) to parody the Asian migrant community's tendency to become more American than the Americans. Thoroughly ironic, Sidhwa takes a hard look at the way frontier violence takes a hold on the ethnic self and causes inevitable assimilation. But unlike Jasmine, Feroza finally does not blend in, and does not enter a Pocahontas marriage that melts her with the WASP American male. Yet as my discussion of these largely prototypical (though from a postcolonial point of view ideologically suspicious) female Asian migrants in these novels will show, despite the "closing of the frontier," the West still represents to them "typical" American life—which, arguably, has never been anything but a "Mythical America."

Jasmine and *An American Brat* certainly replicate previous immigrant patterns of traditional American "treks out West." Their female protagonists cross boundaries and negotiate frontiers just as earlier immigrants did. Yet their form of pioneering has a distinctly Asian nuance. In female immigrant fiction in general, any "call of the West" incorporated into the narrative usually conveys several visions that are central to the immigrant genre: first, "the making everything new" impulse of the immigrant who conceives of America as a utopia and the Promised Land; second, "the great pioneering spirit" of the frontier settlers and colonizers seeking a new *Lebensraum*,[8] seems to be replicated by the immi-

---

8   This term is associated with Nazi Germany and its expansion before and during World War II,

grants' perception of economic advancement; and third, a cultural dialogue that mediates between the past and the present, hovering between assimilation, ethnic nationalism, and hybridization/transnationalism. The typical feature of an immigrant/migrant narrative is its treatment of the myth of a new land, beyond the pale of settlement, where a glorious fresh start can be made. Just as the earlier settlers sought to dominate the wilderness, many new Asian immigrants see America as a beast they must tame. In some ways, many Asian immigrants embrace the age-old American motto, "If we gain the West, all is safe; if we lose it, all is lost."

What is special about Asian women's cultural dialogue staged in the American West is not only their specific Asian-ness but also their gender. Traditionally, pioneering required that women adopt the individualism and self-reliance which we have been taught to view as the result of the frontier process. However, because these new pioneer women come from non-western societies, American frontier individualism seems somehow forced on them. That is, although they may desire to identify as frontier individuals, they are also made uncomfortable in that position, largely because that position is also associated with a tradition of white settler capitalism. Thus, South Asian frontierswomen, for example, must learn to cope with their new-found mobility, but they must also negotiate the negative effects of that independence such as loss of culture, and forced assimilation. These psychological dimensions of pioneer mentality clearly present themselves as major themes for Mukherjee and Sidhwa. It is, therefore, no surprise that both authors combine individualism and proto-feminism as central American myths into which immigrant women are incorporated. Female pioneer predecessors provide them with a legacy of independent and self-reliant womanhood opposed to the seemingly anti-feminist ideals of their cultures of origin.[9]

Mukherjee's Jasmine as Frontierswoman

Mukherjee's novel strongly suggests a reliance on frontier myths and the narratives of Americanization associated with Western locales, mobility (social and otherwise), cowboy/cowgirl lifestyles, and the loss of ethnic culture through the settler capitalism of Western expansion. Furthermore, in *Jasmine* a potential liberation of the female subject is linked to an inevitable Americanization and

---

but it also serves as a metaphor for U.S. expansionism.. The German term is often used in English to indicate a bellicose territorial expansion based on a determined need of one group of people to occupy space populated by what they perceive as inferior peoples.

9   Many postcolonial and Third World writers such as Chandra Mohanty and Kumkum Sangari have corrected the myth that Third World women must be made the charges of western feminists and that there is no indigenous feminist or pro-woman tradition in countries such as India (Mohanty 61-88; Sangari 157-86).

rejection of ethnic and religious cultural restraints. Thus, the mythical and historical American West emerges as the central metaphor of gendered and transnational identity.

As a South Asian woman writer residing in the United States and an American citizen nonetheless, Mukherjee negotiates the promise of American-style individualism, signaling female liberation, with the burden of old world responsibilities and cultural ties, signaling female oppression.[10] She engages the historical, literary, and transnational reality of the myth of the American West as it is linked to issues of migrancy, cultural resistance, and assimilation. In other words, Mukherjee attempts to re-write American literature from Asian and Asian American perspectives by employing Western metaphors to point to the myth of the West as a central American cultural narrative into which all immigrants are invited to participate. Additionally, Mukherjee employs frontier myths to project Jasmine's psycho-cultural development as a character who physically and metaphorically travels further and further west—both in the sense of "western civilization and philosophy" and "West vs. East Coast."

Making the physical move west, Jasmine moves from India to Florida, to New York, then to the Midwest, and finally to California. Making the metaphorical move from east to west, Jasmine, an illegal immigrant, becomes characterized as a "gold digger" out for the Gold Rush that coined the capitalist expansion of American economic history in a different time. Moreover, by choosing or being assigned the different names—Jyoti, Jase, Jazzy, and Jane in different temporal and spatial zones—*Jasmine* illustrates how the multiple subjectivities and different degrees of ethnic negotiation with mainstream American culture are anchored in specific locales of Western scenes and in the myths of emancipation and progress through mobility. "Every night," the narrator of Jasmine discovers, "the frontier creeps a little closer" (16). The Gold Rush mentality adopted by the eponymous character makes her feel that she is able to profit from the uncharted country of America. It is in the West where men take their ideas of justice into their own hands that Indians like Jasmine can belong. But in the Midwest Jasmine is still not an American Indian (a confusing tautology), or even the namesake of "*our* kind [i.e., the Native Americans]," as her mother-in-law reminds her. Jasmine eventually moves to California, and, consequently, perpetuates the state's reputation as the great and last western frontier. California emerges in the text as the new, more perfect, vision of empire. These driving forces of the frontier myth compel Jasmine to leave her Iowa homestead and her disabled husband, for whom she had adopted a traditional female care-giver and exoticized sexual object role.

---

10   As Mohanty and others have documented, any identification of Western liberal feminism with female liberation, and non-western cultural practices with female oppression is, of course, highly problematic and inherently imperialistic.

In Mukherjee's tale, western boundaries are both physical and metaphorical, marking internal and external spaces. The western territory that attracts Jasmine after she tires of the East Coast mirrors the narrator's inner landscape. As many American authors have done before her, Mukherjee uses wilderness legends as the symbolic conveyance of fears about the primitive irrationality of the inner self once it is released from the governing laws of civilization. Specifically, Mukherjee explores, among other things, recent female immigrants' moral and philosophical adaptations of the laws of the land. Both Repression and guilt are associated with the trek out west and with the pursuit of happiness. For Mukherjee's protagonist, the West liberates the inner self so that a chaotic unconscious can be released. Jasmine accepts the irrational as human, and tries to integrate reality and fantasy by responding creatively to the wilderness's savage disorder.

Mukherjee's incorporation of the Mythical West is predominantly worked out in the novel through allusions to the American western novel, *Shane*. Shane is a typical western hero, a lone, rugged individual who arrives in a town, transforms it, and then leaves for the frontier further west. That transformation can be seen either as a restoration of an older moral order, or as a destruction of the community's existing social order. Located in the backdrop of the 1950s novel, *Shane* represents the battle between the old order, the sheep-keepers, and the fast-rising new order of cattlemen. Similarly, in *Jasmine*, a new class of overlords threatens to alter the landscape of farms and agricultural order in favor of golf courses and amusement parks. Jasmine had read the novel *Shane* while in India, and was thus ideologically prepared for the frontier lures of America: "I remember a thin one, *Shane*, about an American village much like Punjab" (40). Some of her identity formation, gained through reading American and British novels, and using them as role models is played out in her American sojourn. Jasmine, like Shane, embodies the American mythology of individualism, and of heroes who clean up towns and ride off into the sunset.

Jasmine is portrayed as just this sort of destructive and paradoxically constructive western hero: Karin, Bud's ex-wife, notices Jasmine's destructive transformative abilities: "Last night, I dreamed that Baden was hit by a tornado. I don't have to ask a shrink to know that you are the tornado. You're leaving a path of destruction behind you" (205). But Jasmine's constructive powers can be seen in her transformation of the small town of Baden, Iowa, from a monocultural enclave to a more multicultural place: Jasmine subverts both the taste buds and the religious certainties of the locals.

Overall, Jasmine's departure for an even more western frontier contains parallels of the American myth played out in the Western novel, but with a distinctive gender difference. Shane was a free individual because he was a man. Jasmine, who adopts the name Jane in her midwestern reincarnation, is more like Calamity Jane, but she is bound by the feminine decorum that society continues to enforce on the frontier. Thus, when Jasmine leaves Bud, deciding not to be plain Jane and reneging on taking care of an older man and attending to his needs, her move may be seen as morally unscrupulous; she leaves a good man who needs and loves her in order to run off with someone else. Yet we must understand that for Jasmine the conflict of old and new, or East and West, is complicated by gender. Her decision to leave, then, is played out in a traditionally female predicament: "I am caught between the promise of America and old-world dutifulness" (241). When Jane/Jasmine decides to leave, she undergoes another name change and, as is implied, another shedding of identities: "I realize I have already stopped thinking of myself as Jane. Adventure, risk, transformation: the frontier is pushing indoors through uncaulked windows" (241).

Jasmine's decision to continue her "pursuit of happiness" allows us to classify the tale as a romance as well as a western novel. Mukherjee thus blends two popular American genres—the romance and the frontier novel—by engaging the romantic promise of the West. A woman going West in the traditional narrative often required a romantic quest. Similarly, Jasmine decides to leave for California only after her former lover Taylor comes to Iowa to resume their relationship. Taylor is the stereotypical romantic hero who comes to whisk her away. The novel ends with a scene of conventional romantic conquest in which Jasmine drives off with Taylor towards the sunset, "greedy with wants and reckless from hope" (241).

Already in India, however, had she not already been part of the so-called global technological revolution and its evocation of frontier terminology? "It was a frontier, especially in India, and no one was staying back to service the goods that were flooding in" (80), she explains. In other words, by going west, Jasmine only changes to a different geographical frontier. The ideological and economic western frontier had already reached her hometown long before she physically removed herself to the West. Thus are the effects of transnational economies and the global interchange of communication and goods.

Given such apparently enthusiastic embracing of American myths, one must wonder if Mukherjee simply replicates the settler-capitalism mentality of earlier immigrant movements and literatures, albeit from a gendered, and non-European perspective. Clearly, Mukherjee presents Jasmine as an "American" pioneer, one who "breaks free" from ethnic customs that seem to have confined her in India such as female subordination, culturally enforced immolation of widows, and female effacements of self. In breaking from what she has known in an effort to create a new world, Jasmine discovers and explores the unexpected individualist anonymity of America. However, by discarding her old Indian life in an effort to embrace her new American one, Jasmine demonstrates the way the reversal of values often leads to reification of those values. In short, Jasmine becomes an immigrant and frontierswoman only by giving up her Indian-ness. Jasmine has thus arrived at the continental boundary of the United States, which is now only an internal limit within a system which extends so far that were she to pursue it to its outermost limits, it would lead her to eventually tread on her own heels.

Jasmine's case shows that a contemporary non-traditional female migrant can fully inherit this particular American myth only when this myth has largely lost its meaning.

The Young South Asian Woman Migrant as American Brat

The American frontier is also being rewritten by Pakistani Zoroastrian Bapsi Sidhwa, who as an expatriate writer engages the American frontier not as a geographical classification but as a trope for change. Sidhwa recognizes that one of the central American myths is that there is still a frontier available, and if it isn't "out there" any more, old and new Americans remake it as they need and when they want it. Yet for Sidhwa, "frontier" and "West" are clearly fuzzy terms, since one generation's western frontier is certainly not the next's, an idea that acquires heightened relevance for Asian migrant women. For women pioneers, going West means leaving loved ones and familiar places, including cultural identities. Feroza Ginwalla, the protagonist of *An American Brat*, anticipates that the American West will provide an opportunity for maximizing her social and cultural assets. Hoping to resist the disintegrating forces encountered through living in the West, first in a small Idaho college town, then in Denver, her initial goal is to shape the frontier into an image to her liking. Clearly, Sidhwa is parodying the dichotomy of the colonialist attitude to the Third World as "uncivilized" and a laughable "civilized" West as Feroza is dumbfounded by the realization that all the advancements of industrial capitalism she encounters have a seedy underside. Whereas the malls and department stores are glitzy, Port Authority Terminal is a dark dungeon of drug addicts, and the freedom and anonymity of American life translates into indifference and anomie.

Sixteen-year-old Feroza Ginwalla is a spoilt upper class Parsee girl from Pakistan who is sent to America to escape the confining politics of femininity advocated by Muslim fundamentalists. Sidhwa's criticism of Pakistani politics in the novel appears heavy-handed as Feroza's nationalist sentiments extend to her admiration for Bhutto but do not amount to an independent political consciousness that would allow the protagonist, unlike the narrator and possibly the author, to mount an open critique of General Zia's policies concerning women.[11] Intended to broaden her mind and build her character in the image of her mother's own liberalism which is suspect in Pakistan because of its ethnic and religious difference from Muslim codes and its seemingly western influence, America is supposed to provide Feroza with responsibility and maturity. But her old-fashioned grandmother wonders if even such temporary emigration means that "the poor child's behaviour [is] so unpardonable that you have to banish her

---

11   Sidhwa records the famous case of the Pakistani rape victim who was found guilty of adultery
     and subjected to imprisonment and beating.

from the country [...]. She's too innocent and young to be sent *there*" (30). The "there" the grandmother fears is the libertine West in which young girls cannot be protected according to the more traditional codes of feminine decorum still enforced despite transnational and cosmopolitan contact in Pakistan. Advised by her young uncle Manek already residing in the United States to get rid of her "gora complex," a feeling of native inferiority towards the supposedly civilized western world, Feroza becomes conscious of the "gravitational pull of the country" (52). As Sidhwa notes, however, in a global society, Pakistanis already know a lot about the United States and share many of the idealizations of mythical America. As Zareen, Feroza's mother also imagines, America eventually becomes to Feroza the land of freedom, a land where state and religion are separated, where girls can aspire to an education, are self-reliant, and do not have to succumb to hyperfeminine gender roles (37-38). First settling on the East coast, however, Feroza's "sense of self, enlarged by the osmosis of identity with her community [...] stayed with her like a permanence [...]. And this cushioning stilled her fear of the unknown" (52). Thus the East represents stasis and continued enslavement by community values to the protagonist which she must escape at the cost of familiarity and connectedness to a larger social fabric that binds her to her home.

America offers a certain invisibility that Feroza has not yet identified as alienation: "busy with their own concerns, none of the people moving about then had even bothered to glance their way or stare at her, as they would have in Pakistan" (52). America gives her freedom indeed but Feroza is too young to analyze the implications of such liberty: "She knew no one, and no one knew her! It was a heady feeling to be suddenly so free [...] of the thousand constraints that governed her life" (58). She quickly learns that bodily odors are taboo, that Manhattan has skyscrapers, that time is all important—and other such classic American moral tales. The mythical and idealized America she sees at first is a "futuristic spaghetti of curving and incredibly suspended roads" (67). The urban wilderness, the "mile upon looping mile of wide highway that waved in and out of the sky at all angles so that sometimes they descended to the level of the horizon of lights in the distance [...] sometimes [appearing] to be aiming at the sky" (67) evokes the first glimpse of (Hollywood-style) western landscape.

After a few months in the States and succumbing to American ideologies, Feroza resolves to avail herself of the "options America offered. With her uncle she would stay—"no matter how long it took—to test their expectations" (116). Feroza, already awakened to protofeminist sensibilities, reflects, "Might not she, too wish to prove herself? Even if she was only a girl? Explore possibilities that were beginning to palpitate and twinkle—as yet unrecognizable—on evanescent new horizons" (117). By documenting Feroza's and Manek's over-eager Americanization, Sidhwa parodies some South Asian migrants' Americanized disdain for the "Third World." Manek, for example, often ridicules his culture's manners and cultural lenses: "But stuck as they were in the Third World, their vision was limited. They imagined, in their usual woolly manner, that a short visit would suffice to give their daughter the sophistication expected from travel abroad" (119). He is also full of wisdom such as "[i]f you want to get into the right college you have to work for it. Nothing is given to you on a plate. You don't know that, because nobody works in Pakistan" (123). But Feroza has already mentally constructed a mythical America, imagining herself free because she can forget the strictures imposed on her conduct as a Pakistani girl. Going off to a small college in Idaho, Feroza becomes the re-incarnated frontierswoman of her class, generation, and educational background, who has been placed in the wilderness: both desirable and exotic to the American gaze. Metaphors such as "virgin land" hail Asian migrant women such as Feroza as the body and voice of the "other" for Americans. By that definition, the western frontier appears in the text metaphorically as the place of the other. Yet Sidhwa reveals the frontier-as-social-margin as a challenge to the migrant woman as it has been for generations of Americans who went west to take the measure of their world. The frontier in *An American Brat* is thus a physical as well as a conceptual boundary between conflicting worlds, and it offers initiation into an new position in the existing social order, without changing the social order as such.

Sidhwa thus re-conceptualizes the Asian migrant woman as the new symbolic feminine in the American landscape. Feroza instinctively chooses territorial expansion as a means of personal development and locates herself within the space of the American West, which, as the narrator explains, is very distant from home, yet borders on the familiar. Sidhwa's employment of frontier mythology signifies that Feroza's journey into her wilderness means that she confronts the forces of her ethnic heritage. The New World for the South Asian migrant woman is a territory that continues to imply cultural annihilation even as it promises rebirth. At the Western Edge of the United States, mythical America appears to her, as it did to generations of previous immigrants, as an image of Eden, a garden of earthly delights. Yet Sidhwa demonstrates through her account of the fateful moments of Feroza's adventurous journey westward an intuitive understanding that America and the Mythical West are still any subjects' encounter with the historically violent. In the Mythical West, where cowboys, miners, and outlaws transformed their old lives, Asian pioneers now seek their luck despite the odds of discrimination, harsh natural laws, and the marginalization of ethnic life. As Asian migrants like Feroza bring a new history and a new sense of locale to the West, is history repeating itself with a twist? Is the West being won all over again by Asian students, professionals, and expatriates?

Going out west and settling on the frontier remains a quintessentially American act, yet Feroza's rite of passage is not necessarily a nationalizing process of assimilation. Feroza merely learns the gunfight justice of the American and Western styles of life built on the free choice of migration opportunities and simultaneous confinement to the margin. As the supposed savage encountering the townspeople, Feroza sets the ground for a narrative exploration of value oppositions. As the Western heroine, Feroza must in the end leave Idaho for Denver, since she cannot be integrated into the non-urban settlement community. Idaho's settler villages, even its college towns, offer no life-sustaining community to a girl out to try her luck and willing herself to succeed in American terms. In Denver, Feroza enters a space where western education produces shared "universal" values and transnational ties, which, for a while at least, make the migrant feel at home. In Denver, she also joins the class of the highly educated cosmopolitans who transcend nationalism or roots in the narrow sense of the word.

Finding New Myths

In conclusion, as Sidhwa and Mukherjee demonstrate in their diverse ways, current migration to the American West fundamentally subverts the myth of the civilized European braving the frontier, because it presents a disruption of this pervasive ideological system. Within a white frontier ideology, it is hard to "place" the new migrants in terms of the nation's long-standing racial/geographic frontiers. Even immigrants such as Mukherjee and her protagonist Jasmine—both from the so-called Third World and arguably not too critical of the United States—displace the myth of a racial/geographic frontier by redefining the national narrative of the frontier. Ultimately, as Mukherjee and Sidhwa show, the current battle about immigration is about re-settling the white frontier and redefining racial definitions of American identity. But as these expatriate South Asian writers also note, current migrants settling the frontier are also in many ways unlike the old ones: they are the offspring of American globalism and European colonial domination, who return from the margins to the center. For these migrants, the United States is simultaneously an economic "promised land" with integrative possibilities and a society steeped in racism and global manifest destiny reminiscent of nineteenth century western imperialism. Moreover, the transnational flow of labor and capital are calling into question the racial frontier as intertwined with the ideal of America's mythical west. Any employment of the frontier myth in contemporary postcolonial migrant women's narratives thus necessarily re-negotiates the national-racial memory associated with the frontier as a place of extinction and genocide. From this perspective we must remember that erstwhile Asian immigration to the West was represented by American nativists as a "Tide of Turbans" and the "Hindoo invasion" (Scheffauner, 1910b, 616; Scheffauner 1910a, 15)[12]; Asiatic Exclusion Leagues at the beginning of the twentieth century successfully lobbied against immigration of Asians, in particular against the "East Indian 'menace'," who were regarded as "untrustworthy, immodest, unsanitary, insolent, and lustful" (Hess 580).

---

12   See also *Proceedings*; Hess 580-83.

One of the primary effects of postcolonialism in the United States is that the West is now at least partly Asian, and that the American West is now "new" and real and no longer conveniently "old" and a dime-novel myth. If we see the American West also as a frontier for American justice, in the words of historian Marilynne Robinson, "the real frontier need never close. Everything, for all purposes, still remains to be done" (10). The complex encounter of Americans born in the United States and newcomers, that encounter fundamental to the best and the worst of the American frontier experience, is far from over; it is still taking place in our contemporary geographic and cultural spaces—whether mythical and material or artistic inspiration and artifact.

Works Cited

Gurian, Jay. *Western American Writing: Tradition and Promise.* Deland, FL: Everett/Edwards, 1975.

Hess, Gary R. "The Forgotten Asian Americans: The East Indian Community in the United States." *Asians in America: The Peoples of East, Southeast, and South Asia in American Life and Culture.* Ed. Franklin Ng. New York, Garland P, 1998. 122-53.

Huseboe, Arthur R. and William Geyer. *Where the West Begins.* Sioux Falls, SD: Center for Western Studies P, 1978.

Immigration and Naturalization Service. *Statistical Yearbook.* 1990.

Lott, Juanita Tamayo. *Asian Americans: From Racial Category to Multiple Identities.* Walnut Creek, London, New Delhi: Altamira P, 1998.

Mohanty, Chandra. "Under Western Eyes: Feminist Scholarship and Colonial Discourses." *Feminist Review* 30 (Autumn 1988): 61-88.

Mukherjee, Bharati. *Jasmine.* New York: Fawcett Crest, 1989.

Proceedings of the Asiatic Exclusion League. (April, 1910).

Pyong Gap Min. "An Overview of Asian Americans." *Asian Americans: Contemporary Trends and Issues.* Ed. Pyong Gap Min. Thousand Oaks, CA: Sage, 1995. 10-37.

Robinson, Marilynne. *Old West—New West: Centennial Essays.* Ed. Barbara Howard Meldru. Moscow: U of Idaho P, 1993.

Sangari, Kumkum. "The Politics of the Possible." *Cultural Critique* (Fall 1987):157-86.

Schaefer, Jack. *Shane.* New York: Fawcett Crest, 1977.

Scheffauer, Herman. "Hindu Invasion." *Collier's* 45 (March 26, 1910): 15.

—. "The Tide of Turbans." *Forum* 43 (June 1910): 616-18.

Sheth, Manju. "Asian Indian Americans." *Asian Americans: Contemporary Trends and Issues.* Ed. Pyong Gap Min. Thousand Oaks, CA: Sage, 1995. 169-98.

Sidhwa, Bapsi. *An American Brat.* Minneapolis: Milkweed Editions, 1993.

Notes on Contributors

ROCÍO G. DAVIS has degrees from the Ateneo de Manila University (Philippines) and the University of Navarre (Spain), where she is presently Associate Professor of American and Postcolonial Literature. In 2000-2001 she was Visiting Professor of Asian American Literature at the University of Illinois-Chicago. She has co-edited *Tricks with a Glass: Writing Ethnicity in Canada* (Rodopi 2000) and *Small Worlds: Transcultural Visions of Childhood* (U of Navarre P, 2001), and has published *Transcultural Reinventions: Asian American and Asian Canadian Short Story Cycles* (TSAR, 2001). She is currently working on a full-length study of Asian American autobiographies of childhood.

CARMEN FAYMONVILLE is Assistant Professor of English and Director of Women's Studies at the University of Wisconsin-Platteville. She has published on Kenneth Rexroth, Judith Ortiz Cofer, Bharati Mukherjee, Victorian Emigration and Postcolonialism, Pedagogy, and is currently writing a book on transnational women writers and national identification.

HELENA GRICE is Lecturer in American Studies at the University of Wales, Aberystwyth, UK. She is co-author of *Beginning Ethnic American Literatures* (Manchester UP, 2001), and author of *Negotiating Identities: An Introduction to Asian American Women's Writing* (Manchester UP, 2002). She has also published in *MELUS*, *Amerasia*, and *Hitting Critical Mass*, and written essays on a series of issues relating to Asian American women's writing.

GEOFFREY KAIN is Professor of Humanities at Embry-Riddle University, Daytona Beach, Florida, where he teaches World Literature, Postcolonial Studies, and interdisciplinary humanities courses. As contributing editor, he has published *R.K. Narayan: Contemporary Critical Essays* (Michigan State UP, 1993) and *Ideas of Home: Literature of Asian Migration* (Michigan State UP, 1997), and numerous critical articles on writers such as Bharati Mukherjee, Prafulla Mohanti, Himani Bannerji, Rohinton Mistry, and Louis Chu. He is presently finishing work on a chapter on R.K. Narayan for the forthcoming book *A Companion to Indian Fiction in English* (Atlantic Books).

AMY LING earned her Ph.D. in Comparative Literature from New York University in 1979 with a dissertation on Thackeray, Zola, and James. She worked to create and disseminate the field of Asian American literature with her book *Between Worlds: Women Writers of Chinese Ancestry* (1990), her chapbook of poems and paintings *Chinamerican Reflections* (1984), and the editing of several multicultural texts, including *The Heath Anthology of American Literature* (1989, 1994, 1998), *Imagining America* (1991), *Visions of America* (1993); *Mrs. Spring Fragrance and Other Writings of Sui Sin Far* (1995), and *Yellow Light: Creating Asian American Arts* (1999). From 1991 until her untimely death in 1999, she was director of the Asian American Studies Program at the University of Wisconsin-Madison.

JOHNNY LORENZ is Assistant Professor in the Department of English at Montclair State University. He received his doctorate in Ethnic and Third World Studies from the Department of English at the University of Texas at Austin, and his M.A. from the University of Miami. His research interests address transamerican literature and cultural studies, and his dissertation, *Haunted Cartographies,* is a study of contemporary epics of disappearance and dislocation. Among his publications is the essay "This Mumbo Jumbo: Magic and Vocabularies in Gloria Naylor's *Mama Day,*" which has been published by U of Delaware P in *Gloria Naylor: Strategy and Technique, Magic and Myth.*

SÄMI LUDWIG is a PD (private docent) at the English Department of the University of Berne in Switzerland. His dissertation was published with Peter Lang: *CONCRETE LANGUAGE: Intercultural Communication in Maxine Hong Kingston's* Woman Warrior *and Ishmael Reed's* Mumbo Jumbo. After extensive research sponsored by the Swiss National Science Foundation at the Universities of California in Riverside and Berkeley and at Harvard University, he will publish *Pragmatist Realism: The Cognitive Paradigm in American Realist Texts* with the U of Wisconsin P in 2002. He is married and has an adopted daughter and an adopted son.

SEIWOONG OH, Associate Professor of English at Rider University in New Jersey, is a specialist in both British Renaissance and Asian American literature. In studying Asian American literature, he is particularly interested in how Asian cultures are translated and perceived in America and elsewhere. His work has been published in such journals as *MELUS, English in Texas,* and *Explicator,* among others.

ALICIA OTANO has a degree in English from Marymount Manhattan College (New York) and a Masters in Literature from the University of Navarre, where she teaches at the Modern Languages Institute. She is currently working on a dissertation on child perspective in Asian American literature.

EULALIA PIÑERO-GIL is Professor of American Literature and Anglo-American Literary Criticism at the Universidad Autonoma of Madrid. Her publications include *Visions of Canada Approaching the Millennium* (2000), *La obra de Marianne Moore: paradigma de una poética femenina* (2001), *Gertrude Stein* (2002), and critical editions on Edgar Allan Poe and Charles Brockden Brown. She has also published numerous essays on Asian American poetry and American modernist poetry.

CAROL ROH-SPAULDING is Assistant Professor of English at Drake University where she teaches fiction writing and Asian American/ethnic American literature. Her fiction and poetry have appeared in several journals and anthologies including *Glimmer Train*, *Ploughshares*, and *Amerasia*. Her awards include a Pushcart Prize and the A.E. Coppard Prize for Long Fiction, for which her chapbook, *Brides of Valencia*, was published (2000). She has completed a collection of short fiction titled *White Fate* and is at work on a novel.

GORDON O. TAYLOR is Chapman Professor of English at the University of Tulsa, in Oklahoma, where he teaches American literature. A native of Los Angeles, he received his B.A. from Harvard College and his Ph.D. from the University of California at Berkeley. Among his publications are *The Passages of Thought* (on psychological representation in American fiction), *Chapters of Experience* (on modern American autobiography), *The Vietnam War and Postmodern Memory* (a guest-edited special issue of *GENRE*), and "'The Country I Had Thought Was My Home'" (on Japanese American Narrative since World War II (in *Connotations*).

KIRSTEN TWELBECK is Assistant Professor of American Culture at the John F. Kennedy-Institute at the Free University of Berlin. Her dissertation on the representation(s) of Korean Americans of different generations in contemporary North American culture is forthcoming in Peter Lang P. Her fields of interest include postcolonialism, feminist theory, and reader-response criticism. She is currently working on a project on the Nobel Prize in American literature.

ROBERT VORLICKY is Associate Professor of Drama and Coordinator of the Honors Program at the Tisch School of the Arts, New York University. He is author of *Act Like a Man: Challenging Masculinities in American Drama* (U of Michigan P, 1995), editor of *Tony Kushner in Conversation* (U of Michigan P, 1998), and of *From Inner Worlds to Outer Space: The Multimedia Solo Performances of Dan Kwong* (Cassell, 2002). He is the recipient of fellowships from the National Endowment for the Humanities, the Fulbright Association, and Senior Scholar at TSOA. He is President of the American Theatre and Drama Society (1999-2002).

DOROTHY J. WANG is Assistant Professor at Northwestern University. She received her Ph.D. from the University of California at Berkeley; her dissertation examined the role of rhetorical tropes in the work of three contemporary Asian American poets.

ZHOU XIAOJING teaches Asian American literature and studies at the State University of New York, Buffalo. She is the author of *Elizabeth Bishop: Rebel "in Shades and Shadows"* and of numerous articles on Asian American literature published in various journals and anthologies. She is currently working on a book-length study on Asian American poetry.

FORECAAST

(Forum for European Contributions
to African American Studies)

Maria Diedrich; Carl Pedersen;
Justine Tally (eds.)

Mapping African America

History, Narrative Formation, and the Production of Knowledge

The world of African America extends throughout the northern, central, southern and insular parts of the American continent. The essays included in this volume take the creation of that world as a single object of study, tracing significant routes and contacts, building comparisons and contrasts. They thus participate in the reworking of traditional approaches to the study of history, the critique of literature and culture, and the production of knowledge. All are engaged in an effort to locate the African American experience within a wider pan-African vision that links the colonial with the postcolonial, the past with the present, the African with the Western.

Mapping African America sketches lines that, far from limiting our geography, extend our knowledge of the Africanist influence on and their participation in what is generally called "Western" culture. This creative challenge to traditional disciplines will not only enhance the reader's understanding of African American Studies but will also help forge links with other academic fields of inquiry.

Bd. 1, 1999, 256 S., 59,80 DM, br., ISBN 3-8258-3328-3

Stefanie Sievers

Liberating Narratives

The Authorization of Black Female Voices in African American Women Writers' Novels of Slavery

Three contemporary novels of slavery – Margaret Walker's *Jubilee* (1966), Sherley Anne Williams's *Dessa Rose* (1986) and Toni Morrison's *Beloved* (1987) – are the central focus of *Liberating Narratives*. In significantly different ways that reflect their individual and socio-political contexts of origin, these three novels can all be read as critiques of historical representation and as alternative spaces for remembrance – 'sites of memory' – that attempt to shift the conceptual ground on which our knowledge of the past is based.

Within a theoretical framework informed by recent black feminist and narratological discussions, the study analyses in particular the textual strategies that Walker, Williams and Morrison use to conceptualize and authorize these liberatory imaginative spaces – spaces in which African American women become central historical agents. It shows how revisionary shifts in thematic emphasis require careful reconsiderations of a literary text's formal organization to allow for the representation of a 'free' black and female subject.

Bd. 2, 1999, 232 S., 49,80 DM, br., ISBN 3-8258-3919-2

Justine Tally

Paradise Reconsidered

Toni Morrison's (Hi)stories and Truths

Toni Morison's *Paradise* (1998) arrived on the scene amid vociferous acclaim and much consternation. Third in the trilogy begun with *Beloved* and *Jazz,* this fascinating yet complicated the novel has sown as much confusion as admiration. How does it work? How does the novel close the trilogy? Indeed, a major complaint among reviewers, why does Morrison overload us with so many characters and stories?

In this first book-length study of *Paradise,* Justin Tally securely links the work to Morrison's entire oeuvre and effectively argues that while all of the novels of the trilogy are deeply analytical of the relationship of memory, story and history, the historical narrative: memory is fickle, story is unreliable, and history is subject to manipulation. A master narrative of the past is again dictated by the dominant discourse, but this time the control exerted is black und male, not white and male. Though this stranglehold threatens to deaden life and put the future on hold, Morrison's narrative disruptions challenge the very nature of this "paradise" on earth.

With these considerations, *"Paradise" Reconsidered* locates the author at the center of the on-going literary and cultural debates of the late 20th century: the postmodern discussion of history, particularly Afro-centrist history, the production of knowledge, the class divisions that are shattering the black community, and questions of "race" and essentialism. What does ist mean to be "black"? And who is the white girl anyway? *A learned and at the same time accessible early reading of a highly complex novel. Further Morrison scholarship will need to return to Tally's sophisticated and courageous explorations of this text.* Professor Maria Diedrich, University of Muenster

Bd. 3, 1999, 112 S., 34,80 DM, br., ISBN 3-8258-4204-5

Dorothea Fischer-Hornung; Alison D. Goeller (eds.)

EmBODYing Liberation

The Black Body in American Dance

A collection of essays concerning the black body in American dance, *EmBODYing Liberation* serves as an important contribution to the growing field

LIT Verlag Münster – Hamburg – Berlin – London
Grevener Str. 179 48159 Münster
Tel.: 0251 – 23 50 91 – Fax: 0251 – 23 19 72
e-Mail: vertrieb@lit-verlag.de – http://www.lit-verlag.de

Preise: unv. PE

of scholarship in African American dance, in particular the strategies used by individual artists to contest and liberate racialized stagings of the black body. The collection features special essays by Thomas DeFrantz and Brenda Dixon Gottschild, as well as an interview with Isaac Julien.
Bd. 4, 2001, 152 S., 39,80 DM, br., ISBN 3-8258-4473-0

Patrick B. Miller; Therese Frey Steffen; Elisabeth Schäfer-Wünsche (eds.)
The Civil Rights Movement Revisited
Critical Perspectives on the Struggle for Racial Equality in the United States
The crusade for civil rights was a defining episode of 20th century U.S. history, reshaping the constitutional, political, social, and economic life of the nation. This collection of original essays by both European and American scholars includes close analyses of literature and film, historical studies of significant themes and events from the turn-of-the century to the movement years, and assessments of the movement's legacies. Ultimately, the articles help examine the ways civil rights activism, often grounded in the political work of women, has shaped American consciousness and culture until the outset of the 21st century.
Bd. 5, 2001, 224 S., 48,80 DM, br., ISBN 3-8258-4486-2

Fritz Gysin; Christopher Mulvey (Hrsg.)
Black Liberation in the Americas
The recognition that Africans in the Americas have also been subjects of their destiny rather than merely passive objects of European oppression represents one of the major shifts in twentieth-century mainstream historiography. Yet even in the eighteenth and nineteenth centuries, slave narratives and abolitionist tracts offered testimony to various ways in which Africans struggled against slavery, from outright revolt to day-to-day resistance. In the first decades of the twentieth century, African American historians like Carter G. Woodson and W. E. B. Du Bois started to articulate a vision of African American history that emphasized survival and resistance rather than victimization and oppression. This volume seeks to address these and other issues in black liberation from interdisciplinary and comparative perspectives, focusing on such issues as slave revolts, day-to-day resistance, abolitionist movements, maroon societies, the historiography of resistance, the literature of resistance, black liberation movements in the twentieth century, and black liberation and post colonial theory. The chapters span the disciplines of history, literature, anthropology, folklore, film, music, architecture, and art, drawing on the black experience of liberation in the United States, the Caribbean, and Latin America.
Bd. 6, 2001, 280 S., 48,80 DM, br., ISBN 3-8258-5137-0

Justine Tally
The Story of *Jazz*
Toni Morrison's Dialogic Imagination
Ever since its publication in 1992, *Jazz*, probably Toni Morrison's most difficult novel to date, has elicited a wide array of critical response. Many of these analyses, while both thoughtful and thought-provoking, have provided only partial or inherently inconclusive interpretations. The title, and certain of the author's own pronouncements, have led other critics to focus on the music itself, both as medium and aesthetic support for the narration. Choosing an entirely different approach for *The Story of Jazz*, Justine Tally further develops her hypothesis, first elaborated in her study of *Paradise*, that the Morrison trilogy is undergirded by the relationship of history, memory and story, and discusses "jazz" not as the music, but as a metaphor for language and storytelling. Taking her cue from the author's epigraph for the novel, she discusses the relevance of storytelling to contemporary critics in many different fields, explains Morrison's choice of the hard-boiled detective *genre* as a ghost-text for her novel, and guides the reader through the intricacies of Bakhtinian theory in order to elucidate and ground her interpretation of this important text, finally entering into a chapter-by-chapter analysis of the novel which leads to a surprising conclusion.
Bd. 7, 2001, 168 S., 39,80 DM, br., ISBN 3-8258-5364-0

Mar Gallego
Passing Novels in the Harlem Renaissance
An Alternative Concept of African American Identity
Bd. 8, Herbst 2001, ca. 224 S., ca. 48,80 DM, br., ISBN 3-8258-5842-1

Hallenser Studien zur Anglistik und Amerikanistik
herausgegeben
am Institut für Anglistik und Amerikanistik
(Martin-Luther-Universität Halle-Wittenberg)

Martin Meyer; Gabriele Spengemann; Wolf Kindermann (Hrsg.)
Tangenten: Literatur & Geschichte
Die Hallenser Studien zur Anglistik und Amerikanistik wollen an die Tradition des Dialogs unter den inzwischen vielfältig verzweigten Teilgebieten eines einstmals einheitlichen Faches anknüpfen, wie sie durch den Hallenser Anglisten Hans Weyhe und seine Kollegen gepflegt wurde.

LIT Verlag Münster – Hamburg – Berlin – London
Grevener Str. 179 48159 Münster
Tel.: 0251 – 23 50 91 – Fax: 0251 – 23 19 72
e-Mail: vertrieb@lit-verlag.de – http://www.lit-verlag.de
Preise: unv. PE

Der vorliegende erste Band der Reihe ist dem Weyhe-Schüler Martin Schulze gewidmet, dessen Werdegang und Tätigkeit als Hochschullehrer die vielschichtigen Entwicklungen des Faches im Schatten des Ost-West-Konfliktes spiegelt, und dessen Initiative die Hallenser Anglistik die Chance eines Neubeginns verdankt.

Die hier versammelten Beiträge zur englischen und amerikanischen Literatur, zu Geschichte, Sprachwissenschaft und Bildungspolitik eint trotz aller Vielfalt der Blick auf die Wechselbeziehungen zwischen europäischer und amerikanischer Kulturtradition sowie das Bemühen um den Dialog zwischen den philologischen und den historisch-sozialwissenschaftlichen Disziplinen.
Bd. 1, 1996, 278 S., 48,80 DM, br., ISBN 3-8258-2907-3

Wolf Kindermann (Hrsg.)
Entwicklungslinien: 120 Jahre Anglistik in Halle
Das Institut für Anglistik und Amerikanistik an der Martin-Luther-Universität in Halle und Wittenberg feierte im Jahr 1996 sein 120jähriges Bestehen. Als erstes rein englisches Seminar in deutschen Landen kann es auf eine lange Tradition der anglistischen Forschung und Lehre, vor allem auf dem Gebiet von Sprachwissenschaft und Sprachgeschichte, zurückblicken. Namhafte Fachgelehrte, unter ihnen Friedrich E. Elze, Max Förster, Max Deutschbein, Hans Weyhe und Otto Ritter, haben die Geschichte der Hallenser Anglistik mit geprägt. Heute steht das Institut vor einem Neubeginn, der sich aber auch den Entwicklungslinien der Hallenser Anglistik verpflichtet fühlen muß.
Der vorliegende Band soll durch Forschungsergebnisse und Arbeitsproben von Mitarbeitern und Gästen des Instituts die thematische Vielfalt des Neubeginns dokumentieren. Er umfaßt neben einem kurzen Überblick zur Institutsgeschichte Beiträge zur Realismusproblematik in der englischen Literatur des 18. Jahrhunderts, zu H.G. Wells, zur anglo-irischen (Yeats, Joyce, Heaney und Friel) und zur amerikanischen Literatur (Poe, Hemingway und Heller, Zora Neale Hurston und Alice Walker). Ferner finden sich sprachwissenschaftliche Beiträge zu den "Anglo-Saxon Wills", zum Verhältnis von Sprache und Ideologie bei Burke und Paine, zu "Intertextuality in Press Correspondence", zum "Pendel des sprachlichen Handelns" sowie ein Beitrag zum Stellenwert von Einstellungen im Fremdsprachenunterricht.
Bd. 2, 1997, 240 S., 49,80 DM, br., ISBN 3-8258-3304-6

Pamela Winchester
Indian Myth and White History
Bd. 3, 1997, 240 S., 48,80 DM, br., ISBN 3-8258-3446-8

Gisela Hermann-Brennecke;
Wilhelm Geisler (Hrsg.)
Zur Theorie der Praxis & Praxis der Theorie des Fremdsprachenerwerbs
Der Band thematisiert die reziproke Einheit empirisch orientierter Theorie und theoriegeleiteter Praxis fremdsprachendidaktischer Fragestellungen. Während sich Theorie als Ergebnis und Prozeß der Fremdsprachenforschung im Wechselspiel mit und an der fremdsprachlichen Unterrichtspraxis als ihrem Gegenstand ausrichtet, liefert die Praxis die Basis, von der Forschung überhaupt erst ihre Impulse empfängt. Beides geschieht immer unter der Prämisse, die eigenen Voraussetzungen, Bedingungen und Grenzen unter Einbeziehung des Verhältnisses zu anderen Bezugswissenschaften kritisch zu hinterfragen.
Die hier vorgelegten Beiträge behandeln verschiedene Aspekte des Theorie-Praxis-Bezugs, eine Thematik, die die Forschung und Lehre von Wolfgang Butzkamm, dem zu Ehren dieser Sammelband erscheint, wie ein roter Faden durchzieht. So stehen neben wissenschaftstheoretischen, paralinguistischen, quantenphysikalischen, empirischen und mentalistischen Reflexionen auch solche zum Umgang mit Literatur, Bilingualismus, Mehrsprachigkeit, gesprochener Sprache und ihrer Kontextualisierung aus suggestopädischer Sicht. Gleichwertig und reziprok.
Bd. 4, 1998, 224 S., 49,80 DM, br., ISBN 3-8258-3840-4

Gisela Hermann-Brennecke (Hrsg.)
Frühes schulisches Fremdsprachenlernen zwischen Empirie & Theorie
Die hier versammelten Beiträge behandeln Zugriffe auf frühes schulisches Fremdsprachenlernen in verschiedenen europäischen Ländern, in der russischen Föderation sowie in den USA und berichten von den dabei gesammelten Erfahrungen. Sie wollen zu weiteren Forschungsaktivitäten anregen und dadurch zu bildungspolitischen Entscheidungsprozessen beitragen.
The present collection of articles deals with various approaches to foreign language learning at primary school in different European countries, in the Russian Federation and in the USA. The results presented want to stimulate further research activities and to contribute to processes of educational decision making.
Bd. 5, 1999, 216 S., 49,80 DM, br., ISBN 3-8258-4351-3

Martina Ghosh-Schellhorn (ed.)
Writing Women Across Borders and Categories
Generally held to be rigid, borders and categories are nonetheless expanded when those bounded by the demarcations of hegemony, challenge its strictures. Significant instances of this

LIT Verlag Münster – Hamburg – Berlin – London
Grevener Str. 179 48159 Münster
Tel.: 0251 – 23 50 91 – Fax: 0251 – 23 19 72
e-Mail: vertrieb@lit-verlag.de – http://www.lit-verlag.de
Preise: unv. PE

constructive transgression can be found in the
women's writing with which this collection of
essays by international critics engages. Whereas
in travel writing by women (Sarah Hobson,
Dervla Murphy, Jan Morris) 'transgression' is
seen to have settled into a familiar strategy,
in autobiography (Ann Fanshawe. Margaret
Cavendish, Christine Brooke-Rose), cultural
analysis (Virginia Woolf, Marianna Torgovnick,
Donna Haraway), and fiction (Michelle Cliff,
Jeanette Winterson, Ellen Galford, Fiona Cooper),
women have succeeded in creating an innovative
space for themselves.
Bd. 6, 2000, 176 S., 39,80 DM, br., ISBN 3-8258-4639-3

Claudia Franken
Gertrude Stein, Writer and Thinker
*Gertrude Stein, Writer and Thinker, "presents
the first sensible overview which includes a
demonstration of the 'content' which may be
found in each of Stein's presumably 'abstract' key
works" (Robert Bartlett Haas, Foreword).*
This study offers a guided commentary on the
about and the "literariness" of her works which
helps the reader to understand and appreciate her
writing and thinking. Exploring Stein's figures of
thought within the context of the philosophies
of William James and A. N. Whitehead and
considering the aesthetic and ethical significance
of texts of all phases and genres of her writing,
this commentary convinces us that Stein was
indeed one of the 20th century's most original and
complex authors.
Bd. 7, 2000, 400 S., 49,80 DM, br., ISBN 3-8258-4761-6

Angela Kuhk
Vielstimmige Welt
Die Werke St. John de Crèvecœurs in deut-
scher Sprache
"Das Werk hat unter den Händen des Teutschen
Übersetzers noch gewonnen." Die europaweite
Begeisterung für die Werke Crèvecœurs äußerte
sich auch in einer Flut an deutschen Übersetzun-
gen: Zwischen 1782 und 1802 entstanden mehr
als 30 Schriften, die auf die Zeilen des berühmten
"Amerikanischen Landmanns" zurückgingen.
Erstmals erfolgt hier eine bibliographische Erfas-
sung und eine chronologische Vorstellung dieser
Texte wie auch der Rezeptionsdokumente.
Ausführliche Übersetzungsanalysen zu den The-
men Indianer, Quäker, Sklaverei, deutsche Ein-
wanderer, Walfang, Flora und Fauna liefern neue
Beiträge zum deutschen Amerikabild im ausgehenden 18. Jahrhundert und erlauben einen
detaillierten Einblick in die vielstimmige Welt
Crèvecœurs.
Bd. 8, 2001, 480 S., 49,80 DM, br., ISBN 3-8258-4882-5

Wolf Kindermann;
Gisela Hermann-Brennecke (eds.)
**Echoes in a Mirror: The English Institute
after 125 Years**
This volume is published in honor of the 125th
anniversary of the English Institute at the Martin-
Luther University in Halle-Wittenberg, one of
the earliest of its kind in Germany. Its long
tradition of research in historical linguistics had
a considerable impact on literary, cultural and
educational studies. Many of the scholars who
taught and researched here over the past 125 years
tried to uphold academic standards, scholarly
values, and personal integrity even in turbulent
times of ideological pressure and political turmoil.
Even now, 12 years after the wall came down, the
process of restructuring that it triggered has not
come to an end. In spite of this, faculty and staff
are standing their ground by linking up with the
legacy handed down to them.
This volume presents current research at the
Institute in a collection of essays on *Beowulf*,
"Elizabethan Parliaments", "Black Vernacular
English", "Denotational Incongruencies",
"Newspaper English", "Interrogating Whiteness",
Edgar Allan Poe, Charlotte Lennox, T. S. Eliot,
Salman Rushdie, David Lodge, and on empirical
issues related to foreign language acquisition
research and to teacher training programs.
Bd. 9, 2001, 264 S., 39,80 DM, br., ISBN 3-8258-5675-5

**Erlanger Studien
zur Anglistik und Amerikanistik**
herausgegeben von
Rudolf Freiburg und Dieter Meindl

Rudolf Freiburg; Jan Schnitker (Hrsg.)
**"Do you consider yourself a postmodern
author?"**
Interviews with Contemporary English Writers
This book presents a collection of twelve
interviews with eminent English contemporary
writers held during a period of four years. The
book allows an illuminating insight into a very
lively and thought-provoking literary culture,
stirred not only by recent ideas of postmodernism
but also by the manifold issues of nationality,
culture, and gender subjected to permanent
redefinitions towards the end of the twentieth
century. The interviews with Peter Ackroyd, John
Banville, Julian Barnes, Alain de Botton, Mau
reen Duffy, Tibor Fischer, John Fowles, Romesh
Gunesekera, Tim Parks, Terry Pratchett, Jane
Rogers, and Adam Thorpe cover topics such as

LIT Verlag Münster – Hamburg – Berlin – London
Grevener Str. 179 48159 Münster
Tel.: 0251 – 23 50 91 – Fax: 0251 – 23 19 72
e-Mail: vertrieb@lit-verlag.de – http://www.lit-verlag.de
Preise: unv. PE

the relationship between writer and public, the role of the literary tradition, the relevance of contemporary literary theory for the production of literature, images of nationality, intertextuality, changes in the attitude towards language and meaning, and the reception of literary texts by critical reviewers and literary critics.
All the interviewers have worked for the *ECCEL* (*Erlangen Centre for Contemporary English Literature*).

Bd. 1, 1999, 248 S., 39,80 DM, br., ISBN 3-8258-4395-5

Hannah Jacobmeyer
Märchen und Romanzen in der zeitgenössischen englischen Literatur
Im Zentrum einer vielfach konstatierten Renaissance des "Wunderbaren" in der Kultur des ausgehenden 20. Jahrhunderts stehen die Formen und Strukturen von Märchen und Romanze. Gelten sie uns einerseits als Merkmale einer prämodernen Narrativik, so sind sie andererseits zu Konstanten von Literatur geworden, die sich durch die Jahrhunderte bis in die sogenannte postmoderne Literatur hinein nachweisen lassen. Anhand ausgewählter zeitgenössischer Texte der englischen Literatur zeigt die Autorin, wie Märchen und Romanzen fortleben - aber auch, wo sie sich überschneiden und auf welche Weise sie in eine endlose, intertextuelle "Echokammer" eingebunden werden. Romanzenmuster erlauben zudem, Einsicht in die Gemeinsamkeiten hoher und "trivialer" Literatur zu nehmen. Autoren der detailliert analysierten Märchen und Romanzen sind u. a. Salman Rushdie, A. S. Byatt, Graham Swift, Angela Carter und Barbara Cartland.

Bd. 2, 2000, 224 S., 68,80 DM, br., ISBN 3-8258-4686-5

Anglophone Literaturen
Anglophone Literatures
Hamburger Beiträge zur Erforschung neuerer englischsprachiger Literaturen
Hamburg Studies
in the New Literatures in English
Herausgeber/General Editor: Gerd Dose

Gerd Dose; Bettina Keil (Eds.)
Writing in Australia
Perceptions of Australian Literature in Its Historical and Cultural Context
A Series of Lectures Given at Hamburg University on the Occasion of the 1st Festival of Australian Literature in Hamburg 1995
This volume is concerned with the fascinating process of deconstructing self-sufficient "Anglo-Australian" national identity, and sheds light on the intense and sustained efforts of Australian writers to contribute to the country's self-definition as a post-colonial and multi-cultural society against the traditional predominance of a "White" British culture that aims at cultural homogeneity. Another focus of the book is on the unique experience of Australian landscape and nature, which has been a major subject of Australian writing since the 19th century and as a theme has never lost its topicality and irresistible appeal. WRITING IN AUSTRALIA is a must for everyone who wants to embark on the study of this new terrain of literary study which is growing in importance so rapidly.

Bd. 1, 2000, 232 S., 38,80 DM, br., ISBN 3-8258-2796-8

Susanne Braun-Bau
Natur und Psyche
Landschafts- und Bewußtseinsdarstellung in australischen Romanen des 20. Jahrhunderts
Die Untersuchung australischer Romane lädt zu einer Reise durch literarische Landschaften ein. Sie beginnt zur Jahrhundertwende mit Joseph Furphy als frühem Vertreter des modernen Romans und zeigt eine Entwicklung auf, die schließlich in der Auflösung realer Landschaften in eine *Psychogeographie* bei Gerald Murnane gipfelt.
Mentale Prozesse sind Filterinstanzen, die zwischen die Landschaft und ihre literarische Umsetzung treten. Die literarische Umsetzung dieser 'Filter' wird analysiert, um ein umfassendes Erklärungsmodell für die kominierende Buschbildlichkeit in der Literatur Australiens, die bis heute fortwirkt, zu entwerfen. Das Stereotyp des menschenfeindlichen *Outback* erweist sich als Frustration der perzipierenden Figur, die eine an britische Konventionen geprägte Bewußtseinshaltung auf die Natur projiziert. Diese mentale Haltung ist den Naturgegebenheiten Australiens unangemessen.
Dabei ermöglicht die breite Auswahl von Romanen die Ableitung einer historische Stufenfolge, bei der sich im Verhältnis von Protagonist und Landschaft eine zunehmende Bewußtseinsdominanz herauskristallisiert. Die Untersuchung liefert daher einen wichtigen Beitrag zur australischen Literaturgeschichte und stellt ein Stufenmodell als Analyserahmen für die (post-)moderne Romanentwicklung vor.

Bd. 2, 1996, 264 S., 58,80 DM, br., ISBN 3-8258-2824-7

Horst Prießnitz; Marion Spies (Hrsg.)
Neuere Informationsmittel zur Literatur Australiens
Ein bibliographischer Essay
Der bibliographische Essay richtet sich an literaturwissenschaftliche Interssenten auf der Suche nach Basisinformationen zur Literatur- und Kul-

LIT Verlag Münster – Hamburg – Berlin – London
Grevener Str. 179 48159 Münster
Tel.: 0251 – 23 50 91 – Fax: 0251 – 23 19 72
e-Mail: vertrieb@lit-verlag.de – http://www.lit-verlag.de
Preise: unv. PE

turgeschichte des 5. Kontinents. Gleichzeitig ist er als Hilfe beim Aufbau einer Spezialabteilung mit forschungsrelevanten Informationsmitteln in Bibliotheken konzipiert.

Bd. 3, 1996, 72 S., 19,80 DM, br., ISBN 3-8258-3169-8

Studien zur englischen Literatur
herausgegeben von
Prof. Dr. Dieter Mehl
(Englisches Seminar der Rheinischen
Friedrich-Wilhelms-Universität, Bonn)

Cordelia Borchardt
Vom Bild der Bildung
Bildungsideale im anglo-amerikanischen Universitätsroman des zwanzigsten Jahrhunderts
Bd. 8, 1997, 272 S., 58,80 DM, gb., ISBN 3-8258-3214-7

Beatrix Hesse
Shakespeares Komödien aus der Sicht der Pragmatischen Kommunikationstheorie
Dieses Buch untersucht sechs von Shakespeares frühen Komödien *(The Taming of the Shrew, A Midsummer Night's Dream, The Merchant over Venice, Much Ado about Nothing, As You Like It* und *Twelfth Night)* im Hinblick auf die Beziehungsstrukturen zwischen den Dramencharakteren. Das methodische Instrumentarium geht auf Watzlawick et al., *The Pragmatics of Human Communication* zurück. Zentrale Aspekte der Analyse sind u. a. das Spannungsverhältnis zwischen der Inhalts- und Beziehungsebene der Kommunikation, zwischen verbaler und nonverbaler Kommunikation (z. B. der Einsatz von Körpersprache, von Requisiten und Kostümen im Schauspiel) und solchen Beziehungen, die auf Gleichheit, und solchen, die auf Ungleichheit beruhen.
Bd. 9, 1998, 208 S., 34,80 DM, gb., ISBN 3-8258-4047-6

Ulrike Horstmann
Die Namen in Edmund Spensers Versepos
The Faerie Queene: Immortal Name, Memorable Name, Well-becoming Name
Zu den auffälligen Merkmalen von Edmund Spensers Versepos *The Faerie Queene* gehören die offensichtlich bedeutungsvollen Namen. Viele von ihnen sind leicht zu entschlüsseln, aber damit beginnt ihre Faszination erst. Die Namen erfüllen die unterschiedlichsten Funktionen im Text: Sie tragen bei zur Charakterisierung von Figuren und Orten und untermalen die Atmosphäre von Situationen. Sie verbinden und kontrastieren Figuren und bauen Spannungsfelder zwischen der Bedeutung eines Namens und den Namenträgern

auf. Spenser folgt nicht dogmatisch einem philosophischen Konzept der Bedeutung von Namen, sondern setzt die Namen je nach Bedarf ein, sowohl für allegorische Sinngebung als auch zur Schaffung von Komik.
Aufbauend auf einer neu entwickelten Typologie der Bedeutungskonstitution durch Namen in literarischen Texten, konzentriert sich die vorliegende Untersuchung der Namen in *The Faerie Queene* dementsprechend weniger auf die etymologische Bedeutung von Namen als vielmehr auf das Wechselspiel von Namen und Bedeutungen im Text. So kann anhand von Hauptfiguren wie dem Redcrosse Knight, Una und Guyon gezeigt werden, daß die Deutung der Namen neue und fesselnde Ansätze zur Interpretation bietet.
Bd. 10, 2001, 320 S., 49,80 DM, br., ISBN 3-8258-4872-8

Christa Jansohn
Zweifelhafter Shakespeare
Zu den Shakespeare-Apokryphen und ihrer Rezeption von der Renaissance bis zum 20. Jahrhundert
Die Arbeit gibt einen historischen Überblick über die Geschichte der Shakespeare-Apokryphen, analysiert die Problematik apokrypher Dramen und stellt am Beispiel von *Arden of Faversham* exemplarisch die Rezeptionsgeschichte von der Renaissance bis zum 20. Jahrhundert in England, Amerika und Deutschland dar. Zudem wird die nur in einem Manuskript überlieferte und äußerst schwer zugängliche Verarbeitung von Jacob Geis' Bühnenbearbeitung des Dramas *(Elisabethanische Tragödie, Arden von Feversham,* 1931) kritisch ediert.
Bd. 11, 2000, 448 S., 68,80 DM, gb.,
ISBN 3-8258-5133-8

Axel Stähler
"Perpetuall Monuments"
Die Repräsentation von Architektur in der italienischen Festdokumentation (ca. 1515 – 1640) und der englischen *court masque* (1604 – 1640)
In den (höfischen) Festen der Renaissance und des frühen Barock kam der Architektur – etwa von Triumphbögen und Saaleinrichtungen oder Proszeniumsbögen, aber auch der in Bühnenbildern dargestellten Architektur – eminente Bedeutung zu: bei der Definition des festlichen Repräsentationsraumes und als Bedeutungsträger. Diese interdisziplinär angelegte Studie konzentriert sich in einer komparatistischen Untersuchung auf die Repräsentation von Architektur in den gedruckten Beschreibungen italienischer Feste zwischen 1515 und 1640 und in den publizierten Texten der englischen *court masque* der frühen Stuartzeit (1603 – 49), in denen sowohl das italienische

LIT Verlag Münster – Hamburg – Berlin – London
Grevener Str. 179 48159 Münster
Tel.: 0251 – 23 50 91 – Fax: 0251 – 23 19 72
e-Mail: vertrieb@lit-verlag.de – http://www.lit-verlag.de
Preise: unv. PE

Festwesen als auch die italienische Festdokumentation als immer wieder anzitiertes Referenzsystem stets präsent war. Ihr Erkenntnisinteresse ist weniger auf das Repräsentierte gerichtet als auf den Repräsentati- onsmodus, es zielt demgemäß nicht primär auf die Rekonstruktion der dokumentierten Festarchitektur, sondern gilt vor allem der Festdokumentation selbst, die also nicht so sehr in ihrer Wirklich-keit-abbildenden als vielmehr in ihrer wirklichkeitbildenden Funktion in den Blick genommen wird, als eigene Gattung mit distinktiven Merkmalen, mit eigenständiger literarischer, kunstliterarischer und ästhetischer Qualität.
Bd. 12, 2001, 584 S., 69,80 DM, gb.,
ISBN 3-8258-5142-7

Anne-Julia Zwierlein
Majestick Milton
British Imperial Expansion and Transformations of *Paradise Lost,* 1667–1837
This study investigates how Milton's texts, above all *Paradise Lost,* were read in the context of eighteenth- and early-nineteenth-century British empire building. Milton's epic was implicated in the articulation and criticism of early modem colonialist discourse; it also lent itself easily to later imperial and anti-imperial appropriations. Milton the 'national poet' emerged from the strife between Whigs and Tories for his legacy; this book analyses Milton's presence in a number of discourses that are characteristic of the Whig model of secular history: the discourses about empire, language and literary criticism, travelling and astronomy, agriculture, commerce and *Pax Britannica,* as well as the slave-trade. The temporal frame extends from the Restoration through the loss of the American colonies to the Second British Empire and 'Milton in India'. Eighteenth-century British national epics, commented Milton editions and poetic Milton recreations invented a tradition for the British Empire and reintroduced the Virgilian concept of *translatio imperii,* transforming Milton's allegories of divine power into descriptions of secular authority. This study contextualizes traditional stories about 'Milton and Romanticism' by examining mostly 'minor' writers; still, Dryden, Johnson, Pope and Blake feature in some detail. The epilogue shows that even postcolonial rewritings of Milton make more sense in the light of the eighteenth-century Milton and his presence in the nineteenth-century British colonial education syllabus.
Bd. 13, 2001, 512 S., 128,00 DM, gb.,
ISBN 3-8258-5432-9

Astrid Laupichler
Lachen und Weinen: tragikomisch-karnevaleske Entwicklungsräume
Bd. 14, Herbst 2001, ca. 456 S., ca. 69,80 DM, gb.,
ISBN 3-8258-5824-3

Anglistik / Amerikanistik

Jost Hindersmann
MLAIB und ABELL
Periodische Fachbibliographien, CD-ROM- und Online-Datenbanken zur Anglistik
Bd. 4, 1997, 96 S., 19,80 DM, br., ISBN 3-8258-3358-5

Holger Boden
Two World Wars and One World Cup – Krieg, Sport und englischer Humor
Bd. 5, 1998, 112 S., 29,90 DM, br., ISBN 3-8258-3851-x

Jörg Rademacher (Hrsg./Ed.)
Modernism and the Individual Talent/Moderne und besondere Begabung
Re-Canonizing Ford Madox Ford (Hueffer)/Zur Re-Kanonisierung von Ford Madox Ford (Hüffer). Symposium Münster June/Juni 1999
Bd. 6, Herbst 2001, ca. 220 S., ca. 49,80 DM, br.,
ISBN 3-8258-4311-4

Ulrike Ernst
From Anti-Apartheid to African Renaissance
Interviews with South African Writers and Critics on Cultural Politics Beyond the Cultural Struggle
Bd. 7, Herbst 2001, ca. 208 S., ca. 39,90 DM, br.,
ISBN 3-8258-5804-9

Aldous Huxley Annual
A Journal of Twentieth-Century Thought and Beyond

Jerome Meckier; Bernfried Nugel (eds.)
Volume I (2001)
2001, 300 S., 67,80 DM, br., ISBN 3-8258-4370-x

LIT Verlag Münster – Hamburg – Berlin – London
Grevener Str. 179 48159 Münster
Tel.: 0251 – 23 50 91 – Fax: 0251 – 23 19 72
e-Mail: vertrieb@lit-verlag.de – http://www.lit-verlag.de
Preise: unv. PE